THE VOLATILE POWDER KEG

THE VOLATILE POWDER KEG

Balkan Security after the Cold War

Edited by

F. Stephen Larrabee

A RAND Study

The American University Press

The American University Press
4400 Massachusetts Avenue, N.W.
Washington, D.C. 20016

Printed in the United States of America
British Cataloging in Publication Information Available

Distributed by arrangement with
University Publishing Associates[SM]
4720 Boston Way
Lanham, MD 20706

A RAND Study
RAND books are available on a wide variety of topics.
To receive a list of RAND books, write or call
Distribution Services, RAND, 1700 Main Street, P.O. Box 2138,
Santa Monica, CA 90407-2138, (310) 393-0411, extension 6686.

Library of Congress Cataloging-in-Publication Data

Larrabee, F. Stephen.
The Volatile powder keg / edited by F. Stephen Larrabee.
p. cm.
Includes bibliographical references.
1. Balkan Peninsula—Politics and government—1989- 2. National security—Balkan Peninsula. 3. Balkan Peninsula—Foreign relations—1989- I. Title.
DR48.6.L37 1994 949.6—dc20 94–12476 CIP

ISBN 1–879383–22–5 (cloth : alk. paper)
ISBN 1–879383–23–3 (pbk. : alk. paper)

The paper used in this publication meets the minimum requirements of American National Standard for Information Sciences—Permanence of Paper for Printed Library Materials, ANSI Z39.48–1984.

Contents

PART 3: THE ROLE OF EXTERNAL ACTORS AND INSTITUTIONS

Preface

This book was initially conceived in the fall of 1990 before the outbreak of the Yugoslav conflict. The original goal was to examine the basic underlying trends in the Balkans that might contribute to instability in the area and make the region a problem for Western policymakers. A second goal was to analyze the role that Western institutions might play in containing and dampening tensions in the region.

The basic impetus for the book stemmed from my belief that the Balkans were again likely to become a major source of instability, and that Western scholars and policymakers would have to pay greater attention to the region. The outbreak of the war in the former Yugoslavia unfortunately has confirmed the validity of my initial concern, while giving the book even more timeliness and relevance.

Initial drafts of the chapters in the book were discussed in September 1991 at a conference in Rhodes, Greece, cosponsored by RAND and the Hellenic Foundation for Defense and Foreign Policy in Athens. The Rhodes conference was attended by policymakers and scholars from the Balkans, Europe, the former Soviet Union and the United States. It provided an invaluable opportunity for the authors to refine their ideas and exchange views with scholars and policymakers in the region directly involved in the events under discussion.

The chapters were revised several times in the aftermath of the Rhodes conference. Trying to keep abreast of the fast pace of events as Yugoslavia disintegrated and the war spread proved to be a daunting—and often frustrating—challenge, for both the authors and the editor. No sooner were chapters completed, than some dramatic new development required important substantive changes and updating. Yet, ultimately, the volume is richer, more comprehensive, and more timely as a result of the revisions than it otherwise would have been.

The book should be of interest to policymakers and scholars seeking to understand the policy dilemmas created by the recent changes in the Balkans. It is the first comprehensive effort to look at internal developments in the Balkans and their implications for Western policy. It unites in one volume two distinct sets of analysts who all too rarely interact—regional specialists on the Balkans and European security specialists. This was done intentionally to encourage cross-fertilization and to highlight the broader security implications of developments in the Balkans.

The volume is divided into three parts. Part 1 focuses on the problems of domestic change in the Balkans. The opening chapter by Nikiforos Diamandouros of the University of Athens examines the general problem of transition from authoritarian to democratic rule and provides a framework for viewing the political transitions discussed in the various country chapters. The subsequent chapters in that section provide a comprehensive discussion of domestic changes in the various individual countries throughout the region. Elez Biberaj of the Voice of America examines the prospects for democratic development in Albania. Duncan Perry of the Radio Free Europe/Radio Liberty Research Institute focuses on Bulgaria, while Daniel Nelson of Old Dominion University assesses the prospects for democratic change and stability in Romania.

Christopher Cviic of the Royal Institute for International Affairs examines the forces that led to the collapse of the Yugoslav federation and the prospects for a peaceful settlement of the Yugoslav conflict. Thanos Veremis, Director of the Hellenic Foundation for Defense and Foreign Policy, highlights the challenges to Greece as it enters the 1990s. Finally, Graham Fuller of RAND examines the prospects for change in Turkey and their implications for Turkish foreign policy.

Part 2 of the volume is devoted to regional security problems. Ian Lesser of RAND focuses on the changing strategic environment in the Mediterranean and its implications for regional security along the Balkan periphery. Tom Hirschfeld, a former RAND analyst now at the Center for Naval Analyses, examines the role that arms control and confidence-building measures could play in enhancing stability in the region, while Radovan Vukadinovic of the University of Zagreb in Croatia analyzes the prospects for regional cooperation.

Part 3 focuses on the role of external actors and institutions in enhancing security in the Balkans. James Steinberg, formerly at RAND, and now Director of the Policy Planning Staff in the State Department, examines the role of Western security organizations, especially the EC, in the Yugoslav crisis, while Loukas Tsoukalis, Director of the Hellenic Centre for European Studies, focuses on the economic role of the European Community (EC) in the region.

My chapter concerns the changing role and interests of the Soviet Union/Russia and the United States in the Balkans. In the final chapter, Uwe Nerlich, Deputy Director of the Stiftung Wissenschaft und Politik in Ebenhausen, Germany, addresses the new challenges to the West posed by developments in the Balkans, and how these developments may affect the evolution of Western security organizations.

Preparation of this volume was supported with RAND Flexible Funds, as allocated by the International Policy Department. These funds are made available through RAND's three Federally Funded Research and Development Centers (Project AIRFORCE, National Defense Research Institute, and the Arroyo Center), and are intended to permit exploratory research on national security issues.

Many people contributed to making the book a reality. Two in particular deserve special mention. The first is Jonathan Pollack, Corporate Research Manager for the International Policy Department at RAND, who supported the initial project and stayed the course despite many frustrating delays. Without his encouragement, patience, and trust the book never would have been completed. The second is Thanos Veremis, the Director of the Hellenic Foundation for Defense and Foreign Policy, who hosted the conference in Rhodes. The Rhodes conference provided an important occasion for cross-fertilization and initiated what I hope will be the first of a number of collaborative efforts between RAND and the Hellenic Foundation in the future.

I would also like to thank Peter B. Kaufman for his skillful editing of the manuscripts, which improved the clarity and flow of the volume. Thanks also are owed to Cynthia Kumagawa of the RAND Publications Department, who was responsible for the marketing and distribution of the volume, and to Carol Richards of the International Policy Department at RAND, who supervised the typing of the manuscripts. Special thanks also go to Sandy Dougharty, Cathy Janeff, Judy Rohloff, and Sabrina Cowans who typed the various chapters and patiently endured innumerable last-minute changes and revisions.

In addition, I would like to thank Doris Siegel, Barbara Kliszewski, and Carole Simms of RAND all of whom contributed in various important ways to the production of the manuscript, and Debbie Elms, whose superb organizational skills helped to make the review conference in Rhodes an outstanding success.

Finally, no acknowledgment would be complete without a special word of gratitude to my wife Agi, who patiently suffered through several drafts of the manuscript and whose constant physical and moral support, especially during the difficult final stage of the project, made the completion of the volume possible.

F. Stephen Larrabee
March 1994

INTRODUCTION

Balkan Security after the Cold War: New Dimensions, New Challenges

F. Stephen Larrabee

The Balkans[1] traditionally have been a source of instability and political turmoil. In the nineteenth and early twentieth centuries the breakup of the Ottoman Empire prompted a proliferation of ethnic disputes, the growth of virulent nationalism, and great-power intrigue, earning the region the reputation as the "powder keg of Europe." This combustible combination led to two Balkan wars and eventually set off the spark that ignited World War I.

The Cold War tended to dampen many of these conflicts. After Yugoslavia's defection from the Soviet camp in 1948, the Balkans remained divided along bloc lines, and Yugoslavia served as a neutral buffer zone. From time to time, conflicts did erupt—such as the Cyprus conflict in 1974. The superpower rivalry kept most of these conflicts in check, however. As a result, the region receded into the background as an area of major political concern.

The Return of History

With the end of the Cold War, however, the Balkans have reemerged as a major source of international concern. The collapse of communism has unfrozen long-dormant ethnic conflicts and given new impetus to nationalist forces throughout the region. As the crisis in Yugoslavia has demonstrated, these conflicts seldom remain localized. What was initially viewed as a local conflict of little strategic importance—an atavistic "tribal war"—has become a major international crisis which has had enormous political consequences for European stability and security.

[1] For the purpose of this study, the Balkans are defined as including Albania, Bulgaria, Greece, Romania, Turkey, and the republics of the former Yugoslavia.

Indeed, when future historians look back on the early post-Cold War period, the conflict in Yugoslavia is likely to be seen as a major failure of Western policy that seriously undermined the prospects for creating a stable security order in post-Cold War Europe.

The conflict in the former Yugoslavia is the most acute conflict in the Balkans; unfortunately, it is not the only one. Hungary and Romania are at odds over the rights of the Hungarian minority in Transylvania; friction between nationalists and the Muslim minority has also surfaced in Bulgaria; in Greece, the issue of the Turkish minority has resulted in strains in relations with Ankara; and in Serbia, repression of the Albanian population in Kosovo has produced growing tensions with Albania.

What we are witnessing in the Balkans today is not the "end of history," as Frank Fukuyama predicted, but the "return of history." The end of the Cold War has unleashed long-submerged historical antagonisms that threaten to turn the Balkan peninsula into a cauldron of ethnic conflict, which could further aggravate the already acute crisis caused by the conflict in the former Yugoslavia. Indeed, the Balkans could become the main obstacle to creating a stable security order in post-Cold War Europe.

Post-Communist Transitions and Regional Stability

One reason for the recent upsurge of instability in the region lies in the domestic changes unleashed by the collapse of communism. Since 1989, Albania, Bulgaria, and Romania have embarked upon an effort to create democratic political systems and market economies. The process of democratization in these countries, however, has been marked by considerable turmoil and unrest.

The reasons for this, as Nikiforos Diamandouros suggests in his opening chapter, are related to the specific features of political systems in the Balkans—the legacy of 500 years of Ottoman rule, the lack of strong democratic institutions and traditions, and the absence of a strong "civil society." None of the newly emerging democracies in the former communist states of the Balkans has a strong legacy of democratic rule. All were under some form of autocratic or military rule during the interwar period, which was then followed by nearly forty-five years of communist rule. Hence, the countries of the Balkans never sufficiently developed the experience, behavioral patterns, and norms associated with political democracy.

In particular, the Balkan countries never developed a strong "civil society." In Central Europe, "alternative" dissident groups such as Solidarity (Poland), the Democratic Forum (Hungary), and the Civic Forum (Czechoslovakia) emerged. These groups served as the embryos of political parties and organized political participation when communist power collapsed in these countries. As a result, in Poland and Hungary (Czechoslovakia was an exception), the collapse of communist power was relatively gradual and was preceded by a certain "preparatory stage" during which these groups engaged in a dialogue with the communist regime regarding the change of the system.

In the communist states of the Balkans, by contrast, the repression of dissent was much greater, and no organized "civil society" was permitted to emerge (Yugoslavia, especially Slovenia, was a partial exception). Hence, when communism collapsed, there were few organized groups or institutions to channel political participation. As a result, the process of democratization in the post-communist states of the Balkans has been more chaotic and violent than in Central Europe.

Indeed, the pattern of transition in the Balkans has differed substantially from that in Central Europe, where the democratic opposition won the initial "founding" elections held in 1990. In the Balkans, by contrast, the former Communists were initially able to retain power by changing their name to Socialists and draping themselves in the mantle of reform—primarily because the democratic opposition was weak and disorganized. This was true in Serbia and Montenegro as well.

Yet, despite the slower pace of change in the Balkans, the democratic forces in the region have gained increasing strength. The Union of Democratic Forces (UDF) in Bulgaria, headed by Filip Dimitrov, won the parliamentary elections in October 1991. Similarly, the Democratic Alliance, headed by Sali Berisha, emerged victorious in the March 1992 elections in Albania. In Romania, the neocommunists, represented by President Ion Iliescu and his Democratic National Salvation Front—since renamed the Party of Social Democracy of Romania (PSDR)—won the September 1992 elections. But the Front's margin of victory was substantially smaller than in the May 1990 elections. The Democratic Convention—an alliance of approximately fifteen opposition groups—made a strong showing, although it failed to win.

Within the former Yugoslavia, Slovenia has made significant progress toward creating both a stable democracy and a functioning market economy since declaring its independence in June 1991. The reasons for this relatively stable transition lie in Slovenia's ethnic homogeneity—90 percent of the population are ethnic Slovenes—and the fact that civil society was more highly developed in Slovenia than elsewhere in the former Yugoslavia. Slovenia was also fortunate in that, unlike Croatia, it largely escaped the ravages of the war in the former Yugoslavia.

In Croatia the situation is less clear-cut. President Franjo Tudjman was democratically elected, but he has shown an increasing authoritarian streak. Moreover, market reform has not progressed as far as in Slovenia. Nevertheless, a functioning political opposition exists despite some political constraints; and discontent with Tudjman's autocratic rule is growing, including within Tudjman's own party, the Croatian Democratic Community (HDZ), which has shown increasing signs of fragmentation and internal dissent.

In Serbia, by contrast, the trend has been toward increasing authoritarianism and centralization of power. Since the end of 1992, President Slobodan Milosevic has tightened his grip on power, first forcing the resignation of Federal Prime Minister Milan Panic at the end of December 1992, and then ousting Federal President Dobrica Cosic in a carefully organized parliamentary coup in May 1993. Milosevic's control of the media and the key organs of power, especially the army and police, have prevented any serious challenge to his authority.

The Resurgence of Nationalism

Another problem is posed by the revival of nationalism. Historically, nationalism has been a strong force in the Balkans. The collapse of communist rule, however, has given it even more potency. Nationalism has come to fill the political and ideological void left by the erosion of communism. Throughout the region, politicians have sought to bolster their legitimacy by appealing to nationalism, and numerous groups have emerged with strongly nationalist agendas.

The most visible example of this has been in Serbia, where Serbian President Slobodan Milosevic has both encouraged and exploited appeals to Serbian nationalism as a way of expanding his power base. As Christopher Cviic points out in his chapter, Milosevic's repression of the Albanian population in Kosovo and his efforts to portray himself as the protector of all Serbs—even those residing outside Serbia's borders—contributed greatly to the crisis in the former Yugoslavia. Croatia and Slovenia feared that Milosevic's calls for central control were simply a cover for a campaign to restore Serbian dominance and create a Greater Serbia, which drove them to demand more autonomy and eventually complete independence.

Yet, Milosevic has by no means been alone in his attempt to exploit nationalism for his own purposes. President Franjo Tudjman has done the same in Croatia. His increasing emphasis on Croatian nationalism, after his election in April 1990, was one of the prime factors in radicalizing the Serb minority in Croatia and greatly contributed to accentuating ethnic tensions—which ultimately led to the outbreak of ethnic conflict—in Croatia.

Nationalism continues to be a strong force in Romania as well. One of the disturbing developments in Romania since 1989, as Daniel Nelson points out in his chapter, is the way in which political groups in Romania, especially the National Salvation Front (FSN) and its splinter party, the Party of Social Democracy of Romania (formerly the Democratic National Salvation Front),[2] have sought to exploit nationalist sentiments. The growth of extreme nationalist groups such as Vatra Romaneasca highlights this danger, as does the strong showing by Gheorghe Funar, the head of the extremist Party of Romanian National Unity (PRNU), in the first round of presidential elections in September 1992. Funar campaigned on a strongly nationalist, anti-Hungarian platform, and his strong showing underscores the continuing potent force of nationalism in Romania.

In Bulgaria, too, nationalism has reemerged as a potent political force. In the Bulgarian case, as Duncan Perry notes, the nationalist impulse has been directed primarily against the Turkish minority, which constitutes about 10 percent of the population. The more liberal attitude toward the Turkish minority adopted by Todor Zhivkov's successors has been opposed by many Bulgarians, however. In January 1990, anti-Turkish demonstrations took place in several large Bulgarian cities. More recently, nationalist groups forced the government to shelve its plan to introduce Turkish language instruction into Bulgarian schools in Turkish-speaking areas of the country.

The Bulgarian Socialist Party (BSP) has sought to appeal to nationalist sentiments to boost its sagging popularity. In the October 1991 parliamentary elections,

---

[2] At its national conference in July 1993 the Democratic National Salvation Front (FDSN) changed its name to the Party of Social Democracy of Romania (PSDR).

it openly attempted to play the nationalist card, exploiting voter concerns about the Turkish minority. Similarly, in the presidential election in January 1992 President Zhelyu Zhelev's opponent, Velko Valkanov, campaigned on a strongly nationalist platform, accusing Zhelev, a firm advocate of restoring full rights to the Turkish minority, of selling out Bulgarian national interests to Ankara. Valkanov ultimately lost—but only by a narrow margin and only after the election had been forced to go to a second ballot.

The growth of nationalism, however, has not been limited solely to the former communist countries of the Balkans. The emergence of an independent Macedonia has revived Greek fears that the new Macedonian state might raise territorial claims against Greece and has sparked a new wave of nationalism in Greece. Former Greek Prime Minister Constantine Mitsotakis tried to steer a moderate course on the Macedonia issue, but, as Thanos Veremis points out in his chapter, his room for maneuvering was severely constrained by his narrow majority in parliament. Mitsotakis's successor, Andreas Papandreou, has consciously sought to exploit popular fears of Macedonian irredentism to bolster his own popularity and deflect attention away from Greece's pressing economic problems.

This resurgent nationalism has contributed not only to greater domestic instability in many countries in the region, it has also inhibited the development of regional cooperation. As Radovan Vukadinovic notes in his chapter, Balkan politics since 1989 have been marked by greater fragmentation and conflict rather than increased cooperation. As a result, the earlier progress toward strengthening multilateral cooperation in the region has largely stalled.

The Yugoslav Crisis

The dangers of violent nationalism are well illustrated by the disintegration of Yugoslavia, discussed in detail by Christopher Cviic in his chapter. Cviic sees the causes of Yugoslavia's disintegration in the rise of Serbian nationalism and smoldering Serb resentment against Tito's effort to keep Serbia weak. This nationalism, Cviic argues, was shrewdly manipulated by Slobodan Milosevic, the current president of Serbia, for his own political purposes. Some may dispute Cviic's thesis or give other factors greater emphasis, but few would deny the destabilizing impact that the Yugoslav conflict has had on the region.

Yugoslavia's disintegration has created a dangerous power vacuum in the Balkans and has left a legacy of unresolved conflicts that could further destabilize the region. The first problem is posed by the conflict in Bosnia. The Bosnian Muslims have been unwilling to sign a peace settlement on the grounds that such a settlement legitimizes Serb aggression and results in the partition of Bosnia. They appear to hope that the devastating impact of the sanctions on the Serb economy will eventually force the Serbs to compromise. However, without a massive Western intervention, including the use of ground troops—which seems highly unlikely—the Serbs are likely to retain most of the areas that they have "ethnically cleansed."

In the end, Bosnia will probably be partitioned: the Croat parts of Bosnia will eventually be incorporated into Croatia, while the Serb areas of Bosnia will become part of Greater Serbia. The Bosnian Muslims will probably be relegated to a small rump state. Such an outcome is unlikely to end the conflict completely, however. Many Bosnian Muslims are likely to consider such a partition illegitimate and imposed upon them against their will. They may continue the struggle surreptitiously through terrorism or sabotage, or both, and could turn to radical Islamic states such as Iran for support. Thus, one of the long-term outcomes of the conflict could be an intensification of the historical Christian-Muslim schism in the Balkans.

Having achieved most of what he wanted in Bosnia, Milosevic may be willing to compromise on the Serb areas of Croatia. Milosevic has on several occasions shown a willingness to back off when it suited his larger interests. He may be willing to do so again, especially if in return he can get some or all of the sanctions lifted.

In the short run, then, some sort of autonomous status for Krajina may prove acceptable to Milosevic. Over the long run, however, most of the areas in Bosnia currently held by Serbs will be incorporated into a Greater Serbia. A highly nationalistic Greater Serbia could emerge as the most powerful state in the Balkans and pose a threat to its neighbors.

A third problem is posed by Kosovo, whose population is 90 percent Albanian. Indeed, Kosovo could be the next flashpoint in the region. Under the 1974 constitution, Kosovo, while remaining formally a part of Serbia, was granted a great deal of autonomy and enjoyed the de facto status of a republic. Since 1989, however, President Milosevic has sought to curtail the rights of the Albanian population. In the summer of 1990, the last vestiges of self-government were eliminated when the Serbian parliament ordered the closing of the parliament in Kosovo.

In the past, most Kosovars favored Kosovo's becoming an independent republic within Yugoslavia because this course seemed to hold the best prospect for achieving greater prosperity and political freedom. However, as Elez Biberaj points out in his chapter, with the disintegration of the Yugoslav federation and the collapse of communist rule in Albania, there has been a shift in the Kosovars' perception of their future. Faced with the prospect of growing Serbian repression within a Serbian-dominated rump Yugoslavia, many Kosovars increasingly view independence or union with Albania as a more attractive long-term option.

Thus far, the Albanian minority has not resorted to open rebellion, principally from fear of harsh Serbian retaliation. The situation in Kosovo is highly unstable, however, and an outbreak of unrest—either unprovoked or provoked—cannot be discounted. Indeed, having achieved their main goals in Bosnia, Serbian ultranationalists could feel free to settle scores in Kosovo.

Any unrest in Kosovo would put the United States in a very difficult position. Both President Bush and President Clinton have warned Milosevic that the United States would not tolerate further repression in Kosovo. This was a unilateral threat—the allies did not make such a pledge and therefore are not obligated to uphold it. If unrest did occur in Kosovo, and was brutally suppressed by the Serbs—as undoubtedly it would be—the United States would be confronted with the need to make good on its commitment or face a serious erosion of its credibility.

Any conflict in Kosovo would almost certainly spread to Macedonia. Macedonia's population is between 30 and 40 percent Albanian. Thus, it would be difficult to keep any war in Kosovo localized. Thousands of Albanian refugees would come streaming into Macedonia. Many Albanians in Macedonia would also join their brethren fighting in Kosovo. As a result, Macedonia would probably be dragged into a conflict. Albania, Greece, and Bulgaria—as well as Turkey—might also be drawn in. The result could be a full-scale Balkan war.

Even if an expansion of the war could be avoided, it has already had serious repercussions that extend far beyond Bosnia's borders. The West's de facto acceptance of Serbia's "ethnic cleansing" (and, to a lesser extent, Croatia's as well) has set a dangerous precedent and could encourage leaders in other parts of Eastern Europe and the former Soviet Union to set up "ethnically pure" states by violent means. Those who call for ethnic tolerance are likely to be discredited and overwhelmed by more radical nationalists, who can point to the Serbian precedent and argue that there is little danger in pressing forward with their radical ethnic agendas.

Perhaps the most serious consequence, however, has been the discrediting of Western security institutions, all of which proved unable or unwilling to halt the slaughter in Bosnia. The most badly damaged has been the European Community. The EC's mediation in the Yugoslav crisis was widely touted as the EC's debut on the international stage. Its inability to prevent a destructive civil war raises serious questions about its readiness for assuming custody of continental security.[3]

The credibility of the United Nations and NATO have also been badly damaged by their inability to stop the conflict. Thus, one of the major lessons of the Yugoslav crisis is the need to revitalize these institutions and adapt them to deal more effectively with the security problems facing Europe in the post-Cold War era. As the Yugoslav crisis demonstrates, these problems are chiefly the result of the proliferation of ethnic conflicts and territorial disputes rather than traditional cases of armed aggression by one state against another.

The Greek-Turkish Conflict

Greek-Turkish differences over Cyprus and the Aegean present another potential source of conflict in the Balkans. These disputes are not new, but they assume greater significance given the overall deterioration of the security situation in the Balkans. As long as they remain unresolved, there is a chance that some unforeseen incident could touch off a conflict, which almost occurred in 1987 when Turkey sent an exploration vessel into a disputed part of the Aegean.

Cyprus continues to be an obstacle to a broader Greek-Turkish rapprochement. During the summer of 1991, there were signs that the Cyprus problem might—with U.S. help—be moving closer to resolution. The Bush administration's efforts, however, failed to yield concrete results. A quadripartite conference on Cyprus, announced by President Bush for September 1991, never materialized. Since then, the intercom-

[3] See Michael Brenner, "EC: Confidence Lost," *Foreign Policy*, no. 91 (Summer 1993): 29.

munal talks, conducted under UN auspices, have failed to make substantial progress on the "set of ideas" advanced by UN Secretary General Boutros Boutros-Ghali.

The prospects are poor for an imminent dramatic breakthrough on the Cyprus issue. The death of Turkish President Turgut Özal in 1993 removed one of the few Turkish politicians from the political scene who had shown any serious interest in promoting a resolution of the conflict. Turkish Prime Minister Tansu Ciller has no experience in foreign affairs. Moreover, she is preoccupied with the economy and the Kurdish insurgency. She is thus unlikely to take bold initiatives on Cyprus, especially those that would be opposed by the Turkish military whose influence has increased since Özal's death. Greek Prime Minister Andreas Papandreou also shows little interest in taking steps that might facilitate a settlement of the Cyprus dispute.

Meanwhile, Greek-Turkish bilateral relations continue to be marred by differences over the Aegean. The "Davos Process," initiated by Özal and Papandreou in early 1988 in Davos, Switzerland, led to a short-lived thaw in relations and raised hopes that a true rapprochement might follow. The rapprochement soon fizzled, however, as both leaders found themselves under increasing domestic pressure. Since then, there has been little progress in easing bilateral tensions. In addition, relations have been strained by incidents involving the Turkish minority in Thrace.

The continuing tension in Greek-Turkish relations is all the more disconcerting because both countries have engaged in a significant military buildup—with Western help—during the last several years. Greece spent almost $2 billion on importing weapons in 1992 while Turkey spent more than $1.5 billion on foreign arms. Moreover, as a result of the practice of "cascading" under the Conventional Forces in Europe (CFE) treaty, Greece and Turkey have received large quantities of heavy offensive weapons free of charge.[4] While these arms have been designed to help these countries modernize their antiquated forces, it is questionable whether pouring such an enormous quantity of arms into a region rife with conflict represents a wise policy on the part of the West.

Clearly, breaking the deadlock in the Greek-Turkish dispute will not be easy. Yet, it is precisely here that there may be a role for the type of confidence-building measures (mutual pull-back zones, "open skies" regimes, and so forth) discussed by Tom Hirschfeld in his chapter. Such measures would not resolve all the bilateral differences between the two countries, but they could help reduce the sense of insecurity on both sides and create a better atmosphere of mutual trust, which might eventually make the resolution of some of the other more intractable bilateral issues easier.

The Bulgarian-Turkish agreement on confidence-building measures, signed in December 1991, could be a useful model in this regard. In addition to expanded military-to-military contacts, the agreement provides for numerous Confidence and Security Building Measures (CSBMs), such as inspections and prior notification of

---

[4] William Drozdiak, "Greece, Turkey Amassing Arms," *The Washington Post,* September 30, 1993. Also, "Fueling Balkan Fires," *Basic Report 93–3* (Washington: British-American Security Information Council, September 22, 1993).

maneuvers that go beyond those provided for in the 1990 Paris Conventional Forces in Europe Agreement. Many of these could easily be adapted to the Greek-Turkish context. The two sides might also consider signing a bilateral "open skies" agreement similar to the one signed by Hungary and Romania in April 1991, which provides for greater transparency and a specified number of overflights of each other's territory. The Hungarian-Romanian agreement shows that military cooperation is possible even when political relations are poor.

None of these measures, of course, is a substitute for a broad political dialogue, but they could help to reduce tensions between the two sides and lay the groundwork for a broader political dialogue at a later date. Moreover, the initiation of a dialogue on confidence-building measures would have the added advantage of involving the respective militaries directly in the negotiating process, thereby sensitizing them to the threat perceptions and concerns of the other side. As the Bulgarian-Turkish rapprochement since 1989 underscores, such military-to-military contacts can play an important role in fostering an overall relaxation of tensions between mutually suspicious adversaries.

Over the longer term, however, there is a need to establish a broader security regime in the Balkans. A promising start in this direction was made at the Conference on Security and Cooperation in Europe (CSCE) Ministerial in Rome in December 1993, which mandated the Forum for Security Cooperation (FSC), the successor to the CFE negotiations on conventional force reductions, to examine regional stability in Southeastern Europe. These discussions are not likely to make significant progress until a settlement in Bosnia has been reached and Serbia has been readmitted to the CSCE. However, once they get going, the main concern of most Balkan states is likely to be focused on the regional military balance within the former Yugoslavia—and in the Balkans as a whole—rather than on the old East-West balance that preoccupied negotiators during the CFE talks. Indeed, one of the central issues is likely to be obtaining constraints on, and reductions of, Serbian forces and equipment in order to prevent a Greater Serbia from posing a threat to its neighbors.

Shifting Regional Alignments

The increasing instability in the Balkans since 1989 has coincided with, and, to some extent, contributed to, the emergence of new regional alignments. Before 1989 the Balkans were essentially divided into two blocs, with Yugoslavia acting as a neutral strategic buffer between them. As a result of the disintegration of Yugoslavia and the end of the Cold War, however, new patterns and political alignments are beginning to emerge that could transform the character of security relations in the region over the next decade.

The close cooperation between Serbia and Greece provides a case in point. Close ties between the two countries have deep historical roots. The collapse of the former Yugoslavia, however, has given these traditional ties a new dimension and intensity. Both countries share a common concern about the emergence of an independent

Macedonia as well as a desire to prevent the expansion of Turkish influence in the Balkans. These common concerns have contributed to close cooperation between the two countries since 1991 that at times has bordered on a de facto alliance.

The recent rapprochement between Bulgaria and Turkey provides another example of the regional realignments that have begun to emerge with the end of the Cold War. For most of the Cold War period, relations between Bulgaria and Turkey were strained. As Duncan Perry points out in his chapter, however, since 1989 relations have undergone a far-reaching improvement. This process was highlighted by the signing in May 1992 of a Treaty of Friendship and Cooperation that calls for a broad expansion of ties in various political and economic areas. Military ties have been expanded as well.

The Turkish-Bulgarian rapprochement, however, has contributed to a cooling of Sofia's relations with Athens. The cooling was reinforced by Bulgaria's rapid recognition of Macedonia as an independent state in January 1992. Although relations have improved somewhat since then, many Greek officials remain suspicious of Bulgaria's long-term intentions, especially regarding Macedonia. They fear that at some point Bulgaria might conspire—with Turkish backing—to raise claims against Greek territory. They have, therefore, viewed the Bulgarian-Turkish rapprochement with some misgivings.

Meanwhile, the breakup of the former Yugoslav federation has led to a revival of traditional interests on the part of many neighboring states on the periphery of the Balkans. Italy, for example, has "rediscovered" the Balkans. Italy played an active role in the EC's mediation efforts in the Yugoslav crisis and has intensified ties to Slovenia and Croatia. It has also quickly moved to reestablish its traditional influence in Albania.

Italy's politics, moreover, are in a state of great flux. What type of foreign policy the new coalition headed by media magnate Silvio Berlusconi, which includes the Fascists, will pursue is unclear. However, one possibility is that Italy could pursue a more nationalistic policy in the Balkans, expecially vis-à-vis Croatia and Slovenia.

Hungary, too, has begun to play a more active role in the Balkans. Budapest has provided strong diplomatic and moral support to Croatia and Slovenia, with which it has close historic and economic ties. All three cooperate closely within the Central European Initiative (formerly, the Hexagonale). Relations with Serbia, by contrast, have deteriorated as a result of the Serbian repression of the Hungarian minority in Vojvodina and violations of Hungarian airspace by the Yugoslav air force.

Finally, Austria has become more actively involved in the region as a result of the Yugoslav crisis. Along with Germany, Austria was one of the strongest supporters of the right to self-determination for Slovenia, and ultimately Slovenia and Croatia probably will draw economically and politically closer to Austria, just as Hungary has during the past decade. All three are likely to view Austria as a bridge to the European Union if, as expected, Austria soon becomes a full member of the EU.

Actually, during the next decade, several new regional constellations could emerge in the Balkans. The first could be a "Central European constellation" composed of Austria, Hungary, Slovenia, and possibly Croatia, if Croatia undertakes a program of serious economic and political reform. All four countries were once part of the Austro-Hungarian empire and share strong historic, economic, and cultural ties. The Central European Initiative provides a regional framework for such cooperation and could give it new impetus.

Serbia, Romania, and Slovakia could also intensify cooperation, possibly forming an informal alliance. All three countries have large Hungarian minorities and share a common concern about possible Hungarian irredentism. This, in effect, would revive the interwar Little Entente (Romania, Yugoslavia, and Czechoslovakia).

Finally, there is the possibility of a "Muslim axis" composed of Turkey, Bosnia, and Albania. Turkey has generally maintained a low-key profile in the Balkans during the postwar period. However, with the end of the Cold War, Turkey has begun to play a more active role in Balkan affairs. It has lent strong political and moral support to the Bosnian Muslims. It has also stepped up military cooperation with Albania. These moves have reinforced fears in Athens of the emergence of an "Islamic arc" in the Balkans on Greece's northern border.

Germany: *Drang Nach Süden?*

Germany has also emerged as a potential new actor on the Balkan scene. Germany is the strongest economic power in Europe. Moreover, it traditionally has had strong interests in the region. During the interwar period, Germany was the dominant economic power in the Balkans, and several Balkan countries, especially Bulgaria and Yugoslavia, were highly dependent on Germany economically.

The strong German support for Croatian and Slovenian independence has created suspicions that a powerful united Germany is intent on reestablishing a sphere of influence in the Balkans. Such fears, however, are exaggerated. The German support for recognition of Croatia and Slovenia had more to do with Germany's attachment to self-determination than with any new *Drang nach Süden* on Germany's part or desire to carve out a new sphere of influence in the Balkans. Having just achieved unification on the basis of self-determination, Germany found it hard politically to deny the same rights to Slovenia and Croatia. Moreover, recognition was seen by many Germans as one of the few means of leverage available to the West to influence the situation in the former Yugoslavia.

In retrospect, Bonn's decision to push for rapid recognition of Slovenia and Croatia can be seen as a serious mistake. It directly contributed to the expansion of the conflict to Bosnia. But the dispute was essentially over tactics—how best to stop the fighting in Croatia—not over spheres of influence. Strong regional and cultural ties do exist between parts of Germany (particularly Bavaria) and Slovenia and Croatia, but overall Germany's economic interests in the Balkans are quite limited, especially when compared to German interests during the interwar period.

Croatian hopes that there would be a large influx of German capital into Croatia have largely been disappointed. Germany has concentrated mainly on providing humanitarian and technical assistance. In addition, German industrialists have been reluctant to invest heavily in Croatia because of the highly unstable political situation and lack of meaningful reform.[5] German investment in Albania, Romania, and Bulgaria to date has also been quite modest.

This seems likely to continue. For the next decade, the German priority will probably be reconstructing the former German Democratic Republic (GDR). This will limit the amount of capital and resources available for investment elsewhere, especially the Balkans. Moreover, Germany remains constrained by its constitutional difficulties from becoming deeply involved militarily in the Balkans. Hence, Germany is unlikely to become the new *Ordnungsmacht* in the Balkans.

Germany cannot afford, however, to ignore the Balkans entirely. Instability in the Balkans has direct consequences for Germany, as it is a "front-line state" for many refugees from the region. The Federal Republic has already accepted more than 200 thousand refugees from Bosnia and Croatia. Moreover, the largest number of asylum seekers come from Southeastern Europe, especially Romania. This large influx of asylum seekers has added to the Federal Republic's growing domestic problems and will force it to maintain an active interest in Balkan affairs.

The Role of the EC*

The asylum problem highlights the close linkage between instability in the Balkans and European security. Not only Germany has been faced with a large influx of refugees. Italy, Greece, Turkey, and Hungary also have been confronted with large waves of refugees resulting from the upheavals in the Balkans, which compounds the extensive economic and social problems already confronting these countries.

Henceforth, the countries in Europe must think much more systematically not only about developing more effective means to prevent and contain conflicts in the Balkans, but also about the broader problems associated with economic development. In this instance, the role of the EC, discussed in detail by Loukas Tsoukalis in his chapter, is likely to be critical. While the Balkans (with the exception of Greece and Turkey) have to date been of only marginal importance for the EC, the progressive integration of the economies of the post-communist states in the Balkans should effect closer future economic ties with the EC. Trade and investment between the EC and the Balkan countries should increase rapidly over the next few years.

Institutional ties have also been broadened. In late 1992, the EC signed association agreements with Romania and Bulgaria similar to those signed with Hungary, Czechoslovakia, and Poland in December 1991. The EC has also played a major role in providing financial assistance to Albania. Albania, however, must first un-

[5] Judy Dempsey, "German Business Slow to Follow State on Croatia," *Financial Times*, 5 Feb., 1992.

* The official name of the European Community was changed in November 1993 to the European Union. However, as most chapters were completed before that date, the original name European Community is often used throughout the text, except in circumstances which specifically refer to the European Union.

dergo a more limited trade and cooperation agreement before moving to the higher stage of association.

Yet as Tsoukalis points out, the Community's policy toward these countries will not be without problems. The long-term demands of these countries will impose certain costs on EC members, especially in terms of trade liberalization. An increased import penetration from the Balkan countries will require further adjustments inside the EC. Until now, the EC has been reluctant to liberalize its import policies, especially in areas important to East European countries, such as agriculture and textiles. Without better market access, however, many of the reforms initiated to date in these countries may fail.

Turkey presents a special problem for the EC. Despite the impressive growth rates it has experienced in recent years, in terms of economic structures, Turkey is still closer to many developing countries than to the advanced industrial countries of the West. Its purchasing power is approximately two-thirds of that of the poorest countries of the Twelve. These economic factors, together with an expanding population and other religious and cultural differences, help to explain why the EC has had so much difficulty in dealing with the Turkish application for membership.

Meanwhile, the movement toward greater European cooperation on security and defense, embodied in the Maastricht Treaty, has tended to leave Turkey, which is not a member of either the EC or the Western European Union (WEU), feeling increasingly isolated. The decision at Maastricht to offer Turkey associate membership in the WEU was designed in part to counteract this feeling. It has been seen by Turkey, however, as underscoring Turkey's "second-class citizenship" and has further reinforced its feeling of estrangement from Europe.

The real danger, as Ian Lesser points out in his chapter, is less that of strategic neglect broadly defined, but rather the narrower and more potent risk of exclusion from the European security equation and its effect on Turkey's relations with the West. As the EC moves to develop a common foreign and security policy, it will be more difficult for the Community to accept the additional burden of direct exposure in the Middle East which Turkish membership in the EC or WEU would impose.

Turkey's Changing Role

Turkey's role in the Balkans, however, could become more important in the coming decades. For most of the postwar period, Turkey largely neglected the Balkans; it concentrated instead on strengthening its ties to the West and later to the Middle East. Although some effort was made to improve bilateral ties with individual Balkan countries, the Balkans were largely regarded as secondary in importance.

As Graham Fuller points out in his chapter, however, the end of the Cold War has dramatically changed Turkey's strategic environment. On the one hand, the collapse of the Soviet Union has reduced the saliency of the Soviet threat and the importance of the U.S. military tie. On the other, as a result of the disintegration of the USSR and Yugoslavia, a whole new "Turkic world" has opened up, stretching from the Balkans to Central Asia. This factor has increased the tendency among parts of the Turkish elite to rethink Turkey's options and interests, including in the Balkans.

One of the most important indications of Turkey's new interest in the Balkans—and beyond—is the Black Sea Economic Zone cooperation initiative. Launched by the late President Turgut Özal in 1989, the project is designed to promote private-sector activity and stimulate the free movement of goods and services among the member states. In addition to Turkey, the group also includes Bulgaria, Romania, Greece and Albania, as well as six member states of the former Soviet Union—Ukraine, Russia, Azerbaijan, Armenia, Moldova and Georgia.

The Black Sea Initiative is part of Ankara's broader effort to develop a more active foreign policy and exploit opportunities created by the end of the Cold War. To some extent, it also represents a hedge against Turkey's current difficulties with Western Europe and the possible rejection of its membership bid by the EC. How successful the initiative will be remains to be seen. Özal's death removed the main backer of the scheme from the Turkish scene. His successor, former Prime Minister Süleyman Demirel, is unlikely to give the project the same high priority as Özal did. Nonetheless, because it provides a means for Turkey to play a leadership role in the region, it is not likely to be dropped.

Politically, Turkey has also made important political inroads in the Balkans in the last few years. The rapprochement with Bulgaria has already been noted. In addition, ties with Albania have been strengthened, especially in the military area. Relations with Romania have also visibly improved. Finally, Turkey has moved to strengthen ties with Bosnia and Macedonia, both of which have large Muslim minorities.

The war in Bosnia has also increased the pressures on Ankara to play a more active role in the Balkans. Although the Bosnian Muslims are ethnic Slavs, not Turks, they are remnants of the Ottoman Empire. Turkey, therefore, feels a close cultural affinity and moral responsibility for their well-being. Moreover, there are over two million Bosnians in Turkey—the result of several waves of emigration since 1878, when Turkey began to withdraw from the Balkans. They represent a strong interest group and lobby in Turkey. Turkey, therefore, has been the strongest advocate within the Western alliance of helping the Bosnians.

The danger is that the Bosnian crisis could add to the strains and fault lines already emerging between Turkey and its Western allies. Indeed, in the future, the "Muslim factor" could play an increasingly important role in Turkish policy, especially in the Balkans. There are over four million Muslims in the former Yugoslavia. In addition, there are about one million Muslims, many of them ethnic Turks, in Bulgaria. Greece also has a large Muslim population (120,000), more than half of whom are ethnic Turks.

As turmoil in the Balkans spreads, these communities may look increasingly to Turkey for support. Turkey's response will depend greatly upon broader trends within Turkish society and the Balkans. However, playing the "Islamic card" has certain risks. Internally, it could strengthen the hand of the radical Islamic forces in Turkish society, while externally it could further estrange Turkey from Europe. In addition, it could revive the traditional Muslim-Christian schism in the Balkans and create new strains with Turkey's Balkan neighbors, especially Greece and Bulgaria.

The United States and Russia: Benign Neglect or Strategic Reengagement?

The end of the Cold War has also raised important questions about the future role of the United States and Russia in the Balkans. During the Cold War, the Balkan region was seen as a strategic pawn in the political struggle for influence between the two superpowers. With the end of the Cold War, both powers initially appeared to lose interest in the area. Indeed, the most striking aspect of the initial phases of the Yugoslav crisis is the marginal role played by the two superpowers. Both preferred to sit back and let the Europeans manage the crisis.

This period of strategic disengagement, however, appears to be ending. Both the United States and Russia have lately shown signs of "reengagement." Indeed, Bosnia has proven to be one of the most vexing problems facing President Clinton. His handling of the problem has raised major doubts in the minds of many Europeans about the degree to which the United States can be counted on to directly engage itself in future European conflicts.[6]

At the same time, the conflict in Bosnia is likely to continue to present major challenges to the Clinton administration. If there is a settlement in Bosnia, the West European allies will be looking to the United States to make good on its commitment to provide substantial peacekeeping troops and will probably tie their own troop commitments to the size of the U.S. commitment. A failure of the United States to live up to its commitment to provide substantial peacekeeping forces would have serious repercussions not only for a settlement in Bosnia but for U.S.-European relations more broadly. It would be seen as a strong signal that the United States did not intend to play a major role in Europe's future and could lead to intensified efforts to create a separate European defense alternative to NATO.

Bosnia could also have an impact on U.S. relations with Russia. The initial pro-Western policy pursued by Foreign Minister Andnei Kozyrev has been replaced by a more independent and differentiated policy that has tacitly supported the Serbs. Indeed, Russia's policy since mid-1992 strongly suggests that it is determined to remain a player in the Balkans and even to increase its influence there. This Russian support for Serbia could pose an obstacle to improved ties between Russia and the United States especially if Russia moves in a more nationalist direction. At a minimum, the United States will have to be sensitive to Russian interests in the area in order to obtain Moscow's support in the UN for any eventual peace settlement.

---

[6] See in particular Francois Heisbourg and Pierre Lellouche, "Maastricht ou Sarajevo," *Le Monde*, June 17, 1993. Also Leo Wieland, "Führungsmacht mit beschränkter Führungskraft," *Frankfurter Allgemeine Zeitung*, June 23, 1993.

Restructuring Western Security Institutions

The developments in the Balkans since 1989 highlight the changing nature of the security dilemma in Europe in the post-Cold War era. Today the basic security challenge is not the threat of possible Soviet invasion, as it was during the Cold War, but the proliferation of ethnic conflicts and territorial disputes. Many of these are located on Europe's southern periphery—especially in the Balkans. But, as this volume makes clear, they are not peripheral. They are at the core of Europe's new security dilemma.

The Yugoslav crisis has highlighted the weaknesses of current security institutions to deal with these new threats. All told, the much touted new security "architecture" has not accorded itself well. The EC made a valiant attempt at mediation, but, as James Steinberg's chapter demonstrates, its efforts were hampered by the lack of internal consensus about objectives as well as the absence of any military mechanism to support its diplomacy. As a result, the parties concerned, especially Serbia, felt free to ignore its mediation, and the numerous cease-fires were violated almost as soon as they had been signed. These weaknesses must be addressed if the EC—now EU— is to play a more effective diplomatic role in future dispute resolutions.

In particular, the EU will need to develop a strong foreign policy arm. The agreement at Maastricht to create a small foreign policy secretariat is a small but important step in this direction. As Steinberg notes, this could help the EU to develop a capacity to respond more quickly to future crises. The EU will also need to acquire the capacity to mount collective military action. The creation of a separate European defense capability remains controversial, however, and is, in part, dependent on the evolution of the WEU. Therefore, it may be some time before such a capability is actually developed.

The Conference on Security and Cooperation in Europe (CSCE) has been another casualty of the Yugoslav crisis. In the Yugoslav crisis, the CSCE did little more than endorse actions undertaken by the EC. If the CSCE is to be effective in the future, the unanimity rule will have to be modified so that decisions can be made quickly. Adoption of the principle of "consensus minus one," approved at the Berlin CSCE meeting in June 1991, was a step in the right direction. However, at some point the CSCE may have to accept some form of majority rule if it is to be more than a forum for discussion.

NATO too needs to be restructured to make it more relevant to the post-Cold War world.[7] In the past, NATO has been careful to avoid involvement in "out-of-area" conflicts—that is, conflicts that do not involve direct aggression against member states. Yet, as Uwe Nerlich points out in his concluding chapter, few of the threats that NATO will face in the future are likely to require collective defense against an armed attack on NATO members, as stipulated by Article 5 of the Washington (NATO) Treaty. Rather, the most likely threats will be posed by Yugoslav-type conflicts on NATO's eastern periphery.

---

[7] For a detailed discussion, see Ronald D. Asmus, Richard Kugler and F. Stephen Larrabee, "Building a New NATO," *Foreign Affairs* 72, no. 4 (Fall 1993): 2–24.

The real question, as Nerlich notes, is whether NATO should be confined to an alliance of last resort, which would dramatically reduce its political and strategic utility, or whether it will be reformed in a manner that corresponds to the new political and strategic environment. With the end of the Cold War, the boundaries between "in-area" and "out-of-area" have become increasingly blurred. Formally, Eastern Europe, the Balkans, and the former USSR are all "out-of-area." Conflicts in these areas, however, have important consequences for alliance members—as the Yugoslav conflict underscores. Unless these conflicts are contained, they could set off a chain reaction that could directly touch on important alliance interests, even if they do not result in a direct armed attack on an alliance member.

The changed nature of the post-Cold War security environment requires NATO to rethink its approach to the "out-of-area" issue. NATO must transform itself from an alliance devoted primarily to collective defense in the event of armed attack to one concerned with enhancing security in the broadest sense. Such a reorientation would not require a formal revision of the NATO treaty but rather a shift in emphasis from collective defense against armed attack (Article 5) to the management and prevention of crises that affect alliance interests (Article 4). This would allow the alliance to deal more effectively with the key security problems facing Europe in the post-Cold War world.

At the same time, there is a need to work out a rational division of labor between NATO and other security institutions, particularly the WEU. In particular, it will be important to avoid a potentially destructive rivalry between the two organizations as each tries to prove that it is better equipped to handle the crises emerging in post-Cold War Europe. At the Helsinki Conference in July 1992, for instance, NATO and the WEU decided to send separate naval task forces into the Adriatic to monitor the UN-imposed sanctions against Serbia. The result was that two separate naval forces ended up patrolling the Adriatic—neither of which had powers of enforcement. The two task forces were eventually merged under NATO command in June 1993. Nevertheless, the initial dispatch of two separate task forces highlights the general danger of competition and duplication that must be avoided if both organizations are to contribute effectively to dampening and resolving future local crises.

The creation of the Combined Joint Task Force (CJTF), announced at the January 1994 NATO summit, goes a long way toward addressing this problem. It allows the WEU to draw on NATO assets in the case that the United States decides it does not want to involve itself in a conflict. Yet the exact division of labor between the various participants is not clear. Nor is it clear who will provide the forces. Moreover, as the Yugoslav conflict has demonstrated, the basic problem is not a lack of mechanisms but of political will. All the mechanisms in the world are of little value if there is not political will to use them.

NATO also must continue to refine its relations to the CSCE. The decision taken at the NATO summit in June 1992 to allow NATO to participate in peacekeeping operations under CSCE auspices on a case-by-case basis is an important step in this direction. But NATO's role should not be confined solely to peacekeeping in the classical sense—that is, interposing forces to maintain an agreed-upon cease-fire.

There may be instances in which the international community may be required to intervene to create or enforce peace against the will of the belligerents. It is precisely in these situations that NATO's unique assets may prove most valuable, either under UN or CSCE mandate.

Finally, the Balkan crisis has underscored the need to rethink the role of the UN in managing regional crises. The UN played a critical role in the Yugoslav conflict, especially in providing peacekeeping forces. There are disadvantages, however, in relying on the UN to try to solve all problems. Achieving consensus for UN action is time-consuming and gives non-European actors a disproportionate role in European affairs. It also risks overburdening the UN. It would be far better if regional organizations shouldered the main burden for crisis prevention or crisis management in Europe, with the UN providing the legitimizing authority for the actions taken by regional organizations such as NATO, the WEU, and CSCE. This would allow the UN to concentrate its peacekeeping efforts on those crises where it alone can be most effective and avoid spreading itself too thin.

The experience in Bosnia has underscored the need for more effective cooperation between the UN and NATO. One important lesson learned is the need for early consultations in the planning process. Such consultation can speed up the planning process and also help to clarify military options. A second lesson derived from the Bosnian experience is the need for enhanced communications and unity of command. Finally, complex peacekeeping operations require a clear mandate, a clear demarcation of responsibilities and a clear definition of the mission from the outset.

Bearing in mind these lessons should help to enhance cooperation between the UN and NATO in any future European crises. At the same time, however, NATO needs to retain its own identity. It should not just become a military subcontractor to the UN. It needs to maintain its capacity for independent and unilateral action if it is to remain an effective instrument for dealing with the new security threats in post-Cold War Europe.

PART 1

Domestic Change and Regional Stability

I

Prospects for Democracy in the Balkans: Comparative and Theoretical Perspectives

P. Nikiforos Diamandouros

For theorists of regime change and, more specifically, of transitions to democracy, the ongoing attempts at democratization in East Central Europe and the Balkans present a special case. Unlike previous transition experiences, all of which involved a move away from authoritarian regimes linked to market economies at various stages of development, the East European transitions constitute the first empirical cases of an attempted change away from posttotalitarian regimes in which centrally planned economies were a central feature.[1]

Viewed from this perspective, the systematic study of the particular problems associated with this set of transitions can be said to produce valuable insights for theorists, policymakers, and East European area specialists, while significantly increasing our understanding of the broad process of democratization that is rapidly gathering momentum around the world.[2]

---

[1] For a theoretical discussion of authoritarian and posttotalitarian regimes, see Juan J. Linz, "An Authoritarian Regime: Spain," in *Cleavages, Ideologies, and Party Systems,* ed., Erik Allardt and Yrjo Littunen (Helsinki: Transactions of the Westermarck Society, 1964), 291–342 and Linz, "Totalitarian and Authoritarian Regimes," in *Handbook of Political Science*, 3, ed. Fred I. Greenstein and Nelson W. Polsby (Reading, Mass.: Addison-Wesley, 1975), 264–350, which, on 336–350, also contains an initial discussion of "post-totalitarianism," viewed as a subtype of authoritarianism. For a more recent, more expanded, and more systematic treatment of this latter concept, see Juan J. Linz and Alfred Stepan, "Democratic Transitions and Consolidation: Eastern Europe, Southern Europe and Latin America," unpublished ms., (1991), ch. 1.

[2] Spurred, in part, by the wave of democratizations around the world, the renewed scholarly interest in democracy has resulted in a number of important, comparative and/or theoretical contributions

Within the broader universe of these concerns, the ongoing transitions in Poland, Czechoslovakia, and Hungary have, for various reasons, already attracted the attention of numerous scholars. Increased familiarity with the histories, politics, and cultures of East Central Europe; the renewed political significance and weight these countries carry within the region and in Europe as a whole; and the longer road toward democracy that they have already traveled, partly account for the interest they have attracted.[3]

Conversely, the study of transitions in the countries in the Balkans can be said to suffer from significant neglect—a state of affairs that this volume seeks partially to redress. This chapter has three aims—first, to outline briefly central features of democratic transitions that are derived from the experiences of other countries; second, to focus on the specific problems that the former communist countries in the Balkans are encountering as they attempt to negotiate their own transitions to democratic politics and to a market economy; and third, to provide a tentative assessment of both the prospects for consolidation of democracy and the type of democratic politics likely to emerge in each case.

Transition and Consolidation

A basic distinction in the burgeoning literature on democratization concerns the difference between transition and consolidation. These constitute separate and qualitatively different phases of the democratization process and should, for that reason,

---

on the subject. Some of the more recent of these include Larry Diamond, Juan J. Linz, and Seymour Martin Lipset, eds., *Democracy in Developing Countries*, 4 vols. (Boulder, Colo.: Lynne Rienner, 1988–1991); Samuel P. Huntington, *The Third Wave: Democratization in the Late Twentieth Century* (Norman, Okla.: University of Oklahoma Press, 1991); Adam Przeworski, *Democracy and the Market: Political and Economic Reforms in Eastern Europe and Latin America* (Cambridge: Cambridge University Press, 1991); Philippe C. Schmitter and Terry Lynn Karl, "What Democracy Is and Is Not," *Journal of Democracy* 2, no. 2 (Summer 1991): 75–88; Robert A. Dahl, *Democracy and Its Critics* (New Haven: Yale University Press, 1989); and the somewhat earlier but important contributions by Arend Lijphart, *Democracies: Patterns of Majoritarian and Consensus Government in Twenty-One Countries* (New Haven: Yale University Press, 1984) and G. Bingham Powell, Jr., *Contemporary Democracies: Participation, Stability, and Violence* (Cambridge, Mass.: Harvard University Press, 1982).

[3] The comparative study of East European transitions is still sparse but growing. Among the more recent works on the subject, see Adam Przeworski, *Democracy and the Market*; F. Stephen Larrabee, "Uncertain Democracies: Regime Change and Transitions," unpublished ms., 1991, which has the advantage that it deals equally with both East Central and Southeast European transitions; the special issue of *Daedalus* 119, no. 1 (Winter 1990); David Stark and Victor Nee, eds., *Remaking the Economic Institutions of Socialism: China and Eastern Europe* (Stanford: Stanford University Press, 1989); Timothy Garton Ash, *The Magic Lantern: The Revolution of 89 Witnessed in Warsaw, Budapest, Berlin and Prague* (New York: Random House, 1990), which deals with the early phase of the transitions; and the various papers presented at the conference on "Dilemmas of Transition from State Socialism in East Central Europe" (Center for European Studies, Harvard University, March 15–17, 1991).

be kept analytically distinct, although they often overlap in practice and are not always easy to distinguish. The important benefit derived from this analytical distinction is that it renders more readily intelligible the extent to which the content, nature, and, more generally, dynamics of transition directly affect the way in which democratic politics becomes consolidated (or fails to do so). In so doing, it also highlights the fact that the nature of democratic consolidation profoundly influences the quality of democracy.

Briefly, the transition is the earliest phase in the larger process of democratization. It immediately follows upon the end of the predecessor regime and constitutes the critical period during which (1) agreement concerning the fundamental rules of the democratic game is generated and (2) the rules, once formulated, are validated by means of free, popular elections that produce a government whose authority to conduct its business is not subject to an effective veto by other actors in the political system. It follows that the transition is characterized by great uncertainty and flux in which leadership and politics and, more generally, micro-level considerations assume center stage, while, conversely, longer-term social and economic factors diminish in importance.[4]

A central feature of the transition is the emergence or reemergence of actors such as political parties, trade unions, and business associations and their direct and central involvement in the negotiations leading to the rules of defining the democratic game. The nature and style of these negotiations, the degree of contestation associated with them, the recourse to, or avoidance of, pacts in reaching agreement concerning these rules—all will be greatly affected by the degree to which these actors show themselves willing to forgo a zero-sum logic in their dealings and to privilege

---

[4] The comparative literature on transitions is certainly rich by now. Among the more important contributions, see Guillermo O'Donnell, Philippe C. Schmitter, and Lawrence Whitehead, eds., *Transitions from Authoritarian Rule. Prospects for Democracy* (Baltimore: Johns Hopkins University Press, 1986) and especially Parts III "Comparative Perspectives" and IV "Tentative Conclusions About Uncertain Democracies"; Geoffrey Pridham, ed., *The New Mediterranean Democracies: Regime Transition in Spain, Greece and Portugal* (London: Frank Cass, 1984); Scott Mainwaring, *Transitions to Democracy and Democratic Consolidation: Theoretical and Comparative Issues*, Kellogg Institute for International Studies, Working Paper 130 (Notre Dame: University of Notre Dame, 1989); Juan J. Linz, "Transitions to Democracy," *The Washington Quarterly 13* (Summer 1990): 143–164; Giuseppe Di Palma, *To Craft Democracies: An Essay on Democratic Transitions* (Berkeley: University of California Press, 1990); and Juan J. Linz and Alfred Stepan, "Democratic Transitions and Consolidations," unpublished ms. (1991), where "transition" is conceptualized in terms very similar to the ones used in this analysis. See also, Julián Santamaría, ed., *Transición a la democracia en el Sur de Europa y América Latina* (Madrid: Centro de Investigaciones Sociológicas, 1982) and Enrique A. Baloyra, ed., *Comparing New Democracies: Transitions and Consolidation in Mediterranean Europe and the Southern Cone* (Boulder: Westview Press, 1987). On the role of leadership in transitions, see Juan J. Linz, "Innovative Leadership in the Transition to Democracy: The Case of Spain," paper presented at the Conference on Innovative Leadership and International Politics, Leonard Davis Institute for International Relations, Hebrew University, Jerusalem, June 8–10, 1987; and Gianfranco Pasquino, "Political Leadership in Southern Europe: Research Problems," *West European Politics* 13, no. 4 (October 1990): 118–130.

instead positive-sum approaches. Such approaches are capable of generating a climate of consensus and trust and of preparing firm foundations for the nascent democratic regime.

Though usually short, a transition may take a long time to complete. The four-month-long Greek transition in 1974 constitutes a good example of the former, while the sixteen-year-long (1974–1990) Brazilian transition is surely the lengthiest on record to date. The length of a transition is not necessarily a major factor affecting either the consolidation or the quality of democracy. To the extent, however, that the content and scope of any transition does profoundly affect both consolidation and the democracy issuing from it, an excessively brief or excessively protracted transition may well leave its mark on what follows. Thus, to pursue further the Greek and Brazilian examples, the brevity of the former—owing, in large part, to the need to move quickly to defuse the enormous pressures generated by the Cyprus crisis and the threat of armed conflict with Turkey, and to the desire of the forces leading the transition to minimize the time available to new (PASOK) or resurfacing (communist) forces to organize—effectively meant that the Greek transition lacked the type of negotiated transaction that was so salient a feature of the Spanish one, and which could have imparted a more consensual quality to the democracy that eventually emerged. Conversely, the very length of the Brazilian transition constituted telling evidence of the many obstacles (that is, and above all, the ability of the military effectively to control the pace of events) that hampered completion and that substantively contributed to the fragility that characterizes current attempts to consolidate Brazilian democracy.[5]

The relative importance of elite and collective actors in a given transition as well as the relation between them is another dimension of transitions worth noting. Consistent with the conceptualization of transition as a phase in the broader democratization process that privileges leadership in politics, the literature on the subject has tended to pay disproportionately greater attention to elites (parties, trade unions, business associations, and so forth) than to collective actors. A principal reason for

---

[5] On the Brazilian transition, see, among others, Alfred Stepan, ed., *Democratizing Brazil: Problems of Transition and Consolidation* (New York: Oxford University Press, 1989); Stepan, *Rethinking Military Politics: Brazil and the Southern Cone* (Princeton: Princeton University Press, 1988); Thomas Bruneau, "Brazil's Political Transition," in *Elites and Democratic Consolidation in Latin America and Southern Europe,* ed. John Higley and Richard Gunther (Cambridge: Cambridge University Press, 1992), 257–281; and Luciano Martins, "The 'Liberalization' of Authoritarian Rule in Brazil," in *Transitions from Authoritarianism,* part II, ed. O'Donnell, Schmitter and Whitehead, 72–94.

On the Greek transition, which, so far, has not been adequately studied, see Harry J. Psomiades, "Greece: From the Colonels' Rule to Democracy," in *From Dictatorship to Democracy: Coping with the Legacies of Authoritarianism and Totalitarianism*, ed. John H. Herz (Westport: Greenwood Press, 1982), 251–273; Constantine Arvanitopoulos, "The Political Economy of Regime Transition: The Case of Greece" (Ph.D. dissertation, The American University, 1989); and P. Nikiforos Diamandouros, "Regime Change and the Prospects for Democracy in Greece, 1974–1983," in *Transitions from Authoritarian Rule*, ed. O'Donnell, Schmitter and Whitehead, part I, 138–164.

that has been that, with few exceptions (for example, Portugal), the empirical universe on which scholars have, to date, based their theoretical conceptualizations concerning transitions has consisted of cases in which elites actually played the central role in shaping the course of events.

In this regard, it is worth noting the powerful influence of the Spanish experience upon students of transitions. The peaceful, reform-oriented, and transacted nature of that transition (aptly captured by the terms *ruptura pactada* and *reforma pactada*) and the intensive interelite negotiations and carefully constructed pacts that became its distinguishing feature helped produce a settlement capable of generating and sustaining broad social and political consensus concerning the way to exit from the authoritarian regime and to build a democratic successor. These are some of the major reasons that it is widely regarded as the most elegant and compelling transition model to date.[6]

The critical role played by elite actors in the Spanish transition has tended to obscure the extent to which collective actors, though certainly not dominant, do constitute an important element in the transition process. In a recent paper, Sidney Tarrow has argued that collective actors should be thought of as setting the "structure of opportunity" within which elites can operate in guiding the transition toward a hoped-for successful completion. Such a concept underscores the need to recall that, despite their admittedly critical role, elite actors do not operate in vacuo during transitions and that, in various ways, collective actors can either enlarge or restrict the political space available for elite action. In the process, this can substantively affect not only the nature and scope of the transition but also subsequent phases of the democratization process.[7]

---

[6] Though it focuses on democratic consolidation rather than transition, the edited volume by John Higley and Richard Gunther, *Elites and Democratic Consolidation in Southern Europe and Latin America,* contains a good discussion concerning the importance of elites in democratization. See, especially, Michael Burton, Richard Gunther and John Higley, "Introduction: Elite Transformations and Democratic Regimes," 1–37. Specifically with regard to the role of elites in transitions, see John Higley and Michael Burton, "The Elite Variable in Democratic Transitions and Breakdowns," *American Sociological Review* 54 (1989): 17–32. For a critical view of the elite approach, see Paul Cammack, "A Critical Assessment of the New Elite Paradigm," *American Sociological Review* 55 (1990): 415–420.

The literature on the Spanish transition is extensive. Notable analyses of this case include Jose Maria Maravall and Julián Santamaría, "Political Change in Spain and Prospects for Democracy," in *Transitions from Authoritarian Rule,* ed. O'Donnell, Schmitter and Whitehead, part I, 71–108; Jose Maria Maravall, *The Transition to Democracy in Spain* (London: Croom Helm, 1982); Paul Preston, *The Triumph of Democracy in Spain* (London: Methuen, 1986); Donald Share, *The Making of Spanish Democracy* (New York: Praeger, 1986); Robert Fishman, *Working-Class Organizations and the Return to Democracy in Spain* (Ithaca: Cornell University Press, 1990); and Richard Gunther, Giacomo Sani and Goldie Shabad, *Spain After Franco: The Making of the Competitive Party System* (Berkeley: University of California Press, 1986).

[7] On the role of collective actors in providing the "opportunity structure" in transitions, see Sidney Tarrow, "Transitions to Democracy as Waves of Mobilization With Applications to Southern Europe" (Paper delivered at the Social Science Research Council conference on "Democratization in Southern Europe," Delphi, Greece, 4–7 July 1991).

In contrast to transitions, consolidations involve the legitimization and institutionalization of the democratic rules of the game at both the elite and mass levels and the elimination of nondemocratic solutions as viable alternatives to the existing regime. By its very nature, consolidation is a longer-term process involving, among other things, the reassertion of social, economic, and other macrostructures that were relatively quiescent during transition. The length of the consolidation phase varies, depending on the criteria used to determine its completion. Thus, while some scholars consider a concrete event, such as change (at least once or, according to others, twice) in governmental incumbency, as tangible evidence of the completion of consolidation, others prefer more complex, qualitative criteria stressing changes in attitudes, behavior, structures or, more generally, political culture. In the latter more extreme case, consolidation may well take from a decade to as much as a generation to complete.[8]

Because the countries of the Balkans, which constitute the central focus of this chapter, are still far from the consolidation stage of their democratization process, the following analysis will be concerned primarily with the dynamics and morphology of transitions and will only deal with consolidation to the extent that the treatment of a particular transition requires it. This is particularly true of the concluding section of the chapter, which attempts to extrapolate from the transitions of individual countries in the region and to assess their prospects for consolidation and democratic politics.

A final issue that is theoretically important concerns the meaning of "democracy." The pertinent literature as well as the more specialized work on democratization points to the existence of two major schools of thought on this subject. The substantive or maximalist conception of democracy preferred by some seeks to extend the principle of equality beyond the realm of politics to that of society and the economy. It follows that such a view of democracy accords little legitimacy to the alternative, minimalist conception that considers equality at the political realm (or what is often referred to as "procedural democracy") as an end worth pursuing in and of itself. According to exponents of the maximalist definition, political democracy can serve as a front behind which profound social and economic inequalities can survive, thrive, and even become partially legitimated. At best, it can be thought of as a stage in the evolution of democracy toward a more meaningful or substantive content.

What I refer to as the minimalist definition has, during the past decade, acquired

---

[8] The literature on democratic consolidation, though still limited, is beginning to expand. See, especially, Geoffrey Pridham, ed., *Securing Democracy. Political Parties and Democratic Consolidation in Southern Europe* (London: Routledge, 1990); and John Higley and Richard Gunther, eds., *Elites and Democratic Consolidation in Latin America and Southern Europe.* For the position that consolidation may require as much as a generation to complete, see Geoffrey Pridham, "The International Context of Democratic Consolidation: Italy, Spain, Greece and Portugal in Comparative Perspective," in *The Politics of Democratic Consolidation in Southern Europe* (forthcoming), ed. P. Nikiforos Diamandouros, Richard Gunther and Hans Jürgen Puhle.

increasing support even among scholars, especially in Latin America, who had earlier been inclined to privilege the maximalist definition in their analyses of the prospects for democracy in that region. Central to the minimalist definition of democracy is an emphasis on procedural criteria guaranteeing equality at the political realm by means of periodic, regularly held, free, and competitive popular consultations, in which there are few restrictions to participation and civil liberties are carefully protected. It is this more restricted definition that has gained salience in works concerning democratization and that also informs the analysis that follows.[9]

Transition Parameters

What types of factors are likely to affect a given transition? More broadly, what are the structures or forces that serve as wider parameters of the transition that domestic actors involved in that transition must consider in formulating their strategies? In this context, one can distinguish three broad large clusters—the country's long-term heritage, the legacy of the preceding regime, and the international context within which the transition occurs. The specific way in which these three interact and the particular weight that conjunctural circumstances may assign to one or all of them will directly affect the dynamics of the transition and will inevitably affect the course of the ensuing democratic consolidation. Much like collective actors, these factors can be thought of as serving to set Tarrow's "opportunity structure" that can either enhance or restrict the freedom of movement enjoyed by elites as they seek to solidify.[10]

Long-Term Heritage

By "long-term heritage," I mean the cumulative political, cultural, social, and economic capital that each society brings into the transition. This heritage is intimately related to the history and particular configuration of state-society relations in a given country. The relative strength or weakness of civil society or, more generally, the relative development or underdevelopment in it of Montesquieu's *corps intermédiaires* and the legacy of a mediated or unmediated exercise of power will profoundly affect the dynamics of the transition and its eventual trajectory. So, too, will the capacity of elites to generate agreement concerning the fundamental rules

---

[9] For a similar analysis, see Michael Burton, Richard Gunther, and John Higley, "Introduction: Elite Transformations and Democratic Regimes," in *Elites and Democratic Consolidation in Latin America and Southern Europe*, ed. Higley and Gunther, 1–38. A minimalist conception of democracy is also a salient feature of Di Palma's *To Craft Democracies*.

[10] In this sense, Tarrow's notion of the "opportunity structure" seems, in certain ways, to parallel the concept of "antecedent conditions" which Kirchheimer distinguished from "confining conditions" in his influential article concerning regime change. On this, see Otto Kirchheimer, "Confining Conditions and Revolutionary Breakthroughs," *American Political Science Review* 59, no. 4 (December 1965): 964–974.

that are critical—not only to the success of the transition but also to the nature of consolidation and the quality of the resulting democratic regime.[11]

A particularly important subset of these long-term factors concerns the culture of conflict resolution upon the transition and the number of salient and divisive structural issues or problems that remain unresolved at the moment of transition. With respect to the former, the prevalence or relative marginality of zero-sum, as opposed to positive-sum, conceptions of conflict resolution may directly affect the degree to which the transition will follow a path reminiscent of the Spanish *reforma pactada* model. In this instance, negotiating a series of critical agreements between and among important elite actors will effect a climate of consensus and trust that will probably have commensurately benign effects on the consolidation and the resulting democratic politics in that country.

The number of unresolved and potentially divisive long-term problems that are carried into the transition can greatly complicate its successful completion and may even contribute to its failure. This is especially true if the prevailing culture of conflict resolution in the society tends to privilege zero-sum over positive-sum approaches and, therefore, impedes consensus-building. Good examples of such issues are the lack of settled and uncontested state boundaries, continuing uncertainty concerning national identity, or the survival or resuscitation of primordial sentiments that are particularly divisive cultural cleavages capable of undermining the course of the transition.[12]

How do the foregoing considerations apply to the transitions now in progress in the former communist countries in the Balkans? A central feature of these transitions is that they are occurring in what I call post-Ottoman societies burdened by a pronounced, though varied, sultanistic heritage. As used originally by Max Weber and elaborated more recently by Juan Linz, "sultanism" is an ideal type describing

---

[11] For Montesquieu's discussion concerning structures of intermediation, see Baron de Montesquieu, *The Spirit of the Laws* (New York: Hafner, 1962), 66–70 and 120–125.

[12] The unsettled or contested nature of state boundaries constitutes a major factor complicating the transitions in the Balkan states. Its significance is accorded particular attention by both Linz and Stepan, "Democratic Transitions and Consolidations," unpublished ms. (1991) and Claus Offe, "Capitalism by Democratic Design? Democratic Theory Facing the Triple Transition in East Central Europe," *Social Research* 58, no. 4 (Winter 1991): 865–892. On the concept of "primordial sentiments" (that is, "the . . . attachment[s] stem[ming] from the assumed 'givens' of social existence [, the] congruities of blood, speech, custom, and so on [which] are seen to have an ineffable, and, at times overpowering, coerciveness in and of themselves") and on their impact on state-building and, especially, nation-building processes, see Clifford Geertz, "The Integrative Revolution: Primordial Sentiments and Civil Politics in the New States," in *Old Societies and New States,* ed. Geertz (New York: The Free Press, 1963), 105–158. See also, Edward Shils, "Political Development in the New States," *Comparative Studies in Society and History* 2 (1960): 265–292 and 379–411 as well as Shils, "Primordial, Personal, Sacred and Civil Ties," *British Journal of Sociology* (June 1957). Finally, it is worth recalling the emphasis that Locke placed on the significance of "trust" as a requisite of smooth state-society relations. On this, see especially Peter Laslett's comments in his introduction to John Locke's *Two Treatises of Government* (New York: Mentor, 1965), 126–130.

regimes distinguished, above all, by the highly personal and arbitrary nature of rule, by the absence of the rule of law, the unmediated and despotic exercise of power, low institutionalization, the absence of intermediary structures, and, hence, the weakness of civil society. By implication, the term also points to the debility of democratic heritage in such a regime. This characteristic is especially pertinent in any attempt to assess the nature of transitions in the Balkans, to place them in comparative perspective, to consider the prospects for their successful completion, and to speculate about the type of regime likely to emerge from them.[13]

The Legacy of the Preceding Regime

The legacy of the predecessor regime as distinct from the country's long-term heritage is another, more circumscribed, parameter that is certain to affect a transition. The specific structures—political, cultural, economic, or social—which a preceding regime bequeaths to its successor constitute a reality that the transition must confront or, at least, cope with. The degree of extrication from that legacy eventually attained by a transition will greatly affect its capacity to contribute to a more successful consolidation and to the quality of the democratic regime likely to emerge.[14]

In this context, the Balkan transitions add an important theoretical dimension to the treatment of this subject. For, along with the transitions in the rest of East Central Europe and in certain of the successor states of the Soviet Union, they allow us to focus on the problems of democratization peculiar to posttotalitarian, as opposed to authoritarian, regimes. Before the advent of the East European transitions, the universe of empirical cases on which the study of this subject was based concerned authoritarian regimes in which limited, though not responsible, political pluralism, often with roots in the antecedent regime, frequently coexisted with a significant social and economic pluralism. By contrast, one of the central problems complicating and hindering the transitions to democracy in East Central Europe and the Balkans stems from a structural feature typical of most posttotalitarian regimes—the

---

[13] On the concept of "sultanistic regimes," see Max Weber, *Economy and Society: An Outline of Interpretive Sociology*, ed. Guenther Roth and Claus Wittich (Berkeley: University of California Press, 1978), 231–232; Juan J. Linz, "Totalitarian and Authoritarian Regimes," in *Handbook of Political Science*, Vol. 3, ed. Greenstein and Polsby, 259–263 for an earlier discussion of the concept; and Juan J. Linz and Alfred Stepan, "Democratic Transitions and Consolidation," unpublished ms. (1991), ch. 1, for a greatly revised and expanded treatment.

[14] The problem of how a successor regime (and, especially, a democratic one) deals with the legacy of its nondemocratic predecessor is a central theoretical as well as policy concern for students and practitioners of democratic politics. It constitutes the main focus of John H. Herz, ed., *From Dictatorship to Democracy*, and, especially, Herz, "Introduction: Method and Boundaries," in the same volume, 3–12. See also Di Palma's treatment of this topic in the context of his discussion of the transfer of loyalties to democratic regimes in his *To Craft Democracies*, 27–43. On the somewhat different topic of how the legacy of the predecessor regime affects democratic transition and consolidation, see Leonardo Morlino, "Democratic Establishment: A Dimensional Analysis," in *Comparing New Democracies*, ed. Enrique A. Baloyra, 53–78.

absence of meaningful pluralism in the economic realm, and basic unfamiliarity with the nature and workings of the economic market.[15]

More generally, the nature and extent of social, economic, or political pluralism in a nondemocratic regime constitute factors that vitally affect the ensuing transition. The relative strength or weakness of structures capable, because of previous learning made possible in the context of limited pluralism, of negotiating with the state in producing the agreements necessary for democratization, will decisively influence the trajectory traveled by a particular transition. It will also, in many ways, spell the difference between its eventual success, stagnation, or outright failure. In the case of the Balkan states, the lesser degree of pluralism typical of posttotalitarian regimes has combined with a sultanistic heritage to produce formidable confining conditions that powerfully affect the transitions now in progress and, more generally, the democratization process as a whole.

The International Context

The international context within which a transition occurs is a third factor to be considered. It is important to note that the experience of the countries in this broader region has significantly diverged from that in both Latin America and Southern Europe, where, with the partial exception of Portugal and Greece, the international factor did not directly and prominently affect the transitions.[16]

---

[15] The degree to which the Hungarian involvement in "controlled market experiments" contributed to the development of economic pluralist structures and, as such, greatly facilitated this country's capacity to cope with the stresses and strains of the economic transition underscores the significance of the problem arising from the absence of such pluralism in most of the region.

On the nature of authoritarian regimes and on the extent to which they allow for significant social and economic pluralism, see (beyond the already cited works of Juan J. Linz, "An Authoritarian Regime: Spain," "Totalitarian and Authoritarian Regimes," and [with Alfred Stepan] "Democratic Transitions and Consolidations"), Guillermo A. O'Donnell, *Modernization and Bureaucratic-Authoritarianism: Studies in South American Politics* (Berkeley: Institute of International Studies, University of California, 1979); David Collier, ed., *The New Authoritarianism in Latin America* (Princeton: Princeton University Press, 1979); James M. Malloy, *Authoritarianism and Corporatism in Latin America* (Pittsburgh: University of Pittsburgh Press, 1977); and Hans Binnendijk, "Introduction: Prospects for Success in Transitions from Authoritarianism," in *Authoritarian Regimes in Transition,* ed. Binnendijk (Washington, D.C.: Foreign Service Institute, United States Department of State, 1987), ix–xxvi.

[16] The emphasis that pertinent analyses have accorded to domestic factors influencing transitions has tended to obscure the extent to which the international environment constitutes an important dimension of the overall context within which transitions occur. And, as such, it has an impact on transitions which, naturally, varies from case to case. The salience of the international factor in the East European transitions is correctly underscored by F. Stephen Larrabee in his "Uncertain Democracies: Regime Change and Transitions," 11–14 and 49–53. To date, the most influential work on this topic has been by Lawrence Whitehead and, more recently, Geoffrey Pridham. For the former, see Lawrence Whitehead, "International Aspects of Democratization," in *Transitions from Authoritarianism*, part III, ed. O'Donnell, Schmitter and Whitehead, 3–46 and "Democracy by

There are at least three levels on which the impact of international factors on the East Central and, more particularly, the Balkan transitions must be understood. The first concerns the circumstances under which the transitions were triggered. The withdrawal of the regional hegemon that had, for over four decades, effectively and repeatedly blocked any attempt at liberalization (Prague Spring), let alone democratization, was the critical event that helped to launch the regional transitions. The vital significance of the role of the hegemon (the Soviet Union) for launching the transitions is underscored by two additional observations. First, in the late 1980s, the Soviet Union and, especially, Mikhail Gorbachev, had indeed attempted to promote what previous Soviet regimes had steadfastly refused to allow: a liberalization of the East European regimes, which would have been in line with the unfolding of *perestroika* in the Soviet Union and would have produced what were hoped to be more viable and durable regimes. This policy was clearly articulated in many of Gorbachev's announcements beginning in late 1987, which stressed that members of the Soviet bloc were free to pursue their own road to the fuller development of socialism. In addition, throughout the two-year period that began with the open encouragement of liberalization in late 1987 and ended with the collapse of the East European communist regimes in late 1989, Gorbachev, on numerous occasions, acted in ways that helped to accelerate the pace of change in Eastern Europe.[17]

Second, the event that effectively launched the transitions in the entire region was the Soviet refusal to come to the defense of the Honecker regime in early October 1989. Once, as a result of this development, the abandonment of the Brezhnev Doctrine of limited sovereignty had been convincingly demonstrated, the old regimes began to fall, and countries throughout the region entered the uncertain and turbulent waters of transition.

The failed putsch of August 19, 1991, in the Soviet Union should, finally, be considered as an additional international factor positively affecting the transitions in Eastern Europe. More specifically, the collapse of hardline opposition to *perestroika* in the Soviet Union eliminated even the slimmest possibility of a desperate Soviet attempt to influence negatively the course of events in East Central

---

Convergence and Southern Europe: A Comparative Politics Perspective," in *Encouraging Democracy: The International Context of Regime Transition in Southern Europe,* ed. Geoffrey Pridham (Leicester: Leicester University Press, 1991), 45–61. For Pridham, see his "International Influences and Democratic Transition: Problems of Theory and Practice in Linkage Politics," in *Encouraging Democracy*, ed. Pridham, 1–28. For a recent work that critically and constructively surveys the literature on the subject, see Basilios Evangelos Tsingos, "Underwriting Democracy, Not Exporting It: The European Community's Effect on the Greek Transition to Democracy" (M.Phil. thesis, St. Magdalen College, University of Oxford, 1992).

[17] On the importance of the regional hegemon for triggering the transitions in Eastern Europe, see, among others, F. Stephen Larrabee, "Uncertain Democracies," 11–14; René Nevers, "The Soviet Union and Eastern Europe: The End of an Era," *Adelphi Papers*, no. 249 (London: International Institute for Strategic Studies, 1990); and Charles Gati, *The Bloc That Failed: Soviet-East European Relations in Transition* (London: I. B. Tauris, 1990).

Europe and the Balkans by lending its support to hardliners in these countries. More important, events in the Soviet Union spurred the further acceleration of the democratization process, by eliminating the residual capacity of hardline elements in various countries in the region to derail it.

The second level at which the international factor exerted itself in the East Central and Balkan transitions concerns the role of the European Community (since renamed European Union) and of the United States in these events. In this regard, it is important to distinguish between the broader crisis that the collapse of the Soviet bloc and the end of the old order effected at the regional and international levels in Eastern Europe and the narrower and more domestic process of the transition to democracy in the individual countries within that region.

As far as the first is concerned, undoubtedly the United States was, from the outset, more inclined to consider the crisis a European affair that should properly be left to the Europeans and, more specifically, to the European Union (formerly EC) to handle. And it is also true that, despite the enormous problems that this entailed, the EU, with Germany at its helm, was eager to play a central role in managing the crisis.

The same observation cannot be made with regard to the transitions *stricto sensu*, where the role of the EC has tended to be much less prominent. This is especially true in regard to the Balkans, where, admittedly, the Yugoslav crisis has tended to absorb most, if not all, of the EC's energies and attention, to the inevitable detriment of the requirements of the transitions in the broader region. While individual member states, especially Germany, have shown greater interest in this process, it is the United States that has been most visible in this regard, in both East Central Europe and the Balkans.

Although the full role of the United States in these events is still difficult to assess, it is worth noting that it has taken multiple forms and has not been confined at the formal, governmental level. Indeed, much of the American input in the transitions has been the result of activities by semiofficial or private organizations that have invested considerable material and human resources in advising leading transition actors about alternative courses of action and in providing them with sorely needed infrastructure. Examples of many such private initiatives include the Soros Foundation, the Charter-77 Foundation–New York, the German Marshall Fund, and the American Bar Association. Although the motivation behind this impressive mobilization of resources varies from organization to organization, it is safe to assume that it represents a mixture of domestic American constituencies with overlapping commitments to economic and political liberalism, democratic principles and anticommunism, and is led by an equally varied set of actors in which East European expatriates, businessmen, policy specialists and academics figure prominently.[18]

---

[18] The story of the greater European Community involvement in the management of the East European crisis and of the more prominent American presence in the politics of the transitions has yet to be systematically studied. For an interesting policy-oriented document addressing some of these issues, see *The Community and the Emerging European Democracies: A Joint Policy Report* (London: Royal Institute of International Affairs, 1991). I wish to thank Ambassador Eythymios

The international environment has affected the ongoing transitions in Eastern Europe in yet another significant way. It has served as a marketplace of ideas, or, more specifically, provided models for political and economic reconstruction that the transition leaders in each country in the region can import and adapt to the needs of their societies. Although "democracy" and the "market" appear to be the undisputed choices of all the emerging regimes in the region, however, the particular type of democracy or market that is likely to prevail in each country remains less clear.[19]

Insofar as the transitions in question are concerned, there exist two major variants of each model. On the level of politics (democracy), the choice is between traditional parliamentarism of the continental variety ensuring the ascendancy of the legislature over the executive, and some form of semipresidentialism, influenced by the experience of the Fifth French Republic. In numerous cases, however, it also has drawn upon distinct indigenous traditions and has been equipped with a strong executive that is popularly elected and, thus, has been invested with direct popular legitimacy capable of effectively competing with that of the legislature. In this connection, it is also worth recalling Linz's observation that the order in which founding elections occur (that is, legislative before presidential or vice versa) may have a significant impact not only on the dynamics of the transition but also on democratic consolidation and on the quality of the ensuing democracy.

Linz's more general point concerning the drawbacks associated with privileging presidentialist over parliamentary institutional arrangements in transitions to democracy is worth remembering for two major reasons. The first is that the "winner-take-all" logic of presidentialism, which works against consensus-building and inhibits the emergence of positive-sum outcomes, is ill-suited for the needs and requirements of transitions—delicate processes whose eventual success hinges on the capacity of the central actors involved in them to reach agreements concerning new rules of the game and to generate the climate of conciliation which, in turn, will enhance the chances of democratic consolidation. The second is that the societies of East Central Europe and, especially, the Balkans lack a cultural, historical, and political heritage of consensus politics and are rather prone to confrontational, zero-sum conceptions of the political game that are more likely to become exacerbated rather than curbed by adopting a presidentialist system.

A quick survey of recent developments in the Balkans concerning this issue provides mixed signals. On the one hand, Albania and Bulgaria (as well as the countries in the northern frontier of Eastern Europe) have opted for a parliamentary,

Stoforopoulos, director of the Greek Institute for International and Strategic Studies, for bringing to my attention this publication, which is the joint product of six European institutes of international affairs. For a glimpse of the role played by nongovernmental organizations, see Herman Schwartz, "Constitutional Developments in East Central Europe," *Journal of International Affairs* (Summer 1991): 71–89 and *TransAtlantic Perspectives 24* (Autumn 1991): 10–12, for an account indicating the strong interest that the German Marshall Fund of the United States has taken in this matter.

[19] The demonstration effect concerning democracy as the dominant model of political organization at present is extensively discussed in Juan J. Linz and Alfred Stepan, "Democratic Transitions and Consolidations," ch. 2 as well as in, among others, Di Palma, *To Craft Democracies*, 183–199.

rather than a presidential, system of government. At the same time, it is worth noting that, in the Bulgarian case, as of January 1992, the president is popularly elected, thus deriving his democratic legitimacy independently of, rather than through, parliament. Reflecting both the sultanic heritage of Ceausescu's regime and, more generally, the more problematic nature of its own transition, Romania has adopted a mixture of the two systems, which accords greater power to the presidency than do the other two countries. It is instructive to note, however, that the newly installed president of Albania, Sali Berisha, is seeking expanded powers which, if granted and rendered permanent, could significantly erode the parliamentary nature of the political system in that country. Moreover, the quest (Albania) or provision (Romania) for enhanced presidential powers in these countries (which, incidentally, parallel Lech Walesa's similar bid in Poland) seems to inscribe itself in the tradition of "strong leadership" historically characteristic of the political cultures in these societies.

Seen in this light, the apparent decline in the fortunes of the Bulgarian presidency and the commensurate increase of the power of the government and of the prime minister can be said to constitute additional, though tentative, evidence indicating the enhancement of the democratization dynamic in that country. Whether this will turn out to be so will, to a great extent, depend on the ability and willingness of the political forces in control of the Bulgarian parliamentary system to prevent the rising tensions between the government and President Zhelyu Zhelev from being cast in a zero-sum pattern of conflict and of promoting, instead, consensus-oriented positive-sum solutions (including a much talked-about amendment to the constitution) capable of defusing, if not solving, the problems arising from the clash between the two institutions.[20]

A second, though less salient, dimension of this competition between alternative modes of political organization concerns the choice between a centralized (unitary-model) as opposed to a decentralized (federal-model) form of state. The latter is considered better able to resist, if not to prevent, the kind of concentration of power that in the predecessor regimes was one cause of enormous abuses. All of these issues will form part of the larger package concerning the choice of suitable institutional arrangements addressed by the constitutional documents that will eventually emerge from the transition process in each country.[21]

On the level of economics, finally, some variant of a mixed-economy model seems

---

[20] For a good sample of Juan Linz's views on how the choice of presidentialism or parliamentarism is likely to affect the transition to democracy, see his "Democracy: Presidential or Parliamentary. Does It Make a Difference?" unpublished ms. (1984) also published as "Democracia: Presidentialismo/ Parlamentarismo. ¿Hace alguna diferencia?" in *Hacia una democracia moderna: La opcion parlamentaria,* ed. Oscar Godoy Arcaya (Santiago: Universidad Catolica de Chile, 1990), 41–108; "Perils of Presidentialism," *Journal of Democracy* 1 (Winter 1990): 51–69; and "The Virtues of Parliamentarism," *Journal of Democracy* 1 (Fall 1990): 84–92. See also the concurring remarks by Di Palma, *To Craft Democracies*, 216 note 13 and Przeworski, *Democracy and the Market*, 34 note 44.

[21] The issue of the merits and demerits of federalist and unitary states was one of the central themes in the international conference on the prospects for democracy in Bulgaria organized by the Center for the Study of Democracy, December 17–20, 1990.

to compete with a conception of the free market that appears to be closer to theoretical discussions of unbridled nineteenth-century capitalism than to any actual form of "extant capitalism."

The debates concerning the adoption of either of these alternative models and, especially, the often unrealistic assumptions that inform them should be understood at two levels. The first concerns the strong desire, shared by elites and masses in these countries, to adopt models of political and economic organization that are as far removed as possible from the culture and practices of the predecessor communist regimes and the centrally planned economies intimately associated with them. This explains the strong attraction that American (or, more precisely, what are often naively presumed to be American) market and political arrangements exercise upon leaders and followers in these countries. These arrangements represent a cultural and ideological commitment to the concept of freedom which, at the moment, is extraordinarily appealing to the majority of citizens of East Central Europe and the Balkans who need to exorcise a painful past and build a promising future.

Second, the search for exogenously derived models of political and economic reconstruction serves as a poignant reminder of the weakness, if not absence, of indigenous democratic and capitalist traditions in most of these countries. Indeed, with the exception of the Czechoslovak democratic experience of the interwar period and the much more recent Hungarian engagement in "controlled market experiments," the remainder of the countries in the region face the formidable challenges of the dual transition confronting them with hardly any significant indigenous cultural capital concerning the meaning and workings of democratic politics and the market mechanism. Once again, this is particularly true of the Balkans, where the sultanistic and posttotalitarian heritages combine to confront the transitions in the region with an even more acute democratic and capitalist "deficit."[22]

To sum up: the profound influence of the international environment upon the East European transitions constitutes a distinguishing feature of the democratization process peculiar to this region, which sets it apart from both the Southern European and the Latin American experiences. One of the most significant, long-term consequences of totalitarian and posttotalitarian regimes in this region has been the

[22] On the historical background that explains the weakness of the democratic and market structures in the Balkans, see, among others, Leften S. Stavrianos, *The Balkans Since 1453* (New York: Holt, Rinehart, Winston, 1958); Iván Berend and György Ránki, *The European Periphery and Industrialization 1780–1914* (Cambridge: Cambridge University Press, 1982); John R. Lampe and Marvin R. Jackson, *Balkan Economic History, 1550–1950: From Imperial Borderlands to Developing Nations* (Bloomington: Indiana University Press, 1982); Charles and Barbara Jelavich, *The Establishment of Balkan National States, 1804–1920* (Seattle: University of Washington Press, 1977). For the more recent period, see Joseph Rothschild, *East Central Europe Between the Two World Wars* (Seattle: University of Washington Press, 1974); Rothschild, *Return to Diversity: A Political History of East Central Europe Since World War II* (New York: Oxford University Press, 1989); Robert Lee Wolff, *The Balkans in Our Time* (Cambridge: Harvard University Press, 1956); and Nicos P. Mouzelis, *Politics in the Semi-Periphery. Early Parliamentarism and Late Industrialisation in the Balkans and Latin America* (London: Macmillan, 1986).

great debility of civil society and of the domestic structures associated with it. This development has commensurately augmented the role that the international factor has played in the tortuous road to the dual transition to political democracy and the market economy in East Central and, especially, Balkan societies and states.

Transition Trajectories

What are the specific problems confronting the Balkan states, as they negotiate their individual transition trajectories and as they attempt to establish political democracies for the first time in their histories? If the dual nature of the transition has already been described as a major factor complicating the broader democratization process in these countries, the simultaneity of the political and economic transition further exacerbates the constraints and burdens plaguing the delicate democratization process in societies with little learning and few collective memories concerning either democratic politics or market principles.

The issue of "overburdening" acquires greater significance in light of a further difference clearly distinguishing the transitions in the Balkans from those to its north. To wit, they were initiated and, initially at least, controlled by elites identified with the predecessor, posttotalitarian regime. Indeed, if the capacity of the old regimes to play such a central role in the early stages of the transition underscores the weakness of civil society structures in all of the region, it also serves as a strong indication that, precisely because of this weakness, the transitions in the Balkans are more than likely to be protracted, troublesome, and inconclusive.[23]

The central role that the reform elements in the old regime have played in the unfolding of the transition to democracy in the Balkans deserves further comment, because it points to the emergence of a discernible and distinctive pattern of democratization peculiar to this region. This involves (a) an initial phase in which reform elements in the crumbling posttotalitarian regime initiate the transition and, despite weak and disorganized opposition, manage to win the first elections by efficiently

[23] F. Stephen Larrabee, in his "Uncertain Democracies," insists on the significance of the "dual nature" of the transitions, both as a complicating or "burdening" factor and as a distinguishing feature of the democratization process in Eastern Europe. See also Di Palma, *To Craft Democracies*, 76–108. In the article just cited (p. 19), Larrabee also points to the central role played by reform elements in the old regime in shaping the distinctive pattern of the "delayed, two-step" transition to democracy in the Balkans. (For a similar analysis, see also Offe, "Capitalism by Democratic Design?" 887–892.) It is perhaps worth noting, in this context, the extent to which the rural-urban cleavage figures prominently in the dynamics of the "delayed" pattern of democratic transition in the Balkans. The degree to which the forces of the old regime had been able to retain their control of the rural areas underscores their capacity to appeal to the less modernized sectors in these societies, to those strata that feel most ambivalent about the loss of state protection and the sharp increase in uncertainty implicit in the transition from a command economy to the market mechanism. As such, this same development is a poignant reminder of the lingering hold of powerful, antiurban, antibourgeois, and, more generally, anticapitalist traditions—long a salient feature of the political cultures of these societies—on contemporary Balkan politics.

using their administrative experience and lingering political strength in rural areas and among the less educated and less competitive strata; (b) a second stage is marked by the burgeoning of the opposition forces, increasing popular pressures for reform, and the growing incapacity of the old-regime elements in control of the government to consolidate their electoral victory and effectively to impede change. The result is (c) the calling of new elections in which a disparate coalition composed of various opposition forces triumphs and ensures the end of the old regime. In this third stage, in which Albania and Bulgaria, but not Romania, now find themselves, the democratic forces belatedly enter upon a critical moment in the democratization process, on the successful negotiation of which hinges the eventual fate (success, stagnation, or failure) of consolidation. It is at this phase, finally, that the structural problems associated with the debility of civil society structures in the region begin to resurface and to affect the day-to-day operation of the political process.

In this regard, the contrast with the transitions in East Central Europe is instructive. In the latter, civil society was sufficiently strong to have been able to organize in ways that precluded the pattern of regime-led transitions that has occurred in the Balkans. Conversely, the incapacity of the Balkan societies to produce the functional equivalents of Czechoslovakia's Civic Forum, let alone of Poland's Solidarity, has meant that societal mobilization has been, for the most part, inchoate and inarticulate and, as a result, unable substantively to contribute to the deepening of the transition and to the commensurate enhancement of the democratization process.

It is, incidentally, this weakness of civil society (and its obverse: the centrality of the state), themselves the combined long-term heritage of sultanistic rule and totalitarian regimes in the former Ottoman lands, which qualitatively distinguishes the transition pattern in the Balkans from those in East Central and Southern Europe. It is also this fundamental change, which renders the Spanish model of transition so inapplicable to the Balkan cases, despite the superficial similarity that arises from the fact that in both cases the new regime was the result of the slow, peaceful, and carefully controlled self-transformation of its predecessor. For it was precisely the presence of powerful and well-developed structures of intermediation—Montesquieu's famous *corps intermédiaires*—and the high degree of social and economic pluralism that they implied that enabled the peculiar—and, in that sense, atypical rather than prototypical—trajectory of the Spanish transition. In short, because of its long-term heritage and the nature of the predecessor nondemocratic regime, Spanish society possessed, at the critical moment of the transition to democracy, the political, economic, social, and cultural capital that, for reasons just mentioned, is so sorely lacking in the former communist countries in the Balkans.

At the economic level, the dual nature of the transition is, as already stated, a central, generic problem complicating the democratization process in Eastern Europe. Here, too, the weakness of civil society in the former communist states of the Balkans exacerbates the situation in this region and, once again, differentiates it in a rather substantive way from the countries to its north. The behavior of trade unions in the transition serves as a good illustrative example of the problem at hand. More specifically, experience derived from transitions from authoritarian regimes points to the frequent conclusion of explicit or implicit arrangements designed to ensure the economic restraint of labor actors during the critical phase of the transition—in exchange for the political benefits derived, among others, from the acquisition of political freedom and the ability to exercise the freedom of organization. Such arrangements enable the elites managing the transition to decouple political from economic demands, to concentrate on the pressing political problems concerning democratization, and to postpone handling economic issues until a politically more propitious time. Clearly, such a strategy has the major advantage of avoiding the problems associated with "overburdening" a transition and, hopefully, provides for its easier and more successful conclusion.[24]

An obvious question that arises in the context of the East European transitions in general is whether, given the simultaneous nature of the dual transition toward political democracy and a market economy, the type of decoupling achieved in societies exiting from authoritarian rule is possible in our cases. For purposes of this discussion, I should like to focus on a subsidiary, but more directly pertinent, question. Assuming that some degree of decoupling, however limited, is possible, is there a discernible difference in how it is likely to play itself out in the northern as opposed to the southern region of Eastern Europe?

Here, I believe the answer is decidedly affirmative. More specifically, the greater degree of labor organization and the tradition of relative economic pluralism that are observable in East Central Europe (with Poland and Solidarity as the most prominent and obvious examples) and render potentially feasible some element of decoupling, through implicit or explicit arrangements resulting in labor restraint, contrast sharply with the virtual absence of such organizations and tradition in the Balkans.

Two alternative paths with respect to the Balkans derive from this difference. Both have significant implications for the long-term prospects of the democratization process in the region and are directly linked to the problems associated with sultanistic and posttotalitarian heritage. First, in the absence of traditions of organization and relative economic pluralism, there is an increased probability that economic actors will behave unpredictably or even anomically and, in so doing, render decoupling arrangements all the more difficult to effect and commensurately complicate, disrupt, and unduly burden the transition. Such a development might well take the form of wildcat actions or even anomic outbursts by groups, such as the Romanian miners, who have, in the post-Ceausescu period, resorted to violence at least twice to achieve political aims, thereby undercutting the democratic process.[25]

The second potential path stems from the same conditions of weakness in organization and the tradition of relative economic pluralism but leads toward a different

[24] The point concerning the restraint of labor and the consequent capacity to decouple economic from political issues in transitions from authoritarian as opposed to posttotalitarian regimes is forcefully made by Di Palma in *To Craft Democracies*, 76–108, especially 97–101.

[25] The initial occasion of the Romanian miners' "intervention" in the politics of the transition occurred in June 1990, when they were called in by the ruling coalition, made up of reform elements of the previous regime headed by Ion Iliescu, to break up the demonstrations of the students and the

potential outcome. Thus, precisely because of these weaknesses, one can imagine that the pivotal role that both the sultanistic heritage and its totalitarian and posttotalitarian successors have accorded to the state in these countries might enable this latter to contain or repress outbursts of the type described above during the transition period, through various means, including, in extremis, violence. Although such an eventuality might, in the short run, be the functional equivalent of decoupling and enable transition leaders to devote their attention and resources to the political requirements of the transition, its medium- and longer-term cost will be highly damaging for both the transition and the democratization process as a whole. This is so because such an assertion of state power will severely undermine, at a particularly delicate moment in time, the multiple processes through which relations of trust critical to the positive articulation of state and society are slowly being (re)built; and also because it will tend to reproduce and perpetuate the type of state role and behavior that constitute an integral part of the problematic legacy intimately associated with the sultanistic, totalitarian, and posttotalitarian regimes of the past.[26]

At the cultural level, too, the countries of the Balkans face formidable difficulties, as they negotiate their uncertain transitions in search of democracy. In this context, four major items deserve attention—the absence of a democratic tradition in these countries, anticommunism, the resurgence of nationalism, and the resurfacing of cleavages based on primordial sentiments.

As already noted, the absence of a democratic tradition is, with the notable exception of the Czechoslovak experience during the interwar period, a general characteristic of East European—but above all, Balkan—societies. Burdened by a centuries-long period of sultanistic rule under the Ottoman Empire and over four decades of totalitarian and posttotalitarian regimes, the countries in this latter region never developed sufficiently the learning, experience, behavioral patterns and norms associated with political democracy in the sense defined earlier in this chapter.

To be sure, numerous conjunctural factors seem to favor the establishment of democratic politics in this as in other areas of the world. These include (a) an international

---

opposition. The degree of government involvement in the second intervention by the miners in September 1991 is less clear. What is clear, however, is that the disturbances associated with this intervention afforded Iliescu a convenient opportunity to force Prime Minister Petre Roman to resign and, thus, to eliminate a significant pole of opposition to his presidential power.

[26] It is in this context that the significance of collective actors in the Southeast European transitions must be understood. More specifically, if one aspect of the historical weakness of civil society—itself the result of the combined impact of sultanism and totalitarianism—is an incapacity to articulate substantive demands and alternatives to state initiatives, another is its ability to resist, thwart, undermine, and erode state-generated policies by means of noncompliance, evasion, or popular outburst. In this latter sense, collective actors, in the form of inchoate but tangible popular pressures, have indeed been an integral part of the Southeast European transitions, serving for the most part, though not exclusively, as spurs for further democratization and as obstacles to potentially retrogressive moves by the old regimes initially in control of the transitions. For a similar perspective derived from a different cultural, historical, and social setting, see James C. Scott, *Weapons of the Weak. Everyday Forms of Peasant Resistance* (New Haven: Yale University Press, 1985).

environment sensitive to the basic freedoms associated with democracy; (b) the absence of any viable alternative to democracy as a legitimate model for political organization, following the delegitimation of fascism after World War II and of communism more recently; and (c) the presence, within the region, of significant social and political forces willing, if not eager, to engage in the democratic experiment. Still, the obstacles posed by the absence of previous democratic learning are such as to render the transition tenuous and its eventual outcome uncertain.

Somewhat inevitably, anticommunism is, for the moment, a potent force informing the politics and societies of the former communist states in East Central Europe and the Balkans. Viewed from the requisites for a successful transition to democracy, its problematic nature derives from two of its distinctive qualities. First, its essentially "negative" self-definition—a system of thought hostile to communism does not, of itself, promote democracy. On the contrary, it often serves to provide legitimate ideological cover for antiparliamentary and outright antidemocratic forces of the extreme Right, whose activities can seriously undermine the democratization process and, at best, debase the quality of a given democracy. Second, anticommunism can, in combination with other cultural forces such as nationalism or religion, be a highly flammable ingredient that can effectively impede, if not derail, the transition.

Both of these dangers—but especially the second—loom large in the Balkan transitions. In all the countries in the region, the forces loyal to the old regime(s) have sought to strengthen their declining fortunes and to slow down the pace of democratization by adopting increasingly nationalist, if not chauvinist, positions. This development has, in turn, pushed the prodemocratic forces in Bulgaria, Romania, and, it would appear, Albania to espouse extreme anticommunist positions in which nationalist as well as religious images play a central role and osmotically affect the climate of the transition in an adverse way. The overall result is a situation that can both significantly threaten the prospects for a successful conclusion of the transitions in these countries and impede eventual democratic consolidation.[27]

Finally, the threats that the abuse of nationalism poses to the integrity of the transition can be greatly exacerbated, if combined with, or linked to, other powerful cultural and social cleavages such as those associated with ethnic or religious

---

[27] The emergence of divisive political discourses associated with pronounced cleavages based on nationalist, religious and, more generally, primordial sentiments is becoming an increasingly salient feature of the transition in all three countries, especially as competitive politics acquires further momentum in these societies and serves as fertile ground for the emergence on the political scene of groups willing to exploit these cleavages for political advantage. The Romanian experience is a good case in point. There, Gheorghe Funar, the head of the extremist Party of Romanian National Unity (PRNU) received nearly 12 percent of the vote in the September 1992 presidential elections. In the same country, the dominant National Salvation Front (FSN) as well as its splinter party the Party of Social Democracy of Romania (formerly the Democratic National Salvation Front), now headed by Iliescu, have tacitly cooperated with extremist forces such as the Vatra Romaneasca. On the evolving situation in Romania, see Istvan Deak's letter to the editors in *The New York Review of Books*, 16 July 1992, p. 53.

minorities, irredentist aspirations, territorial disputes, and, more generally, divisions based on what anthropologists define as "primordial sentiments." This is especially true in the Balkans, where one of the most problematic legacies of Ottoman rule is the persistence of powerful and unresolved ethnic divisions and irredentist claims which, having survived the communist regimes of the past half century, have resurfaced with renewed vigor and are severely complicating the politics of the transitions in the entire region.

Examples of such cleavages include the Turkish ethnic minority in Bulgaria, whose political expression, the Movement for Rights and Freedom headed by Ahmed Dogan, managed to gain a small but pivotal number of seats in the parliament issuing from the October 1991 elections. It skillfully used its power to become a partner in the Union of Democratic Forces (UDF) government headed by Filip Dimitrov, and to bring down the latter in the October-November 1992 crisis in that country. Another example is the Hungarian minority in the Timisoara area of Romania, where the initial disturbances erupted that toppled the Ceausescu regime. There is also the huge Albanian ethnic minority in the Kosovo region of Serbia, which figures prominently in the powerful irredentist aspirations unleashed by the collapse of the communist regime in Albania. Finally, there is the Greek ethnic minority in Albania, which, like the ethnic Turks in Bulgaria, has already organized itself into a separate political formation that received five seats in the parliament in the March 1991 elections and two seats in the March 1992 elections, despite having been forced to alter its official name to overcome objections emanating from the dominant political parties that it represented an ethnic minority promoting Greek irredentist policies.

The dangers that such cultural cleavages—based, as they are, on highly volatile and explosive primordial sentiments—pose for the transition process arise primarily from their potential superimposition on other salient cleavages in a manner which, instead of attenuating them, will rather tend to reinforce them. The outcome of such an eventuality would almost certainly be the addition of further turbulence, instability, and conflict to what already are delicate and tenuous transitions in the Balkans—a development that would more than likely severely disrupt the transition process and quite adversely affect the chances for democratic consolidation.

As the foregoing analysis has sought to establish, current prospects for democracy in the Balkans are uncertain. The central role played by forces directly associated with the old regimes in launching the transitions in Bulgaria, Romania, and, more recently, Albania, and their successful, initial efforts to contain the pace of change and to minimize losses substantively contributed to this uncertainty and has subsequently enabled it to survive if not to increase.

As of late 1993, the degree and quality of change in the region remains unclear. In Romania, the Democratic National Salvation Front—renamed the Party of Social Democracy of Romania in July 1993—remains in control and has actually obtained a renewed mandate as a result of its victory in the September 1992 presidential and parliamentary elections. In fact, the success of the reform element of the old regime to retain power after two elections (May 1990 and September 1992) underscores the continuing deviation of the Romanian transition trajectory from the pattern observed in the two other Balkan states. The significantly improved showing of the democratic opposition in the September 1992 elections, however, where the latest opposition formation, the Democratic Convention, won 20 percent of the popular vote and eighty-two seats in parliament, as well as the much larger percentage of the popular vote (38 percent) obtained by Emil Constantinescu, the democratic opposition's candidate for president, suggest that Romania seems to be distancing itself gradually from some of the debilitating legacies of Ceausescu's sultanistic regime and to be following the course traveled earlier by Bulgaria and, more recently, Albania.

In the latter country, the last one in the region to enter the uncharted waters of the transition, a comfortable victory at the polls in the March 1992 elections allowed the opposition Democratic Party, headed by Sali Berisha, to unseat the ruling Albanian Party of Labor and to gain control of both the parliament and, through it, the indirectly elected presidency. The democratic opposition's victory followed on the road initially traveled by Bulgaria and conformed to the "delayed" transition pattern distinctive to the region.[28]

To be sure, in Bulgaria, the transition has certainly moved further along than in the other two countries. The October 1991 parliamentary elections, which produced a peaceful change in governmental incumbency and brought the heterogeneous coalition of the Union of Democratic Forces (UDF) to power, as well as the January 1992 presidential vote, which, through Zhelyu Zhelev's election, confirmed the UDF's ascendancy in Bulgarian political affairs, constitute concrete evidence of significant progress in that country's democratic transition. Still, the strong showing of the Bulgarian Socialist Party (BSP, former communists) in both the parliamentary and the presidential elections, as well as Zhelev's failure to get elected in the first round of the voting for president, and the continued fragmentation of the UDF, point to the continuing power of forces associated with the old regime, underscore the uncertainties surrounding the transition, and caution against hasty and overly optimistic conclusions concerning its outcome.[29] Indeed, recent polls suggest growing support for the Bulgarian Socialist Party, which could emerge as the main victor in the next parliamentary elections.

---

[28] For recent developments in the Balkans, see the special issue of *Hérodote* 63 (October-December 1991), entitled "Balkans et Balkanisation." On Romania, see the review article by István Deák, "Survivors," *The New York Review of Books*, 5 March 1992, 43–51. On Albania, see Eliz Biberaj, "Albania at the Crossroads," *Problems of Communism* 50, no. 5 (September-October 1991): 1–16 and, more generally, Biberaj, *Albania: A Socialist Maverick* (Boulder, Colo: Westview, 1990). For the information concerning the barring of the party representing the Greek ethnic minority from participating in the March 1992 elections, see *I Kathimerini* [The Daily], 5 February 1992, p. 2.

[29] In the October 1991 elections, the UDF won 34 percent of the popular vote and 110 seats in parliament. With 33 percent of the popular vote and 106 seats in parliament, the BSP demonstrated its staying power, which has deep roots in Bulgarian society dating back to the interwar period, and indirectly pointed to the tenuous hold on power so far attained by the democratic forces. This latter dimension of the evolving Bulgarian political scene was underscored by the narrow margin (43 percent versus 37 percent) through which in a second ballot, Zhelev managed to win the presidency.

Particularly worrisome, in this context, are two recent developments relating to the emerging patterns of electoral competition in this country and threatening to inject a strongly polarizing climate into the politics of the transition. The first concerns the fact that the Bulgarian Socialist Party's strategy for establishing its proper nationalist credentials by exploiting the tensions, primordial sentiments, and cleavages associated with the presence of a large (10 percent of the population or approximately 1 million) minority of ethnic Turks in the country has caused the UDF to adopt the role of champion of the victims of communism in Bulgaria, to espouse increasingly sterile, anticommunist, nationalist, and, in a number of ways, extremist positions, and to enter into a parliamentary alliance with the Movement for Rights and Freedom representing the ethnic Turks. The October–November 1992 government crisis, caused by the withdrawal of the movement's support from the UDF government headed by Dimitrov; the subsequent failure of the latter to secure the tacit support of the ethnic Turks for a minority UDF government; and the prospect of a BSP mandate or new elections constitute developments that may inject another polarizing twist to the uncertainties of the Bulgarian political scene.

The second pertinent development in this regard points to the resurgence of long-quiescent political cleavages between far Left and Right dating back to the turbulent postwar period and to their superimposition on the type of divisive, contemporary cleavages just described.[30] Although the potential implications of all these developments for the transition and, more generally, for the longer-term prospects for democracy in the region remain unclear, they are nevertheless a pointed reminder of the formidable obstacles to political democracy in each country and, more generally, of the fragility of the democratization process throughout the Balkans.

More specifically, the prospects for democracy in the former communist countries of the Balkans would seem to hinge on three major and closely interrelated factors. First, the capacity of the prodemocratic forces must be sufficient to organize themselves to gain firm control of the transition process and to steer it through the critical phases during which the rules of the democratic game (constitutions, guarantees concerning civil and human rights, etc.) will become defined, agreed upon, and validated by means of free and competitive elections. Second, these forces must be able to maintain their unity and avoid the divisions that are likely to undermine efforts to generate the consensual arrangements necessary for successfully concluding the transition and, especially, for ensuring the prospects for democratic consolidation. Third, there must be the effective control of forces that are hostile to the establishment of full and unencumbered political democracy.

Success in realizing these goals will constitute tangible evidence that these societies are successfully handling the negative aspects of their sultanistic and totalitarian heritages and will greatly enhance the chances that, following a series of protracted transitions, democracy will emerge as the dominant mode of political organization for the first time in the region's history. Conversely, failure to realize

---

[30] I wish to thank my colleague Ilias Nicolacopoulos, a keen analyst of the electoral scene in the Balkans, for these observations.

them can effectively complicate, stall, and potentially derail the transition, with commensurately negative results for the democratic process. If nationalism, primordial sentiments, territorial disputes, and zero-sum approaches to conflict resolution become ascendant once more in the politics, culture, and society of the Balkans and, in the process, cause the fragmentation of the prodemocratic forces in these countries and the resurgence of long-quiescent conflicts dating back to the interwar years and to the 1940s, the prospects for democracy in the former communist states will dramatically decline. In that eventuality, we may well become unhappy witnesses to protracted and inconclusive transitions issuing in alternating cycles of Balkan variants of *democraduras* and *dictablandas.* These will linger on in the margins of broad democratic regions and will be painful reminders of the confining conditions that must be overcome before democratic regimes can prevail in these societies as well.[31]

[31] Of Latin American origin, the concepts of *democradura* ("hard" democracy) and *dictablanda* ("soft" dictatorship) graphically convey the hard-to-define political situations that lie at the interstice between democratic and nondemocratic regimes. "Democradura" would roughly parallel the concept of "pseudodemocracy" used by Michael Burton, Richard Gunther, and John Higley in their treatment of democratic settlements (see Burton, Gunther, and Higley, "Introduction: Elite Transformations and Democratic Regimes," in *Elites and Democratic Consolidation*, ed. Higley and Gunther, 1–80). "Dictablanda" comes close to liberalized, but not democratized, authoritarian regimes. For a similar view concerning Latin America, see Albert O. Hirschman, "On Democracy in Latin America," *The New York Review of Books*, 10 April 1986.

II

Albania and the Albanians in the Post-Communist Period

Elez Biberaj

The Albanian nation is undergoing one of the most critical periods in its modern history. Divided almost evenly between Albania, on the one hand, and rump Yugoslavia and Macedonia, on the other, the more than six million Albanians are confronted with daunting challenges. Although Tirana's communist regime was swept from power in parliamentary elections on March 22, 1992, Albania faces a period of prolonged instability as it embarks on the difficult road of establishing a genuine multiparty democracy and making the transition to a free-market economy. Albania's President Sali Berisha has inherited a country in the midst of a severe economic and social crisis. The economy has virtually collapsed. The rapid crumbling of the centrally planned economic system in 1991 led to dramatic declines in agricultural and industrial production. The gross domestic product per capita is estimated to be below $400, and unemployment as high as 70 percent. Inflation is running at more than 300 percent. Moreover, decades of communist misrule and repression have led to the disintegration of the moral fabric of Albanian society. Only large-scale Western humanitarian assistance has saved Albania from disintegrating into total anarchy and chaos.

Although the communists no longer hold national power, they control the local government in many districts. Despite the diminished role of the Albanian Party of Labor (APL), renamed the Socialist Party at its 10th Congress in June 1991, its tentacles still pervade the administrative structure. Embattled communists are trying to fan political animosities in an attempt to block the democratic process. Although the balance has shifted perceptibly in favor of democratic forces, the post-communist government faces serious challenges in restoring law and order, reviving the economy, and building democratic institutions based on the rule of law in a country lacking a democratic political culture.

Ethnic Albanians in rump Yugoslavia and Macedonia face equally if not more difficult problems. Serbia's President Slobodan Milosevic has forcibly stripped Kosovo of all autonomy and disenfranchised the two million members of the Albanian majority. Since the outbreak of Albanian nationalist demonstrations in 1981, Kosovo has been characterized by a persistent and violent conflict, which has reduced ethnic Albanians to second-class citizens. For more than a decade, ethnic Albanians have lived under virtual military and police occupation.

Ethnic Albanians have refused to accept the legitimacy of Serbian rule, and have declared Kosovo an independent state. Ibrahim Rugova, president of the self-proclaimed Republic of Kosovo, is committed to a peaceful resolution of the conflict with Serbia. Milosevic insists that the issue of Kosovo is nonnegotiable for Serbia.

Albanians on both sides of the border believe that war with Serbia is probable. They fear that once Serbia resolves its conflict with Croatia and Bosnia-Herzegovina, it will turn its attention and resources to a settling of accounts once and for all with the ethnic Albanians. The Albanians in Kosovo are unarmed and, unlike the Slovenes, Croats, and Bosnians in the initial stages of the war with Serbia, do not have their own territorial defense or police forces. Albania's army is no match for the Serbian military; therefore, a full-scale Albanian-Serbian war would have disastrous repercussions for Albania.

Background

Sandwiched between Yugoslavia and Greece, Albania has been faced with an unfriendly external environment for most of the period since its independence in 1912. The exclusion of large, compact, Albanian-inhabited territories, particularly Kosovo and Çamèria, from the Albanian state recognized by the great powers in 1913, as well as subsequent Italian, Yugoslav, and Greek attempts to further partition or dominate Albania, have made the Albanians overly security-conscious. This sense of insecurity has been reinforced by fears that any potential aggressor could easily overrun the country. Although it is a revisionist country interested in regaining its lost territories, Albania's strategic location, small territory, and limited manpower and economic resources have shaped its purely defensive strategy.

Its strategic location has given Albania an importance out of proportion with its size and actual resources and has made it attractive to external powers interested in dominating or expanding their influence in this ever-volatile region. During the interwar period, Albania fell under heavy Italian domination, becoming Europe's first World War II victim. The Italians staged their invasion of Greece from Albania, complicating Tirana-Athens relations for decades. With the collapse of Yugoslavia in 1941, most Albanian-inhabited territories, including Kosovo, were attached to Italian-occupied Albania. For the first time since 1912, the majority of Albanians in the Balkans were united into one administrative state. At the end of the war, however, Kosovo again fell under Yugoslav control.

The smallest and economically least developed state in the Balkans, Albania has been in a less advantageous position than its immediate and significantly more powerful neighbors to provide for its own security and has relied for protection on external alliances and favorable international developments. Enver Hoxha, who ruled Albania from 1944 until his death in 1985, sought to ensure his country's independence and economic development by forging alliances, in turn, with Yugoslavia (1945–1948), the Soviet Union (1948–1961) and China (1961–1978).[1]

Following the invasion of Czechoslovakia in 1968, Albania considered the Soviet Union its main enemy, although, in the official parlance, the two superpowers were considered equally dangerous. Albania improved relations with its two contiguous neighbors, Greece and Yugoslavia, and pledged to come to Yugoslavia's assistance in the event of a Warsaw Pact invasion. There were remarkable similarities between the Albanian and Yugoslav military postures in dealing with a perceived threat from the Warsaw Pact. Albania's 1976 constitution contained provisions similar to those in Yugoslavia's 1974 constitution, stipulating that no citizen had the right to accept the occupation or surrender of the country. Moreover, the constitution prohibited the establishment of foreign military bases and the stationing of foreign troops on Albanian territory.[2]

Hoxha's Albania was the only European state to boycott the 1975 Helsinki summit meeting of the Conference on Security and Cooperation in Europe (CSCE). Tirana claimed that European countries could not ensure their security under the umbrella of the two superpowers. Albania also refused to participate in Balkan multilateral gatherings and concentrated instead on strengthening bilateral ties.

Despite the Albanian government's rhetoric, East-West disarmament agreements and the Helsinki accords, which advocated the inviolability of international borders and confidence-building measures, enhanced Albania's security. Favorable international developments lessened Albania's perception of a hostile external environment. After China suspended its economic and military assistance, Hoxha refused either to seek other sources of foreign assistance or to open up the country. The government, however, gradually toned down its ideological rhetoric and improved ties with neighboring countries, most notably Yugoslavia, Greece, Turkey, and Italy. The APL continued its repressive domestic policies, however, strictly controlling all aspects of life. The consequences of Hoxha's isolationist policy soon became

---

[1] Albania's post-World War II foreign and security policy has been well documented. See Nicholas C. Pano, *The People's Socialist Republic of Albania* (Baltimore: Johns Hopkins University Press, 1968); Peter R. Prifti, *Socialist Albania Since 1944: Domestic and Foreign Developments* (Cambridge: MIT Press, 1978); Stavro Skendi, ed., *Albania* (New York: Praeger, 1956); Anton Logoreci, *The Albanians: Europe's Forgotten Survivors* (Boulder, Colo.: Westview Press, 1978); Ramadan Marmullaku, *Albania and the Albanians* (Hamden: Archon Books, 1975); Eugene K. Keefe, et al., *Area Handbook for Albania* (Washington, D.C.: U.S. Government Printing Office, 1971); William E. Griffith, *Albania and the Sino-Soviet Rift* (Cambridge: MIT Press, 1963); Harry Hamm, *Albania—China's Beachhead in Europe* (New York: Praeger, 1963); and Elez Biberaj, *Albania and China: A Study of an Unequal Alliance* (Boulder, Colo.: Westview Press, 1986).

[2] *Kushtetuta e Republikës Popullore Socialiste të Shqipërisë* [The Constitution of the People's Socialist Republic of Albania] (Tirana, 1976).

evident. After years of continual growth, the Albanian economy began a steady decline in the early 1980s.

In April 1985, Hoxha was succeeded by his close adviser Ramiz Alia. While publicly insisting on continuity with Hoxha's policies, Alia initiated some changes. In foreign policy, pragmatism was given priority over ideology. He tried to stabilize relations with Yugoslavia, which were adversely affected by the simmering dispute over Serbia's harsh treatment of ethnic Albanians, and Tirana's endorsement of demands that Kosovo be granted the status of a republic.[3] Albania significantly increased its cooperation with Greece, which formally lifted the state of war with Albania in 1987; established diplomatic ties with West Germany; and gradually elevated its ties with Warsaw Pact nations to the ambassadorial level. It continued, however, to reject both American and Soviet offers to normalize relations.

Before 1990, Alia took no measures to dismantle the despotic political system and the overcentralized economic management system inherited from Hoxha. While tinkering with some cosmetic economic reforms, Alia continued to insist that the state run the economy. He remained adamant about not taking any action that could threaten the APL monopoly of power.[4]

The Demise of Communist Rule and the Rise of Opposition Parties

In the wake of the break with Moscow in the early 1960s, the Albanian regime had distanced itself from what it termed as "revisionist" parties in power in the Soviet Union and Eastern Europe. In the mid-1970s, as political divergences with China grew, Hoxha maintained that Albania was the only genuinely socialist country in the world. Alia explained the collapse of communism in Eastern Europe in 1989 as the result of the ruling elites in those countries having deviated from Marxism-Leninism. He insisted that Albania's communist regime enjoyed widespread popular support and that developments in Eastern Europe would have no impact on his country.[5]

Despite Alia's optimistic tone, however, Albania faced remarkably similar problems to those in the other East European countries, and the East European revolutions caused the Albanian government to reassess its domestic and foreign policies. At a Central Committee plenum in January 1990, Alia launched what he termed a democratization process, which involved separating the state from the party and taking steps to decentralize the economic system. At another Central Committee meeting three months later, as part of the democratization process, Alia proposed

---

[3] For background on the 1981 demonstrations in Kosovo, see Stevan K. Pavlowitch and Elez Biberaj, "The Albanian Problem in Yugoslavia: Two Views," *Conflict Studies,* nos. 137/138 (1982); and Elez Biberaj, "The Conflict in Kosovo," *Survey* 28, no. 3 (Autumn 1984): 39–57.

[4] For background, see Elez Biberaj, *Albania: A Socialist Maverick* (Boulder, Colo.: Westview Press, 1990).

[5] Tirana Domestic Service in Albanian, 1430 GMT, December 12, 1989, translated in *FBIS-EEU* 89–239, December 14, 1989, pp. 1–4.

measures aimed at improving the human rights situation. In May 1990 the People's Assembly approved changes in the country's penal code that abolished the death penalty for citizens caught trying to escape the country and lifted the ban on religious propaganda. Moreover, citizens were guaranteed the right to travel abroad. The Ministry of Justice, eliminated in the mid-1960s, was reinstituted, with the government committing itself to the rule of law. Although these measures were significant in the Albanian context, they did not represent major reforms; they merely amounted to lifting some of the most drastic restrictions imposed by the totalitarian regime.

Increased domestic pressure for change, developments in Eastern Europe, and the continued deterioration of the situation in Kosovo, forced the Albanian government to announce new diplomatic initiatives. The insistence of East European countries that all trade transactions be conducted in hard currency caused serious problems for Albania and coincided with a deepening economic crisis. Acknowledging that self-reliance had taken a heavy toll, in April 1990 Alia said the government would seek foreign assistance and would permit foreign investments. He also announced a sudden change in the stand toward the superpowers, saying that Albania was interested in reestablishing ties with both Washington and Moscow. This represented the clearest departure from Hoxha's policies, whose main pillar was rejection of all contacts with the two superpowers. Equally important was Alia's request that Albania be admitted as a full member of the CSCE, which required Tirana to bring its human rights legislation up to the level of other CSCE members. At the same time, Tirana expressed willingness to establish diplomatic relations with the European Community (since renamed European Union).

By seeking to expand foreign relations and to improve the regime's image on the international arena, Alia hoped to arrest the declining authority of the ruling APL. In a meeting with the visiting UN secretary general in May 1991, Alia reportedly promised that all citizens would be permitted to travel abroad, political prisoners would be released, and believers would be permitted to open churches and mosques, which had been closed in 1967 when Hoxha's regime proclaimed Albania the world's first atheist country. Alia's failure to deliver on these promises led to widespread disenchantment. Many people came to suspect that the recent measures were intended solely to impress foreigners.

Alia's foreign policy initiatives met with limited success. The downfall of communism in Eastern Europe and the end of the Cold War had resulted in the decline of Western strategic interest in Albania. The United States and Western Europe conditioned the improvement of ties on Albania's progress toward genuine political pluralism, full respect for human rights, and the implementation of reforms that would eventually lead to the creation of a market economy. Socialist Albania had missed its window of opportunity by rejecting Western offers for close ties in the 1960s and the 1970s and by boycotting the Helsinki process. If the Western alliance had been willing to bail out Albania economically during the Cold War, in 1990 it was unwilling to contribute to the survival of Europe's most corrupt and repressive Stalinist regime.

Albania's relations with West European countries suffered a serious setback after more than five thousand Albanians stormed foreign embassies in Tirana in July 1990. With unprecedented international attention focused on Albania, the last communist domino in Europe, Alia permitted the refugees to leave the country. The embassy incident represented a major setback for the APL and was a clear indication that the regime, despite its highly repressive nature, was not invincible. Alia's reluctance to use the armed forces to prevent the refugees from entering foreign embassies suggested the government was sensitive to the political dangers of attempting to suppress such a large number of people. Several countries, including West Germany, closed their embassies and froze relations with Tirana. Pressure on the regime increased to follow the example of other East European countries and allow the creation of opposition parties. Alia argued strongly that yielding to demands for political pluralism and radical economic reforms would exacerbate both economic and political problems and even lead to the collapse of Albania's socialist system.

The Albanian government tried desperately to improve its international image. In the fall of 1990, Alia became Albania's first head of state to participate in a UN General Assembly session. In October 1990, Tirana hosted the second conference of Balkan foreign ministers; the first such conference had been held two years earlier in Belgrade. But to Alia's chagrin, the conference failed to support Tirana's request for full membership in the CSCE, and Albania was the only European country absent from the CSCE summit meeting held in Paris in November 1990.

In response to growing unrest, the regime moved on two fronts. On the one hand it intensified the campaign against regime opponents. On the other hand, the APL leadership introduced the notion of pluralism of ideas, according to which Albanians would be permitted to express their ideas but could not form political parties. Alia also declared that the APL would relinquish its constitutionally guaranteed monopoly of power. A new election law approved in November 1990 provided for multicandidate elections and permitted mass organizations, which until then had been transmission belts for the party for advancing its own candidates.

Alia's new measures failed to placate domestic critics who were advocating political pluralism. In December 1990, following four days of student demonstrations at Tirana University, the Albanian regime belatedly joined its former East European communist allies in sanctioning the establishment of opposition parties. After forty-seven years of unchallenged rule, the communists reluctantly agreed to end the one-party system. Alia's grudging acceptance of political pluralism reflected an ambivalence between his desire to avoid bloodshed and his determination to orchestrate the process of reform, prolonging as long as possible the APL's control of the government.

Within a short period of time, several political parties were formed. The Democratic Party was created on December 12, 1990. Led by a group of intellectuals and students headed by Dr. Sali Berisha, a cardiologist, the Democratic Party challenged the premises of the APL's domestic and foreign policy. It advocated a Western-style, multiparty system based on respect for human and individual rights and the establishment of a free-market economy. It called for the full integration of Albania into Europe and its democratic institutions, denouncing the communist regime's isolation policy. While emphasizing the importance of Albania strengthening ties with Western Europe, the Democratic Party viewed the United States as the best source to help Albania to get back on its feet economically and politically.

In contrast to the APL, the democrats from the outset concentrated on the plight of ethnic Albanians in Yugoslavia. In its program, the Democratic Party committed itself to struggle "for the realization of centuries-long aspirations of the Albanian nation for independence, union and progress in accordance with the spirit of international documents."[6] Berisha, addressing more than 100 thousand people at a rally celebrating the establishment of the Democratic Party, said his party did not consider as permanent the division of the Albanian nation. The Democratic Party, he said, "will fight with peaceful means and in the framework of European integration processes to realize [the Albanians'] rights for progress and national union."[7]

The Democratic Party was followed by the creation of several other political parties, groups and associations, the most important being the Republican, Agrarian, Ecological, National Unity and Social Democratic parties and the Kosovo and Çamëria associations, which advocated the protection of the rights of ethnic Albanians in Yugoslavia and Greece, respectively. While they expressed support for a pluralist democracy, protection of human rights, and emphasized the importance of rule of law, the new parties did not share the Democratic Party's proposal for a radical overhaul of the country's economic system, advocating instead gradual economic changes. In the arena of foreign policy, however, they shared the Democratic Party's objectives of greater interaction with Western countries, the opening of the country to foreign investments, and supported Kosovo's union with Albania in the event of Yugoslavia's disintegration.

On March 31, 1991, Albania held its first multiparty elections in more than half a decade. The election campaign had been conducted in a highly tense political atmosphere, with periodic clashes between opposition supporters, on the one hand, and the army and the police force, on the other. With enormous resources at its disposal and denying the opposition access to the media and the necessary resources to spread its message, especially in the countryside, the APL won 169 seats in the 250-seat People's Assembly. The Democratic Party won seventy-five seats; the OMONIA association, representing ethnic Greeks, five seats; and the communist-controlled National Veterans Organization one seat. The new People's Assembly elected Alia as president for a five-year term. Reformist economist Fatos Nano was asked to form a new government. But despite their election victory, the communists were unable to govern the country. Only two months after the elections, Prime Minister Nano's government was forced to resign as a result of a three-week general strike organized by the newly created Independent Trade Unions. The APL accepted opposition demands that new elections be held in May or June 1992 and agreed to a

[6] *Rilindja Demokratike* (Tirana), 5 Jan. 1991, p. 3. (Emphasis added.)

[7] Ibid., p. 5.

power-sharing arrangement, retaining only eight posts in the 24-member cabinet. Nano was replaced by Ylli Bufi, former minister of food and a member of the APL Central Committee.

At their 10th party congress in June 1991, the communists renamed their party the Socialist Party and elected Fatos Nano as their leader. They also repudiated traditional Marxist principles and modeled their renovated Socialist Party more along the lines of West European social-democratic parties. But they still opposed radical economic reforms. The Socialist Party's program advocated a mixture of state, collective, and private ownership, but rejected total privatization of state ownership.[8]

The coalition government, lacking a broad political base, was unable to implement the changes necessary to remedy the bad economic situation. The communists, controlling an absolute majority in the People's Assembly, blocked the approval of legislation required to implement radical economic reforms and attract foreign investments. The economy remained largely state-owned and directed. By the end of summer 1991, the situation deteriorated dramatically, with increased political tension and a widespread breakdown in law and order. Thousands of Albanians attempted to flee to Italy, which forced the Rome government to launch a humanitarian assistance effort to help the impoverished country. While industry ground to a halt because of the lack of raw materials, the peasants took matters into their own hands, disbanding agricultural cooperatives.

In December 1991, after President Alia failed to meet a series of demands, Berisha withdrew his ministers from the coalition government, accusing the communists of having obstructed the implementation of economic and political reforms.[9] Alia named the minister of food, Vilson Ahmeti, to form a caretaker government and scheduled elections for March 22, 1992.

Berisha's Accession to Power

The decision to enter into coalition with the communists had resulted in a significant decline of popular support for the Democratic Party. Although Berisha came under harsh criticism from President Alia, the communist-controlled media, and even his own ministers in the coalition government, who accused him of launching the country into further turmoil, there was an immediate outpouring of popular support for the Democratic Party's decision to withdraw from the government. Cooperating closely with the powerful independent trade unions, two other opposition parties, the Republican and Social Democratic parties, and the influential organization representing former political prisoners, the Democratic Party launched a well-organized national campaign promising to restore law and order and implement radical economic and political reforms aimed at establishing a market economy and

[8] *Zëri i Popullit* (Tirana), 3 July 1991, pp. 1–3.

[9] Radio Tirana Network in Albanian, 1430 GMT, December 4, 1991, translated in *FBIS-EEU* 91–234, December 5, 1991, pp. 1–3.

a democratic pluralistic system based on the rule of law. Berisha also tried to assure the communists that there would be no revenge against them. He told a foreign journalist that, "if we start to seek revenge, Albania will never get to know democracy. If all those who are guilty were to be punished, then Albania would have to be turned into one gigantic concentration camp."[10]

Although only a year earlier, the communists had won 67 percent of seats in the parliament, in the March 22 election they suffered a humiliating defeat, winning only 27 percent or thirty-two seats in the 140-seat parliament. The Democratic Party won a resounding victory, capturing ninety-two seats. The Social Democratic Party won seven seats and the Union for Human Rights, which was formed after the ethnic Greek organization OMONIA and other ethnically based groups were banned from fielding candidates in the election, two seats. The Republican Party did very poorly, winning only one seat.[11] At a news conference a day after the election, Berisha said the victory of the Democratic Party marked the end of the communist nightmare in Albania and called for national reconciliation:

> In building Albania, we need many things, but what we do not need are hatred and revanchism. The Democratic Party invites all the democratic forces in Albania not to waste time in destruction and confusion, but to devote their talents and energies to building the future. It is true that in the past the dictatorship committed ugly deeds, but it is also true that Albanians as a whole are at the same time accomplices and fellow victims of the regime under which we lived.[12]

Alia resigned as president only days after the final election results were announced. The parliament, controlled by the Democratic Party, approved a series of changes in the Law on Constitutional Provisions, enhancing the president's powers. The document, which was adapted in May 1991 and will be in force until a new constitution is promulgated, had severely curtailed Alia's powers. Democratic Party deputies argued that the new president needed enhanced powers to deal with the serious problems confronting the nation. On April 9, 1992, the parliament elected Berisha as president for a five-year term. In his inaugural speech, Berisha acknowledged the "extremely difficult" tasks in establishing a genuine democracy in Albania and reviving its economy. He again emphasized the importance of national reconciliation:

> We have all been jointly responsible to varying degrees for the survival of the dictatorship, at least for the 99.9 percent vote we gave it out of fear. We were

[10] *Rzeczpospolita*, February 25, 1992, p. 6, transl. in *FBIS-EEU* 92–045, March 6, 1992, pp. 2–3.

[11] Radio Tirana Network in Albanian, 1330 GMT, March 30, 1992, transl. in *FBIS-EEU* 92–062, March 31, 1992, p. 2.

[12] Radio Tirana Network in Albanian, 1310 GMT, March 23, 1992, transl. in *FBIS-EEU* 92–057, March 24, 1992, pp. 4–5.

all also its victims, however. Let this mutual suffering and pain therefore unite us in joint responsibility to build a civilized society such as Spain and Portugal.

The new president also tried to assure ethnic Albanians in Kosovo of Tirana's support. He said he had "unswerving faith that the Albanian cause is a just cause that can be fully solved within the framework of the Helsinki Final Act and the European Community's regional initiative." Berisha also assured minorities in Albania that they will enjoy "all the rights and individual and national freedoms that our Constitution and international documents guarantee for them."[13] In an interview with Radio Tirana, the president said that while Albania currently resembles a "wasteland," he was optimistic about the future.[14]

Aleksander Meksi, a fifty-three-year-old archaeologist and a founding member of the Democratic Party, was selected as prime minister. Having received a clear mandate for change, the democrats moved swiftly to dismantle the totalitarian state network they inherited from the communists. Bold measures were taken to restore law and order, reinvigorate the justice system and root out rampant government corruption. The Foreign Ministry bureaucracy, which reportedly had been staffed predominantly by the secret police, underwent a sweeping purge. More than 50 percent of its personnel were dismissed and all ambassadors replaced. The secret police, renamed in 1991 as the National Intelligence Service, was totally reorganized; 70 percent of its personnel were being replaced.[15]

The military also underwent radical changes. During more than four-and-a-half decades of communist rule, Albanian society was subjected to a greater degree of militarization than any society in Eastern Europe. The armed forces and the much dreaded secret police, Sigurimi, represented the main pillars of Hoxha's dictatorship. A cardinal rule of Hoxha's regime was the total control of armed and internal security forces by the communist party. Probably in no other East European country was the ruling communist party able to exercise such continuous and pervasive control over the military as did the APL. The Constitution promulgated in 1976 designated the first secretary of the APL as the commander-in-chief of the armed forces. Throughout 1989 to 1990, the military hierarchy maintained a high profile and strongly supported Alia's refusal to relinquish the APL's monopoly of power. Alia's momentous decision in December 1990 to sanction political pluralism was followed by the outbreak of spontaneous violent anticommunist demonstrations in Shkodèr, Elbasan, Kavajè, and Durrès. Alia ordered the police and army troops, backed by armored vehicles, to restore order. One of the first and main demands put forth by the Democratic Party was the complete depoliticization of the armed forces. Berisha called for the disbanding of party committees in the military and the inter-

[13] Radio Tirana Network in Albanian, 1606 GMT, April 9, 1992, transl. in *FBIS-EEU* 92–070, April 10, 1992, pp. 2–3.

[14] Radio Tirana Network in Albanian, 1432 GMT, April 9, 1992, transl. in *FBIS-EEU* 92–070, April 10, 1992, pp. 3–4.

[15] *Zëri i Popullit*, 4 July 1992, p. 3.

nal security forces, the elimination of political commissars, and the restoration of military ranks, abolished in 1966. As tensions mounted during early 1991, Alia relied increasingly on the security forces and the military to maintain order and intimidate the opposition. Evidently with Alia's approval, the armed forces supplied arms to members of the organization "the Volunteers of Enver Hoxha," formed by conservative communists in February 1991, and used military vehicles to transport APL supporters and sympathizers to communist-sponsored rallies. Even after the selection of the Democratic Party nominee Perikli Teta as minister of defense in the coalition government, relations remained uneasy between the armed forces and the democratic opposition.

Although the Law on Constitutional Provisions, approved by the People's Assembly in April 1991, provided for the full depoliticization of the armed forces and prohibited political party activities in the military, the Democratic Party saw the armed forces as the last stronghold of communism and potentially a threat to the new government. The armed forces were broadly restructured, the top leadership was swiftly replaced, and young officers were promoted into the top ranks. A well-coordinated campaign was launched to rid the military of communist supporters. While the Socialist Party claimed that widespread purges had crippled the armed forces at a time of an increased possibility of war with Serbia, the new minister of defense, Safet Zhulali, insisted that radical reforms were necessary to create a professional military, whose main task would be to defend the country from outside aggression and not to perpetuate the tenure of a corrupt, totalitarian party.[16] The Albanian military has increased its cooperation with other countries, particularly Turkey and the United States. At a meeting with a visiting NATO delegation in October 1992, Berisha appealed for assistance to reform the Albanian army.[17]

Some observers have suggested that a military takeover in Albania is "highly probable."[18] Although the possibility of a military coup cannot be ruled out, such a development is unlikely. The army is in no position to deal with the nation's many problems and a military takeover will only throw Albania into further political turmoil. And conservatives have been disgraced to such an extent that seemingly they stand little chance of drumming up significant support to stage a comeback.

The post-communist government moved steadfastly to lay the foundations of a market-based economy. The government's program placed a priority on obtaining critical raw materials that would enable vital sectors of industry to resume operation, revive the agricultural sector by assisting individual farmers, and create the legal structure and environment that would attract foreign capital.

The government's program was critically dependent on foreign assistance. In May 1992, the European Community granted Albania most-favored-nation status

---

[16] *Zëri i Rinisë*, 25 April 1992, p. 1; and *Rilindja Demokratike*, 25 July 1992, p. 4.

[17] Radio Tirana Network in Albanian, 1430 GMT, October 16, 1992, transl. in *FBIS-EEU* 92–202, October 19, 1992, pp. 5–6.

[18] Marko Milivojevic, "Wounded Eagle: Albania's Fight for Survival," *European Security Study*, no. 15 (London: Institute for European Defense and Strategic Studies, 1992): 30.

and signed an agreement on trade and economic cooperation.[19] In July 1992, the World Bank granted Albania a credit of $41.1 million to help the government finance the import of spare parts, fertilizers, vehicles, and equipment needed to revive the production of agricultural goods, minerals, and electricity.[20] This was followed with the signing of a standby agreement with the International Monetary Fund.

Meksi's government has placed a priority on privatization in the agricultural sector. By autumn 1992, approximately 80 percent of the land had been returned to private farmers. The government has indicated that service establishments and small shops will be auctioned, while enterprises will be sold or transferred to employees. It has, however, backtracked on privatization of the large industrial enterprises, which requires extensive preparation and capital, and could further exacerbate the problem of unemployment. Meanwhile, natural resources and power-industry enterprises and facilities have been exempted from privatization.

Privatization seems to have caused considerable resentment. Many workers were not in a position to take advantage of privatization because of their lack of capital and experience with the workings of a market economy. The most profitable enterprises and shops were bought by former communist officials, leading to widespread perceptions that the so-called red mafia may have lost political power at the national level but still held a tight grip over the economy.

Berisha has urged the West to provide increased assistance to Albania. In July 1992, the Group of 24 held a meeting in Tirana to assess Albania's needs. It was disclosed that since September 1991, the Group of 24 had granted Albania approximately $900 million, mainly in humanitarian aid and technical assistance.[21] On a per capita basis, Albania has received more Western aid than any other East European country. The Group of 24 pledged to provide urgently needed raw materials and spare parts for the Albanian industry, and pesticides, fertilizer, and seeds for private farmers.[22] In August 1992, the parliament passed the Foreign Investments Law, which creates a legal framework for foreign investments and provides for compensation for expropriation.[23] The government, however, has been unable to devise a clear strategy to attract foreign capital and Albania is still waiting for a surge of foreign investments. Many foreign companies remain wary because of Albania's lack of political stability and fear that the war in the former Yugoslavia could eventually also engulf Albania. In addition, many foreign businessmen apparently feel the effort required to strike deals in Albania is not worth the accompanying risks. They have encountered serious difficulties in dealing with red tape and legal uncertainties as well as Albania's bleak economic outlook.

---

[19] ATA [Albanian Telegraphic Agency] in English, 0818 GMT, May 12, 1992, in *FBIS-EEU* 92–094, May 14, 1992, p. 2.

[20] *World Bank News* (Washington, D.C.), XI, no. 26 (July 2, 1992): 1.

[21] Radio Tirana Network in Albanian, 1330 GMT, July 22, 1992, transl. in *FBIS-EEU* 92–142, July 23, 1992, p. 2.

[22] *Rilindja Demokratike*, 24 July 1992, p. 1.

[23] *Fletorja Zyrtare e Republikës së Shipërisë* [The Official Gazette of the Republic of Albania] (Tirana), no. 4, August 1992, pp. 226–229.

The implementation of austerity measures was bound to affect the Democratic Party's popularity. While a small percentage of the population benefited from the new economic policies, living standards continued to decline as many goods became so expensive that they were beyond the reach of most people. Dissatisfaction with the government's policies was reflected in the results of local elections, held at the end of July 1992. On the eve of the elections, the government had raised consumer prices in accordance with the IMF stabilization program. The Socialist Party made an impressive comeback, winning about 45 percent of the general vote.[24] The Democratic Party's poor showing in the local election adversely affected the government's ability to govern effectively. Berisha has tried to maintain worker support for his radical reforms, but the pain and dislocations brought on by the radical measures taken have led the trade unions to increase pressure on the government for a more gradual approach to reform. In response, the government was forced to modify some aspects of the reform to lessen its impact on the poorest sectors of society.

Despite serious difficulties, in 1993 there were some signs that the economy was beginning, albeit slowly, to turn around. Private markets were thriving in many cities, and many industrial enterprises and factories, shut down for over a year because of the lack of raw materials, had resumed operation. Agricultural production showed a modest increase after a two-year drastic decline. And remittances from refugees abroad were pouring in and expected to amount to as much as $400 million a year.[25] Most observers agree that Albania has good prospects for an economic expansion. It has a relatively well-educated working force, ample hydroelectric and oil resources, and is relatively rich in mineral resources, including chromium and copper. Its beautiful and thus far unexploited Adriatic coast represents excellent prospects for the tourist industry. If the tourist industry were developed, it could become a major source of foreign exchange.

However, Albania's prospects of building a genuine pluralistic democracy are less promising. Since the opposition was legalized in December 1990, Albania has come an extraordinary distance in dismantling the totalitarian state. But it has a long way to go in establishing a genuinely pluralistic democracy. The lack of a liberal political tradition and the absence of a well-entrenched democratic elite represent serious obstacles to democratic institution-building. Nevertheless, Berisha seems committed to move in this direction. Western assistance will be critical in helping Albania build a democratic culture.

Albania's Evolving Foreign Policy

The introduction of political pluralism had an immediate and significant impact on Albania's foreign and security policy. Foreign policy had long been the preroga-

---

[24] Socialist Party candidates swept 23 of 42 municipalities. Radio Tirana Network in Albanian, 1000 GMT, August 13, 1992, transl. in *FBIS-EEU* 92–157, August 13, 1992, pp. 3–4.

[25] ATA in English, 1123 GMT, October 7, 1992, in *FBIS-EEU* 92–96, October 8, 1992, p. 3.

tive of the first secretary of the APL and the Politburo and was not the subject of public debate. The opposition parties challenged the APL monopoly over foreign policy formulation, and called for the full depoliticization of the foreign affairs establishment. For the first time since 1944, foreign policy came under close public scrutiny. While in the past, domestic public opinion had played no role in formulating and implementing foreign policy, the introduction of political pluralism heightened national feelings. Issues long considered taboo, such as the question of ethnic Albanians in former Yugoslavia and Greece, became subjects of heated public debate.

In early 1991, the Democratic Party organized a demonstration to protest then-Foreign Minister Reiz Malile's visit to Cuba and China. The democrats, advocating a reorientation of Albania's policy toward Western Europe and the United States, criticized Malile for having invited Chinese Prime Minister Li Peng to visit Albania, and demanded his resignation.[26] Both Malile and Sofokli Lazri, Alia's chief foreign policy adviser, reportedly exercised a restraining influence on Albania's expansion of ties with the West, advocating instead the development of close relations with the Soviet Union, China, Vietnam, and Cuba. Lazri, who apparently played a critical role in formulating foreign policy, was blamed for the poor state of Albania's relations with West Germany and the deterioration of ties with Italy. The establishment of diplomatic relations with Bonn in 1987 had raised hopes that West Germany would assist Albania's economic development. The much hoped-for cooperation with West Germany never materialized because of the Albanian government's intransigence on human rights issues and rejection of foreign credits and investments. Tirana's refusal to permit an Albanian family that had entered the Italian embassy in 1985 to leave the country had brought relations with Rome virtually to a standstill. Because of opposition criticism, Malile was replaced, and Lazri resigned.

By summer 1991, the renovated socialists, having publicly repudiated Hoxha's devastating isolation of the country, had developed unusually close relations with Italy. A constant theme in the pronouncements of socialist leaders and their media was that Italy, and not the United States, was Albania's "natural ally." Following the escape of thousands of Albanians to Italy in August 1991, most of whom were forcibly repatriated, the Rome government began a program of massive humanitarian assistance. During the election campaign in March 1992, Italy threw its support solidly behind the socialists. The Democratic Party, on the other hand, took a strongly pro-American position.

The new government has emphasized the need to rapidly open up Albania to the outside world. Berisha has taken a very active role in formulating and conducting foreign policy. He has established personal contacts with numerous world leaders and has used these contacts to impress upon them the need to treat Albania as a "special case," forcibly arguing that no European country had suffered more under communism than Albania. Berisha's top foreign policy objective has been to obtain foreign aid to reinvigorate the economy. While he has expressed appreciation for the humanitarian assistance his country has received, Berisha has attempted to convince foreign governments to invest in Albania, expressing concern that continued

[26] Abdi Baleta, "Renewed Toasts," *Rilindja Demokratike,* 30 Jan. 1991, p. 6.

reliance on foreign aid will drive his country into a debt trap. Berisha has also expressed the desire that his country be accepted in European and international institutions and organizations, which will speed up its integration into the world community. The Albanian government has responded to dramatic developments in the Balkans by striving to forge close links with the United States, NATO members, and former Yugoslav republics. Tirana has also urged the international community to engage in preventive diplomacy regarding the possible peaceful resolution of the thorny issue of Kosovo.

Relations with the United States and the Former Soviet Union

Albania's relations with the United States and the former Soviet Union have undergone rapid and positive change. In March 1991, the United States restored diplomatic relations with Albania after a hiatus of more than fifty years. Washington made no secret that this was a deliberate decision aimed at boosting the democratic process in Albania. Democratic Party leaders had all along urged the United States to proceed with the normalization of relations. In a highly unusual development that could not escape the attention of communists in Tirana, the State Department invited Democratic Party leaders Berisha and Gramoz Pashko to attend the signing ceremony.[27]

Washington's support ensured Albania's admittance into the CSCE. In June 1991, Secretary of State James Baker visited Albania to underscore the importance the United States attached to the democratization of the tiny Balkan country. He informed the Albanians that the United States would provide $6 million worth of assistance and that Washington would be prepared to provide additional support if meaningful political and economic reforms were implemented.[28] Following Baker's visit, numerous American delegations visited Tirana to assess Albania's need for humanitarian and technical assistance.

Following the Democratic Party's election victory, Albanian-American relations witnessed a steady and significant improvement in all fields. Although it has had to compete for U.S. assistance with other East European countries and former Soviet republics at a time of diminishing resources, Albania has been the subject of considerable American attention. By November 1992, the United States had granted Albania more than $70 million in humanitarian and technical assistance. In June 1992, Berisha became the first Albanian leader to pay a state visit to Washington, where he held talks with President George Bush and Secretary of State James Baker. During the visit Bush signed a trade agreement giving Albania most-favored-nation preferential trade status.[29]

---

[27] *The Washington Post*, 13 March 1991, p. A–22; and *The Christian Science Monitor*, 18 March 1991, p. 7.

[28] Thomas L. Friedman, "300,000 Albanians Pour into Streets to Welcome Baker," *The New York Times*, 23 June 1991, pp. 1, 8.

[29] For Berisha's Washington visit, see David Binder, "Albanian Leader Tells Bush of His Fear

While the Albanians seemingly have exaggerated expectations of the level of assistance the United States is able or willing to provide, Washington has included Albania in all its East European aid programs and is providing technical assistance in many sectors. The U.S. government has urged private American investments. Albania does offer good investment opportunities, particularly in the oil industry and in tourism. There is also a large, relatively well-to-do Albanian community in the United States, which played an important role in promoting the establishment of diplomatic relations and is eager to help Albania's economic revival. Albanian-Americans have been remarkably effective in lobbying the U.S. Congress and administration on Albanian issues.

The former Soviet Union had tried for years to woo Albania back into the Warsaw Pact by promising economic assistance. Despite significant changes in the international arena even before the East European revolution, the Soviet Union continued to view Albania as an attractive beachhead in the Adriatic. Soviet military strategists apparently never forgave Nikita Khrushchev for his tactless handling of the Albanians, which led to the Tirana-Moscow break and the Soviet withdrawal from the naval base at Sazan, near the port of Vlorë. Before 1990, the Albanian government had rejected Moscow's offers to restore ties, and continued to view the Soviet Union as the principal potential threat to Albania. Tirana's hostility to Moscow was further reinforced by Soviet support for Serbia's crackdown against ethnic Albanians. The Albanian communist regime was one of the harshest critics of Mikhail Gorbachev's *perestroika* and *glasnost'* policies.

The deterioration of the economic situation, however, increased domestic pressures, and the declining authority of the APL forced Tirana to change its stand on many issues, including its stance toward the Soviet Union. Tirana-Moscow relations were restored in the summer of 1990, but the event lacked the enthusiasm and euphoria that permeated the subsequent establishment of Albanian-American ties. Preoccupied with its own domestic problems, Gorbachev's Soviet Union did not take any significant steps to expand relations with Albania. Gorbachev, however, invited Alia to visit the Soviet Union.

Following the disintegration of the Soviet Union, Albania expressed a desire to strengthen relations with the Russian federation. There have been several senior-level delegation exchanges between the two countries. Despite increased political contacts between Tirana and Moscow, however, bilateral economic cooperation remains insignificant and is unlikely to improve in the near future because of Russia's own domestic problems.

Western Europe

Since the beginning of 1991, Albania has moved toward a closer association with Western Europe. Albania has lifted self-imposed constraints that had limited its

---

of Serbia," *The New York Times*, 16 June 1992, p. A–10; and *The Washington Times*, 16 June 1992, p. A–4.

external economic interaction, and has liberalized its legislation to attract and encourage foreign investments and the establishment of joint ventures. Albania's long-term stated objective is full integration into the European Union (formerly EC), with which it established relations in June 1991.

The Albanians have appealed to Western Europe for large-scale assistance to stabilize the economy, whose decline has accelerated with the rapid disintegration of the old system. They have requested technical assistance, improved trade ties and financial aid. The West has been slow to respond to Albania's requests, however, because of the widely held perception that large-scale aid will only prop up an increasingly disintegrating economy. The Albanians appear particularly disappointed that Germany has not played a greater role.[30]

Of all the major Western countries, only Italy has sent significant financial assistance to Albania. Italy has been forced to take an active role because it has been confronted with waves of Albanian refugees. Political tensions that followed the toppling of Hoxha's statue in Tirana on February 20, 1991, led to the illegal emigration from Albania to Italy of approximately twenty-four thousand Albanians. Rome returned several thousand refugees, granted Albania emergency humanitarian aid, and declared it would not accept other refugees. These steps, however, did not prevent other Albanians from fleeing across the Adriatic. In August 1991, approximately 20,000 refugees fled to Italy. This time they were all sent back. Italy has been Albania's leading aid donor, granting its impoverished neighbor more than $350 million during the period from September 1991 to November 1992. Rome also dispatched a contingent of about 900 soldiers to distribute the aid provided by Italy and the European Community.

Immediately following the parliamentary elections in March 1992, Berisha moved to mend fences with the Italians, who had supported the socialists. The relationship between Italy and post-communist Albania is an uneasy one, however. The United States and other countries have been unwilling to undertake a major effort to help Albania escape the poverty trap. Thus Berisha, not unlike King Zog in the 1930s, has little choice but to rely on Italy, while continuing to search for alternate patrons.

But the harsh treatment of refugees and the behavior of Italian soldiers in Albania have led to increased anti-Italian feelings. There is also concern about growing Italian influence; many Albanians fear that Italy will eventually dominate Albania economically and politically as it did in the 1930s. Although Italian aid will help Albania shore up its tattered economy, Tirana runs the risk of locking itself into a client-patron relationship with Rome with far-reaching consequences for Albania's independence.

---

[30] The German embassy, which had been closed down in July 1990 after Albanian refugees stormed foreign missions in Tirana, was reopened only in August 1991. Germany also resumed its economic assistance, which was suspended in 1990. See Hamburg DPA in German 1050 GMT, August 22, 1991, in *FBIS-EEU* 91–164, August 23, 1991, pp. 15–16.

The Balkans

Albania's relations with its contiguous neighbors have historically been characterized by simmering ethnic disputes. Historical obsession with encirclement by a Greek-Yugoslav alliance has led Albania to seek security by turning for protection to distant powers.

The resurgent border and interethnic conflicts in former Yugoslavia and the federation's disintegration have caused a realignment of Balkan states, presenting Albania with both opportunities and risks. The issues of both Kosovo and Macedonia have appeared on the agenda. To deal with a growing Serbian threat, Albanian diplomacy has concentrated on strengthening ties with Turkey, Greece, and Bulgaria and forging a new relationship with independent Macedonia, Croatia, and Slovenia.

Whereas in recent decades Albania had developed excellent political ties with Turkey, bilateral economic cooperation had lagged. In the wake of the accession to power of the Democratic Party, Turkey responded positively to Albanian requests for increased cooperation. In June 1992, Prime Minister Süleyman Demirel visited Tirana and the two countries concluded a treaty of friendship and cooperation. On this occasion, Turkey announced it was granting Albania immediate humanitarian and technical assistance worth $50 million.[31]

To the chagrin of Greece, the two countries have developed a close military relationship, and they signed a defense cooperation pact in July 1992. While details of the agreement were not disclosed, the Turkish defense minister said it reflected "the determination of both countries to cooperate in military education and scientific cooperation."[32] Among the many economic projects being discussed is Turkey's interest in constructing an international highway linking the port of Durrès with Istanbul. Turkey also played an instrumental role in Albania's inclusion in the Black Sea Economic Zone initiative.[33]

Although Albania has significantly strengthened its relations with Turkey, relations with Greece remain strained. Albanian-Greek relations have been adversely affected by the influx of thousands of Albanian refugees into Greece and the contentious issue of the ethnic Greek minority in Albania. An estimated 150 thousand Albanians have fled to Greece since early 1991 in search of jobs and a better life. Such a massive influx of refugees has created difficulties for the Greek authorities, which have blamed the Albanians for the rise in crime and illegal activities. In late 1991, Athens forcibly expelled thousands of refugees. Reports of widespread mistreatment of refugees and several cases of Albanians being killed by Greek border guards caused an uproar in Albania. Tensions were further increased in February 1992, when the Albanian parliament approved a new election law banning ethnically based groups, such as the ethnic Greek organization OMONIA, from partici-

---

[31] Anatolia in English, 1425 GMT, June 1, 1992, in *FBIS-EEU* 92–106, June 2, 1992, p. 2.

[32] Anatolia in English, 1557 GMT, July 29, 1992, in *FBIS-WEU* 92–147, July 30, 1992, p. 58.

[33] Radio Tirana Network in Albanian, 1330 GMT, June 26, 1992, transl. in *FBIS-EEU* 92–125, June 29, 1992, pp. 3–4.

pating in the elections. Athens launched a strong protest, claiming that the election law discriminated against ethnic Greeks. Although a compromise was reached with the formation of the Party for the Protection of Human Rights, ostensibly open to all Albanian citizens but actually composed exclusively of ethnic Greeks, the incident seriously strained bilateral relations. The situation was also exacerbated by irresponsible statements made by some ethnic Greek leaders, who advocated that Greece annex southern Albania.[34]

Following Prime Minister Constantine Mitsotakis's visit to Albania in May 1992, tensions between the two nations decreased, but suspicions persist on both sides. The Albanians fear that prolonged political instability could revive official Greek claims on southern parts of their country—an issue already raised by some circles in Greece.[35] Moreover, Tirana is deeply concerned about a potential alliance between Greece and Serbia. Greece, on the other hand, is worried that Albania will again fall under Italian domination or enter into a close military alliance with Turkey.

Tirana's ties with Bucharest and Sofia have shown no appreciable improvement. Albania apparently does not perceive great advantages in cultivating closer relations with Romania and Bulgaria, which are preoccupied with their own internal problems. However, Tirana's attitude toward Sofia could change in view of developments in former Yugoslavia, particularly Macedonia.

Relations with Former Yugoslav Republics and the Question of Kosovo

Albania has viewed the war in Croatia and Bosnia-Herzegovina with great alarm, fearing that the conflict could spread to Kosovo. The disintegration of the Yugoslav federation coincided with great political and social upheavals in Albania. The Albanian state has never been weaker vis-à-vis its neighbors than at present, and, in the event of a war in Kosovo, could offer little help to the ethnic Albanians. Nevertheless, Albania has considered Slovenia, Croatia, and Macedonia as natural allies against Serbia. High level delegations from Ljubljana, Zagreb and Skopje have visited Tirana for discussions on a wide range of political and economic issues. The Slovenes have expressed interest in establishing joint ventures in Albania in many sectors, particularly in the tourist industry. Economic cooperation with Croatia, however, has lagged because of the war.

Of the three former Yugoslav republics, Albania is most directly interested in closer ties with Macedonia. The two countries have mutual political and economic interests. A viable, independent Macedonia separating rump Yugoslavia and Greece is obviously in Albania's interest. Landlocked Macedonia, facing increased economic pressure from both the north and the south, desperately needs an outlet, and

---

[34] See *Helsinking Sanomat,* March 25, 1992, p. C1, transl. in *JPRS-EER* 92–053, April 30, 1992, p. 1.

[35] Dhim. Mikhalopoulos, "The Albanian Threat Is Real," *To Vima Tis Kiriakis*, June 7, 1992, p. A25, transl. in *FBIS-WEU* 92–141, July 22, 1992, p. 33.

Albania's ports present excellent prospects. The two sides have taken steps to increase their economic cooperation and are considering several important joint projects, including constructing highways and railway lines, establishing a joint airline, and building an oil pipeline with Italian help. In October 1992, Tirana offered Macedonia its facilities to transport oil via Albanian territory.[36]

The dilemma Albanian decisionmakers face is how to reconcile the interests of the Albanian state with those of the large and restless Albanian population in Macedonia. There are between 600 thousand and 800 thousand Albanians in Macedonia, accounting for 30 percent to 40 percent of the total population. They have been subjected to severe repression and discrimination and have demanded full equality with the Macedonians. Ethnic Albanian leaders have urged the European Community not to recognize Macedonia unless Skopje authorities approve constitutional changes recognizing the Albanians as a nation and not a national minority.

President Kiro Gligorov's visit to Tirana in June 1992 marked the beginning of what appeared to be a promising Albanian-Macedonian dialogue. In return for Albania's pledge to recognize Macedonia, Gligorov reportedly agreed to take concrete measures to improve the position of ethnic Albanians. Berisha, for his part, assured Gligorov that Albania had no territorial claims on Macedonia and urged the ethnic Albanians to "be a factor of stability for the Macedonian state."[37] In a subsequent interview with *Le Monde*, Berisha said:

> Albanians, wherever they are, must rely firmly on the Helsinki principles. The Albanians in Macedonia must help stabilize that state because a stable and independent Macedonia is in the whole region's interest. The Macedonians, for their part, must recognize the Albanians' rights, otherwise they will not have any real stability.[38]

Despite serious opposition from Macedonian nationalists, Gligorov has taken steps to meet Albanian demands. Ethnic Albanians, who in April 1992 had declared an autonomous republic in western Macedonia, adopted a more moderate course following the Berisha-Gligorov meeting. In the summer of 1992, ethnic Albanian political parties agreed to join a government coalition. Although the authorities have not yet met the ethnic Albanians' main demand for constitutional changes, tensions between the two ethnic groups seem to have been at least temporarily defused.

The future course of Tirana-Skopje relations will depend greatly on how the Macedonians resolve their differences with the ethnic Albanians. While Berisha has exerted a moderating influence on ethnic Albanian leaders, the latter are likely to reassess their position if their minimum demands for equality with the Macedonians are not met.

---

[36] ATA in English, 0912 GMT, October 13, 1992, in *FBIS-EEU* 92–199, October 14, 1992, p. 2.

[37] ATA in English, 0800 GMT, June 4, 1992, in *FBIS-EEU* 92–108, June 4, 1992, pp. 6–7.

[38] *Le Monde*, June 28–29, 1992, p. 3, transl. in *FBIS-EEU* 92–130, July 7, 1992, p. 9.

Albania's relations with rump Yugoslavia remain tense, with frequent border skirmishes and a massive increase in troops on the border. Tirana has appealed for international intervention to prevent a full-scale conflict in Kosovo.

While tensions in Kosovo were high throughout the 1980s, the situation was exacerbated in March 1989, when Serbia stripped the province of its autonomy. When Albanian members of the Provincial Assembly declared Kosovo's independence from Serbia in July 1990, Milosevic suspended the provincial parliament and government, and shut down the Albanian-language radio, television, and daily *Rilindja*. Rejecting the legitimacy of Serbian rule, ethnic Albanian deputies met clandestinely in the city of Kaçanik and proclaimed Kosovo a republic.[39] While the decision was supported by the overwhelming majority of Kosovars, the Serbian government denounced it as "an unconstitutional act" and a direct attack on the territorial integrity of both Serbia and Yugoslavia, and intensified plans for the Serbianization of Kosovo.

Since September 1990, more than 100 thousand Albanians have been fired from their jobs and replaced by Serbs brought into Kosovo from Serbia. In a stepped-up recolonization of Kosovo, the Serbian parliament adopted a law encouraging Serbs to resettle in the region. Serbian authorities have replaced numerous Albanian professors at the University of Pristina and have shut down all Albanian-language schools that do not accept Serbian school curricula that purposely neglect the study of Albanian culture and history.[40] Ibrahim Rugova, leader of the Democratic League, which claims a membership of some 700 thousand, has stressed a peaceful approach as a means of gaining diplomatic and propaganda advantage over Serbia. Meanwhile, he has had to respond to growing Kosovar frustration over the absence of any improvement of the situation and the failure of his policies to break Serbia's hold over Kosovo. Some activists have urged Rugova to pursue a more assertive strategy against Serbia. Professor Rexhep Qosja, Kosovo's preeminent scholar, has reproached Albanian political parties "for retreating before Serbian policy" and permitting the development of a situation in which Albanians are unprepared to defend themselves.[41]

In September 1991, Albanian deputies of the suspended provincial Assembly met clandestinely and declared Kosovo "a sovereign and independent state" and decided to hold a national referendum. Albanians overwhelmingly approved the Assembly's decision.[42] Serbia's foreign minister responded by saying that the Alba-

[39] Zenun Çelaj, "Kosova Declared a Republic Within the Framework of Yugoslavia," *Zëri i Rinisë* (Pristina), 14 September 1990, pp. 7–9. Çelaj, a prominent journalist and secretary of the Pristina-based Council for the Protection of Human Rights and Liberties, was the only reporter present at the Kaçanik meeting. He was arrested and spent a month in jail for allegedly having attended an illegal meeting. For Çelaj's personal account of imprisonment, see his article "I Was Not Alone," *Koha* (Pristina), 8 Nov. 1990, p. 10.

[40] Helsinki Watch, *Yugoslavia: Human Rights Abuses in Kosovo 1990–1992,* pp. 38–49.

[41] See Qosja's interview in *Fjala* (Pristina), no. 27 (July 1991): 3–5.

[42] Zagreb Radio Croatia in Albanian, 2215 GMT, October 7, 1991, in *FBIS-EEU* 91–196, October 9, 1991, p. 42.

nians constitute a minority in Yugoslavia and, therefore, "do not have a right to self-determination." He said, "There is no way that they can get a republic, let alone a state, of their own."[43]

The Albanians formed an underground government, appointing Bujar Bukoshi, a close Rugova adviser, as prime minister. In the most significant defiance to date of Serbia's sovereignty over Kosovo, ethnic Albanians organized elections in May 1992 for a new parliament and a president. Rugova was elected as president of the Republic of Kosovo. Serbian authorities, however, have forcibly prevented meetings of the new parliament. With the exception of Albania, moreover, no state has recognized the Republic of Kosovo.

With the disintegration of the Yugoslav federation, Albanian ethnic demands have also changed. Although formerly the main demand was that Kosovo be granted the status of a republic within Yugoslavia, now all ethnic Albanian political parties insist on Kosovo's full independence. Rugova has rejected increasing international calls that Serbia grant Kosovo special status and restore its former autonomy. He has also said that the division of Kosovo, an option apparently advocated by increasing numbers of people in Serbia, is unacceptable, because it would still leave about one million Albanians under Serbian rule. Instead, Rugova has advocated the establishment of an independent, neutral Kosovo state, which would be demilitarized and would maintain close links with both Serbia and Albania.[44]

In sharp contrast with Rugova, Qosja has maintained that the only solution to the problem of ethnic Albanians is immediate unification with Albania. He has called on the Tirana government to take a more forceful stand in protecting ethnic Albanians and advocating "national union." Qosja has accused Rugova of betraying Albanian national interests, particularly by participating in the London Conference as an observer and by rejecting the use of mass, popular protests to exert pressure on Serbia.[45] Having insisted on a peaceful resolution of the conflict with Serbia, Rugova must at some point produce tangible substantive progress toward the restoration of political rights to justify his position to a restive Kosovar populace.

Not unexpectedly, Serbia's president Milosevic has not only ruled out the possibility of the establishment of an independent Kosovo state but has also said that Belgrade will not grant Kosovo an autonomous status.[46] He has insisted that "Kosovo will remain a part of Serbia, and this really cannot be discussed under any circumstances."[47]

Albania has expressed alarm at the possibility of an armed conflict in Kosovo

---

[43] *Der Spiegel* (Hamburg), October 7, 1991, pp. 194–195, in *FBIS-EEU* 91–195, October 8, 1991, pp. 52–53.

[44] See Rugova's interview in *Delo* (Ljubljana), October 10, 1992, p. 20, transl. in *FBIS-EEU* 92–200, October 15, 1992, pp. 70–72.

[45] *Zëri* (Pristina), 5 Sept. 1992, pp. 4–5.

[46] Belgrade RTB Television Network in Serbo-Croatian, 2054 GMT, October 9, 1992, transl. in *FBIS-EEU* 92–198, October 13, 1992, pp. 33–43.

[47] Belgrade RTB Television Network in Serbo-Croatian, 1902 GMT, May 28, 1992, transl. in *FBIS-EEU* 92–104, May 29, 1992, pp. 48–54.

and has indicated that, in the event of a war in Kosovo, it will have no choice but to come to the assistance of the ethnic Albanians. Berisha has repeatedly stated that Albania is not demanding a redrawing of borders but has insisted that the ethnic Albanians be permitted to exercise their right to self-determination.[48]

National Unification: Thinking about the Unthinkable?

With the reunification of Germany, the Albanians remain the only divided nation in Europe. Albania has a population of about 3.3 million. Although there are no exact figures, there are believed to be more than 2 million Albanians in Kosovo, and 50 thousand in Montenegro. An estimated several hundred thousand are scattered throughout Serbia proper, with large communities in southern Serbia. The Albanians have the highest birthrate in Europe: 25.3 per thousand in Albania (1989) and 29.9 per thousand in Kosovo (1987). The Albanian population is also Europe's youngest: more than one-third of Albania's total population is under fifteen years of age; 60 percent of Kosovo's population is under twenty-seven years old. Based on current projections, by the year 2000 there will be four million Albanians on each side of the current state boundaries separating Albania and former Yugoslavia. Thus, there will be almost as many Albanians as Serbs in the Balkans, and several times more Albanians than Montenegrins and Macedonians. The question begs itself: How long can such large communities of the same nation remain divided?

Since World War II, Albania's claims to Kosovo have been dormant. Hoxha downplayed the issue, giving priority to state-to-state relations with the former Yugoslavia. Alia was even less supportive of the ethnic Albanians. Most Kosovars who crossed the border during the 1980s to escape prosecution in Yugoslavia for nationalist activity were turned back.[49] In contrast to Hoxha, Alia did not formally endorse ethnic Albanian demands for a republic, stressing that the status of Kosovo was an internal Yugoslav issue. During the Balkan Foreign Ministers' Conference held in Tirana in 1990, Alia received Yugoslav Foreign Minister Budimir Loncar. According to Yugoslav news reports, the Albanian leader "expressed respect for the integrity of Yugoslavia and Serbia."[50] This statement runs counter to the Kaçanik declaration which had proclaimed Kosovo's independence from Serbia.

Post-World War II ethnic Albanian communist leaders in the former Yugoslavia were loyal to Belgrade and did not advocate union with Albania. With its crackdown, Serbia has now relegated the Albanians to the bottom levels of the society. Relying on brute military and police force to maintain peace and order, the Serbian

---

[48] *Le Quotidien de Paris* (Paris), September 11, 1992, p. 17, transl. in *FBIS-EEU* 92–180, September 16, 1992, p. 2.

[49] Sinan Hasani, *Kosovo: Istine i Zablude* (Zagreb: Centar za Informacije i Publicitet, 1986), 203; and Milovan Drecun, "Preparations of the Skipetars [Albanians] for an Armed Rebellion," *Politika* (Belgrade), July 14, 1991, 14, translated in Joint Publications Research Service, *East Europe Report* (Washington D.C.: U.S. Government Printing Office), no. 91–111 (July 30, 1991), 66.

[50] Tanjug Domestic Service in Serbo-Croatian, 1436 GMT, October 26, 1990, in *FBIS-EEU* 90–209, October 29, 1990, pp. 3–4.

government has threatened ethnic Albanians' physical security, locked them out of political institutions and processes, and restricted their access to education, jobs, medical care, and social services. Serbian repressive measures, ostensibly undertaken to fight Albanian "nationalism and irredentism," have actually strengthened independence sentiment and helped unify the ethnic Albanians. Ethnic consciousness among Albanians in Yugoslavia has never been more powerful than it is now.

For decades the question of the unification of the Albanian nation was taboo in both Albania and Yugoslavia. The issue of national union, however, now dominates political debate on both sides of the border. Although Albania and Kosovo have developed independently of each other during most of this century, there is a much stronger sense of unity among Albanians on both sides of the border than is commonly recognized by outsiders. Even during the long absence of free movement across the border, cultural cooperation between Pristina and Tirana universities in the 1970s, the Kosovars' adoption of the standard Albanian literary language, and the explosion of Albanian-language publications, radio, and TV have reinforced the bonds between the two parts of the Albanian nation. Although sentiments for unification are increasing, neither activists in Kosovo nor in Albania have gone beyond rhetorical statements, recognizing the preponderant power Serbia enjoys in relations with both Kosovo and Albania.

Serbia has repeatedly demonstrated the ability to crush forcibly any attempt to wrest away Kosovo. Albanian national movements, however, have surfaced repeatedly. By failing to seek a solution that will meet minimum ethnic Albanian demands, Milosevic has planted the seeds of a bloody armed conflict. Over the long-term, the costs to Serbia of keeping Kosovo under its control eventually are likely to increase. Serbia's economy, already in shambles, will be heavily taxed by the costs that continued military occupation of Kosovo will entail.

Serbia's fear of Albanian irredentism threatens to become a self-fulfilling prophecy. The rift between the Albanians and the Serbs appears unbridgeable. Even granting Kosovo special status or restoring its former autonomy may turn out to be too little, too late. Despite vehement repression, Albanian nationalism in Kosovo is increasing.

As long as the political rights of the Albanian community in Kosovo are not restored, Kosovo will remain a potential source of instability and turmoil. The West must move beyond treating the Albanian problem solely as a human rights issue and actively mediate a solution to the Kosovo issue. Failure to act expeditiously could confront the international community with a more general Balkan conflagration, with hundreds of thousands of Albanian refugees desperately seeking haven in neighboring countries—particularly Greece and Italy.

III

Bulgaria: Security Concerns and Foreign Policy Considerations

Duncan M. Perry*

Throughout the forty-plus years of communist rule in Eastern Europe, the Soviet Union was primus inter pares, and the USSR's bulwark in the Balkans after the mid-1960s was Bulgaria—the only faithful follower of the Moscow line in the peninsula. Bulgaria's past communist orthodoxy, from Moscow's perspective, coupled with its location on the northern borders of Greece and European Turkey, lent it a unique strategic importance. In addition, Bulgaria's proximity to Turkey afforded the USSR a potential stepping-stone to the Turkish Dardanelles and the Bosphorus—the Soviet Union's only naval and maritime passage from its warm-water ports on the Black Sea to the Mediterranean. Bulgaria also served as Moscow's agent in international affairs. Bulgarian personnel acted at times as surrogates for the Soviet Union in matters including diplomatic initiatives, covert activities, training terrorists, conducting arms deals, and spreading misinformation.

Bulgarian national political leaders are now gazing westward, anxious to enter Western trade and security alliances, hoping soon to join the European mainstream. The shift away from Soviet-style government by Bulgaria and the other former Soviet satellites will have an important long-term impact on Bulgaria's economy and security system. Nevertheless, economic ties between Bulgaria and many former Soviet republics, notably Russia, will remain strong for some time to come, as they are bound together by common economic factors including mutual supply, production, market, and distribution interdependencies.

* The author wishes to express his thanks to James F. Brown, Douglas Clarke, Kjell Englebrekt, and Patrick Moore of the Radio Free Europe/Radio Liberty Research Institute in Munich for their helpful comments on an earlier version of this chapter.

Domestic Politics

Contemporary Bulgarian politics are a swirl of ideological, social, and economic crosscurrents. At first they could be characterized as a bipolar struggle between the Bulgarian Communist Party (BCP), which changed its name to the Bulgarian Socialist Party (BSP) in 1990, and the major democratic coalition, the Union of Democratic Forces (UDF), founded in 1989. This changed in 1992 when the Movement for Rights and Freedoms, a predominantly Turkish group and the only other party to be represented in parliament, broke ranks with its erstwhile UDF ally and voted to bring down the government.

The BSP, whose program and direction have evolved from authoritarian communism to a muddled, quasi-social-democratic platform, albeit with strong nationalist overtones, faced off with the UDF, whose constituent organizations included various political orientations including liberals, conservatives, social democrats, environmentalists, and agrarians. During the June 1990 national elections, the BSP secured a narrow majority of 211 seats in the Grand National Assembly, Bulgaria's special legislature convened to draft and ratify a new constitution and various reforms, on the strength of 46.25 percent of the vote, while the UDF came in second with 36 percent of the vote and 144 seats.

To many, the UDF's comparatively poor showing was a significant disappointment. Given that the party had only a few months to build a constituency, however, its performance was not all that bad. In the parliament that was formed as a result of the first free national elections in more than forty years, the BSP and the UDF became locked in struggles that often seemed to be motivated more by interparty enmity than political or ideological differences. Despite the sometimes Byzantine and apparently self-serving activities of deputies and their parties, important legislation related to democratization and the creation of a market economy was finally passed, including, notably, a new constitution on July 12, 1991. During the process, however, the UDF coalition, which was never robust, began to disintegrate. Two factions formed around the issue of whether the constitution should be approved before the fall elections (which eventually were held on October 13, 1991) or after. The BSP, itself somewhat fractured, profited from this split, as votes for the three UDF splinter groups that chose to run on their own tickets actually reduced the number of ballots overall cast for the UDF. In the final tally, the UDF won a narrow plurality of 34.36 percent or 110 seats in the 240-person National Assembly. The BSP gained 33.14 percent and secured 106 seats. The only other political organization to win seats in the legislature was the Movement for Rights and Freedoms (MRF), which won 7.55 percent of the vote and gained twenty-four seats in parliament. None of the approximately thirty-four smaller parties and organizations that ran candidates even secured representation, as none passed the threshold of 4 percent of the vote needed for seats.[1] In effect, more than 20 percent of the electorate failed to gain parliamentary representation because it voted for parties or independents that won no seats.

[1] The Bulgarian Agrarian National Union came close with 3.86 percent of the vote.

The 1991 election was both a victory and a defeat for the democratic forces. The UDF coalition's voter support declined by only 1.64 percent over the percentage of votes won in the 1990 election, despite the defection of three factions representing nearly 10 percent of the voting electorate. This indicates that the UDF actually gained some strength in the year between elections.

In the second round of democratic elections in October 1991, the BSP received 13.11 percent fewer votes than those cast in the last election, a setback of only moderate proportions. The loss was attributable to a combination of factors: continuing adverse press coverage of corruption perpetrated during the communist era, the BSP's indecisive behavior during the abortive August 1991 coup in the Soviet Union, and, finally, the putsch itself and the subsequent diminution of the prestige and power of the Communist Party of the Soviet Union. Rural areas remained the stronghold of the BSP, with people there still opposing radical economic reform and some voters opposed to according full human rights to Bulgaria's ethnic Turks. Although it became the opposition party, the BSP was not without power. As a two-thirds vote of the National Assembly was required for constitutional change, no such action could be enacted without support from BSP deputies.

Perhaps the biggest winner in the 1991 elections was the MRF. Its main concern is the protection and extension of Muslim rights in Bulgaria. In fact, in the elections of both 1990 and 1991, the MRF had the third-largest showing, garnering twenty-three seats (5.8 percent) in the 400-seat Grand National Assembly which promulgated the new constitution, and twenty-four seats in the 240-seat 1991 National Assembly (7.55 percent). The MRF not only made a slight gain over its 1990 showing, but more important, it became a linchpin in the National Assembly as the only other party to win seats. The UDF and the MRF pledged to act together in pursuit of human rights and radical national reform. Neither wished to work with the BSP, but, at the same time, no member of the MRF was invited to join the new cabinet, nor was a seat sought.[2]

The UDF election victory ensured that economic reform would continue, with privatization of industry slated to be among the items demanding the most immediate attention. Efforts to attract more Western investment and assistance also continued. The new government was obliged to address at least some of the MRF's demands concerning the teaching of Turkish in schools and other human rights issues. In the process, the government needed to confront growing anti-Turkish sentiments in some quarters and an opposition party that increasingly had been promoting anti-Muslim nationalism.

The UDF's honeymoon period lasted into the spring of 1992. Until then, its leaders worked relatively closely with the leaders of the MRF. Gradually, however, the two parties fell out with one another over the style of governance fostered by the UDF under the leadership of Prime Minister Filip Dimitrov. The MRF accused the UDF of failing to consult regularly about state matters and claimed that the govern-

---

[2] See Kjell Engelbrekt, "Opposition Narrowly Defeats Socialists in National Elections," *Report on Eastern Europe*, no. 43 (October 25, 1991): 1–3.

ment was not considering MRF interests. Trade unions and even members of the bureaucracy lined up against the government. Meantime, within the ruling cabinet, the prime minister had to confront dissension, notably from the then Minister of National Defense, Dimitur Ludzhev, who was sacked along with the Minister of Industry and Trade, Ivan Pushkarov, and others in a cabinet reshuffle in May 1992.

As if the power struggle with Ludzhev were not enough, Dimitrov also came under fire from the state president, Zhelyu Zhelev, ironically a founder of the UDF, who was reelected to the presidency on January 19, 1992. Zhelev chided the government for being autocratic and for spending too much time hunting communist malfeasants and not enough on reforming the state. In August, he accused the government of engaging in confrontational politics that alienated the unions, the press, and the extraparliamentary opposition and of seeking to cause friction with the presidency. By October, both sides were accusing each other of lying.

While this simmered, in a show of force, the MRF forced the resignation on September 24 of the president of the National Assembly, Stefan Savov, a UDF leader and head of the Social Democratic Party. Confrontation between the erstwhile political allies escalated and MRF leaders considered calling a no-confidence vote on the cabinet. Compounding the Dimitrov government's problems, a scandal broke out in October 1992 over an alleged secret arms deal with the Republic of Macedonia. On October 21, the prime minister was censured by the legislature meeting in closed session. His government fell on October 28, 1992, having narrowly lost a confidence vote in the parliament.

At the end of December 1992, a caretaker government headed by Lyuben Berov, a former adviser to President Zhelev, was approved by parliament. Since then, Bulgarian politics has become increasingly polarized. The right wing of the UDF has waged a vicious attack against President Zhelev—a former leader of the UDF—accusing him of promoting the "recommunization" of the country and demanding his resignation as well as that of Prime Minister Berov, the dissolution of parliament and the convocation of new elections. The UDF's call for new elections, however, could backfire. The UDF has lost considerable support among the public, which has become increasingly disillusioned with its political intrigues and policy of permanent confrontation. They also blame the UDF for the drastic decline in living standards and the country's rising unemployment. All this has worked to the benefit of the BSP, which, thanks to the internal divisions and discord within the UDF, could emerge as the strongest party in the next elections. Indeed, Bulgaria could become the next country in Eastern Europe, after Lithuania and Poland, to witness a comeback by the former communists.

The BSP has been able to capitalize on the public's disillusionment with the UDF's fragmentation and its failure to effectively address Bulgaria's pressing economic problems. While Bulgaria has made significant strides toward creating a market economy, the economic and social costs of the government's reform program has been high. Gross domestic product has fallen by over 33 percent since 1990, and unemployment had reached 17 percent by mid-1993. As a result of this mounting unemployment, the public's patience is wearing thin. Further, there is evidence that, particularly in the economic sphere, members of the former communist nomenklatura, many of whom still occupy important positions in the security and military forces, the bureaucracy and commerce, have been working against reform. In addition to nomenklatura obstructionism, there is resistance from managers, administrators and workers. These problems seem to have been fueled by fears of becoming unemployed or, in the case of the nomenklatura, losing influence and privileged positions.

Bulgaria has also been hard hit by the impact of the UN sanctions against Serbia. The sanctions cost Bulgaria $2–3 billion in lost revenue last year. This has added to its economic woes at a time when it can ill afford such losses. The unwillingness of the West to compensate Bulgaria for these losses has led to bitterness and disillusionment among the population. This has contributed to growing support for the Socialists and could lead to a dangerous growth of anti-Western feeling over the long run.

The Muslim Question

The role of Muslims in Bulgarian politics is a matter of great importance in contemporary Bulgaria. Historically, at least titularly, Bulgaria was a part of the Ottoman Empire from the late fourteenth century until 1908.[3] Although the Ottomans eventually relinquished control of Bulgaria, many ethnic Muslim Turks, augmented by a smaller number of Slavs whose forebears adopted Islam, remained in Bulgaria.

The Muslim and Christian communities did not integrate, and the separation continued after the fall of the Ottoman Empire. During the 1950s through the 1980s, Bulgarian-Turkish relations were generally smooth, but never close. Bulgarians never seemed to overcome the Ottoman " 'yoke' psychosis," that is, the oversimplified notion that Bulgaria existed for nearly 500 years under great oppression perpetrated by Ottoman authorities.[4] Turkey, for its part, had, and continues to maintain, an interest in the well-being of the ethnic Turks and other Islamic peoples in the Balkans.

Relations between Bulgaria and Turkey deteriorated precipitously when the Bulgarian government launched an assimilation campaign intended to transform ethnic Turks into "Bulgarians" in December 1984. The reasons behind this attempt at cultural and religious transmogrification have never been publicly stated. It is probable that the national purification campaign was induced in part by the logic that if the majority population could be mobilized against the Muslims, its attention would be diverted from the increasingly evident national economic crisis. The fact that the non-Muslim population had a shrinking birthrate while the Muslims had an expand-

---

[3] As a result of the Russo-Turkish War and the Treaty of Berlin signed in 1878 by the European powers, Bulgaria was granted the status of an autonomous principality within the Empire. It thus became functionally independent in that year.

[4] J.F. Brown, *Eastern Europe and Communist Rule* (Durham: Duke University Press, 1988), 330–331.

ing one was also used to feed anti-Muslim sentiments which, rooted in the Ottoman yoke syndrome, were easily aroused. Often coupled with this was fear that ethnic Turks wanted either to secede or create an autonomous Turkish region within Bulgaria (which some have likened to a Cyprus-like division of the country). In the end, this attempt to create a "unitary state" failed, but not before at least 100 Muslims died resisting the authorities.[5] With the onset of the assimilation program, basic human rights were denied the ethnic Turks, and even the use of the Turkish language was forbidden. Soon after taking office in 1989, the Bulgarian communist government, which unseated long-time dictator Todor Zhivkov, began a program of reinstating those human rights denied to Muslims, and did so with the support of most political opposition groups, especially the UDF.

Of the 300 thousand to 375 thousand who fled to Turkey in 1989 as a result of Bulgaria's opening its border—an effort to eliminate the "Turkish Question" by physically removing a large number of the ethnic Turks from Bulgaria—about half have returned. When they left, many of their belongings and much of their real estate were sold at low prices to non-Muslims or simply lost to the state. The government has been attempting to find means to return such property. However, many Bulgarians—especially anti-Muslim nationalists and those living in the predominantly Turkish regions who reaped the profits from ethnic Turkish departures—have opposed, sometimes physically, the restitution of both civil rights and property to those Turks who left. Initially, they also criticized the right to have the Turkish language taught to children in schools, but were later overruled.[6] Despite pledges to institute the teaching of Turkish in schools, the government has faltered in the face of opposition from ethnic Bulgarians.

The Muslims of Bulgaria, who constitute between 10 percent and 15 percent of the total population, generally have been nonviolent throughout both the assimilation campaign and subsequent events. Some organized the MRF in 1989, and during the ratification debates in spring and summer 1991 over Bulgaria's newly written constitution, the MRF representatives stridently pushed for making Turkish an official language of Bulgaria. No such measure was passed, but the episode, which involved the walkout of MRF deputies from the legislature, is a warning that Bulgarian Muslims will become more assertive in pursuit of their goals, thus creating a greater likelihood for confrontation between Bulgarian nationalists and Bulgaria's largest minority groups. Meanwhile, the ethnic Turkish minority is becoming more self-confident, more vocal, and more demanding, as witnessed by its tactical alliance with the BSP in the fall of 1992, which resulted in the fall of the Dimitrov government. The MRF will surely continue to pressure the government for greater participation in national affairs and minority rights, and may thus

---

[5] Amnesty International, *Bulgaria: Imprisonment of Ethnic Turks* (London: Amnesty International, 1986), 13–14; Hugh Poulton, *The Balkans: Minorities and States in Conflict* (London: Minority Rights Group, 1992), 129–151.

[6] See Duncan M. Perry, "Ethnic Turks Face Bulgarian Nationalism," *Report on Eastern Europe* 2, no. 11 (March 15, 1991): 5–8.

increasingly become the target of intensified anti-Muslim vituperation or, perhaps, even violence from nationalist quarters. The government will be forced to confront difficult historic social, economic, and political issues in the process.

In a number of cases, the anti-Muslim nationalists have been encouraged in their ethnocentric behavior by members of the former communist nomenklatura seeking to obstruct the government through demonstrations and actions like those in the Turkish regions in February 1991 against the teaching of Turkish in schools. These people continue to argue that they expect Muslim attempts to divide Muslim from non-Muslim regions in Bulgaria. They also suggest that interests in Turkey might employ and underwrite ethnic Turks in Bulgaria who would buy up property and industries, slowly and quietly edging out ethnic Bulgarians and eventually establishing a substantial Turkish hold over internal Bulgarian economic affairs.[7]

But such prospects seem remote. A Turkish invasion was never likely. It is even less likely now in view of the recent Bulgarian-Turkish rapprochement. Moreover, beset by substantial unemployment, high inflation, the need to further industrialize and reform the statist economy, pressure to resolve the increasingly violent Kurdish problem, and a serious fundamentalist-secularist struggle, Turkey is occupied with internal problems. Even if relations with Bulgaria were strained, it is unlikely that Turkey would multiply its troubles by intervening in Bulgaria, especially because Ankara is currently relatively satisfied with Sofia's progress regarding restoration of rights to Bulgarian Turks.

Nevertheless, anti-Muslim nationalists in Bulgaria view themselves and their country as the outermost European bastion against Islam. As concern increases about Islam and Muslim fundamentalism, especially in conservative circles in the West, these nationalists can be expected to emphasize their front-line status. Such behavior could exacerbate tension between Muslims and non-Muslims in Bulgaria and might well damage Bulgarian-Turkish relations, which could result in a loss of assistance from Ankara.

The Military Dimension

During the early days of the democratization process (and again after the August 1991 attempted overthrow of Mikhail Gorbachev in the Soviet Union), many Bulgarians were apprehensive about possible interference in political affairs by the Bulgarian armed forces. Repeated assurances of nonintervention from the military were issued, such as the one on November 14, 1990, when the minister of national defense stated that "there is no danger of a military coup."[8] Less than two years later, on September 2, 1992, Chief of the General Staff Lyuben Petrov made a similar statement.[9] The military has, indeed, publicly refrained from interfering in poli-

---

[7] See Stephen Ashley, "Ethnic Unrest during January," *Report on Eastern Europe* 2, no. 6 (February 9, 1990).

[8] *Duma*, November 14, 1990.

[9] BTA, September 2, 1992.

tics, but it has exerted an influence in other ways. The most obvious has been through influencing the offices of important military figures in public positions following the fall of communism, including the vice-president of Bulgaria (1990–1992), Colonel General Atanas Semerdzhiev, and the minister of defense in 1990, Colonel General Yordan Mutafchiev. Retired Colonel General Dobri Dzhurov, former minister of defense for more than twenty years under communist leader Todor Zhivkov, was instrumental in removing his boss. Now that the military is divided between old and young, advocates of the status quo and advocates of change, it appears that its influence will diminish. Nevertheless, the Soviet imprint on military and security matters in Bulgaria will be felt for years to come, until such time as those trained in or by the former USSR are fired or retired. Some still seem opposed to reform as Bulgaria seeks to locate new allies and establish new security arrangements in the West.

So far, the government has been able to control the damage by those who oppose military reform through retirements. Meanwhile, reform is proceeding. The process is aided by the emergence of younger officers committed to change. An influential organization of mid-level and junior-grade officers in the military, the Bulgarian Legion "Georgi Rakovski," was founded in 1990 by military personnel intent on reform. It has thousands of members—no precise figures are available—and has become a watchdog of the general staff and senior officer ranks.[10] Although it has had nationalistic tendencies, the legion is gradually becoming a more moderate lobbying group. Further, the military doctrine of the Bulgarian armed forces is now under review and clearly changing.

Bulgaria has also begun to establish civilian control over the military and security forces. On November 5, 1991, the first civilian minister of defense, Dimitur Ludzhev, was appointed—an act that symbolically underscored Bulgaria's movement toward greater democracy. In May 1992, Ludzhev was replaced by Alexander Staliiski, a former dissident and a man popular among the MRF because of his strong defense of human rights. The current defense minister, Valentin Alexandrov, is also a civilian.

Relations with the West

When Western organizations extend assistance to Eastern Europe, they tend to divide the region into northern and southern tiers, with comparatively stable Bulgaria lumped in with its volatile and unstable neighbors Albania, Romania, and the former Yugoslav lands. Since the fall of Todor Zhivkov in November 1989, Bulgaria has made a concerted effort to demonstrate to Western nations that it, too, is part of the European mainstream. Bulgaria has troops in Cambodia as part of a UN peacekeeping mission. It offered to assist the United States and its allies in the Persian Gulf War, forswearing a multibillion dollar contract with Iraq in the process, thereby sustaining significant financial losses. As further proof of Bulgaria's will-

[10] See Duncan M. Perry, "A New Military Lobby," *Report on Eastern Europe* 2, no. 40, 1–3.

ingness to conform to Western norms, Bulgaria has been observing the trade embargo against Libya and the rump Yugoslavia, at substantial cost, for both had been important trading partners.

A small state with a population of about nine million, Bulgaria has throughout most of its modern history been under the protection of a great power, first imperial Russia, then Germany, and finally the former Soviet Union. It is now standing by itself for only the second time.[11] At the moment there are no predators. But the unaligned status of the country surely weighs heavily on national leaders, many of whom feel at once pleased about having shed Soviet protection but uncomfortable with not having found a new patron. Militarily, NATO is the only obvious alternative. But so far NATO has been unwilling to expand its ranks and accept new full members.

But even if NATO does eventually open its ranks to new members, Bulgaria's chances of becoming a member in the short-term are less promising than those of the Visegrad countries (Hungary, Poland, the Czech Republic and Slovakia), which are likely to be given top priority by NATO. Thus, for the foreseeable future, Bulgaria will have to be content with membership in the North Atlantic Cooperation Council (NACC) and the new U.S. initiative, "Partnership for Peace." This initiative envisages closer defense cooperation through the conclusion of a bilateral defense agreement with NATO but does not offer a clear-cut security guarantee.

In the economic sphere Bulgaria has made overtures to both the EC (since renamed EU) and the Council on Europe. Association with both organizations would afford Bulgaria a greater opportunity to join Europe, politically and economically. Bulgaria joined the Council of Europe on May 7, 1992, and it has been a member of the CSCE process since its inception.

Relations with the EC have also been strengthened. In December 1992, Bulgaria signed an association agreement with the EC similar to the ones signed between the EC, Hungary, Poland, and the former Czechoslovakia in December 1991. The association agreement provides for greater market access for Bulgarian products to the EC.

The Balkans

The conflict in Bosnia is at the core of Bulgaria's current regional policies. Bulgaria's main concern is to prevent a spread of the war, especially to the newly independent Former Yugoslav Republic of Macedonia, which was founded on September 17, 1991. Should the conflagration spread to Macedonia, it could spark an all-Balkan war and rekindle the nineteenth century contest for possession of this central Balkan region. Bulgaria has also suffered severe economic losses—about \$2–3 billion dollars in 1993—as a result of the imposition of the UN embargo. Bulgaria thus has a strong stake in preventing the spread of the conflict and seeing it

[11] The first was during the reign of Prince Alexander of Battenberg (1879–1886), the interregnum (1886–1887), and the early years of Prince (later Czar) Ferdinand's rule (1887–1896).

ended as soon as possible.

Bilateral relations between Bulgaria and Romania, its only former Warsaw Pact ally in the Balkans, were generally cordial during the communist era. Now they, too, are strained, though the reason in this case is ecological—each blames the other for causing serious environmental damage to its territory.

Relations with Greece improved substantially during the Zhivkov era. Bulgaria's recognition of the Republic of Macedonia on January 16, 1992, led to a cooling of relations. However, relations have gradually improved since then. The two countries signed a military cooperation agreement at the end of 1992. In addition, the Berov government has taken a more cautious attitude toward Macedonia than that of the UDF-led government headed by Prime Minister Filip Dimitrov. Both these developments have contributed to an improvement in the overall climate of relations.

Relations with Turkey have improved markedly since Zhivkov's ouster in November 1989, especially in the military field.[12] Military exchanges—virtually nonexistent prior to 1991—are now frequent. In December 1991 the two countries signed an agreement designed to strengthen security and confidence along the Bulgarian-Turkish border.[13] The agreement calls for an increase in military contacts as well as a number of concrete confidence-building measures, such as prior notification of maneuvers and inspections beyond those contained in the Paris CFE agreement. In keeping with the spirit of this agreement, in July 1992 Turkey unilaterally withdrew several battalions from the Bulgarian border. In May 1992 the two countries also signed a Treaty of Friendship and Cooperation, which provides for expanded ties across the board.

The Macedonian Question

The Yugoslav republics of Slovenia and Croatia declared independence on June 25, 1991, and the federal military, controlled largely by ethnic Serbs and Montenegrins, then mounted a military campaign against both. The conflict in Yugoslavia continues to rage despite the efforts of the UN, CSCE, and the EC to promote a peaceful resolution of the crisis. The key question is, what kind of rearrangement will be built upon the rubble of the former Yugoslavia? Integral to Bulgaria's interests and concerns in this connection is the fate of the Republic of Macedonia, which constitutes more than one-third of geographic Macedonia, most of which was accorded to Bulgaria in 1878 as a result of the San Stefano Treaty that imperial Russia dictated to the Ottoman Empire at the conclusion of the Russo-Turkish War (1877–1878).[14]

---

[12] See Kjell Engelbrekt, "Relations with Turkey: A Review of Post-Zhivkov Developments," *Report on Eastern Europe*, April 26, 1991, 7–10.

[13] For the text of the agreement, see *Bulgarska Armiya*, December 23, 1991. Translated in FBIS-EEU-92–001, January 2, 1992, 5–6.

[14] The Treaty of San Stefano was signed by the Russian and Ottoman governments in March 1878. It was nullified three months later by the Treaty of Berlin.

By the terms of the San Stefano Treaty, Bulgaria's borders were expanded threefold to include Thrace and most of Ottoman Macedonia. The inhabitants of Macedonia were largely Slavs who—the Bulgarians argued—used a language closely resembling Bulgarian. Bulgarians regarded these inhabitants as being of the same nationality, while the Slavs of Macedonia generally had no developed national consciousness at the time.[15] Great-power politics intervened, and Macedonia was lost by Bulgaria three months later at the Congress of Berlin and reawarded to the Ottomans. Since then the "Macedonian question" has festered in the Balkans.

Since the Treaty of Berlin, heated and at times irrational debates over the ethnic composition of Macedonia have flared among Bulgarian, Greek, and Yugoslav (and more recently Serbian) nationalists, with each side claiming the majority of inhabitants of the region as their kin and the territory these people occupy as their birthright. The collection of these disputes has become known as the "Macedonian question."

Bulgaria vigorously pressed its claims to Macedonia. Bulgarian troops occupied Macedonia during the Balkan Wars (1912–1913), World Wars I and II (1914–1918 and 1939–1945) and subsequently relinquished it each time. During World War II, the Yugoslav partisan leader Josip Broz Tito argued that those Slavs living in Yugoslav Macedonia (now called the Federal Republic of Macedonia) belonged to a distinct Slavic nationality called "Macedonian." This maneuver at once deprived Serbs and Bulgarians of legitimate claim to Macedonia. Tito's Macedonia was made up of people who were said to possess a culture sharing characteristics with, but different from, those of the Bulgarians or the Serbs.

Under pressure from the USSR after World War II, the Bulgarian government recognized the "Macedonian" nationality. In the 1956 Bulgarian census, the authorities even listed 187,729 Macedonians living in the Pirin region of Bulgaria. By 1965, however, as relations with Yugoslavia deteriorated, this number shrank to 8,750. By 1968, Bulgaria had changed its policy to one resembling its 1914 position, in which it contended that the Slavs living in Yugoslav Macedonia were by origin Bulgarian, as were those people living in Pirin. The 1975 census showed no Macedonians—only Bulgarians in Bulgaria.[16]

The current Bulgarian perspective on the Macedonian nationality is that Tito created it during and following World War II to diminish, if not invalidate, the legitimacy of any Bulgarian claims on Yugoslav territory or people. It was also a means of defusing a tendentious political problem, for the Serbs had managed to alienate the Slavs of Macedonia before and during the war by their attempts to Serbianize the population. For postwar Bulgaria, the creation of a Macedonian nationality was a reasonable compromise, since, as a defeated power, Bulgaria could not claim Macedonia. But it could hope that the population of Yugoslav Macedonia, if made

[15] See Duncan M. Perry, *The Politics of Terror: The Macedonian Liberation Movements, 1893–1903* (Durham: Duke University Press, 1988), 21–24.

[16] Patrick Moore, "Bulgaria," in *Communism in Eastern Europe*, ed. Teresa Rakowska-Harmstone (Bloomington: Indiana University Press, 1984, 2d ed.), 209.

identifiably separate from Serbs, and given its antipathies toward Serbia, might gravitate toward Bulgaria as the two lands shared significant cultural, linguistic, and historical ties.[17] Bulgaria maintained this line after the Stalin-Tito break in 1948, because the alternative was that Macedonia might be reincorporated into Serbia. Today, Bulgarian nationalists have condemned this policy as a "sellout" by the Bulgarian government in the interest of international communist unity.

Bulgarians generally regard the population of Bulgarian Macedonia as purely Bulgarian. The Greeks consider those people living in Greek Macedonia who speak a Slavic language as Slavophone Greeks. Both Bulgaria and Greece currently reject the notion of a Macedonian nationality within their borders, though according to experts in Skopje, both countries possess a Macedonian minority.[18] The official Bulgarian and Greek positions were categorically affirmed in February 1991 when Greek Prime Minister Constantine Mitsotakis and Bulgarian Prime Minister Dimitur Popov met in Athens and later in Sofia and declared Yugoslav claims regarding Macedonians in both countries "absurd assertions."[19] The complexion of the problem abruptly changed with the September 17, 1991, declaration of Macedonian independence from Yugoslavia. At that juncture, Athens mounted a forceful campaign to ensure that major nations of the world did not recognize Macedonia until such time as the new state's name was changed. At issue were Greek claims to exclusive use of the Macedonian designation because it was a historical birthright. Further, Greece claims that by adopting the name Macedonia, the government in Skopje has not recanted irredentist aspirations for Greek Macedonia. Underlying this is the Greek fear that those Greek citizens of Slavic origin who live in Greece might discover their roots and demand minority rights.

Bulgaria recognized the new republic on January 16, 1992. Turkey followed suit a few weeks later. Among the major powers, only Russia initially braved Greek wrath to recognize the fledgling state. As a consequence of nonrecognition by major world economic powers, notably the EC and the United States, Macedonia was until recently unable to obtain financial assistance from the European Bank for Reconstruction and Development, the World Bank, and the International Monetary

[17] See Robert R. King, *Minorities under Communism* (Cambridge: Harvard University Press, 1973), 188.

[18] If political circumstances force the Bulgarian government to recognize a Macedonian minority within its borders, the move could cause minor reverberations in Greece among the Slavophone population. The likelihood of serious problems seems remote, though, because this group is disappearing as a result of a long-term process of Hellenization. At present, Slavophone Greeks probably do not number more than fifty thousand people, and their national consciousness appears to be Greek. See William H. McNeill, *The Metamorphosis of Greece Since World War II* (Chicago: University of Chicago Press, 1978), for observations concerning Slavs in Greece. See Evangelos Kofos, *The Macedonian Question* (Thessaloniki: Institute for Balkan Studies, 1987); and Duncan Perry, "Macedonia: A Balkan Problem and a European Dilemma," *RFE/RL Research Report 1*, no. 25 (19 June 1992): 35–45; Stefan Trobst, "Makedonische Antworten auf die 'Makedonische Frage' 1944–1992: Nationalismus, Republiksgründung, *nation building*," *SudostEuropa 7/8* (1992): 423–442.

[19] *Otechestven vestnik*, 21 Feb. 1991.

Fund. Further, the economic blockade by both Greece and Serbia, especially of fuel, has had a serious impact on the country's agricultural sector.

Macedonia, the population of which is roughly one-third Albanian, is in a delicate and precarious position. Should the Albanians, who are already seeking functional autonomy, decide that the republic is not viable, they could try to unite with Albania along with the province of Kosovo in Serbia, whose population is 90 percent Albanian. This could lead to a Balkan war, for neither Serbia nor Macedonia would stand quietly by as their territories were dismembered.

Prospects for the Future

The Bulgarian government, intent on reaching out to the West, is steadily if slowly democratizing. Until the elections in October 1991, the fragmentation of parliament resulted in long delays in the passage of legislation that was often poorly conceived. The noncommunist government elected on November 8, 1991, initially worked very well; however, since late 1992, the parliament has again become increasingly fragmented, and tensions between parliament and the president have intensified, leading to increasing polarization of Bulgarian politics.

Bulgaria's main weaknesses remain the shaky economy together with the absence of an established democratic political culture. Political leaders have been successful in developing an economic reform program such that Western agencies, most notably the IMF and the World Bank, are willing to work with Bulgaria as it seeks to recover economically from the disaster of communist rule. Outside assistance is unlikely to match popular expectations, however, which will have a negative impact on Bulgarian morale. Should the population become sufficiently frustrated with the economic dislocation it is suffering, reform could be derailed. The government and the parliament have made major strides toward creating a free-market economy through such legislation as the privatization act, but progress has been painfully slow and often retarded by the cumbersome, at times obstructionist, and untrained government infrastructure.

Demagogic extremism is often a symptom of economic distress. Certainly anti-Muslim factions are visible and vocal in Bulgaria. For democratization to succeed, current leaders recognize that they must contain Bulgaria's irredentist factions and nationalist-extremists and continue the process of according full political rights to Muslims. The sooner the economy improves, the sooner extremism is likely to subside. Democratic reformers will also continue to face resistance from an entrenched holdover nomenklatura. During the last days of the run-up to the 1991 election and subsequently, the BSP, now in parliamentary opposition for the first time, sought to exploit anti-Turkish nationalism. Despite BSP claims that its politicians will work constructively, its policies have been directed more toward the protection, perpetuation, and prosperity of the party, than toward the national good.

Internationally, the main risk comes from a spillover of the war in the former Yugoslavia. Should Macedonia be attacked or otherwise drawn into the war in the former Yugoslavia, Bulgaria could be drawn in as well. Macedonia has deep symbolic and emotional value to Bulgarians. Whether they would enter with the intent of carving Macedonia up or ensuring that the new republic remains independent is unclear. How Greece, Serbia, Turkey, and Albania would line up would depend on the causes and the participants involved, but it is likely that if one country enters Macedonia, others will follow.

On balance, Bulgaria has the potential to be a major stabilizing force in the Balkans. It could set an example through further stabilization and democratization at home, and the statesman-like behavior of its leaders in the resolution of Balkan problems. If political instability increases and extremist factions gain in importance, however, the process of democratization could be obstructed or halted. Ethnic and religious turmoil would likely intensify, making Bulgaria a volatile and unstable backwater and inhibiting its transition to democracy.

IV

Post-Communist Romania's Search for Security

Daniel N. Nelson

Romania's post-communist dilemmas are numerous and severe. As in other states where communist parties ruled for two or more generations, Romania must create democratic institutions and processes while building an entirely new free-market economy.

But Romania is unlike other former Soviet-bloc states in many other respects. A violent uprising in December 1989 was a painful culmination to a quarter-century during which Romanian leader Nicolae Ceausescu's paranoia and megalomania worsened year by year. With only few parallels in the world—such as North Korea under Kim Il Sung—Ceausescu's dictatorship was extreme in its central planning, repression of intellectual and artistic expression, surveillance of citizens, and rejection of any reform.[1]

The National Salvation Front (Frontul Salvarii Nationale, or FSN) emerged in the midst of the December 20–22, 1989, fighting in Bucharest, led by anti-Ceausescu Communist Party elites. Conspiracy theories—that is, that the violence that began in Timisoara on December 17 had been utilized as a pretext by which another group of communists could gain power through a coup in Bucharest—were heard almost immediately thereafter.[2] Disaffected and sidelined from the Front's leadership after spring 1990, Silviu Brucan, one of the early leaders of the FSN, and former Defense Minister Nicolae Militaru added to the conspiracy thesis in 1991 by alleging that the plot against Ceausescu had been planned from within the Communist Party for years.

[1] Among books on these subjects, the most notable are Mary Ellen Fischer's *Nicolae Ceausescu* (Boulder, Colo.: Lynne Rienner Press, 1990) and Trond Gilberg, *Nationalism and Communism in Romania* (Boulder, Colo.: Westview Press, 1990).

[2] An early expression of this view was Vladimir Tismaneanu, "New Masks, Old Faces: The Romanian Junta's Familiar Look," *The New Republic* (February 5, 1990): 7–9.

But none of the accusations about a nomenklatura-based plot against Ceausescu offer any refutation that the confrontation in Timisoara—a week before violence erupted in Bucharest—was entirely independent from intraparty plans to remove Ceausescu. Reverend Laszlo Tökes's defiance and the actions of citizens were genuine and spontaneous, as was the confusion and fear among party authorities and uncertainty within the army. None of these conspiracy theses, moreover, can deny the accumulating history of citizen-based anti-Ceausescu demonstrations that no one claims were "organized" by the nomenklatura—most notably those by the miners in the Jiu Valley in 1977 and 1981, and the industrial labor unrest in Brasov in 1987. The antipathy that surfaced in Timisoara, Bucharest, and elsewhere during December 1989 could not have been manufactured nor planned by either Iliescu or any other conspirator.

But did they (Iliescu, Petre Roman, and the "Front" leadership) "hijack" the revolution? In one sense, what happened is alarmingly simple—people who were, or had been, close to power knew more than anyone else whom to call, how to assemble a "team" quickly, and what actions to take. Ion Iliescu, Petre Roman, Silviu Brucan, Dimitru Mazilu, and others who were part of the Front's early core leadership acted as one might expect them to act—they stepped forward when chaos was at hand, and sought to play principal roles. For someone like Iliescu, who had considered Ceausescu's ouster as essential for Romania, there was no choice but to enter the fray.

Conspiracy theses, however, take this much further, and attribute a dark malevolence to the actions of the early Front leadership—a sinister manipulation, and an unprincipled use of force, intimidation, and misinformation. Such inferences err greatly by their simplicity. Iliescu and the others assumed a personal risk on December 21–22, 1989. Regardless of our moral judgments about their previous roles, it would have been safer and easier for them to remain quiescent—particularly given the absolutely clear impression, by December 1989, that communist regimes in Eastern Europe had no future. Iliescu was under no illusion that a "communist" system could continue, and did not desire anything of the kind.

If old ideology did not motivate the FSN leadership, what did? Some degree of repressed personal ambition among a group of well-educated, urbane Communist Party members—denied advancement during Ceausescu's regime—may have been a factor. But a much more important reason was (and is) "competent nationalism." FSN leaders were the only well-trained, fully prepared, policymakers in Romania who had not been sycophants to Ceausescu. Further, these few people around Iliescu and Roman—numbering just over a dozen—were colleagues and friends, trusting one another enough to unite as a "National Salvation Front" at a time of crisis in Romania. They all cared deeply about Romania, and held a strongly Romania-centric view of the Balkans without being chauvinistic.

Like millions of Romanians, these people had joined the Party, cooperated with its internal security apparatus, and tried to prosper in a reprehensible communist dictatorship. For some observers, this is sufficient to condemn the FSN from the outset. I disagree with this assessment, and regard Romania as fortunate to have had some competent leadership during its first few years after tyranny. Further, since the Romanian people have twice elected Ion Iliescu by substantial margins over his opponents (most recently, in a run-off election in October 1992, with 61 percent of the vote), no one has any grounds for claiming that the majority of Romanians find his erstwhile "communist" affiliation troublesome.

Apart from the FSN's character, however, no one can contest that Romania—to a far greater extent than elsewhere in the former Soviet bloc—was exhausted and despoiled by the severity of Ceausescu's dictatorship, and the cultural, socioeconomic, and political costs Romania incurred because of such tyranny.[3]

Not surprisingly, Romanian post-communism is often viewed as relatively more troubled than that of Poland, Czechoslovakia, or Hungary. Regardless of these countries' many economic and political difficulties, Western observers tend to see Romania's transition to anything resembling democracy as likely to be longer and more conflictual than the transitions in Central Europe.

Domestic Politics

Since December 1989, Romania's unimpeded movement away from Ceausescu's tyranny has been thwarted by several events. In the immediate aftermath of the December revolution, considerable international sympathy for Romania's plight existed. But it was not long before the traditional wing of Romanian politics (the Liberal and Peasant parties) began to reemerge to attack the Front's political control, while intellectuals and students complained of the FSN's "neocommunism" and its "theft" of the revolution—charges that grew more insistent during the spring 1990 electoral campaign.[4] It was also in mid-March 1990 that violence between Hungarians and Romanians in the Romanian city of Tirgu Mures, captured on videotape and shown worldwide, implied that Romania was a state without civic order.

After the May 20, 1990, elections had resulted in an overwhelming, albeit imperfect, victory for the NSF, another chance existed to improve relations with the West.[5] Once again, however, complaints from both the historic parties as well as protests by urban intelligentsia about the conduct of the campaign (protests that included occupation of Bucharest's principal traffic intersection at University Square) tarnished the Front's legitimacy.

The FSN government made matters far worse by forcibly removing demonstrators from University Square on the night of June 13, 1990. There was a violent response to this police action; protesters besieged government buildings and threat-

[3] See Daniel N. Nelson, "The Romanian Disaster," in *Research on the Soviet Union and Eastern Europe*, ed. Anthony Jones (Greenwich: JAI Press, 1990), 83–111. See also, generally, Daniel N. Nelson, *Romanian Politics in the Ceausescu Era* (New York: Gordon and Breach, 1988).

[4] I have detailed these charges and countercharges in a special edition of *Electoral Studies* 9, no. 4 (1990): 355–366.

[5] A comprehensive report is National Democratic Institute for International Affairs/National Republican Institute for International Affairs, *The May 1990 Elections in Romania* (Washington, D.C.: NDI/NRIA, 1990).

ened its existence. Unable to gain army intervention from then-Defense Minister Victor Stanculescu, and with the regular police ineffective or refusing to act, Iliescu publicly appealed to citizens to save the FSN government.

His appeal was heeded with violent abandon by Jiu Valley coal miners—an element of Romania's industrial work force that had been cultivated as FSN supporters. When the miners arrived in Bucharest the next day on commandeered trains and buses, they acted as vigilantes—attacking protesters, students, and innocent bystanders, and ransacking offices and apartments of opposition groups and leaders. The government neither condemned them nor was it able to intervene to stop what has been called a "rampage."

Western governments held the Iliescu-Roman government accountable for apparently condoning such wanton violence. Their disassociation from the FSN government was abrupt and far-reaching. Consequently, Romania's reintegration into Europe and its march toward democracy were dealt a considerable setback.[6]

Far more than the political lineage of Iliescu and Roman, or even the FSN's reluctance to dismantle fully the state's role in society and the economy, these episodes damaged the FSN's chances to achieve credibility as a post-communist government deserving support. Yet, since mid-1990, a draft constitution has been written and approved (by both chambers of parliament on November 22, 1991), and far-reaching economic reform legislation has been written and passed.[7] In addition, some (although far too few, in the opinion of many observers) former Ceausescu loyalists have been tried and sentenced to prison terms, a new broadly based anti-FSN political party (Alianta Civica, or the Civic Alliance) has been formed, and local elections were scheduled (first for November 1991 and then rescheduled for February 1992).[8] These critical steps, in addition to many other acts (for example, halting the illegal, international sale of babies placed for adoption), have begun the arduous task of recreating stronger ties between Bucharest and Western democracies.[9]

---

[6] The flavor of Western commentary on the June 1990 events was a *Washington Post* editorial, "Romania's Stalinists," 17 June 1990.

[7] A compendium of such legislation and administrative reforms, with proposed timelines, is Council for Reform of the Government of Romania, *The White Book of the Romanian Reform* (Bucharest: May 1991). The Council is headed by Adrian Severin, deputy prime minister and de facto economic reform "czar" for the FSN government.

[8] "15 Ceausescu Officials Jailed," *Financial Times*, 26 March 1991. Among those sentenced were former propaganda chief Dumitru Popescu and former foreign minister Ioan Totu, both of whom received five and a half years in prison. A total of twenty-one former Politburo members were tried for genocide. A more complete report on these charges was issued by Rompres on March 25, 1991, and reprinted in FBIS, *Daily Report: East Europe* 91–058 (March 26, 1991), p. 46.

[9] American adoption of Romanian children had led to a substantial black market for infants in Romania that was traumatic for families who wished to adopt and impossible for the State Department to manage. Stories on this dilemma and the Romanian actions are numerous. Several that provide summary information are David Binder, "U.S. Issues Warning of Obstacles in Adopting Romanian Children," *New York Times*, 24 May 1991; Al Kamen, "U.S. to End Waivers for Romanian

All of these achievements were again endangered when, in late September 1991, coal miners' anger at price increases and nonresponsive bureaucracy spilled over once more. Commandeering trains and trams once again, five thousand to ten thousand made their way back into Bucharest to lay siege to the government, now located in the former foreign ministry building. Demanding the resignation of Roman, Iliescu, and their cabinet, they occupied the parliament building as well, intimidating deputies and senators with threats of physical harm and surrounding the presidential palace at Cotroceni. In such an atmosphere, Iliescu once again sought military protection and, as in 1990, the army said that internal political stability was for the government to ensure. Police were likewise reluctant to react with force, as they were both outnumbered and untested.

Petre Roman's resignation was clearly neither voluntary nor orderly. His departure suggests the severe political circumstances in which Ion Iliescu and Petre Roman governed. A mere ten thousand miners could bring the government to a standstill. Roman's resignation was urged on him, not offered, and accepted by all concerned as a sacrifice to ensure a modicum of stability.

In October, after intense discussions, Iliescu asked former Finance Minister Teodor Stolojan to form a government—a "caretaker" government intended to persevere through the spring of 1992 and very little else. Stolojan's government, in fact, had to last through the fall of 1992 because of disputes regarding the timing of a national election and the ground rules for such a ballot. And, far from being a caretaker government, Stolojan himself became the most popular Romanian politician by early 1992.[10] Stolojan, however, steadfastly refused to consider a continuation of his political career, turning down direct solicitations to run for the presidency in 1992 elections.

In part because of his popularity and apolitical identity, Stolojan's government was able to oversee a continued and purposeful economic transition toward a free market, while improving the country's sense of civil order. First steps were taken toward selling state-owned enterprises, new currency was issued, exchange controls largely eliminated, and foreign credits and investments began to return incrementally.

Local elections in February 1992 were conducted freely and fairly, and led to a substantial redistribution of subnational power. In major cities, a coalition of anti-Front parties—the Democratic Convention—won mayoralty races and captured local councils.

Owing to the FSN's losses in that election vis-à-vis its overwhelming June 1990 victory, and because of increasing personal friction between President Ion Iliescu and Prime Minister Petre Roman, the Front split acrimoniously in early 1992 into two parties—the Democratic National Salvation Front (FDSN), headed by Iliescu,

---

Adoptions," *Washington Post,* 27 July 1991 and an Associated Press dispatch, "Romanians Put Strict Curbs on Adoptions," carried in the *Washington Post,* 17 July 1991.

[10] Data from national surveys conducted in December 1991 and January 1992, by the Institute for Marketing and Survey Research, Bucharest, directed by Dr. Alin Teodorescu.

and the National Salvation Front (FSN), headed by Roman. The two parties then competed against each other in the September 27, 1992, parliamentary and presidential election (with Roman, recognizing his own political liabilities, stepping aside to nominate an unknown, Caius Dragomir, as the FSN's candidate for president). The FDSN achieved a plurality of more than 27 percent of the vote, and became the parliament's largest party, while Roman's FSN had the support of only 10 percent of the electorate and Dragomir did not garner even 5 percent of the presidential vote.[11]

Rebuffed by moderate opposition parties and unable to govern alone, Iliescu's party—renamed once again as the Party of Social Democracy of Romania (PSDR)—had to rely on a tawdry group of nationalist allies to the left and right. The government of Prime Minister Nicolae Vacaroiu, which was installed after the fall 1992 elections, exhibited a responsiveness to such parliamentary "allies" by moving aside some principal economic reformers and by replacing Defense Minister Spiroiu in March 1994. Yet, Vacariou's cabinet did preserve governmental stability at a time when anything else would have been disastrous.

We should remember, however, that the larger contest underway is one in which Romanian-specific events elaborate but do not define the future of Eastern Europe. From the Baltic to the Balkans, post-communist Eastern Europe has three essential goals—accelerating the transition to a market economy, institutionalizing democratic processes, and finding a new basis for national security. The pursuit of these goals must be simultaneous. Yet, their interaction is not necessarily synergistic.

Indeed, there is ample reason to suspect that both the creation of a market economy and the recasting of national security planning involve political conflicts that undermine fragile protodemocracies. Freeing prices from government control, establishing a fully convertible currency, selling off state-owned enterprises and assets—these and other fundamental steps will create considerable pain before any gain is seen. New post-communist governments can ill afford an evaporation of public trust and support when such political legitimacy is one of the very few strengths on which today's new East European leaders can rely.

Yet, where market economic principles have been most completely implemented, governments have quickly begun to confront a significant increase in popular antagonism toward the new authorities as no better than the old (that is, communists), popular doubt that anything will ever truly improve, and purposeful citizen apathy (a "pox on all their houses" attitude) that defies amelioration through any political technique.[12] Survey data also suggest that the rapid imposition of democratic pro-

---

[11] Final percentages were reported in the Romanian press; see, for example, *Romania Libera,* 1 October 1992, p. 1; exit poll prognoses reported on Romanian television on September 27 had been highly accurate. See a report on such prognoses by IRSOP in *Evenimentul Zilei*, 28 September 1992, p. 1.

[12] For comparison, political apathy and the dangers such a phenomenon represents to democratization in the Polish case is discussed in David Mason, Daniel N. Nelson, and Bohdan Szklarski, "Apathy and the Birth of Democracy: The Polish Struggle," *East European Politics and Societies* 5, no. 2 (Spring 1991): 205–233.

cesses before institutional supports (free media, broadly based parties, independent trade unions) are built yields political acts much less meaningful than otherwise, acts that provide little or no support for democracy.[13]

It is far too easy to presume that free markets and free governments can be created soon or without conflict. And it may be wrong to assume that both democracy and the free market are coextensive with security for citizens or their government.

Romania is a case in point. A deeply embedded democracy and a robust market economy—even if such desiderata were to take firm root tomorrow—would not add up to irrevocable security for the state, government, or nation. A free market and a free government are necessary but insufficient for Romania's national security. New bases for a secure Romania must be found within a threat-rich, low-capacity environment that envelops the country, while being compatible with the norms of a free-market democracy.

Internally, Romania confronts numerous dangers to stability and well-being, some of which are perceptions magnified through the lens of Bucharest's political and economic uncertainties. Principal among these are (1) ethnonationalism, (2) the political strains of marketization, (3) the resistance of an old nomenklatura to change, and (4) widespread suspicion and apathy of citizens toward political authority. (Civil-military relations—also a difficult matter in Romania today—will be discussed in a separate section.)

Ethnonationalism inflames the Balkans as nowhere else in Europe because of the fiendishly complex interweaving of nations and borders. Romania's heterogeneity gauged by ethnic identity, language, religion, economic maldistribution of resources, and other measures of intrastate differences pales by comparison to Yugoslavia. Yet, if one includes Hungarians (more than two million), Gypsies (very conservatively two million, with some estimates of over three million) and other smaller minorities, at least 17 to 18 percent of Romania's population is non-Romanian. This sizable minority population is more volatile politically because the Hungarians are the largest component of a diaspora of critical interest to Budapest, while the Gypsies are the fastest growing part of the population.

The debate about Transylvania extends well beyond the framework of this essay. During the latter years of communist rule, both Hungarian and Romanian regimes engaged in arcane disputation, using questionable scholarship, about who was in Transylvania first, and which culture had preeminent claim in the region. To Hungary, the 1920 Treaty of Trianon (under which Hungary ceded Transylvania to Romania) is anathema, while to Romania, it justifiably returned the region to its cultural heirs after Austro-Hungarian aggrandizement.

Since 1989, however, issues between the governments have turned less on historical debate than on matters of immediate policy. These concerns are detailed below. Yet, the Romanian government has also had to confront a small, albeit quite

---

[13] See Mason, Nelson, and Szklarski, "Apathy and the Birth of Democracy," wherein a number of studies are cited concerning Poles' attitudes about the efficacy of participation in the post-communist setting.

dangerous group—Vatra Romaneasca (Romanian Hearth)—that has organized in Transylvania and elsewhere in the country as a reactionary, nationalist political force. Vatra has published a rabidly anti-Hungarian, antisemitic, weekly newspaper called *Romania Maré*, which has become the mouthpiece for diatribes against all minorities and moderation. *Romania Maré* has a large circulation throughout the country, and appears well-financed. Other extreme nationalist periodicals such as *Europa* also are sold widely in Romania.

To call Vatra or its media "ideological" would be far too generous; their claim to fame is the neofascism that they propagate. Vatra is suspected of having ties to former Securitate agents, or even to remnants of the Iron Guard of the 1940s. Vatra's ties to the FSN and FDSN are alleged by various opposition parties. These linkages, however, denied both by people around Iliescu and in Vatra, are merely inferential, not factual. Their overlap lies in the powerful appeal of nationalism, not in any shared ethnic hatred. The leftist nationalism of Iliescu is not rooted in antisemitism nor does it share any ideological space with the neofascism of Gheorghe Funar (the most prominent extreme right presidential candidate in the September 1992 elections). Yet, people who voted for someone like Funar will, if a choice exists, cast their run-off ballots for a nationalist of the Left, not candidates who are perceived to be creations of international financial and political interests. Whatever its genesis, Vatra sustains itself through ethnic hatreds that promote a mirror-image response from Hungarians and the other groups attacked.[14]

A June 29, 1991, "Roundtable on the Dangers of Extremism," organized by the Democratic Anti-Totalitarian Forum, the National Peasants' Party, the National Liberal Party, and others, issued a warning about the dangerous growth of "leftist and rightist extremism," especially "actions that tolerate and encourage xenophobia, chauvinism, [and] antisemitism."[15] This coalition indicted, by implication, policies or actions of the FSN government. The Romanian Ministry of Culture, however, responded by issuing a statement at the end of July 1991 condemning the nationalist extremism of several publications.[16] Former Prime Minister Roman has likewise characterized four newspapers and periodicals as "racist, chauvinistic and nationalist" and threatened to ban them.[17] And in July 1993 President Iliescu lashed out against these extremist periodicals and asked prosecutors to investigate their finances. The underlying antagonisms on which such publications thrive, and to which they contribute, however, are products of factors not amenable to government proclamations.

---

[14] A very good synopsis of Vatra Romaneasca's lineage, tactics, and implications, including descriptions of its principal organ *Romania Maré* and citations from its leaders, is Dennis Deletant's "Convergence Versus Divergence in Romania: The Role of the *Vatra Romaneasca* Movement in Transylvania" (Paper delivered at the Society for Southeast European Studies 75th Anniversary Conference, December 8–14, 1990).

[15] See "Declaratie," in *Romania Libera,* 2 July 1991, p. 2.

[16] See this Ministry statement published in *Romania Libera,* 24 July 1991, p. 1.

[17] As quoted in *RFE/RL Daily Report*, #150, August 8, 1991, p. 2.

Vatra, operating openly in the new political environment, seems to be gaining members; in its national union conference in Cluj during mid-May 1991, the strength and considerable confidence of its membership was evident.[18] Vatra's organizational efforts may extend into the Romanian Army and Interior Ministry, and allegations of Vatra funding for activities of the Party of National Unity of Romanians within military units have been made.[19]

Detracting from Romania's image abroad, while adding to the perception of intolerance domestically, were impressions of antisemitism in the country emphasized by the visit of Elie Wiesel in early July 1991. Wiesel came to honor the several hundred thousand Jews who were taken from Romania to Nazi extermination camps in World War II. Both *Romania Maré*'s coverage of Wiesel's visit and the interruption of his address in Iasi by people denying that Jews' deaths occurred or were abetted by the Antonescu regime added to the image of a nation that did not want to come to grips with its past.[20] The fact that then Prime Minister Roman and President Iliescu both acknowledged the commemoration, and sent representatives to the Wiesel speech, was generally not observed in the foreign press.

Taken together, ethnonationalism and residual images of intolerance create an atmosphere in which the pluralism and accommodation critical to democracy are imperiled. These are an omnipresent threat to Romania's post-communist transition.

For now, this threat is latent, with two extremist candidates receiving a smaller proportion of the total presidential vote in September 1992 than did Jean Marie Le Pen's political party in France during that country's local elections. Further, intolerant or hateful opinions concerning minorities are evident in only a small proportion of responses to public surveys in Romania. What is now a small problem could become larger, however, were deprivation to rise, external threat to be seen as more imminent, and political leadership to be viewed as weak. Indeed, by early 1994, the demands of Romania's left and right extremists had become more vocal and contributed to Defense Minister Spiroiu's ouster.

Marketization represents an equal or greater challenge. Thus far, the Romanian government's efforts to create a free-market economy have been more limited than in Poland or Hungary; privatization, free prices, and other measures have, however, been initiated.[21] Important legislative action is now beginning to be introduced. A law to privatize some agriculture was passed in February 1991, and President Iliescu

---

[18] This is the interpretation both of American diplomats then stationed in Romania as well as a number of European and U.S. scholars who have conducted research in Romania during 1991.

[19] See a report on this matter by Constantin Vranceanu in *Romania Libera,* 6–7 July 1991, p. 3.

[20] See Henry Kamm, "Romanians Are Told of Nation's Role in Mass Killing of Jews," *New York Times,* 2 July 1991, and Henry Kamm, "Anti-Semitic Taunt at Wiesel Talk in Romania," *New York Times,* 3 July 1991, p. A8.

[21] A comparative discussion of privatization efforts in Eastern Europe acknowledges Romania's attempts, and notes the very minimal steps by Czechoslovakia and Bulgaria. See Marvin Jackson, "The Progress of Privatization," *Report on Eastern Europe* 2, no. 31 (August 2, 1991): 40–45.

signed a far-reaching privatization law on August 14, 1992, to distribute immediately 30 percent of Romania's capital stock to the population via shares in joint-stock companies, while the state will hold the other 70 percent and be responsible for its eventual sale.[22]

Unfortunately, the opposition parties protested the privatization law by walking out before a vote, leaving the FSN majority to pass unilaterally such important legislation. But before this legislation, price increases had been used as the primary mechanism for marketizing; the critical step of creating a new form of ownership, however, has now begun. With this step has come heightened unemployment, as enterprises that cannot operate profitably have either been forced to close or have become much smaller. Prices continue to escalate. An economy already in a tailspin will suffer further through at least the mid-1990s, and the political costs to any government will be grievous. These impending conditions were among the principal causes of workers' anger in September 1991, and contributed to the rise of social tensions in 1992–1993.

The already severe loss of public support suffered by the FSN government and its successors since the May 1990 elections has not been solely or largely because of accusations about "neocommunism" or the miners' invasion of Bucharest in June 1990. Rather, the principal issue, especially during 1991, was the disastrous deterioration of the economy. In the May 1990 elections, the FSN's parliamentary candidates accumulated over two-thirds of the popular vote. By late March 1991, only 31 percent of a national sample indicated that they would vote for the FSN—although it remained the party with the largest proportion of public support.[23] Unquestionably, a 50 percent increase in Romanians' cost of living in the three months between October 1990 and January 1991 contributed to the government's diminished approval rating.[24] Huge price increases after price controls on basic foodstuffs were ended on April 1, 1991, contributed to an erosion of the Front's popular approval.[25] Just before these price increases were instituted, 74 percent of the same national sample acknowledged that they were worried or very worried about the shock of price liberalization.[26]

Not surprisingly, strikes became more frequent and more widespread in 1991,

[22] See the announcement of Iliescu's action in a Rompres dispatch of August 14, 1991, reprinted in FBIS *Daily Report: East Europe* 91–158 (August 15, 1991), p. 31.

[23] See Institutul Roman Pentru Sondarea Opiniei Publice (IRSOP), "Politograma IRSOP la un an de la alegeri" (Bucuresti: IRSOP, 1991), April 10, 1991.

[24] According to the Bucharest periodical *Economistul* (March 3, 1991), a survey of 2,400 goods and services indicated a 50 percent cost-of-living increase between October 1990 and January 1991.

[25] Reuters reported on April 2 about the consequences of such price increases. See "Romania Upset and Resigned at Rise in Basic Food Prices," *New York Times,* 2 April 1991, p. A–2; also "Romanians Face Big Price Rises," *Financial Times,* 2 April 1991.

[26] This survey was conducted by IRSOP March 26–31, 1991, with a sample of over 2,200 individuals. See IRSOP's report, "Politograma IRSOP."

[27] *Financial Times,* 19 June 1991, reported these incidents in an article entitled "Romanian Strike Spreads."

hitting key sectors such as transportation, health, and education.[27] By August, the railway work stoppages were continuing, while the major Brasov truck factory, defense industry workers, and others were also out on strike.

Correspondingly, public opinion polls noted a further decline in Front support, although individual FSN leaders obtained more confidence than any non-FSN personage. Interestingly, the September 1991 miners' violence led to a slight increase in FSN support, up to 34 percent as people grasped for stability and reassurance.[28]

During early 1991, the political distress of the FSN government because of economic calamity was evident; disputes between then Finance Minister Theodor Stolojan (later prime minister) and State Secretary Anton Vatasescu in March (reportedly over the second stage of price liberalization and the social safety net to accompany those price increases) led, indirectly, to a cabinet crisis.[29] Roman eventually acted to create a stronger team on economic matters, appointing Eugen Dijmarescu to the finance and economics posts, joining cabinet member Adrian Severin and Mugur Isarescu (governor of the Romanian Central Bank) as the key policymakers concerning the country's economic transition. By late September, of course, the government's political hemorrhaging had extended much further, making it vulnerable to another incursion by coal miners.

The old nomenklatura—all of those individuals whose posts of responsibility and career were based on party loyalty—numbered in the hundreds of thousands. Post-Ceausescu Romania faces, as do all of the East European states, a difficult passage toward establishing a new leadership or managerial elite. Such an endeavor is impossible if an entirely non-Party past is required as a criterion for holding government posts. Simply put, there are insufficient numbers of people who simultaneously have no Communist Party background *and* possess adequate skills and training to assume executive, legislative, or judicial positions.

Indeed, it is vital to recognize that Romania's ability to be governed at all in the first year or two after December 1989 rested with a very small group of well-trained, cosmopolitan individuals. This cohort of fewer than ten people were friends and colleagues, had encountered each other as instructors at the Communist Party Higher Academy (the Stefan Gheorghiu Academy), and had been critical of Ceausescu and many of his policies. To condemn these people outright simply because of their past Communist Party membership, or their service to Romania during the Ceausescu era, would be to ignore their deeper commitment and larger talents.

But criticisms have been widespread, directed at Iliescu and Roman individually, at their staffs and cabinet, and at their inability to clear out the larger mass of apparatchiks still in place around the country. Roman, of course, tried to direct all criticisms at Iliescu after the split. At the FSN congress in March 1991, charges that the FSN government had concentrated power "around technocrats" were heard, and

---

[28] These data were discussed thoroughly in Petre Datculescu, "Romanian Political Dynamics and Public Opinion," in *Romania After Tyranny,* ed. Daniel Nelson (Boulder, Colo.: Westview, 1992). Comments on FSN post-September 1991 popularity are in *Curierul National,* 9 Nov. 1991, pp. 1–2.

[29] Bucharest Domestic Service reported on this episode on March 22, 1991, in a dispatch reprinted by FBIS *Daily Report: East Europe* 91–057 (March 25, 1991), p. 36.

that Roman and Iliescu had enabled "political bargain-hunters" to creep in "from the old bureaucracy."[30] Resignations from within the FSN were made with the same kind of accusation; Claudiu Iordache, who had been a leader in Timisoara's uprising in December 1989, resigned from an FSN party position, claiming that the Front was simply keeping communists and their policies in power.[31] Sharper condemnation came from the newspapers of traditional parties, whose editors never doubted that the communists retained political control.[32]

More problematic than holdover communist bureaucrats is the concern that the Securitate—the secret police—have been given a new lease on life. President Iliescu and Prime Minister Roman acknowledge that many erstwhile Securitate agents remain in the newly reconstituted Romanian Intelligence Service (SRI, in its Romanian initials), headed by Virgil Magureanu.[33] Aware of such concern, the SRI has tried to create a more open appearance, granted a number of interviews, and generally sought to portray itself as a defender of Romanian laws and security.[34] But the gap of mistrust has not been bridged.

There is little doubt that the minimal turnover of local-level officials in Romania has also been detrimental to the effectiveness of economic reform and political pluralism. Calls for local elections in 1992 were a direct consequence of suspicions that each county *(judet)* requires a thorough political housecleaning before democratic forces or policy reforms can really have a chance. The Romanian government was also thwarted by its limited control over local and regional authorities.

The Role of the Military

The loyalty of Romania's military to a post-Ceausescu democratic transformation is uncertain. Lines of authority between civilian leaders and the army had grown tenuous during the communist period as Ceausescu constrained resources available to the military, denied to the high command a preeminence for national defense, and isolated the armed forces from technological imports that could have helped it to modernize.[35]

The dubious role of the regular army in the first days of the anti-Ceausescu revolt—especially in Timisoara when, from December 17 to 20, army units used force against citizens—did not help the military's reputation. The army's defense of its role in December 1989 has become repeated and vigorous now that senior officers

---

[30] See the *Christian Science Monitor's* report on "Romanian's Party Congress," 19 March 1991.

[31] See the *Washington Post*, "Official Quits High Party Post," 14 March 1991.

[32] See, for example, Sorin Stafan, "Regimului Frontul Salvarii Nationale," *Dreptatea,* 4 April 1991, p. 3.

[33] Such concern reaches the Western press. See, for example, Stephen Engelberg, "Uneasy Romania Asks: Where Are Spies Now?" *New York Times,* 13 February 1991.

[34] For example, see the revealing two-part interview of Major General Mihai Stan, First Deputy Director of SRI, by Stefan Mitroi in *Tineretul Liber,* 8–9 February 1991.

[35] Daniel Nelson, "Ceausescu and the Romanian Army," *International Defense Review* 22, no. 6 (January 1989): 737–742.

have their story straight. The defense minister and principal commanders argue that the army performed precisely as it should, given the information fed to it; the army thought the nation was threatened, the first stage of which was for a foreign power to foment internal revolt. This scenario was in their manuals, and was the scenario portrayed to them by Ceausescu's people in the last week of his regime. As the reality of the situation clarified, army spokesmen claim the army did precisely what it should have done, and immediately acted to protect the Romanian people (against the Securitate). This, at least, is the forceful assertion from the defense minister and the country's leading officers.[36]

In March 1994, Gheorghe Tinea, a state secretary in the foreign ministry, was appointed Romania's first post-Ceausescu civilian defense minister. The previous defense ministers, General Nicolae Militaru, General Victor Stanculescu and General Constantin Nicolae Spiroiu were all military officers. That Militaru and Stanculescu were moved from their posts reveals two aspects of the weak link between civil and military authority; Militaru was opposed from within the army, while Stanculescu was opposed from outside the military.

Victor Stanculescu had the severe political problem of being associated with the 1989 events in Timisoara. Switched to the ministry of industry in early 1991, he retained considerable power in national-security decisionmaking until his removal from the cabinet in October 1991. And, even from outside the cabinet, his voice is still heard within the army.

Stanculescu's unwillingness or inability to commit forces in Iliescu's behalf in June 1990 and the mounting liability that he represented long before his departure from the cabinet are suggestive. Within the army are all the cleavages, from nationalist to communist, that splinter post-Ceausescu Romanian politics—and the high command considers the army's unity, not the national interest, its priority.

Many signals of these intra-army tensions emerged forcefully in 1990–1991. Although the army repressed the "Action Committee for Democratization of the Army" (CADA) in 1990, other groups remain active, from the Left and Right. The high command's sensitivity to such organizations, and particularly to their contacts with the press, is clear, as is their larger concern about army unity and discipline.[37]

The same concern about discipline, however, creates a deterrent for any more direct military involvement in politics. A coup or overt intervention is highly unlikely because of the army's doubt about itself, notwithstanding frequent pronouncements about Romanians' loyalty to the army and vice versa. The army does not want confrontation with anyone, and vastly prefers its reclaimed role as sole defender of the national frontiers. This is not a military force, or an officer corps, that finds appeal in acting as a praetorian guard.

Defense Minister Spiroiu, however, was convinced that no civilian was yet pre-

---

[36] Interview with General Constantin Spiroiu, October 1–2, 1992, Ministry of Defense, Bucharest, Romania, and discussion with his principal staff officers.

[37] See Aurel Peruz and Gavrila Inoan's interview with Defense Minister Spiroiu in *Tineretul Liber,* 25 October 1991, pp.1, 3.

pared to head the defense ministry. As late as the fall of 1992, he believed that the problems of the armed forces in Romania could be understood only by someone in uniform—although, he insisted, they would abide by a civilian minister if one were named.[38] Perhaps as a consequence of this doubtful approach to civilian command, the relationship between the ministry of national defense and the Romanian parliament remains distant, for members of parliament know very little about the army and vice versa. However, there have been recent efforts to introduce greater civilian control over the military. In the spring of 1993, Ioan Mircea Pascu, a former foreign policy adviser to President Iliescu, was appointed deputy minister of defense. Finally, in March 1994, Gheorghe Tinea was appointed Romania's first civilian defense minister in the post-Ceausescu period. This appointment, brought on by right- and left-wing extremist criticism of Spiroiu, is no guarantee of civilian authority in the ministry of defense, which will depend on larger ongoing reforms, not personalities.

The most debilitating threat from within the Romanian political system, however, is a pervasive doubt about the relevance of political authority to resolving problems and meeting demands. The National Salvation Front saw, even before it splintered, its once formidable level of confidence wither as economic conditions worsened while FSN personages were unable to shake popular suspicions about their past or current motives. This is not, precisely speaking, a case of popular indifference to the public realm. Instead, it is a purposeful turning inward, begun long ago in the misery of Ceausescu's dictatorship, away from a public political environment from which there was nothing to be gained.

External Environment

Romania's security environment remains precarious. Externally, Romania finds itself buffeted by seriously strained relations with Hungary, the danger of widening post-Soviet war or disintegration that exacerbates issues such as Moldova, the worrisome possibility of a greater Serbia emerging from Yugoslav disintegration, and latent tensions with Bulgaria. Beyond immediate borders, Romania's greatly depleted economic condition, social conflict and general political imbroglio makes the country susceptible to various external threats.

Among parties and groups within Romania, there is little consensus about either a definition of security or the relative importance of such internal and external threats. Foreign and defense policy agreement breaks down quickly when specific decisions are required and alternatives are debated. Yet, broadly similar outlooks—for example, stressing nonnegotiable Romanian sovereignty in Transylvania, residual Romanian interests in Bessarabia (specifically Moldova), and a need to address Soviet and Russian interests while moving closer to Western Europe, the United States,

[38] Author's interview with General Spiroiu, October 1–2, 1992, Bucharest, Romania.

[39] Compare, for example, chapters by Ioan Mircea Pascu, who has served as counselor to President Iliescu for foreign policy, and the views of Sorin Botez, foreign policy adviser to the National Liberal Party, in *Romania After Tyranny*, ed. Daniel N. Nelson (Boulder, Colo.: Westview, 1991).

and Japan—have denoted core Romanian interests for almost all political actors.[39]

Complexities and challenges of Romania's security environment are acknowledged by the Romanian government. Former Defense Minister Spiroiu, in a July 1991 interview, for example, noted:

> Today experts maintain increasingly that threats may come primarily from internal sources in the form of unexpected consequences from East European reform processes, or they could also be economic, social or national [; in addition] there are various nonconventional threats such as terrorism, drug trafficking, the environment, etc.[40]

Romania's ability to respond creatively and quickly to a new security environment is constrained by the country's relative isolation from the West during the first two post-Ceausescu years, by disastrous economic conditions, and by the lack of a firm domestic political consensus.[41]

Relations with the West

Strenuous endeavors by both the presidency and the foreign ministry have been made to repair Romania's damaged relations with industrial democracies. There is, to be sure, a sensitivity about being isolated, and a strong tendency among Romanian officials to suspect that the West responded negatively to Romania's May 20, 1990, election because the outcome was not what the West had desired. Yet, Romanian officials also acknowledge that Romania's poor image is a product of the country's bureaucracy, disorder, sociopolitical instability, strikes, and corruption.

In part because Romanian plans for a market economy began to materialize and local elections were planned, the Bush administration reacted favorably in late 1991 by waiving the Jackson-Vanik amendment—a critical first step toward renewing most-favored-nation (MFN) status. Although submission of MFN to Congress for approval did not happen until after local elections were held, Romania has now begun to reenter financial markets once closed to it by the United States. Symbolic American participation in balance-of-payments support from the Group of 24, initially through a small $10 million grant for agricultural assistance, helped reassure other non-European Community states (most notably Japan and wealthy Middle East countries) that Romania should no longer be ostracized.[42]

The Bush administration's changing views about Romania were derailed just after the September 27 national election in Romania. The U.S. House of Representatives rejected by a resounding margin the administration's proposal to grant MFN

---

[40] Interview with General Constantin Nicolae Spiroiu in *Adevarul,* 18 July 1991 (author's translation).

[41] See the commentary by Dumitru Tinu in *Adevarul,* 16 May 1991.

[42] A visit by the governor of the Romanian Central Bank to Washington in December 1991 secured this cooperation by the U.S. government in G–24 efforts.

to Romania. The vehement opposition to MFN for Romania enunciated by Hungarian-born U.S. Representative (from California) Thomas Lantos was wrongly seen in Bucharest as the sole reason for the defeat of MFN. There is no question that U.S.-Romanian relations were set back by the House rejection. Most Romanians were incredulous that Americans could deny to their country a more open trading relationship when the same privilege had been granted to the dictator, Nicolae Ceausescu, and to Saddam Hussein until the invasion of Kuwait, and is still enjoyed by Beijing's leaders, who slaughtered civilians in June 1989. MFN status was finally restored in October 1993. By then, however, the absence of Western markets had already caused considerable economic harm.

Relations with the European Community and with NATO, on the other hand, have significantly expanded. Romania joined in the new North Atlantic Cooperation Council established after the Rome NATO Summit in November 1991, and in early 1994 it became one of the first former members of the Warsaw Pact to join NATO's Partnership for Peace programs. In November 1992, it signed an association agreement with the EC (since renamed EU) similar to that signed by Hungary, Poland, and Czechoslovakia in December 1991. However, Romania still suffers from President Iliescu's neocommunist image.

Relations with the East

Romanian borders are not endangered today by threatening armies. Almost without exception, however, political actors in Bucharest view the potential for future dangers to be significant.

Hungary's "threat" to Romania is not military. Rather, the Magyar diaspora in Transylvania is thought to be a cauldron in which Hungary's involvement can only be disruptive. Romanian decisionmakers are, for the most part, suspicious about any Hungarian government presence—through consulates, educational exchange programs, investment initiatives, and so forth—in Transylvania.

Several important and highly specific points of contention exist. Hungary wants to reopen a consulate in Cluj-Napoca (Koloszvar), to reestablish an autonomous Hungarian university in the same city, to open more border crossing points between the two countries, and to begin investment programs in that part of Romania. There are no territorial claims necessarily implied by any of these actions, but each has (as seen from Bucharest) the potential to further develop local loyalties toward Budapest, and to diminish Bucharest's control over this part of Romanian territory.

More broadly, and particularly in Washington, Romanians perceive a "Hungarian lobby" exerting anti-Romanian viewpoints. Romania expressed a quite different view—that is, that a broad treaty of understanding, cooperation, and goodwill is first required to establish the "norms of bilateral relations," after which "a future

---

[43] See, for example, the exchange of letters during late June and early July 1991 between Hungarian Foreign Minister Geza Jeszenszky and Romanian Foreign Minister Adrian Nastase as reported on Bucharest Programul Unu Radio, reprinted in FBIS *Daily Report: East Europe* (July 10, 1991), p. 29.

accord on a series of concrete actions" is feasible.[43] In 1991, both sides accused the other of having the proverbial cart before the horse, and neither defused the tension. At international forums—for example, at the July 1991 CSCE Geneva meeting on ethnic minorities—the two countries clashed once again regarding the Romanian ethnic minority policy.[44]

In 1992, at the urging of the European Community, Hungary and Romania began direct discussions about a bilateral treaty. The negotiations, however, have been slowed over two issues—Hungarian demands that Romania include a clause in the treaty committing it to improve the treatment of the Hungarian minority, and Romanian demands that Hungary explicitly agree to renounce any attempt to change the present borders between the two countries. Until these issues are resolved, the prospects are slim for a major improvement in relations.

Ironically, while political relations with Hungary are troubled, military relations are quite good. Both countries' militaries have sought to advance bilateral confidence- and security-building measures, including the signing of an "open skies" agreement in spring 1991. Although largely symbolic (involving only four overflights a year), the accord breaks new ground and strongly implies that neither army has anything it wants to hide from the other in order to mount an attack.

Despite such an important step, however, Romanians recall with evident dislike a remark made by Hungarian Prime Minister Jozsef Antall concerning his role as premier of 15 million Hungarians—the number in the state of Hungary plus all the diaspora in the aggregate. There is also the memory of Hungary's redeployment of forces from its western border to its eastern frontier with Romania in 1989 and 1990, a measure that the West appears to have understood but that rankled Romanian sensitivities.

The potential for conflict with Ukraine, or with Russian nationalists in Moldova, weighs heavily on Romanian security planners. Were Bessarabia not a part of the historic animosity between Moscow or Kiev and Bucharest, the potential for a genuinely cooperative relationship might exist. Romanians still constitute 60 percent of the population in the republic of Moldova, however, which asserted its independence in August 1991.[45] The Prut River, which served as the Soviet-Romanian border since the end of World War II, has insulated Romania from few if any of the dangers arising from the USSR's dismemberment. Defense ministry internal discussions did, in 1991, begin to consider the implications of a Ukrainian army and

---

[44] The author discussed the Hungarian view with Foreign Minister Geza Jeszenszky in Washington, D.C., in late July 1991. The angry Romanian rejection of Hungarian complaints was carried by Rompres on July 19, 1991, and reprinted in FBIS *Daily Report: East Europe* 91–139 (July 19, 1991), p. 25.

[45] According to the Soviet census of 1989, there were 3.3 million "Moldovans" and 145,000 "Romanians." But there is no linguistic or cultural distinction between these two labels. Of all Moldovans, 2.5 million are in the union republic of that name, constituting two-thirds of the republic's population in 1989. After some migration to Romania, it is safe to estimate that at least 60 percent of Moldova's population is ethnically and linguistically Romanian.

tensions over Bukovina and Bessarabia generally, while the Romanian foreign ministry sought to initiate negotiations concerning the eventual return of lands the Soviets annexed to Ukraine fifty years ago.[46]

No Romanian government can turn its back on the plaintive appeals of people in Moldova for closer cultural and economic ties. Since the August 26, 1991, declaration of Moldovan independence, Chisenau and Bucharest have significantly improved economic and cultural ties. While Romania hopes eventually to unite with Moldova, unification is not an immediate policy objective. Public attitudes in Moldova do not support immediate unification. The September 1992 presidential election in Romania resulted in a defeat for Mircea Druc, a former Moldovan prime minister who changed citizenship to run for the Romanian presidency. Druc's defeat, and the poor showing of Dragomir and Constantinescu, who both argued for firmer Romanian moves toward unification, have served to defuse the pressure for unification, though union still remains a long-term goal for the Romanian government.

Since the escalation of fighting between the ethnic Romanian majority of Moldova and Russians of the breakaway Trans-Dniestria in 1992, the Romanian government has been concerned to avoid any action that would worsen fighting. Rumors and accusations about Romanian engagement in the fighting in Moldova have circulated widely in the Western and Russian press. Some Romanian citizens apparently have crossed the Prut individually to join in the fight against "Trans-Dniestria" and Russians—a fact acknowledged by Romanian intelligence, military, and political figures. But there is no evidence of systematic Romanian government intervention in the conflict.[47] Government-to-government agreements to provide military training for officers were signed in 1992, but these do not constitute a concerted Romanian effort to affect the military outcome. However, the powerful Russian 14th Army based in Moldova, commanded by General Lebed, has often provided fire support, logistics, and weapons to the anti-Romanian fighters.

The FSN, FDSN, Democratic Convention, and other parties all seek to drape themselves in the flag of nationalism, of which Bessarabia is a prime symbol; all speak in veiled terms that imply eventual reunification, and of "eliminating the consequences of the Molotov-Ribbentrop Pact."[48] At the same time, they all recognize

[46] See Ilie Paunescu's commentary on territorial disputes with Ukraine in *Dreptatea,* 12–13 November 1991, p. 1.

[47] During my trips to both Moldova and to Romania in 1992, I conducted interviews with Ioan Talpes, head of Romania's Foreign Intelligence Service; General Constantin Spiroiu, minister of national defense; Ioan Mircea Pascu, foreign policy adviser to President Iliescu, and others. In interviews with residents along the Prut, in Iasi, Chisenau, and other areas, I also inquired about reports of Romanian detachments entering Moldova, arms shipments across the Prut, etc. During these interviews, I was unable to obtain any corroboration for these reports, although I heard a number of stories about individuals who made personal decisions to join in the fighting.

[48] A conservative view is expressed editorially in *Dreptatea,* 26 October 1991, p. 1, regarding Bessarabia"s "reannexation." Radio Free Europe/Radio Liberty *Daily Report* #222 (November 22, 1991), p. 4, cited Romanian Orthodox Patriarch Teoctist about the reunification of all historic Romanian provinces into a renewed Romanian state.

existing political realities. Iliescu, for instance, has pointed out that "the two banks of the Prut are not the only actors involved" in the Moldovan issue.

One of the most heavily criticized steps taken by the Romanian government was signing a Treaty of Friendship and Cooperation with the Soviet Union in 1991. Typically, Iliescu was attacked for "selling our country to our great Eastern neighbor for another 15 years."[49] In an interview discussing the treaty, former Foreign Minister Adrian Nastase responded by pointing out the advantages to Romania of retaining close ties with the Soviet Union—the raw materials, potential markets, and so forth. Further, he pointed out that the treaty clarified thorny bilateral issues, including Romanian treasures taken by the Red Army, and Serpent's Island, occupied by the USSR since the war.[50] Romanian officials involved with foreign policy defended, as well, clauses providing mutual guarantees against entry into hostile alliances or the use of one's territory for an attack on the other. According to Romanian decisionmakers, these were well within the framework of a sovereign state deciding how it should best pursue interests with large neighbors.

But Romania's concerns ran deeper. The Soviets—particularly the Soviet military—were edgy about Moldova, and had sent additional troops to the republic in late 1990. Romania's justifiable concern was that, along with tension on the Hungarian border, a much more ominous adversary could emerge if provoked beyond the Prut River. That the treaty clearly denied to Romania any territorial ambition beyond the Prut—that is, to reunite Bessarabia with other Romanian territory—was condemned by many in Romania's anti-FSN opposition. Yet, the treaty's reassurance to Moscow was meant to enable Bucharest to continue developing ties with the Moldovan government.

The disintegration of the USSR made the Romanian-Soviet treaty moot. The fears that had motivated the Romanian decision to sign a treaty in 1991 became palpable in 1992, however, as Russian nationalism surfaced as a result of Moldova's independence. Former Russian Vice President Aleksandr Rutskoi, Defense Minister Pavel Grachev, and others have been vocal in their view that Russian military power may be needed to ensure "Russian rights" in Moldova—a threat that creates an ominous dilemma for Bucharest. Russian intervention in Moldova—under the guise of "peacekeeping"—presents a dilemma for Romania. To confront Moscow militarily would be suicidal; yet, to stand idly by and watch Moldova, with its ethnic Romanian majority, be overrun by Russians would be unacceptable in terms of Romanian domestic politics.

Farther west, Romania faces an enlarged, well-armed, nationalist Serbia under Slobodan Milosevic. In July and August 1991, the Romanian-Yugoslav border was reinforced because of the sizable movements of the Yugoslav People's Army (JNA) into and through Croatia. There was an obvious concern that, were fighting to continue, guerrilla units might seek sanctuary in Romania or try to resupply forces from Romanian territory. The Romanian military has also discussed possible responses,

---

[49] For instance, Gabriel Marculescou's "Guilty Silence," *Romania Libera*, 12 November 1991, p. 1.

[50] See the interview by Nastase in *Dimineata*, 10 April 1991.

were Yugoslav federal forces to intrude into Romanian territory in "hot pursuit." In all of this there has been considerable worry in Bucharest that an entirely unwanted neighboring war might complicate already weighty national security concerns.

As fighting spread from Slovenia to Croatia and then to Bosnia-Herzegovina in 1991–1992, Romania was powerless to affect the strife. At first, Bucharest nervously advocated EC and CSCE action to preclude dismembering Yugoslavia. Some agents of the former Ceausescu regime may have taken Yugoslav warfare as an opportunity to sell black market weapons.[51] And, former Foreign Minister Nastase and the Stolojan government in 1991–1992 acknowledged that sanctions against Serbia had been ignored by Danube river cargo vessels, as well as train and truck transporters who had chances to make enormous profit.

The amount of this trade is impossible to quantify. Until June 1992, however, manpower and equipment necessary for full-scale enforcement of the international embargo—inspections of vessels, aircraft, and trucks bound to and from Serbia or territory in Croatia or Bosnia held by Serbs, and seizure of those found to be carrying contraband—were not being earmarked for the task. Part of the reason was budgetary—Romania would be a huge loser if the sanctions were employed tightly, whereas it would gain a modest but important increment in hard-currency trade if a blind eye and deaf ear were turned to the problem. Enforcement of the sanctions was tightened under American and West European pressure in mid-1992, and the closing of the Danube has been costly to Bucharest. But Romanians do not regard Serbs as an adversary and are disinclined to make an enemy of Belgrade.

Romania and Serbia share common concerns about Hungarian irredentism. This shared interest worked to moderate Romania's reactions to the Serbian military offensive into Croatia and Bosnia-Herzogovina, and to dampen Romanian enthusiasm for economic sanctions against Belgrade. This one issue of overlapping interest, however, will be insufficient to surmount both Romanian concerns about Serbia's long-range intentions and Bucharest's evident desire to support the UN.

Throughout the Balkans, Romania's policy has sought improved ties whenever possible. With Turkey and Greece, a careful balance of solicitation has thus far moved Romania in a positive direction with both. Romania's reaction to the Turkish Black Sea Economic Zone proposal has been far more positive than Bulgaria's, with an obvious attempt to use Ankara's idea to some advantage vis-à-vis Bulgaria.

Regarding Bulgaria, however, troubles have increased rather than diminished. Ostensibly, the problem is pollution of Ruse, a Bulgarian city on the Romanian-Bulgarian border, by Romanian factories across the Danube. Such complaints, dating back to the mid-1980s, are valid, but they are heavily exploited by Bulgarian politicians. Bitter and angry exchanges took place concerning the issue during 1991, making it even clearer that, beneath the surface, all is not well between the two countries.

Romania's military is woefully underprepared for any concerted attack. Its equipment is very outdated; its training poor. Efforts are being made by the post-Ceausescu

---

[51] See *Vjesnik* (Zagreb), 7 May 1991, p. 4.

government to depoliticize the army and to professionalize it. Former Defense Minister Spiroiu emphasized the need to give "top priority to qualitative aspects in all areas of national defense," and specifically referred to equipment and the standard of conscripts as matters requiring urgent attention.[52] For the near term, however, Romania's 170,000 active-duty personnel remain an unlikely guarantor of the nation's security. Involvement in economic activity, which had absorbed almost eighty thousand of the military's active personnel in 1989, had a debilitating effect on readiness and equipment-maintenance.[53] Romania is now too poor to reverse this effect in the near future.[54]

To reinforce its security, Romania seeks to strengthen its ties to regional and multilateral security organizations. The aforementioned associate status in the European Union (formerly EC) is one such linkage. In addition, it has participated in Danubian cooperation, the Black Sea Economic Zone, and Balkan cooperation generally. President Iliescu has spoken of interlocking "harmonious relationships amidst the new all-European architecture and its subregional components."[55] Former Foreign Minister Nastase advocated a web of regional and subregional structures that are "temporary, until the establishment of a pan-European security system."[56]

Most of all, perhaps, Romania fears being separated from the rest of Europe—isolated in the Balkans to contend, alone, with its internal and external threats. In particular it opposes dividing East-Central from Southeastern Europe. Such a division, in the Romanian view, would perpetuate the difference between haves and have-nots, both in terms of economic access to the West and the availability of security guarantees. Romanians of all parties are also uncomfortable with the notion of recreating a buffer zone between Russia and the countries of Eastern Europe.

Prospects for the Future

Romania must confront numerous intractable problems that make the country less secure than most of the other formerly communist states of Eastern Europe. It has neither the military nor the economic capacity to confront such threats. Indeed, it is Romanian diplomacy that must deal with the country's security needs for the foreseeable future.

A wide range of initiatives has been inaugurated; none of these alone can satisfy Romania's security needs. Yet, Romanians have begun the arduous reentry into

[52] See the interview of Spiroiu by Octavian Andronic in *Libertatea,* 4–5 July 1991, pp. 1–2.

[53] Ibid.

[54] For a more complete discussion of Romania's military in the post-Ceausescu era, one should consult Larry Watts, "The Romanian Army in December and Beyond," in *Romania After Tyranny,* ed. Daniel N. Nelson (Boulder, Colo.: Westview, 1991).

[55] See the text of his address to a seminar on "Perceptions and Concepts of Security in Eastern Europe" in Bucharest on July 4, 1991, as reprinted in FBIS *Daily Report: East Europe* 91–131 (July 9, 1991), p. 3.

[56] A full elaboration of Nastase's views is in Lucia Verona's interview of the foreign minister in *Az,* 25 May 1991, pp. 1, 4.

Europe, with considerable promise that—provided domestic political democratization and economic reform continue—Romania's insecurity can be diminished during the 1990s.

Romania's immediate future—into the mid-1990s—will be fraught with intrastate and external dangers. From within, extremism of the Left and Right, although not yet powerful, could be made vastly more threatening to values and processes of free market and free government. Continued economic pain, without very evident support from advanced industrial democracies, will be a readily available catalyst for the growth of neofascism and neocommunism.

To expect democracy to flower autonomously during the trauma of creating a market economy, particularly in Romania after a quarter-century of tyranny, is naive. Each halting step toward a free-market democracy must be supported proportionally more for Romania than, for example, Hungary, since the process of change was begun long ago in the latter case, in a country that is much smaller and more homogeneous.

Ideally for Romania, a consensual core for the country's post-communist politics would emerge from the multiparty coalition formed in late 1991—the Democratic Convention—and a reunified Social Democratic Left. But none of the immediate post-communist political organizations fared well in 1992–1993, as the Front split along the lines of personality into the FSN (Roman) and FDSN (Iliescu), and the components of the convention began to be pulled apart. In the latter case, the Liberal Party split away entirely.

From its overwhelming May 1990 electoral victory, the FSN and its president, Ion Iliescu, lost half of its support by the time of the February 1992 local elections. But this "loss" did not translate into any other party's unambiguous "gain." Instead, the various parties in the convention have been unable to identify viable national candidates who can appeal beyond the urban intelligentsia. While parties other than the Front (such as the National Peasant Party) have very wide support, there have been no new leaders who have emerged to garner the trust of workers and peasants.[57]

As a consequence, a much less popular Iliescu and his party, the FDSN—which was renamed the Party of Social Democracy of Romania (PSDR) at its July 1993 congress—still managed to win a plurality in parliament (both houses) with about 28 percent of the vote in the September 1992 national elections, and almost half of the presidential vote in a field of six candidates in the first round of voting. Iliescu's appeal to the workers' and peasants' fear of change, and the failure of the Democratic Convention candidate, Emil Constantinescu, to do more than mount a standard American-style campaign, ensured that a strong center did not emerge.

External threats are not imminent, but are likely to grow during the 1990s, partly owing to domestic political uncertainties. The more economic pain weakens politi-

---

[57] Surveys by IRSOP, and independent data collection efforts directed by Alin Teodorescu on the one hand, and Pavel Campeanu on the other, have all confirmed this failure of opposition parties to generate any charismatic following or sense of trust in specific leaders.

cal legitimacy, the more likely it becomes that Romanian parties will try to use nationalism to increase their political appeal, which may then exacerbate relations with their neighbors. The significant presidential vote (more than 10 percent) achieved by a right-wing extremist, Gheorghe Funar, in the September 27, 1992, election underscores the dangers in this regard.

The West cannot dispel any of the threats to Romanian security. But the United States and other industrial democracies can, without great outlays of budgetary resources, reinforce the slender threads of democratic processes in Romania. Diplomatic attention is cheap, and small contributions to highly visible assistance programs can help stabilize democracy and convince Romanians that their sacrifices during and since Ceausescu were not for naught.

It is imperative that the United States follow up the restoration of most-favored-nation (MFN) status with substantial trade incentives to U.S. firms who wish to invest in Romania. MFN provides a green light to investors concerned about the stability of a country and American confidence in the viability of its leadership. Western investments are a lifeline for countless Romanians struggling to implement the transition to a free-market economy and a clear sign of support for intelligent, and respected economists heading the National Bank and ministry of finance.

Symbolically, the key step that the United States could take to improve relations with Bucharest is to recognize Romanians' immense sacrifice during and after Ceausescu, and to acknowledge the "good news" about this Balkan state rather than repeat well-worn stories about orphans, AIDS babies, pollution, and miners' rampages.

The best insurance that Romania will move toward free-market democracy is for Romanians to reject extremism. And the best way to guarantee that such rejection holds will be to mitigate the conditions that lead workers, peasants, and others to respond favorably when fanaticism of the Left or the Right offers its false solutions.

V

Yugoslavia: The Unmaking of a Federation

Christopher Cviic

States usually break up in the wake of military defeat, which is the way in 1917–1918 four European empires—the Hapsburg, the Ottoman, the Prussian, and the Russian—met their end. It was Japan's military humiliation of European colonial empires overseas in 1941–1942 that set in train the process of decolonization which eventually extended to parts of the world beyond Asia. The new thing about breakups in our own day is that they happen in peacetime by implosion, rather than as a result of military defeat. Czarist Russia's successor, the Soviet Union, dissolved itself in December 1991 by agreement among its major constituent republics—though it could be argued that the Soviet army's military failure in Afghanistan during the period since 1979 had contributed to the state's demise.

No military factors, either direct or indirect, were involved in Yugoslavia's demise in 1991. The outside world did not expect—and most definitely did not want—its breakup, which occurred precisely at a time when Europe was beginning to make arrangements for the post-Cold War era, with the stability of the existing states as one of its cornerstones. In that sense, there could not have been a greater contrast here with Yugoslavia's first breakup in 1941, which resulted from the Nazi German and Fascist Italian invasion, assisted by Hungary and Bulgaria, and followed by the establishment of a number of quisling regimes in regions not annexed by any of the victors.

The reasons for Yugoslavia's demise in 1990–1991 are numerous and complex, but they all sprang from its internal contradictions as a multinational state. In a nutshell, Yugoslavia broke up because the nations that constituted it had come to reject it—either totally or just in its current form—as incompatible with their national aspirations. Because in the post-Cold War era outside interests were no longer ready to underpin its existence at any cost—as they would have done earlier, considering its strategic significance to the East-West balance in Europe—the disintegration was allowed to happen. That it occurred against the background of a bloody war, instead of by agreement among the parties (as in the Soviet Union), was owing to one very important factor. In the Soviet case, the largest republic, Russia, wanted to break away from the Soviet center just as much as the non-Russian republics did. In Yugoslavia's case, the largest republic, Serbia, was closely identified with the central power of the Yugoslav state and was unwilling to tolerate the state's replacement by a loose confederation as the non-Serbs demanded.

For the Serbs, Yugoslavia's most numerous people (36 percent of the total population in 1981, the year of the last complete census), the problem was that under communist rule—particularly in the last decade of the life of President Tito, who had rebuilt the country in 1945—the undisputed hegemony they had enjoyed in the 1918–1941 period had been gradually undermined. They wanted more, not less, Yugoslavia. This contrasted with what the non-Serb majority wanted—the continuation of Yugoslavia in some form, but with only as much power reserved for central institutions as suited the individual federal republics and autonomous provinces.

The conflict over those very different and mutually exclusive visions of Yugoslavia did not start in the past few years. It became acute, however, only when various cohesive factors had weakened to the point that they could no longer preserve the status quo.

For four and a half decades after 1945, no challenges to Yugoslavia as a state could be seriously mounted. Yugoslavia was firmly held together by a charismatic leader, President Tito, at the head of a loyal Communist Party and army that he had led to victory in 1944–1945. The break with the Soviet Union in 1948 created a bond between the regime's supporters and its opponents. The latter considered the alternative to Tito—a return to direct rule from Moscow—as far worse than the Titoist version of socialism that offered the peoples of Yugoslavia a measure of prosperity, particularly in the two decades before Tito's death in 1980. Last, but by no means least, whatever the citizens of Yugoslavia felt about their state—whether or not they wanted it—the outside world did, and acted accordingly. To keep afloat an independent (even if communist) Yugoslavia, and thus prevent it from "going over" to the Soviet Union, was a major aim of the Western powers during the Cold War. They showed their seriousness by providing the Tito regime with a large amount of all kinds of aid. Even more important, they made it clear that they would not tolerate any threats—not only to its independence but also to its territorial unity and integrity. In this matter, there was a standoff with the Soviet Union, which preferred the status quo under Tito to a possible lurch toward internal democratization and a parallel slide into membership in the Western bloc.

All these cohesive factors disappeared one by one during the 1980s. Tito's death in 1980 was followed by a severe financial crisis that shook the population's confidence in its rulers' ability to go on delivering economic prosperity. The Cold War ended in 1989, and with it the need to fear a possible Soviet takeover. The Communist Party of Yugoslavia (official name since 1952: the League of Communists of

Yugoslavia) officially broke up at its congress in Belgrade in January 1990. It had long been divided into "reformist" and "dogmatic" wings as well as (and more important) along territorial lines: one party organization for each of the six federal republics (Bosnia and Herzegovina, Croatia, Macedonia, Montenegro, Serbia, and Slovenia) and the two autonomous provinces (Kosovo and Vojvodina).

For the first time in Yugoslavia's history since 1918, the territorial units composing it as well as their populations felt that they could decide their future without anyone from the center in Belgrade—let alone abroad—dictating their decision to them. But the peoples of Yugoslavia disagreed profoundly about what should happen next. What they did not disagree about was that they had a raw deal in Yugoslavia.

An Auction of Grievances

For many years, particularly since the mid-1960s, the most vociferous complainants about Yugoslavia had been the Serbs. But the first full public expression of the Serbian case against post-1945 Yugoslavia came in a memorandum prepared in 1985–1986 for the Serbian Academy of Arts and Sciences in Belgrade by a working group of historians, demographers, economists, and lawyers under the chairmanship of the academy's vice-president and one of Serbia's best-known writers, Antonije Isakovic. The memorandum, which was leaked to the Yugoslav press in 1986 but had been known in outline before, alleged inter alia that:

- The federal government in Belgrade had ever since 1945 discriminated against Serbia in the economic field while at the same time favoring the two western republics, Croatia and Slovenia, and leaving in the hands of men from these republics the power of economic decisionmaking. The memorandum's authors argued that the "anti-Serb bias" in the pre-1941 Communist Party of Yugoslavia was inspired by the anti-Serb attitude of its directing body (until its dissolution by Stalin in 1943): the Communist International (Comintern) in Moscow.
- The partition of Serbia into three parts under Tito's 1974 federal constitution weakened Serbia by de facto dismembering it, particularly as the two autonomous provinces of Kosovo and Vojvodina were allowed direct participation in decisionmaking at the federal level, thus bypassing Serbia.
- The Serbs in Kosovo as well as in Croatia were subject to policies aimed at either driving them out altogether (as in Kosovo) or assimilating them (as in Croatia). In both cases, the memorandum alleged, what was happening to the Serbs was tantamount to "genocide."

From all the evidence they claimed to have marshaled, the memorandum's authors concluded that the policy of "strong Yugoslavia, weak Serbia" pursued by President Tito (himself half Croat and half Slovene) and his second-in-command, Edvard Kardelj (a Slovene), had serious disadvantages. Serbia was, therefore, entitled to press for a revision of the "unequal" 1974 constitution.

The Serbs' disenchantment with Yugoslavia was paralleled by a growing anti-Yugoslav feeling among the country's non-Serbs, notably the Slovenes and the Croats.

The former had from 1918 until relatively late into the post-1945 period been fervent supporters of the Yugoslav state, seen both as a market for Slovenia's goods and a protection against German and Italian imperialism. During the mid-1960s, however, the Slovenes, a small nation constituting only 8 percent of Yugoslavia's total population, became alarmed at the growing trend toward cultural "Yugoslavia" which they considered a threat to their national identity. Another reason for growing Slovene disenchantment with Yugoslavia was their conviction that, in the economic field, they were putting into Yugoslavia much more than they were getting from it. As an important hard-currency exporter, Slovenia resented the centralized system of currency control that allowed the center in Belgrade to maintain a large army and civil service as well as to sink valuable resources into poorly managed investment projects in Serbia and other less developed areas. The fear of "creeping Serbianization" and resentment of economic mismanagement were not, however, considered by the majority of Slovenes as an argument for leaving Yugoslavia altogether. Rather, most Slovenes wanted to turn the country into a looser grouping with some common institutions. A factor that contributed toward the new thinking in Slovenia was the awareness that, in a peaceful Europe, the old threat from the West had disappeared. Austria and Italy were no longer seen as imperialist predators, but as friendly neighbors and attractive economic partners offering an opening to the West.

Like the Slovenes, the Croats in the past had viewed Yugoslavia as a framework for the protection of national territory, above all from Italy, which had been promised in 1915 most of the Croat Adriatic coast as well as the islands as a reward for entering World War I on the side of the Entente. After the breakup of Austria-Hungary in 1918, Italy proceeded to occupy most of the territories in question but later restored some of them to Croatia, then a member of the Yugoslav kingdom. Earlier than the Slovenes—perhaps because of their geographical proximity to Serbia—the Croats abandoned the view of Yugoslavia as a friendly haven from Italian imperialism. This feeling of alienation from Yugoslavia, originally a Croat nineteenth-century idea, received a new impetus from the murder of two Croat deputies by a Montenegrin deputy in the Belgrade parliament in June 1928. Stjepan Radic, leader of the pacifist Croatian Peasant Party, who had been wounded in the same attack, died that August. In January 1929 King Alexander introduced a personal dictatorship, which was particularly harsh in Croatia. In the same year, Ante Pavelic, a lawyer from Zagreb, founded the *Ustase* (Insurgent) movement to fight for Croatia's full independence. Pavelic, sentenced to death in absentia, obtained the cooperation of several neighboring governments, notably those of Bulgaria, Hungary, and Italy. In 1934 King Alexander was assassinated by a Macedonian terrorist working closely with the *Ustase*.

In 1941, after failing to persuade Vladko Macek, Radic's successor as leader of the Croat Peasant Party, to take over running the quisling Croat state, the Italians and the Germans put Pavelic and his *Ustase* in charge. Pavelic's regime embarked on a policy of genocide directed against Croatia's Serbs and Jews. Many thousands perished in *Ustase* concentration camps alongside thousands of Croat opponents of the regime. The shadow of Pavelic's monstrous regime continued to hang over Croatia in post-1945 communist Yugoslavia despite the fact that many more Croats had fought on the side of the Tito partisans than on Pavelic's side. The Croats also resented the Serbs' preponderance in Croatia's civil service, police, army, and the economy—far in excess of their actual share of the population in Croatia (11.6 percent, according to the 1981 census). The sacking by Tito in 1966 of Aleksandar Rankovic, a powerful Party figure and former secret police boss, and a Serb by nationality and sympathy, ushered in a period of liberalization throughout Yugoslavia. It sparked off a national cultural and political revival in Croatia and generated increasing support for a greater autonomy for Croatia within Yugoslavia. This "Croatian Spring" was crushed by Tito in a series of purges in late 1971 and throughout 1972. The purges had a politically and culturally stultifying effect in Croatia, which lasted nearly two decades and were comparable to the post-1968 purges in Czechoslovakia. They also had an important side effect in that they helped to strengthen proindependence sentiment in Croatia—just as King Alexander's dictatorship had done after 1929.

The Gainers

Important groups in Yugoslavia, however, representing just under a half of the total population remained strongly in favor of the Tito nationality policy, under which they had gained important concessions. This applied above all to the Bosnian Muslims, the Macedonians, and the Montenegrins. The Bosnian Muslims, descendants of Croat Catholics and members of the Bogomil sect who embraced Islam after Bosnia came under Ottoman rule in 1463, received recognition as a separate ethnic group at the end of the 1960s and were given the status of one of the three constituent nations of the Bosnian republic of the Yugoslav federation. (Previously, Bosnian Muslims had been "claimed" both by the Croats and the Serbs.) The Macedonians were recognized as a nation in their own right after 1945 and were given their own republic. The Tito regime hoped in that way to tie the Macedonians more closely to Yugoslavia and to forestall any future Bulgarian attempts to renew their old claim to Macedonia. (Bulgaria occupied Macedonia during the 1941–1944 period, during which the previously strong pro-Bulgarian sentiments faded among the Macedonian population, which was exposed to a campaign of forcible Serbianization during 1918–1941.) The Montenegrins, historically always considered a part of the Serbian nation, were given a separate republic of their own in 1945, thus reviving within the Yugoslav federation Montenegro's independent statehood, which had been extinguished when it joined Yugoslavia in 1918.

Among the gainers of the Tito nationality policy were also the two big national minorities, the Albanians and the Hungarians. The Albanians, most of them concentrated in the Kosovo province of Serbia, were one of the most oppressed groups in pre-1941 Yugoslavia and continued to be regarded as an "unreliable national element" within Serbia during the Rankovic era (Rankovic took a personal interest in the Albanians until his downfall in 1966). During the period of liberalization, which began in 1966, the Kosovo Albanians' lot improved. Kosovo's autonomy was upgraded, the province obtained increased economic development aid, and Pristina, the capital, obtained its own university. Under the 1974 constitution, Kosovo, together with Vojvodina, Serbia's other autonomous province, had its status upgraded by becoming a constituent element of the Yugoslav federation, able to participate directly in decisionmaking at the federal level, thus bypassing Serbia. The Hungarians welcomed the upgrading of the Vojvodina province, where most of Yugoslavia's Hungarians live. The Hungarians had already been enjoying broad cultural autonomy in the province, with their own press, radio and TV programs, university departments, theaters, and so on. To this was added after 1966 greater political representation, albeit within the official Party-controlled framework.

In sum, the Tito regime's nationality policy failed principally because it was not rooted in a democratic system and legitimized by freely elected representatives of individual nations and national minorities. Even so, it represented an improvement over the strongly Serb-flavored centralism of pre-1941 Yugoslavia, which had begun too late to move toward its own version of federalism. The attempt in Tito's Yugoslavia to satisfy non-Serbs, however, antagonized the Serbs without fully satisfying the Croats and the Slovenes. When Serbia began its campaign of reassertion after Tito's death, the Croats and the Slovenes first hoped that the campaign would lose momentum. When it did not, they decided to leave rather than risk being crushed by the Serbian steamroller. This left the other groups with no choice but to follow suit.

The Center Hits Back

The 1974 constitution had given Tito the position of president-for-life. In that capacity, he chaired meetings of Yugoslavia's collective state presidency composed of representatives of Yugoslavia's eight federal units—the six federal republics (Bosnia and Herzegovina, Croatia, Macedonia, Montenegro, Serbia, and Slovenia) and the two provinces of Serbia (Kosovo and Vojvodina). The eight were elected for a four-year term by secret ballot in their respective assemblies in the republics and provinces, to which they remained accountable. Given the separate federal status of Serbia's provinces of Kosovo and Vojvodina, the member for Serbia represented only Serbia proper without the provinces.

After Tito's death in May 1980, the presidency became the collective head of state. To help its smooth functioning, the position of president of the presidency was created on the principle of strict annual rotation among the eight federal units. The duties of the presidency included (apart from purely ceremonial and representative functions) appointing the federal government; signing the laws passed by two federal assembly chambers (one representing the republics and the provinces on the basis of parity and the other all citizens as such); and, most important of all, acting as commander-in-chief of the Yugoslav People's Army. In this last function, the presidency had the right to introduce the state of emergency in the country in a response to a potential outside threat. The introduction of a state of emergency in response to a domestic crisis, however, required unanimity among all the eight federal units. The 1974 constitution thus combined federal and confederate elements, balancing the substantial autonomy of the individual federal units with a centralism inherent in the supremacy of the federal over the republican and provincial legislatures.

Until the spring of 1990, Yugoslavia's supreme legislature was the Federal Assembly in Belgrade. Of its two chambers, that of the republics and the provinces whose members were appointed by republican and provincial assemblies was the more powerful, as it had the right to veto decisions of the federal government. If supported by the presidency, the federal government could implement a controversial decision as an emergency measure—but only for a period of up to two years. In the course of 1989–1991, the emergency procedure became the norm rather than the exception, indicating the appearance of deep divisions among the federal units. At first those divisions were mainly over economic matters—notably the size of the federal budget and methods of financing it—but gradually, purely political aspects took over.

Political divisions among the federal units sharpened in the 1989–1991 period and led to changes that undermined the 1974 constitution and thus also the authority of the federal state. By the end of the 1980s, a serious split had emerged within the ruling party. On one side were the hardliners (particularly strong in the party organization in the Yugoslav army) and the leadership of the republic of Serbia. On the other side stood party reformists, with a strong presence in the top ranks of the party in Slovenia and Croatia (by then Croatia had at long last shaken off the legacy of the post-1971 repression). What united the former group was the aim they both shared—that of recentralizing Yugoslavia by removing the confederal features of the 1974 constitution. The latter not only resisted the push for recentralization but also worked to strengthen political pluralism and civil liberties. The polarization soon became acute. Open confrontation between the two factions opened the way for the collapse of the entire postwar political system.

The Milosevic Campaign

It was from Serbia that the initiative came that led to the collapse of the political status quo. Serbia's aim was to increase its influence within the Yugoslav federation. If the Serbian Academy's memorandum provided the theoretical basis for Serbia's reassertion in Yugoslavia in the post-Tito period, action came from Slobodan Milosevic, who became Serbia's leader in 1986 at the time of the memorandum's publication. Within a year, Milosevic, a man of the Communist Party apparat but also a gifted populist politician, began his campaign of Serb reassertion among the Serb minority in Kosovo—a region of particular historical significance to the Serbs. It was in Kosovo that the Turks in 1389 inflicted a crushing defeat on Serbia that eventually led to its subjection to Ottoman rule for another five centuries. During those centuries, the Serbs continued to dream of revenge for Kosovo. As a participant in the Balkan Wars against Turkey (together with Bulgaria, Greece, and Montenegro), Serbia was able to take Kosovo from the Turks, with its ancient Serbian monasteries and other historical monuments recalling the fact that the province had once been part of Serbia. By the time it had returned to Serbian rule, however, Kosovo had changed its population pattern—the number of Serbs living there had diminished, largely because of emigration, while the number of Albanians had increased.

From 1918 to 1941, the Yugoslav government tried to alter the demographic balance in Kosovo by pressuring local Albanians to emigrate while offering land to Serb colonists (particularly ex-soldiers) together with financial and other incentives. The Albanians' high birthrate continued to work in their favor, however. When Yugoslavia was reconstituted in 1944–1945 and Kosovo once again found itself part of Yugoslavia, this demographic trend continued and indeed accelerated. In 1961 the census showed that Albanians constituted 67 percent of Kosovo's total population. By 1981 their share had increased to 77 percent of the total. According to the estimates made for the 1991 census (boycotted by Kosovo's Albanians), their proportion had risen to over 90 percent while that of the Serbs had dropped to below 10 percent (compared with 18.4 percent in 1961 and 13.2 percent in 1981).

Apart from the high Albanian birthrates, an important factor in the declining Serbian numbers was net Serb emigration from the province. The Serbs attributed it to Albanian "terror" aimed at the creation of an "ethnically pure" Albanian Kosovo. The Albanians claimed that the Serbs were leaving in search of better employment opportunities than in the extremely poor Kosovo, helped on their way by handsome prices paid for their houses and farms by the land-hungry Albanians.

Milosevic used a visit he paid to Kosovo in the spring of 1987 to adopt a high profile as a defender of the Serbs there. He promised that "nobody would ever again beat them." In October 1987, he used the Kosovo Serbs' alleged plight as an excuse to purge the Serbian party of rivals he accused of having been "soft" on the Albanians, since the 1981 demonstrations in Kosovo in favor of making it the seventh republic of the Yugoslav federation. The unrest had been followed by tough repressive measures against the local Albanians and by purges of Albanians in the Kosovo party. Milosevic claimed, however, that none of that represented an adequate response to Albanian "separatism" and "irredentism" and promised to do much more.

In 1988 Serbia began to use its state apparatus and mass media to organize hundreds of demonstrations by Serbs throughout the republic in support of Serbia's "unification" and against the state leaders of the two provinces who were resisting it. The campaign, officially called the "antibureaucratic revolution" and combining elements of xenophobic antinationalism and Chinese-style "cultural revolution" was a direct challenge both to the central party authority and to the collective federal leadership. One of the biggest rallies in Serbia was that in June 1989 marking the six hundredth anniversary of the Kosovo battle. The campaign claimed its first success in October 1988 when the leadership of Vojvodina, a mixture of Serbs and Hungarians accused of "autonomism," resigned after a series of mass rallies in Novi Sad, the province's capital. In January 1989, the "anti-bureaucratic revolution" crossed over into Montenegro. Following a series of rallies swollen in size by Milosevic supporters bussed over from Kosovo, the Montenegrin leadership also resigned and was replaced by pro-Milosevic men. The "pacification" of Kosovo took longer because of the bitter resistance of the local population and Albanian party cadres to the Milosevic takeover. Mass demonstrations and two general strikes were held in the province in 1988–1989 to protest the proposed abolition of the province's autonomy under the guise of Serbia's "unification." Dozens of people, all Albanians, were killed in clashes with the police and the security forces brought in from other parts of Yugoslavia to quell the unrest. The resistance in Kosovo finally was broken, though not unanimously (Slovenia alone voted against), by the intervention of the Yugoslav army approved by the presidency. In March 1989 Kosovo's assembly, surrounded by tanks and police, ratified the amendments to Serbia's constitution giving the Serbian government in Belgrade control over Kosovo's police, courts, and territorial defense as well as the power to change the constitution further without reference to Kosovo or its assembly. The Serbian assembly in Belgrade had already adopted these amendments, as had the now Milosevic-controlled assembly of Vojvodina. These changes, which ended the two provinces' right to act independently of Serbia within the federal Yugoslav institutions, were unprecedented in postwar Yugoslav history. This was true not only because they effectively eradicated two federal units, but even more because they were implemented unilaterally and in open defiance of federal authorities.

The most important consequence of the changes was that Serbia substantially increased its influence in the federation. The changes abolished any basis for the provinces' separate representation at the federal level. But Serbia never took the logical next step. This would have been their de jure removal from federal bodies. Serbia pretended, however, that all that was involved was a reorganization of its internal arrangements, which would not require any such change. The other four republics (since January 1989 Montenegro had entered Serbia's orbit) watched with dismay, unwilling to sanction the new situation but unable to reverse it. In the end, they acquiesced in what was a significant shift in Serbia's favor in the internal Yugoslav balance of power. On the federal level, Serbia now controlled three of the collective presidency's eight votes, instead of one as previously. (Informally, it could also count on Montenegro, which actually gave it four).

In the summer of 1990, Kosovo's assembly refused to approve the new Serbian constitution. It was punished for this by the Serbian authorities in Belgrade who ordered its immediate dissolution. This should have caused a constitutional crisis throughout Yugoslavia. Without a functioning assembly, Kosovo's representative in the federal bodies (the assembly, the government and the presidency) had become illegitimate and so had, logically, those bodies themselves. The crisis of Yugoslavia's state system, however, was quickly overshadowed by another, even more important one—that of the ruling party.

The Onset of Democracy

The crisis involving the party was brought to a head in the autumn of 1989 by the decision of the Slovene assembly to amend the Slovene constitution to allow for multiparty elections to take place in the spring of the following year. In December 1989, Croatia followed Slovenia's example by ordering a constitutional change to allow for such elections in Croatia, which were also held in the spring of 1990. Both republics thus followed Serbia's example in openly defying a major provision of the 1974 constitution by deciding to replace one-party rule by the multiparty system. In both republics, the change was approved by the republican branches of the Communist Party, without reference to (let alone the approval of) the central Party bodies and in advance of the all-Yugoslav Communist Party Congress convened for January 1990. When the Congress met in January 1990, no agreement on political and economic reforms could be reached and the Party fell apart.

Multiparty elections duly took place in Slovenia and Croatia in April–May, followed by elections in Bosnia and Herzegovina (October), Macedonia (November) and Serbia and Montenegro (December 1990). In Kosovo the elections were boycotted by the majority Albanian population. In Slovenia a broad coalition called Demos won the election and the post of prime minister afterward but the presidency of Slovenia went in a separate election to Milan Kucan, leader of the reformed communists. In Croatia the election was won by the right-of-center Croatian Democratic Union under the leadership of Franjo Tudjman. It achieved a majority of seats but not of votes. In Bosnia and Herzegovina the three "national" parties representing the Muslims, the Serbs, and the Croats won shares of the vote closely corresponding to their share of the total population and decided to form a coalition government. The parties were the Party of Democratic Action (representing the Muslims), the Serbian Democratic Party, and the Croat Democratic Union. In Macedonia the nationalist Macedonian "Revolutionary Organization—Democratic Party of Macedonian National Unity" (VMRO-DPMNE) won a third of the vote, not enough to form the government, and went into a coalition with the reformed communists. Kiro Gligorov, a prominent reform communist politician from the Tito era, was elected president. In Serbia and Montenegro the communists won convincingly. In Montenegro the League of Communists won 66 percent of all votes and 83 seats in a 125-strong assembly. In Serbia the Socialist Party (renamed Communist) won 77 percent of votes and 194 seats in a 250-strong assembly. Slobodan Milosevic was reelected president in Serbia, also with a large majority.

The republican elections altered the composition of federal bodies under the direct jurisdiction of the republics—the chamber of republics and provinces and the presidency—but not that of the second federal chamber constituted by all-Yugoslav elections. Such elections were supposed to be held in 1989 but were repeatedly postponed. The chamber's mandate was repeatedly prolonged by agreement with the republics but in violation of the federal constitution. This delegitimized the federal government: it neither had the constitutional right nor the practical instruments to impose its will upon the federal republics.

A serious blow was struck to the entire federal system in May 1991 by Serbia when it refused to go along with what should have been a routine "proclamation" of Stipe Mesic, Croatia's representative in the presidency as its president for one year. Serbians maintained that Mesic was "against Yugoslavia." This left Yugoslavia without a head of state for the first time since 1945. More important, it left the Yugoslav army without its commander-in-chief. Without the presidency, moreover, the federal government could not resort to rule by decree. The work of the federal assembly also was blocked, since its decisions required formal approval from the presidency before becoming law. It was during this period that Yugoslavia entered its most serious and, as it turned out, terminal crisis.

A month before the Mesic case blew up, Croatia and Slovenia had submitted to the other republics a joint proposal for the transformation of Yugoslavia into a loose union of sovereign states modeled on the organization and work of the European Community, with variations introduced to meet Yugoslavia's special needs. Thus, a common currency, foreign policy, and defense were to be retained—possibly also a common parliament—but the prerogatives of all central institutions were to be considerably reduced. Serbia and Montenegro rejected the proposal and indicated that they favored a federation more centralized ("a functioning federation") than Yugoslavia's under the 1974 constitution. The Serb-Montenegrin model envisaged that the two-chamber federal assembly would be retained but with the composition of both chambers modified. Instead of the republics having the same number of deputies regardless of their size and population (as under the 1974 constitution), the number of deputies would depend on the numerical strength of each nation. The provinces of Kosovo and Vojvodina would lose their direct representatives in both chambers. According to this model, the power of the federal center would be enlarged, especially in the economic sphere. In the event of their proposal being rejected, the two republics also declared their intention to seek a re-drawing of Yugoslavia's internal borders in a way that would ensure that all Serbs (and Montenegrins) lived within the same state. This proposal was unacceptable to Croatia and Slovenia. In June 1991 Bosnia and Herzegovina and Macedonia produced a third model that sought to combine features of the first two, though it leaned more toward the Croat-Slovene proposal in its affirmation of republican sovereignty.

Matters came to a head on June 25, 1991, when first Croatia and then, a few hours later, Slovenia declared independence. Both said that they had despaired of seeing Yugoslavia transformed in any way acceptable to themselves. Both based their decisions on referendums held on December 23, 1990, in Slovenia and on May 19, 1991, in Croatia. In Slovenia 93.2 percent of all registered voters took part in the referendum. Of those voting, 95 percent said "yes" to the question of whether they wanted Slovenia to become a sovereign, independent state, while only 4 percent voted against. In Croatia, the number of those participating in the referendum was smaller—86 percent of all registered voters. This reflected the situation in certain rural areas where the Serbs formed the majority and which were in a state of rebellion against the government in Zagreb. But of those who did vote in the Croatian referendum, 94 percent said "yes" to the proposition that Croatia should be a sovereign, independent state, possibly in some form of association with the other republics, as proposed by Croatia and Slovenia earlier in the year. Only 4 percent voted for the alternative, that Croatia and Slovenia should remain part of a Yugoslav federation, as envisaged by Serbia and Montenegro. Analysis of the voting figures revealed that a substantial proportion of Croatia's Serbs, most of whom live in the cities, had voted for independence, just as many Russians and other Slavs had voted for independence in the Baltic countries.

Europe's First War since 1945

In the wake of their independence declarations both republics reiterated their willingness for further talks about peaceful "dissociation." But their tactics differed. Croatia adopted a wait-and-see attitude. In contrast, Slovenia took over the control of customs and frontier posts as well as the control of airspace over its territory. The federal army thereupon attempted to wrest control of the border and the airspace from the Slovenes. It claimed that it was doing so in pursuit of its constitutional obligation to protect the territorial unity and integrity of Yugoslavia. Such an obligation existed in the Yugoslav constitution, but the army did not receive proper authority for its action against Slovenia. It could not receive it because the body that could have given it in its capacity as the army's commander-in-chief—the presidency—was paralyzed by the nonelection of Stipe Mesic as its head in May, when Serbia blocked what would have been a purely formal procedure. The lack of consensus required for such an action was emphasized by the fact that the presidency's Slovene member, Janez Drnovsek, had gone to Ljubljana after the proclamation of independence. The army claimed that the federal government, including Prime Minister Ante Markovic, had backed its action, but Markovic denied this. The federal government indeed had condemned the Slovene action as both "illegal and illegitimate," but had not ordered a full-scale attack on Slovenia and told the army to implement it. This was an important episode that marked the army high command's readiness to dispense with its previous insistence on at least some constitutional cover for its actions.

Slovenia provided the army with an unpleasant surprise. Its resistance was better organized and more determined than had been expected by the authorities in Belgrade. Not only did the Slovenes manage to keep the posts they had occupied, but they also succeeded in preventing the army from occupying the Ljubljana airport and knocking out the republic's radio and television transmitters. Within a few days, the Slovenes had managed not only to stall the army's advance and surround numerous units, but also to take more than fifteen hundred federal officers and soldiers prisoner. They also captured a quantity of arms and equipment, including tanks and armored cars. The Slovenes were able to put up the resistance they did because of their good organization and high morale, in contrast to the army's lack of organization and extremely poor morale (some soldiers were told they were being sent to fight an Austro-German invasion). The Slovenes also managed at least partly to match the army's firepower. This was because they had imported some antitank and antiaircraft rockets from Singapore and various Western countries. They also had some of their own arms. The attempt by the army high command in Belgrade to disarm Slovenia in April–May 1990 on the eve of the communists' departure from power was partially foiled—Slovenia managed to retain about 40 percent of its territorial defense arms and equipment. (A similar operation, also in the spring of 1990, in Croatia succeeded owing to the cooperation of the predominantly Serb defense apparat; it left the republic virtually disarmed.)

Underestimating the Slovenes' will and ability to resist was one of the army high command's miscalculations. Another was that the West would either endorse its "disciplinary action" in Slovenia or, at worst, condemn it only verbally. But things turned out differently. Pictures on television screens around the world of Yugoslav army tanks crashing through improvised barricades on country roads and military aircraft strafing Alpine villages had an immediate impact, not least on the European Community. From the earliest days, the EC had been the principal actor in the joint Western effort to find a peaceful way out of the Yugoslav crisis.

Behind this policy lay Western worry that the (inevitably messy) breakup of a state composed of so many disparate units was likely to be costly and that the bill for the establishment of a number of successor states would have to be paid by the West. There was also the fear that the disintegration of Yugoslavia would reopen a number of old territorial disputes involving virtually all of the neighbors (Kosovo, Macedonia, Vojvodina, perhaps even Istria and parts of Dalmatia). True, the Cold War had ended and Yugoslavia had lost its previous strategic importance between East and West. But the possibility of new conflicts involving a broad area of Southeastern Europe was certainly not welcome. There was another consideration on the minds of Western policymakers. It was that Croatia's and Slovenia's secession would set precedents for secessions elsewhere (Czechoslovakia, the Soviet Union, India) as well as close to home (France, Italy, Spain, and the United Kingdom). Over and above all, there was quite simply a reluctance to contemplate the demise of a state into which the West—the United States in the early days and the European Community latterly—had poured a huge amount of money and to which it had devoted much diplomatic support.

The outbreak of armed conflict galvanized the EC into action. On June 29 the European Council decided to send an EC "troika" consisting of the foreign ministers of Italy (the previous president), Luxembourg (president until the end of June) and the Netherlands (president for the July–December period) to Yugoslavia on a mediating mission. The EC troika visited Belgrade and Zagreb at the end of June and managed to get agreement on the following points: an immediate cease-fire in Slovenia in return for the Slovene commitment to end the blockade of army barracks and various units surrounded in parts of the republic; a three-month moratorium on the implementation of the Croat and Slovene declarations of independence; and the reconstitution of the Yugoslav presidency in Belgrade under Stipe Mesic following Serb agreement to lift the blockade on his election. There was jubilation in EC circles when the troika returned. The jubilation proved to be premature.

The first cease-fire was broken almost as soon as it was signed, the first of many such broken cease-fires in Yugoslavia. A group of fifty unarmed EC monitors was immediately dispatched to Slovenia to observe the implementation of the cease-fire, with the possibility open that they might also be sent to Croatia. Germany's proposal that Croatia and Slovenia be recognized was shelved in the EC. Germany's argument that recognition would act as a deterrent against further army attacks both in Slovenia and Croatia was not accepted by its EC partners.

Throughout July and August, fighting in Croatia not only continued but also spread to various parts of the republic. It involved the Croatian National Guard and other security formations (including some privately raised ones) on one side and, on the other, the Yugoslav federal army and the Serb irregulars in Croatia supported by volunteer units brought over from Serbia and popularly referred to as the *Cetniks*. The war in Croatia led to steady loss of territory by the Croat government in Zagreb. The European Community's four-month job as mediator effectively ended in November when the UN became the center of the next stage of international efforts concerning Yugoslavia.

In September the United Nations had passed a resolution calling for peace in Yugoslavia and instructing all its members to observe an embargo on arms exports to all sides in the conflict. In October, the UN's special envoy, Cyrus Vance, visited Yugoslavia to study the possibility of sending a peacekeeping force there. Hopes were raised that peace might be achieved by the unexpected acceptance in November by both Serbia and Croatia of the principle of stationing of UN peacekeeping forces in various areas of Yugoslavia. The way was cleared for such a force by a vote in the Security Council. Despite the agreement in principle to such a force by the federal government, the governments of Serbia and Croatia and the federal army, the plan to send a peacekeeping force to Yugoslavia hit a number of snags toward the end of 1991. The main difficulty centered on the question of where the force should be stationed: along its borders with Serbia and Bosnia, as Croatia demanded; or in and around the Serb-held territories within Croatia. The Yugoslav federal army first agreed and then withdrew its agreement to its evacuation from the Serb-held enclaves to make way for UN peacekeepers. This confirmed the suspicions on the Croat side that all the army and its Serb allies wanted was to use the UN to freeze the present territorial position—as had happened in Cyprus after the Turkish invasion and partial occupation of the island in 1974. What also made the Croats suspicious was the Serbian side's refusal to allow the stationing of a UN force inside Bosnia, as demanded by the political leaders of the Muslim-Croat majority, representing just under two-thirds of the entire population of the republic.

Deadlock within the EC over what to do next, and the apparent inability of the UN to intervene, led to a confrontation between Germany and most of the other EC members at a meeting in Brussels on December 16. Germany reinstated its proposal for immediate recognition of Croatia, Slovenia, and any other republics that asked for it. It argued that recognition could help stop the war by giving a clear signal to the army and the Serbs that their campaign against Croatia could not succeed in the long run, because the world would not accept the territorial gains made by Serbia by force.

Germany's EC partners opposed recognition—not in principle, but over the timing. They advanced the argument that recognition at that moment would undermine the UN's peacekeeping effort as well as perhaps provoke the Serbs and the army into extending the war into Bosnia and Macedonia. These critics received public backing from President Bush, UN Secretary General Javier Pérez de Cuéllar and Cyrus Vance. But Germany persisted and so, in the end, EC ministers worked out a compromise. It was that the EC would "implement" recognition of those Yugoslav republics that requested it on January 15, provided they met certain conditions: respect for democracy and minority rights and acceptance of UN and EC peace efforts. Croatia and Slovenia as well as Bosnia and Macedonia all applied (Bosnia over the strong protests of its Serbian leaders). Serbia and Montenegro did not apply.

Several things happened at the end of 1991 to speed up the final demise of Yugoslavia. Federal Prime Minister Ante Markovic, who had for months been the subject of fierce attacks in Serbia for allegedly hindering the war effort against Croatia (as well as being criticized in Croatia for not speaking out against the war), resigned on December 20. Stipe Mesic had already resigned in November as president of the Yugoslav presidency, the post which he was able to occupy in July only thanks to strong EC pressure on Serbia to lift its veto. Meanwhile, an arbitration panel established by the EC reported its own expert opinion that Yugoslavia was in a "state of dissolution." Serbia protested against this view and the EC's proposed procedure for the recognition of individual republics as an attack on Yugoslavia. Germany, which had already angered Serbia by introducing back in November a ban on trade links with Serbia and Montenegro as aggressors in the war against Croatia, angered it still further by announcing on December 23 that it had recognized Croatia and Slovenia and that it was only postponing the formal exchange of ambassadors until January 15. Germany's critics voiced their misgivings over the German actions, seeing them as German muscle-flexing and predicting that it would aggravate the situation. The United States was particularly vehement in its criticism of the German action, calling it "utterly irresponsible."

At first these fears appeared to be justified. The federal army increased its attacks against various Croatian cities, which even included some attacks with surface-to-surface missiles. But early in January, Cyrus Vance announced that both sides in the conflict had accepted the broad plan for sending as many as ten thousand UN peacekeepers to twenty-eight districts of Croatia (including places like Vukovar, occupied by the army after a siege lasting several months) before the Yugoslav army's withdrawal from Croatia. The agreement was condemned as a sellout by some local Serb leaders in Croatia and by the more extreme nationalists in Serbia itself, but it reflected an important shift in both the army's and the Serbian government's assessment of their prospects. Here the situation had shifted somewhat in the Croats' favor, leading stage-by-stage to a sort of stalemate. The army still retained its superior firepower and, thus, the ability to go on inflicting material damage on Croat cities, but suffered increasing problems with manpower—notably a shortage of skilled personnel for the armored units and the air force. The army's low morale, evident particularly during the siege of Vukovar, meant that the use of infantry had to be limited, not least because of the poor discipline and training of the Serb irregulars increasingly used to fill the gap left by former recruits from Croatia, Slovenia, Macedonia, and also Bosnia.

The Croats, on the other hand, improved their performance partly as a result of better weapons (mainly obtained from army barracks and stores where federal soldiers could be persuaded to surrender), but partly also because of their higher morale, which was understandable considering that they were defending their territory. (The correspondingly large number of Serb desertions was owing to the lack of such motivation among many Serbs, particularly those from Serbia proper.) The Croats also benefited from a more professional leadership provided by the armed forces' new commanders, notably General Anton Tus, chief of the general staff and, until June 1991, commander of the Yugoslav air force. While the Croats were not in a position to recapture their lost territories in the foreseeable future, the federal army for its part could no longer hope to occupy the whole of Croatia and impose on it a quisling government. The army's financial base was shrinking, with little hope of foreign assistance as long as it remained involved in the war for Serbia, its main base of operations. Croatia felt the pinch even more, with so much of its infrastructure devastated and hundreds of thousands of displaced people and injured soldiers and civilians to cope with. But Croatia's plight in this respect was eased by considerable humanitarian aid from the West and by the strong and continuing sense of national solidarity at home.

It was against the background of the emerging military and political stalemate that both Serbia and the army leadership began to revise their previous attitude to the UN's involvement in Yugoslavia. They had accepted it on the surface but had effectively sabotaged it by the constant breaches of cease-fires in Croatia and, even more important, through the refusal (obviously inspired from Belgrade) of Bosnia's Serbs to agree to a UN presence, which had been requested both by the Muslims and the Croats in the republic (according to provisional 1991 census results, Muslims make up 43 percent of the total population, Serbs 31 percent, and Croats 17 percent). The Croats, too, had entertained serious doubts about the UN presence. In the end, Croatia accepted the stationing throughout the republic wherever necessary. In early January 1992 both Serbia and Croatia accepted the UN proposals as outlined once again by Cyrus Vance. The January mission by Cyrus Vance was a peace effort in the right place at the right time—when both sides felt it might be to their advantage to talk and deal. Germany's recognition of Croatia and Slovenia in advance of the January 15 deadline for EC countries appeared not to have hindered the peace process under UN auspices but rather to have helped it. The war on the territory of Croatia drew to a close in early 1992, with the future shape of the rest of the former Yugoslav federation still unclear.

Toward Greater Serbia?

One thing, at any rate, was clear by the beginning of 1992: Yugoslavia was no longer likely to be put together again either by its own peoples or outsiders. This seemed to be reluctantly accepted by the community states as well as the United States in December when together with Croatia and Slovenia, Bosnia and Herzegovina as well as Macedonia all applied for recognition by the EC. One of the most vivid symbols of the final and irrevocable end of Yugoslavia was the monetary parting of the ways. On October 7, 1991, Slovenia had introduced its own currency—the tolar; on December 23, Croatia issued its own transitional Croat dinar; and on December 24, the Serb-dominated National Bank of Yugoslavia in Belgrade issued a new dinar for the rump of Yugoslavia (but with no mention of the republics as in the past). But in early January 1992, Serbia called all the parties and groups supporting the idea of Yugoslavia to a special assembly in Belgrade. The assembly, composed of the representatives of the ruling (renamed) communist parties in Serbia and Montenegro as well as leaders of Serbian groups in Croatia and Bosnia and Herzegovina, was part of Serbia's attempt to emulate Russia's bid after the Soviet Union's dissolution in December 1991 for recognition as the Soviet state's successor. The Belgrade pro-Yugoslavia assembly made little political impact, largely because it was boycotted by the Serbian opposition, which saw it as a Milosevic regime gimmick, and by all significant non-Serb parties in the other four republics.

Serbia's (and Montenegro's) pressure for international acceptance of the continuity of the Yugoslav state received a serious blow on January 15 when all EC states officially recognized Croatia and Slovenia while deferring the recognition of Bosnia and Herzegovina and Macedonia. An EC-sponsored report published on the eve of recognition stated that Slovenia fulfilled all conditions for recognition; that Croatia did also, except for some defective legislation concerning the position of national minorities; that Macedonia fulfilled all conditions too, having specifically renounced any territorial aspirations beyond its current territory; but that Bosnia and Herzegovina's recognition had to await a clear expression of popular will, perhaps in a referendum.

The report was only an advisory one, but EC governments followed it broadly. For example, certain governments stated that Croatia would have to remedy its legislation in line with the report, which its leader, President Franjo Tudjman, promised immediately in a comprehensive declaration. On Macedonia, EC governments deferred to Greece, which had demanded that, as a condition of recognition, Macedonia should change its name, thus removing any ambiguity concerning any claims to Greek territory that was part of the historic Macedonia. Having made a gesture toward Greece, the governments quietly started preparations for recognition in the near future. The continued nonrecognition of Bosnia was an attempt to assure extra time for the arrival in the republic of UN peacekeeping forces and for an agreement among the republic's three nations that would avert its division. EC recognition policies were not accompanied by the perhaps logical step of the derecognition of the Yugoslav state. This was done to allow time for negotiations on both Macedonia and Bosnia, but above all to avoid giving an excuse for an antipeace strike by the hardline rejectionist elements in the federal army and the Serbian leadership.

Nevertheless, the EC moves made it virtually impossible for Serbia to assert its position as the legal heir of Yugoslavia while pursuing the aim of a greater Serbia. Henceforth that aim had to be pursued much more openly. Serbia's war aims had never been explicitly stated, partly because Serbia's policy has been characterized by much opportunism of the "grab-what-you-can-while-you-can" variety. The maximum aim, shared by the federal army, was to keep the old Yugoslavia together under tighter central control from Belgrade. The alternative, scaled-down demand was for a greater Serbia including large chunks of Croatia as well as the republics of Bosnia and Herzegovina, Macedonia, and Montenegro. (Both of these aims implied Serbia's inheriting the Yugoslav state's international assets and membership in international bodies.) The minimalist version was also acceptable to the federal army, but even this smaller variant was in doubt after January 15.

It remained open to Serbia and the federal army to defy the UN's efforts to demilitarize the Serb-held enclaves in Croatia. But that would have exposed the army to the virtually impossible task of ensuring control of those areas at a time of almost complete withdrawal from other parts of Croatia and with direct and secure communications only with eastern Slavonia (including the city of Vukovar). Besides, the federal army faced the better-armed and disciplined Croat forces, politically backed by international recognition of Croatia. In other words, the army could no longer claim that it was intervening in a civil war to protect Yugoslavia's integrity as well as the security of Croatia's Serbs.

The Croatian Serbs' position had paradoxically weakened with the intervention of the UN, which emphasized their isolation (except in eastern Slavonia) from the main Serbian body. Not surprisingly, leaders of the Serb enclaves, notably Milan Babic, the boss of the Knin region in central Croatia, initially opposed the Vance plan. His opposition produced the first serious rift in the Serbian camp. Verbal support offered to the Serbs in Croatia by the army and the Serbian government in Belgrade failed to satisfy the Serbs in the enclaves. But there was little they could do to buttress their position in the longer term and they had to back down under strong pressure from Belgrade, including threats to stop shipments of food and consumer goods from Serbia, which had kept the Serbian-controlled enclaves afloat. The Croatian Serbs' attempt to consolidate their territorial gains and make them demographically irreversible through the policy of "ethnic cleansing" *(etnicko ciscenje),* the forcible expulsion of non-Serbs, outraged foreign opinion and strengthened the Croats' resolve to win the territories back one way or another. Thus, ironically, the bid to detach these regions from Croatia may eventually bind them to it more closely—except perhaps in the east, where Serbia has a better chance because of geographic proximity of captured territories such as Baranja (which lies between the Drava and Danube rivers).

With Macedonia becoming an independent state in 1992 (though not, at first, recognized by most states) and Bosnia managing to resist (at a huge cost in human lives) the Serb attempt to annex it, even the minimalist version of greater Serbia looks unrealizable, not the least because of its economic weakness, aggravated by the huge cost of prosecuting a war first in Croatia and then an even longer and bloodier one in Bosnia. There remains the possibility of a greater Serbia much smaller than originally planned, consisting of Serbia with Kosovo and Vojvodina with Montenegro, but even that appears unlikely. First, there is the uncertain political situation in Montenegro. In a referendum at the end of February 1992, Montenegro voted in favor of union with Serbia. The poll was low, however, and opposition is steadily growing to the policy of close union with Serbia on the grounds that such a policy is exposing Montenegro to international political isolation and economic ruin. Italy's reported attempts to detach Montenegro from Serbia by attractive economic offers of cooperation remain a threat to Serbia's hold.

Furthermore, Belgrade faces the dilemma of either making a deal with the Albanians of Kosovo that would restore to them most of the autonomy they had gained after 1974, or continuing the occupation of all or most of Kosovo and risking the danger of an explosion of Albanian discontent. Similarly, a deal with the Hungarians of Vojvodina would be a sensible course, not least because of Serbia's need to repair relations with Hungary, its northern neighbor. Such concessions, still anathema to most Serbs, would at least offer the prospect of political consolidation in Serbia and of some improvement in Serbia's international position, which would lead to more favorable financial and economic treatment. Serbian attitudes, however, would have to change profoundly for an eventual return to the two provinces' former autonomy to become politically acceptable. Such a change can occur only as a consequence of the visible failure of Serbia's war of conquest.

The army's overwhelming presence in Bosnia at the end of the war in Croatia (most military units had, by early 1992, withdrawn to Bosnia) offered the Belgrade regime and its Serbian allies in Bosnia a chance to impose a solution by force—a de facto partition of Bosnia and the annexation to Serbia of Bosnia's predominantly Serbian parts. (In Bosnia, local Serbian leaders had claimed all along that although they constituted only 31 percent of the population, they—as a predominantly rural people—were entitled to 64 percent of the territory.) One of the great attractions to Belgrade of this option was the prospect it offered of linking the Serb-controlled enclaves in Croatia with those in Bosnia and, ultimately, Serbia itself—a concept encapsulated in the Belgrade slogan *Srbija od Vozdovca do Obrovca* (Serbia from Vozdovac, a district of Belgrade, to Obrovac, a small town on the northern Croatian Adriatic coast). A powerful attraction to the army was the retention of most of Bosnia, a key strategic area and also the location of the bulk of former Yugoslavia's defense industry.

It was this option that the Serbian leaders tried in April 1992 when Serb paramilitary units crossed the Drina river (the historical border between Bosnia and Serbia) and attacked a number of predominantly Muslim towns on the Bosnian side, massacring many of their inhabitants and forcing the rest to flee. Simultaneously, the combined army-paramilitary forces surrounded a number of cities, including Sarajevo, the capital. Serb forces managed very quickly to occupy over two-thirds of the republic's territory but failed to force the official leadership in Sarajevo with its Muslim president (but also Serb and Croat members) to surrender on Serbia's terms. By the end of 1992, the military situation in Bosnia had approached something resembling a stalemate, despite the army's continuing superiority over the Bosnian government forces in firepower. An important factor here was the Muslims' rising morale in contrast to the Serbs' poor morale and discipline. After huge atrocities committed against them by the Serb irregulars (but also the army), the Muslims started to fight back and score some successes.

An important factor was the cooperation between the predominantly Muslim Sarajevo government army and the predominantly Croat forces of the Croatian Defense Council (HVC), which had a base in western Herzegovina and was supported militarily and economically from Croatia proper. It was through those Croat-controlled regions and Croatia itself that the Sarajevo government first managed to receive arms from abroad to supplement those it had captured from the former Yugoslav army barracks, thus at least partially beating the arms embargo in force equally against all the republics of former Yugoslavia. The Muslims, however, failed to roll back the Serbian forces from the areas occupied by the Serbs—though they did manage to defend Sarajevo. In the spring of 1993, having suffered huge military and civilian casualties at the hands of the Serbs, and with some half a million refugees driven out of Bosnia (most of them Muslim), the Muslims turned on the Croats in Bosnia with a view to compensating themselves for the territory lost to the Serbs. A factor here was the Muslims' fear that Croatia and Serbia would, in any case, divide Bosnia between themselves, leaving the Muslims only a few enclaves, if that. The Muslims' fears were fueled by the well-documented reports since 1990 of official Zagreb-Belgrade talks about dividing Bosnia, held in the absence of the Muslims. The suspicion of a Serb-Croat partition destroyed the confidence and cooperation that had initially existed between the Muslims and the Croats united against a common enemy—Belgrade. In the fighting in 1993, the Croats lost substantial territory to the Muslims—including most of the mixed Croat-Muslim areas that had been assigned to the Croats as part of the negotiations held in Geneva since the international conference on former Yugoslavia in London in August 1992, under the chairmanship of Lord Owen and Cyrus Vance. The fighting between the Croats and the Muslims in the first half of 1993 enabled the Serbs to make further significant territorial gains at the expense both of the Croats and of the Muslims and to tighten their noose around Sarajevo.

Despite its military successes, Serbia's long-term future remains extremely bleak, mainly because of its economic weakness. UN sanctions imposed in May 1992 on the rump Yugoslavia (Serbia and Montenegro) took a long time to start having an impact, but their long-term effect was never doubted in Belgrade, especially in terms of denial of access to international credits. In order to avert sanctions, the Belgrade leadership announced, in April 1992, a complete formal disengagement from Bosnia, including the withdrawal of the Yugoslav army from there and the handing over of its heavy weaponry to the forces of the newly proclaimed "Serbian Republic of Bosnia and Herzegovina." These moves failed to impress the EC, the United States, or the UN. The latter refused to accept the new rump Yugoslavia as a legal successor of the former Yugoslavia. Indeed, its leadership was threatened with a total international blockade if the war in Bosnia continued. It was this need to prevent total international isolation and to have the sanctions lifted that led to the appointment, with Milosevic's full backing, of Dobrica Cosic, a famous nationalist writer, as president of the new Yugoslavia after elections in May. In June, Milan Panic, an American-Serbian businessman with strong links in Belgrade, was appointed prime minister of the new state. Dismissed at first as a puppet of Milosevic, Panic started developing a strategy of his own involving a normalization of relations with Croatia, ultimate recognition of Bosnia and Herzegovina, and even concessions to the Albanians of Kosovo. Panic's moves, at first regarded by many observers as tactical and cosmetic, angered hardliners both in Serbia proper and in Bosnia and Croatia and brought him into collision with Milosevic. Since Cosic appeared to stand squarely behind Panic, the clash developed toward the end of 1992 into one between Milosevic and Cosic.

The clash ended with Panic's ouster from the position of federal prime minister in December, following elections in the same month in which Milosevic's Socialist (formerly Communist) Party won, with the ultranationalist Radical Party of Vojislav Seselj gaining the position of the second largest party. Cosic's position was considerably weakened, and he was finally ousted as federal president in May 1993. At the end of 1993, Milosevic continued to hold all the main cards, relying on his full control over Serbia's large and well-armed security forces, the administration, the media, and the countryside. This meant that if anybody were to negotiate Serbia's retreat from Croatia and Bosnia and lead it back into world bodies, it would be Milosevic, rather as Saddam Hussein did for Iraq after the Gulf War. Milosevic had outmaneuvered the other possible rivals by dividing Serbia's fragmented opposition and by marginalizing Prince Alexander Karadjordjevic, son of the late King Peter II. Initially very popular, the prince came to Serbia in the spring of 1992 apparently with the intention of becoming the figurehead of a new, more liberal regime relying on the opposition Democratic Party. Milosevic succeeded, however, in neutralizing the prince's potential appeal as the messenger of peace and international respectability by bringing Panic into play. An important factor in the prince's failure to make any impact in Serbia was his lack of political charisma and his poor choice of advisers. He thus had to return to London, his place of permanent residence, outsmarted by Milosevic and unlikely to be able to make another bid for the Serbian crown.

The opposition remains divided into a (much smaller) faction that argues that more decisive action to restore Serbia's international respectability and resume dialogue with all its neighbors is needed; and a (much larger) faction that is accusing Milosevic of not being fully behind the Serbs in Croatia and Bosnia, and worse than that, being ready to betray the Serbs there. What is helping Milosevic against his ultranationalist critics is the war-weariness of the Serb people and the growing impatience of many Serbs from Serbia proper *(Srbijanci)* with the "people from over there" *(precani)*—meaning the Serbs in both Croatia and Bosnia who have dominated Serbia's domestic political agenda and external policy for so long. Unless a sudden upsurge of social discontent occurs, necessitating large-scale use of force and a division within the core Milosevic group, Milosevic is likely to remain in the saddle for the foreseeable future.

An important role in the outcome of the struggle for power in Belgrade will be played by the army. The situation, particularly in the economic field, is well understood by the army. Its leaders realize that a collapsed Serbian economy could not support even a smaller Serbian army of the future that they are in the process of creating (virtually all the remaining non-Serbian senior officers were retired in March 1992, along with many Serbs too closely associated with the Tito era and, even more important, the defeats in Slovenia and the army's extremely poor performance in the Croatian war in 1991). But the army also has—apart from its military needs and its pride—what is referred to these days as an existential problem. This is the question of pensions for officers and NCOs retiring from the service as well as that of salaries, housing, and so on for those wishing to remain. As the example of the former Soviet army has shown, it is partly a matter of face-saving—armies must not be humiliated—but even more one of pounds, shillings, and pence. Any solution to the former federal army's problem will involve a large "constructive bribe." The question is who will pay it. There is not much money left over in the West for the strategically downgraded Yugoslavia. Most signs point to a wish by the army leadership, aware of its manpower and other problems, to disengage from all but core Serbian areas. The withdrawal from Macedonia was completed in March 1992, while the full break with the forces in Bosnia may take considerably longer. Rogue local commanders in league with militant local Serb politicians in Bosnia could delay the process of disengagement, but they cannot derail it completely. Nevertheless, even when that is completed, the story will not have ended. The danger of a conflict will remain.

The danger point will be reached in 1994–1995 when public opinion in Serbia begins to realize that, despite the victories of Serbian arms in Croatia and Bosnia, Serbia will not be able to retain its wartime gains and may, after all, be condemned—as some Serb opposition figures had been predicting all along—to an eventual reduction to the size of the preindependence *pashalik* without Montenegro, perhaps without Vojvodina, and, above all, without Kosovo. This will be the moment of opportunity for extremist xenophobic groups such as that led by Vojislav Seselj, a close approximation of a fascist boss; or a military figure such as General Ratko Mladic, the charismatic commander of the Bosnian-Serbs. To avert the danger of another Balkan war by a revisionist Serbia trying once again to act as the Piedmont of a larger Balkan state, a policy of containment will be needed—by whatever polite name it is given. Such a policy will have to involve incentives as well as threats and could be best implemented within a broader Balkan grouping, including not only states of the Orthodox tradition such as Romania, Bulgaria, and Greece (as well as Macedonia), but also Albania. The prospect of friction and instability will, however, remain.

One of the biggest problems will be how to maintain over a period of time an essentially united Bosnia. Any deal leading to its being carved into "ethnically pure" areas to be annexed by Croatia and Serbia and a small Muslim statelet in the middle would be dangerous considering the close intermingling of the three main population groups—the Croats, the Muslims, and the Serbs—which remains even after the outbreak of war in April 1992, and the large-scale population transfers that occurred as a result of it. These will not be accepted voluntarily by the Muslims who are, above all, the principal victims. International opinion still supports the idea of a united Bosnia within its present borders. Western policy failed to force united

Bosnia's acceptance on Croatia as well as Serbia and the Serb-led former federal army after the referendum at the end of February 1992 during which the republic's Croats and Muslims (60 percent of the total population) voted solidly in favor of independence—together with some Serbs who supported this option. But a heavily decentralized Bosnia as a buffer state within its historic borders, which Tito's Yugoslavia had accepted and confirmed in its 1974 constitution, still remains the only realistic solution.

Bosnia's chances of remaining an entity within its historic borders were enhanced by the Croat-Muslim agreement reached under U.S. sponsorship—and heavy pressure—in 1994. Under that agreement, Bosnian Croats and Muslims agreed not only to stop fighting each other but also to form a federation on the territory controlled by them, also open to the Serbs to join at a later date. Under a special agreement with the Croat government in Zagreb, the federation was to be given access to Croatian Adriatic ports as well as a customs union and a defense agreement with Croatia. Though not keen to join the federation, Bosnian Serb leaders did not reject the idea outright, perhaps aware of the harm their intransigence in the matter could do the campaign for the lifting of UN sanctions against Serbia and Montenegro waged by their powerful backer in Belgrade, Slobodan Milosevic.

To ensure some sort of permanence and economic viability for a continuing Bosnian entity, however, it will be essential to anchor it in an international compact, either formal or, perhaps, an informal one to start with. An international regime for Bosnia could be devised by the United States and the European Union, in cooperation with Russia and backed by the United Nations. Turkey could also play an important role here as a backer of its fellow Sunni Muslims in Bosnia. Bosnian Serbs' fears of being swamped within Bosnia by an ever larger Muslim community (the Muslims have a much higher birthrate than either the Croats or the Serbs) could be met by internationally backed guarantees such as were advanced by the EC early in 1992. Failure to reach a solution that ensures justice for Bosnia's Muslims, who suffered so heavily in the war, would bring about the very situation that so many in Europe feared: a radicalization of Bosnian Muslims, perhaps even a resort by them to international terrorism—in short, another Palestine in Europe. Another consequence would be further acts of copycat "ethnic cleansing" elsewhere, encouraged by the success of Serb "ethnic cleansing" in Croatia and Bosnia. Bosnia could become a major destabilizer for Europe and beyond.

Macedonia is perhaps even more of an international problem than Bosnia because of the historic rivalries over it among its three Balkan neighbors—Bulgaria, Greece, and Serbia. The pre-election period in the autumn of 1990 saw an upsurge of nationalist sentiment—both among the republic's Macedonian majority and its large Albanian population (nearly 30 percent according to the latest estimates).

However, the result of the November 1990 election produced a sort of stalemate. The Macedonian nationalist party VMRO-DPMNE, consciously recalling the old revolutionary movement of pre-1941 days called VMRO, won only 32 percent of all votes and 38 seats in a 120-member parliament, which was not enough to form a government. It was forced to form a coalition with the reformed Communists who obtained 26 percent of all votes and 31 seats. Quarrels among the leaders of the largest party led to the election of a respected reformist figure from the Tito era, Kiro Gligorov, as president. The Albanian Party of Democratic Prosperity of Macedonia was the third largest with 14 percent of all votes and 17 seats. The need to cooperate with the other coalition partners has restrained the influence of the more assertive and, at the same time, more pro-Bulgarian wing of VMRO-DPMNE.

Moderation in Skopje, Macedonia's capital, is well received in Bulgaria. The two countries have been growing closer. In contrast, relations with Greece have continued to deteriorate right up to and beyond the referendum on independence at the end of 1991, which produced a large, but not overwhelming, majority in favor. Many Albanians boycotted the referendum and, at an unofficial one of their own in January 1992, voted for autonomy for their parts of Macedonia. The referendum was declared illegal by the government.

Greece's bid to stop Macedonia's recognition after its referendum was resisted by Bulgaria and Turkey, both of which recognized Macedonia early on (as well as the three republics of Bosnia, Croatia, and Slovenia) to the chagrin of Greece, which claims to fear Macedonian irredentism and rejects as "cultural imperialism" Macedonia's name. As a result of bitter Greek opposition, the EC at its meeting in Lisbon in April 1992 postponed the recognition of Macedonia pending a resolution of the name problem. Greece also instituted a virtual blockade of the republic. Although it achieved de facto recognition by being accepted as a member of the UN in the spring of 1993, Macedonia remains weak and vulnerable. It has suffered badly as a result of the war in Croatia and Bosnia, not the least because of the sanctions imposed by the UN on Serbia. In the longer term, Macedonia could become once again an appendage of Bulgaria, with Turkey's backing. Bulgaria's political leaders have their hands full with the domestic situation, however, and are too busy to bother over Macedonia. Chauvinist aspirations toward Macedonia played a relatively minor role during the presidential elections in the autumn of 1991. Such Bulgarian aspirations, however, could be renewed with the result that Macedonia might be driven to seek other allies to help it preserve its independence.

The present outlook is that all these different pressures could cancel each other out and actually enable Macedonia to survive as a buffer state—especially as relations with the Albanian minority have improved and the opening of the border with Albania has reduced tensions among Macedonia's Albanians. This was one of the grounds for the special EC-sponsored commission's verdict in December 1991 that Macedonia fulfilled all conditions for recognition. One of the possible roads to reconciliation between the Macedonians and their Albanian minority would be the granting of a degree of autonomy to the Macedonian Albanians who live in the west of the country. Given the need to secure the state against outside pressures, notably from Greece, some such accommodations will likely be reached. Guarantees given to Greece, that Macedonia has no territorial ambitions, have not so far appeased Greece. Much publicity has been given in Greece to traumatic fears going back to the time of the civil war in 1946–1949, fomented from the north (including today's Macedonia). Greece, however, has resisted Serbia's calls for a partition of Macedonia between Serbia and Greece—thus far, at any rate.

In addition to various conflicts over Macedonia, there is Kosovo, perhaps the most serious flashpoint in the Balkans, largely because of the harshness of the Serb occupation and the steadily deteriorating social and economic situation in the province as well as throughout Serbia. If a more democratic structure is not forthcoming from Belgrade soon, tensions in Kosovo will continue to rise. Eventually, there is likely to be an explosion. Then Albania could become involved, but also, one by one, Greece, Turkey, and Bulgaria as well as Macedonia, Montenegro, and Serbia. Kosovo's Albanians have, since the suppression of the province's autonomy in 1989, displayed remarkable discipline and self-restraint, motivated largely by their effort to avoid giving Serbia a pretext for another crackdown in Kosovo, perhaps to be followed by mass expulsions to Albania as part of a long-term plan for the "ethnic cleansing" of Kosovo. The key question is whether this self-restraint will last.

The External Factor

The conflict in Yugoslavia in 1991 had a surprisingly small impact outside the country's borders. That was one of the reasons that the outside powers could afford to stay out for such a long time. The overflow of refugees from Croatia and Serbia's Vojvodina province troubled Hungary, but the worst effects of this extra burden on the Hungarian economy were attenuated by large-scale international aid provided to deal with the problems by various charitable bodies and international agencies in the West. In addition, Hungary marginally benefited economically from the re-routing of transit routes normally passing through Yugoslavia. Greece's trade and transport links with Western Europe suffered as a result of the war in Yugoslavia, but not to a disastrous degree. Austria and Italy coped with the inflow of refugees.

Western governments, including the United States government, continued to hope that Yugoslavia could be put together again. Essentially they waited for the conflict to burn itself out before talks could begin on another Yugoslavia. That calculation was upset by the better-than-expected resistance of the vastly outnumbered and outgunned Croats and the poorer-than-expected performance of the federal army. The CSCE mechanism established for the resolution of conflicts under its November 1990 Paris Charter was briefly brought into play, but then became neutralized by the opposition of certain states—notably Spain, Turkey, and the (then still existing) Soviet Union—who did not want precedents set for possible CSCE measures one day against themselves or their friends. For NATO the war in Yugoslavia was an "out-of-area" matter; it kept a low profile. For the Western European Union, there was no geographical restriction, but also no recognizable security threat. In August, when serious fighting began in Croatia, France suggested a WEU peacekeeping force, but the idea was dropped after serious objections by several member states, notably Britain, Germany, and Portugal. Britain's main objection was that (as Britain knew all too well from its own experience in Northern Ireland) such forces could aggravate the conflict and themselves become the target for hostility by locals. This left the EC and the UN.

The latter could not be brought into play in the early part of the conflict because of the objections by mainly non-European members such as China and India to the UN acting in domestic affairs of states (at the time, the war in Yugoslavia could still be plausibly described as a civil war within a sovereign country). As has been noted previously in this chapter, the EC enthusiastically assumed the role of the principal actor. Its effectiveness was reduced, however, by its own unresolved dilemma over what it was trying to do. Was the EC an honest broker, not taking sides but just offering diplomatic mediation? Or, was it a potential participant on the side of the victim and against the aggressor? The EC tried to avoid being pushed out of the former role into the latter one. In the end, it was forced—largely under pressure from Germany—to do something to stop the conflict. Germany's insistence that something be done provoked a split within the EC and aggravated the already existing tensions arising from Germany's unification. The EC tried to preserve at least the facade of unity in the run-up to the Maastricht meeting in December 1991, which debated the future course of European monetary and political integration. But at a meeting after the Maastricht one, the Germans forced their partners to accept that recognition must be offered to republics that want it.

The EC's failure to end the conflict led to a decision in October to bring in the UN. The UN envoy of the all-but-defunct federal government in Belgrade was asked to request such intervention. This device was insisted on by the nonaligned, many of whose members feared that authorizing a peacekeeping UN operation in what was still technically a sovereign state (though admittedly one in an advanced stage of dissolution) could create an undesirable precedent. At the start, however, the UN faced the same snags as the EC had previously—Cyrus Vance, U.S. secretary of state under President Carter, appeared to have negotiated a cease-fire only to find it almost immediately broken.

The breakthrough came at the end of the 1991. On the ground, the federal army was licking its wounds after the costly battle of Vukovar, a siege that had cost it many lives but even more prestige and credibility. Draft-dodging and desertions in Serbia were increasing amidst rising war-weariness of the entire population. Faced with serious manpower shortages and a Croatian enemy that was beginning to fight well and even take the offensive here and there, the army was already considering how best to extricate itself from a war it knew it could not win. The final push was given in December as the army started to retreat from certain areas together with its local Serb militia allies. Germany recognized Croatia and Slovenia. Continuing the war against an internationally recognized state suddenly became more dangerous, not because of any certainty that Western governments would rush to Croatia's defense but because there existed a possibility that they might. Against a Croatia and Slovenia that could now reckon with financial assistance from the West, Serbia could not muster any significant allies except, in the Balkans, Romania and to a certain extent Greece. Russia, which had just emerged out of the Soviet Union's collapse, was too preoccupied with itself to help. It was in this situation that Slobodan Milosevic, on behalf of both Serbia and the army, sued for a UN-sponsored peace, enabling them both to avoid the highly unpleasant necessity of yielding to the EC and to Germany in particular, which had for months been routinely demonized in the closely controlled Belgrade media. In the EC, the United States, and the UN, the German initiative was condemned as irresponsible and likely to lead to a widening of the conflict to Bosnia—and perhaps also to Kosovo—and Macedonia. Against all expectations, however, the cease-fire—the fifteenth since July—held. However, the EC's hopes that early recognition of Bosnia—in April 1992—would do the trick by acting as a deterrent against a Serbian invasion were disappointed. In the absence of any serious warnings of EC action to forestall such an invasion, Serbia attacked, unleashing Europe's largest and bloodiest conflict since 1945.

Will the UN add the former Yugoslavia to the growing list of countries where it has, since the end of the Cold War, been able to make a contribution? This is unlikely considering its failure to enforce the Vance Plan in Croatia, where "ethnic cleansing" by the Serbs in UN-protected zones had continued without interruption, and its still greater failure to contribute significantly to the end of the conflict in Bosnia in 1992–1994, despite an extensive humanitarian engagement on the ground. Nor does the European Union (formerly EC) emerge from the conflict in Yugoslavia with a great deal of credit. Hopes in June–July 1991 that the Community's intervention there would help erase the Persian Gulf War fiasco and prove that it did, after all, have an effective foreign and security policy were disappointed. The Community's difficulty was that Yugoslavia did not represent a really important strategic stake to any of its members any more than it did to the United States. While the Germans wanted almost from the start at least to do something to show domestic opinion that they were trying to stop an awful war close by and well reported in the media, the others did not. Therefore, the EC kept the lid on the Germans, who held back in the interest of preserving at least an outward unity in the run-up to the important Maastricht meeting in December 1991. Meanwhile, the EC sent monitors to observe cease-fires that broke one after the other, giving rise to the bitter joke: "What is the shortest unit of time?" "Why, the Yugosecond: the time that elapses between the signing of a cease-fire and its breaching."

The EC also laid on a peace conference at the Hague which began early in September 1991, under the chairmanship of Lord Carrington, former British foreign secretary, held many sessions, did a lot of useful spadework in clarifying various minority, border, and other issues, but in the end adjourned without a result because the army and Serbia still thought they could win. The EC's insistence long into the conflict that it was an honest broker and not taking sides is easy to understand. To have publicly named the aggressor (Serbia and the army) and the victim (Croatia) would have required a follow-up action, some sort of naval or aerial move such as the frustrated EC monitors suggested in a leaked secret report to Brussels in December. When recognition came, first by Germany in December 1991 and then by the rest of the Community in January 1992, the war had already reached a sort of stalemate. It had burnt itself out, at least for a while, allowing the peace process to start in earnest. The larger responsibility lies with the EC for so stubbornly clinging to the status quo in Yugoslavia at the beginning. Perhaps one of the (all too obvious) lessons here is the need for greater flexibility toward fragmenting states, a phenomenon now more frequent than in the Cold War era.

When the Soviet Union started to break up, the EC and more hesitantly the United States recognized realities sooner, perhaps because there was a vital Western interest at stake: the prevention of nuclear proliferation and even a war involving nuclear weapons between the republics.

Cynics have attributed the distinctly laid-back attitude of the United States in the Yugoslav conflict to an ulterior motive: a deliberate attempt to show the Europeans that they cannot do without NATO and the United States. It is more likely that the Bush administration after the Gulf War simply did not want to get involved in a particularly complicated regional conflict in an area of little immediate significance to the United States. Domestic Yugoslav lobbies in the United States were not able to change the *ohne mich* (leave me out) American policy, which was also reinforced by the deep American distaste for anything that leads to the breakup of states and is likely to cost the international community (the United States in particular) a lot of money to put right. Some powerful critics like former President Richard Nixon, *New York Times* columnist Anthony Lewis and former British Prime Minister Lady Thatcher chastised this attitude but made little headway, even when the more activist Clinton administration came to power in 1993.

This changed in early 1994 in the wake of a mortar bomb explosion, widely blamed on the Serbs, in the main Sarajevo market on February 5, in which 65 (mainly Muslim but also Croat and Serb) Sarajevans were killed and more than 200 injured. Under strong U.S. pressure, NATO issued an ultimatum to the Serbs to cease their bombardment of Saravejo, one of the "safe areas" designated by the UN Security Council in May 1993, and to pull back within 10 days their heavy weapons—or else risk retaliatory action by NATO. The Serbs complied with the ultimatum, though with the aid of face-saving Russian mediation enabling them to claim they were withdrawing in response to Russia's urging and not the NATO ultimatum. Within days of the Serb pullout, American F-16 jet fighters, on air patrol over Bosnia monitoring the observance of the October 1992 UN Security Council resolution banning military flights over Bosnia, shot down four Serbian fighters which had been bombing Muslim positions in Central Bosnia. Behind this new U.S. activism in NATO (as well as the U.S.-led initiatives for Croat-Muslim peace in Bosnia and for an accommodation between the Croat government and the rebel Serbs in Croatia) lay several motives. One of them was the desire by an increasingly hard-pressed Clinton administration to repair America's international image dented by botched-up foreign interventions—the one in Somalia initiated in the dying days of the Bush administration and the one in Haiti ordered by Clinton. The other—and perhaps more important—was the perceived need to reinvigorate an ailing NATO faced with a deteriorating political situation in Russia and its neighborhood following the success of hardline anti-reformist and neo-imperialist forces in the December 12 election.

The prospect in mid-1994 was for the United States continuing to play a leading role in the Balkans within a NATO-UN framework while also trying to keep Russia on board as long as possible as a useful (albeit a junior) partner nudging the reluctant and fractious Serbs towards compromise. An example of this was the so-called "Contact Group" formed in the second half of April 1994 after another confrontation—this time over the Serb offensive against the "safe area" of Gorazde in Eastern Bosnia—by the United States, the European Union and Russia to coordinate international diplomacy over Bosnia. From the Russian point of view, high-profile diplomatic involvement in the Balkans by diplomats like Vitaly Churkin acting alongside America's Charles Redman helped the Yeltsin government in its efforts to defend itself from domestic critics accusing it of being America's stooge. But talk of a U.S.-Russian-imposed "new Yalta" in the Balkans was wide of the mark, not least because of the lack of interest in Balkan ventures by the Russian military. In fact, all signs in mid-1994 pointed to Russia—whatever its ultra-nationalists might say—lacking both the motivation and the capability to reach back into its former zone of control in the Balkans or, for that matter, in East Central Europe and remaining fully occupied with the rebuilding of its sphere of control in its "near abroad."

The tragedy that occurred in Croatia in 1991 and in Bosnia in 1992–1994 could still be repeated elsewhere in the Balkans, though there is a possibility that the worst may not happen. Two things need to be done to avoid the worst-case scenario, a war involving Kosovo, Sandzak, Macedonia and the neighboring states.

1. The most urgent requirement is for a flexible but durable formula for a political settlement in Bosnia. One possibility here would be to make the European Union—within a UN-approved framework and with NATO's help—the official guarantor of Bosnia's unity and territorial integrity, with some local operational involvement on the model of the proposed EU governorship of Mostar. There is a precedent for such a solution, the one adopted at the Congress of Berlin in 1878. Serbia, backed by Russia, wanted to take Bosnia from a slowly disintegrating, defeated Turkey. The uprisings in Bosnia in 1875–1876 paved the way. But Austria-Hungary, backed by Germany and Britain, frustrated this Serbian ambition. Bosnia, while still under Turkish sovereignty, was handed to Austria-Hungary to administer as a separate body. (This time the European Union, empowered by the UN, would have something like trusteeship powers.) The arrangement worked well until in 1908 Austria-Hungary in a panic annexed Bosnia to insulate it from Serbia. The new version of the Berlin Congress formula, for which Russian backing would have to be secured, could offer a solution for today.
2. The other important move would be to build on the small but so far quite effective U.S. military presence in Macedonia and agree on an international guarantee of Macedonia's independence and territorial integrity, to be signed by the United States, the European Union, Russia and all the neighbors (including Turkey), approved by the UN and perhaps monitored by the CSCE. Greece's opposition would present a formidable obstacle, which would have to be overcome, but at least in some other respects the situation is more favorable than formerly in Croatia and Bosnia. Macedonia has, in President Kiro Gligorov, a shrewd and capable leader who has so far proved equal to the tasks he has been faced with. Macedonia, unlike Bosnia and Croatia before, is de-

militarized, the Yugoslav People's Army having withdrawn from there in 1992. The economic and social situation is not explosive, though the Skopje government's relationship with the Albanian minority remains complicated, to say the least.

The Balkans, the powder keg of Europe, could easily explode once again as the twentieth century ends. Through constructive action, however, that explosion is preventable. There is nothing inevitable about it. But it will not be a "quick fix." Purposeful, patient leadership—above all by the United States—so woefully absent in the earlier phases of the crisis in the former Yugoslavia will be needed to see the Balkans through the remaining years of our century into the next one without further wars.

VI

Greece: The Dilemmas of Change

Thanos Veremis

Situated in the turbulent Balkan neighborhood and open to economic refugees and illegal immigrants from north and east, Greece occupies the most precarious geographic position among European Community members. A steadfast ally of the West throughout the Cold War period and the most stable and prosperous country in the Balkans, Greece has witnessed a marked deterioration of its security environment since 1989. Besides having to absorb over 300 thousand destitute Albanian refugees, Greece is faced with the emergence of an independent Macedonian state, which for forty years has laid claim to parts of Greek territory. In addition, relations with Turkey remain strained owing to differences over Cyprus and the Aegean.

Greece is firmly committed to the territorial status quo in the Balkans and views the resurgence of nationalism in its northern neighborhood with great concern. Internal strife in Yugoslavia could spill over into adjacent areas, causing problems for Greece that range from a further influx of refugees to the resurgence of irredentism. Although such challenges have not been addressed effectively by either NATO or the European Community (now European Union), Greece considers its security enhanced by membership in both institutions. The most pressing challenge that the Greeks face during this period of rapid transformation, however, is shedding old ways of thinking and preconceptions that hold Greek politics hostage. Finally, Greece must address the problem of its ailing economy, which constitutes a major obstacle to its ability to play an effective role in the Balkans.

PASOK's Legacy

As a member of NATO and the EU, Greece is in a privileged position in a region characterized by increasing instability. Yet these advantages were not readily apparent to more than half of the Greek electorate during a good part of the 1980s. The Communist Party remained staunchly pro-Soviet in a rapidly changing world, while the Pan-Hellenic Socialist Movement (PASOK), led by Andreas Papandreou, appealed to the disaffected social strata of the society. Papandreou also capitalized on the ill feelings generated by American policy in Greece during the junta period and after the 1974 Cyprus crisis, arguing that "foreign imperialism" was responsible for the country's misfortunes. When the ratification of Greece's accession treaty with the European Community was brought before parliament for discussion in 1980, Papandreou and his deputies absented themselves from the debate.[1] Furthermore, the leader of PASOK promised to withdraw Greece from NATO once he had gained power.

The combination of socialism, nationalism, and populism that comprised the ideological triad of PASOK was unique in Greek politics. Even more striking was the movement's mass appeal to a heterogeneous public and its reliance on grassroots organizations and regional committees all over Greece. Although the movement's origins roughly coincide with resistance against the Greek military dictatorship, Papandreou became an interlocutor in the Right-Left debate on the civil war. To the dismay of the communists, he sought to usurp their wartime record of resistance against foreign occupation and even included in his ticket Marcos Vaphiades, the commander-in-chief of the communist forces during the civil war (1946–1949). A latecomer on the Greek political scene who had made his academic mark in the United States during the 1940s and 1950s, Papandreou championed the cause of the vanquished Left in the 1970s, when the last embers of the civil war cleavage were dying out. Although many of the issues and divisions caused by the civil war were of little concern to the younger generation, this did not impede PASOK's growing popularity nor its ability to maintain power from 1981 to 1989.

PASOK's rhetoric rekindled fears of past police-state practices and evoked the cleavage that had divided Greek society for almost three decades. Meanwhile, PASOK's widespread promises of social benefits and handouts appealed to the less privileged members of Greek society. During PASOK's tenure in power, the government promoted significant income redistribution and social benefits, but these policies were not accompanied by economic growth and were financed by loans. This, in effect, meant that the cost of social policy would be borne by future taxpayers.[2]

Papandreou's illness and his absence from the administration of power during the summer of 1988 resulted in a major turning point in PASOK's political fortunes. The various scandals that erupted in the winter of 1988–1989 severely hurt the party politically. Although PASOK's electoral percentage fell from 45.8 to 38 percent in the June 1989 elections, the New Democracy Party with 43 percent of the vote was

[1] Thanos Veremis, *Greek Security Considerations* (Athens: Papazissis, 1980), 86–87.

[2] Loukas Tsoukalis, "The Austerity Programme: Causes, Reactions and Prospects," in *Greece on the Road to Democracy: From the Junta to PASOK,* ed. Speros Vryonis, Jr. (New York: Aristide Caratzas, 1991), 197.

unable to form a government and entered a coalition of limited mandate with the communists. The electoral system, a variant of proportional representation, was set up by PASOK so as to prevent the formation of a one-party government. In the elections of November 1989, the New Democracy received 46 percent of the vote, but was unable to form a government.

Because the communists were reluctant to cooperate with PASOK, all three opposition parties in parliament formed a government of national unity under the octogenarian former banker Xenophon Zolotos as a way out of the impasse. Several months later, the deterioration of the economy forced the Zolotos government to resign. A new election was held in April 1990. New Democracy finally managed to secure the narrow margin required to form a government. PASOK won 39 percent of the vote, and the alliance of left-wing forces declined to 11 percent.

The Economic Dimension

In the last decade the poor state of Greece's economy has emerged as an important internal and external problem. If its economy had been in a healthier condition, Greece would have been in a better position to extend aid and investments to its Balkan neighbors after the collapse of communism in 1989. Given its modern harbor in Thessaloniki, Greece could become a centerpoint of commercial activity in the Balkans. Greece's economy, however, will have to undergo significant restructuring—which previous governments failed to implement—before Greece can take full advantage of the opportunities opened up by recent changes in the Balkans.

The high growth rates of the 1960s declined as a result of the 1973 oil shock. Still, GDP grew by 6 percent a year on average during the decade of the 1970s. The rate of growth in the 1980s declined to 1.6 percent a year, and by 1987 Greece's had dropped below Portugal's (until then the poorest member of the EC)—although in Greece a more equitable distribution of income has eradicated poverty. The main reason for this decline was the government's failure to restructure the economy after the second oil price shock when most developed countries moved away from labor-intensive industries to output with higher technological content. These readjustments led to rising unemployment, which Greek governments considered socially divisive. Instead of allowing uncompetitive firms to fail, PASOK undertook expensive measures to salvage them and made them the responsibility of the public sector.

Although EC membership revived foreign investment in Greece, the end of protectionism hit indigenous firms hard. High levels of consumer demand have always outstripped domestic supply, causing high imports and inflation, but PASOK's redistributive income policies further fueled private demand and worsened the chronic trade imbalance. Transfers from the EC cushioned the current account deficit while at the same time encouraging demand and contributing to a growing trade deficit. The persistent trade imbalance owed much to the high unit labor costs and low productivity. The income policy under the 1985 stabilization program reduced, within two years, unit labor costs below those in the EC, but, when the policy was suspended, the problems returned.

High inflation since 1974 is largely due to cost-push through wage increases unmatched by a corresponding rise in productivity. The slowdown in growth rates in the 1980s, however, is somewhat misleading because it fails to consider the existence of a rigorous parallel economy that defies fiscal control. As Robert McDonald has noted, "monitoring the self-employed—particularly tradesmen, professionals and landlords—is notoriously difficult and the large number of small industrial and retail establishments makes inspection of books difficult."[3] Remittances from seamen and émigrés constitute another source of untaxable income that cannot therefore be monitored accurately. Thanks to a rigorous parallel or "paraeconomy," the GDP may actually be 29 percent higher than officially recorded.[4]

The remedies for the ailing economy adopted by the New Democracy under Prime Minister Constantine Mitsotakis did not differ substantially from those employed during the successful term of PASOK Finance Minister Kostas Simitis (1986–1987). New Democracy's stabilization program strived to lower inflation to single figures, to curtail public-sector borrowing requirement (PSBR) to a level that would reduce aggregate public-sector debt as a proportion of GDP, and to cut the current account deficit to a level at which it could be sustained by nondebt capital inflows. The EC decided to grant Greece a 2.2 billion ECU loan linked to commitments on economic policy. For the above to bear fruit, austerity measures should be stringently applied that will curtail the spending power of the average Greek and will trim the public sector to more manageable levels.

Although initially slow in applying austerity measures, Prime Minister Mitsotakis had drafted a medium-term recovery program by 1991. The budget deficit was projected to reach 9.9 percent in 1993, and the public-sector borrowing requirement was expected to fall from 17.8 percent to 3 percent of the GDP in 1993. Inflation was targeted to drop from an average of 20.4 percent in 1990 to 7 percent by the end of 1993.[5] Yet these targets will be difficult to achieve. In September 1992 a barrage of measures by the government affecting social insurance, privatization of transportation, and reforms in education provoked a series of strikes that jeopardize the prospects of recovery.

High defense spending has been a consistent burden on the economy. During the last decade, Greece has ranked first among NATO countries in military expenditures as a proportion of GDP (6.6 percent in constant prices). Furthermore, the average conscription period of twenty-two months is the longest in NATO.[6] In keeping with détente in Southeastern Europe, the tripartite government of Novem-

---

[3] Robert McDonald, *Greece in the 1990s. Taking Its Place in Europe*. EIU (Economist Intelligence Unit) Economic Prospects Series. Special Report No. 2099, February 1991, p. 75.

[4] Ibid., pp. 19, 39, 53, 64, 68, 75; Panayotis Pavlopoulos, *The Paraeconomy in Greece* (Athens: IOBE, 1987).

[5] Robert McDonald, "Prospects for the Greek Economy," *Yearbook 1990* (Athens: Hellenic Foundation for Defense and Foreign Policy, 1991), 240–252. Also, McDonald, *Yearbook 1991*, 89–91.

[6] *Enhancing Alliance Collective Security: Shared Roles, Risks and Responsibilities, in the Alliance* (A Report by NATO's Defense Planning Committee, December 1988), 50.

ber 1989–March 1990 agreed on significant defense cuts, a trend that continued during the first two years of the Mitsotakis government, but was later reversed.

Foreign Policy Developments: The PASOK Legacy

During Papandreou's first tenure as prime minister, Greece sought to pursue a more "independent" foreign policy. Certain aspects of PASOK's foreign policy, however, were veritable exercises in irrelevance. At a time when the nonaligned movement was in general decline, Papandreou chose to establish ties with essentially anti-Western neutrals of northern Africa and the Middle East. When the Reagan-Gorbachev tug of war on disarmament was beginning to bear positive results, he joined the leaders of five other major states (Mexico, Argentina, Sweden, India, and Tanzania) to promote world denuclearization and continued to press for nuclear-free zones in the Balkans. Finally, Papandreou's reluctance to join with the United States and Western Europe in condemning the Soviet Union on issues such as the introduction of martial law in Poland and the downing of the KAL airliner won his government points with Moscow but created ill will in Washington, whose support was far more important for Greek security.

Stripped of its declaratory aspects, PASOK's policy toward the West did not actually differ widely from that of many Community members. Soon after his advent to power in 1981, Papandreou quietly abandoned his threat to withdraw from NATO and hold a plebiscite to decide Greece's membership in the EC. Furthermore, instead of closing the U.S. bases in Greece as he had threatened, he signed a new defense cooperation agreement in 1983. This agreement maintained the bases for five more years—although publicly he sought to portray the move as the beginning of their removal. Without any visible benefit for Greece, Papandreou consciously tried to create the impression of being the maverick of the Western alliance. It has often been claimed that the electoral support that Papandreou derived from his much publicized rebellious image justified—in his own calculations—the damage this caused to Greece's position in the West. Such claims, however, are highly debatable and underestimate the long-term damage to Greek interests caused by Greece's isolation from the overall Western consensus on foreign and security issues.

PASOK reflected a resurgent isolationism in certain segments of society that sought to protect themselves from Western competition and the dislocations of adjustment posed by closer integration with Europe. Based on a parochial sense of moral superiority but acknowledging the economic power and technology of the West, PASOK opted for the fantasy of the "third way."[7]

Both major parties, PASOK and New Democracy, shared similar perspectives regarding the problems between Greece and Turkey. Unlike former Prime Minister Constantine Karamanlis, who had conducted bilateral discussions with Turkish officials without success, Papandreou had insisted from the outset that any discussion

---

[7] Thanos Veremis, "Greece," in *Politics and Security in the Southern Region of the Atlantic Alliance,* ed. Douglas Stuart (London: Macmillan, 1988), 137, 139.

with Turkey would be tantamount to sacrificing Greek security. The Davos meeting between Papandreou and (then) Turkish Prime Minister Turgut Özal in February 1988 therefore represented a significant deviation from PASOK's basic foreign policy stand. Almost a year earlier, a crisis caused by Turkey's decision to send a research vessel escorted by warships into the disputed continental shelf region—around the islands of Lesbos, Lemnos, and Samothrace—had brought the two states close to an armed clash. The crisis was eventually defused, but it underscored the delicate state of relations between the two countries in the Aegean.

Furthermore, the enormous burden of defense spending on the Greek balance of payments and the long military service, which detracted from the government's populist image, convinced Papandreou that he needed to reduce the prospect of a possible outbreak of war between Greece and Turkey. In the spring of 1988, however, Turkish Foreign Minister Mesut Yilmaz raised the question of the "Turkish" minority in Greek Thrace and dismissed any possibility of a Turkish military withdrawal from Cyprus before the two communities came to an agreement. The Greek side soon came to the conclusion that Turkey wanted to exclude Cyprus from the Davos package while simultaneously giving priority to the issue of the Muslims in Greek Thrace. Although some progress was made in developing a set of confidence-building measures regarding accident prevention in international waters of the Aegean, the "Davos spirit" gradually lost momentum and ground to a halt in 1989.

Foreign Policy Priorities under the New Democracy

After winning the election in April 1989, the New Democracy's main task was to curtail the huge internal and external deficits while improving Greece's image as a dependable member of the West. Both priorities were associated with Greece's two main foreign policy considerations: (1) the evolving shape of the European Community, which will determine Greece's economic future; and (2) the forms of Western collective defense and security cooperation, which will assure Greece's security.

Greece, along with other southern EC members, favors an acceleration of the Community's political union through a "deepening" of its institutions.[8] In Greek eyes, broadening EU membership to include countries of the European Free Trade Area (EFTA) and the former Eastern bloc will dilute the purpose of the intergovernmental conference on political union and possibly diminish the prospects for economic and monetary union. Although Greece is ill prepared to enter the European monetary union, it is well aware that should the EU delay its political union Greece could find itself isolated in the explosive Balkan peninsula. In the field of security, many Greek policymakers favor the absorption of the WEU by the EU over the long run.

The Maastricht Treaty on European Union, adopted in December 1991, was greeted with satisfaction in Athens and was ratified in the Greek parliament with the support

---

[8] Jacques Delors, "European Integration and Security," *Survival* (March/April 1991): 99–110. See also Roberto Aliboni, ed., *Southern European Security in the 1990s* (London: Pinter Publishers, 1992).

of all parties except the Greek Communists. At Maastricht, Greece was also invited to become a member of the WEU. However, the EC's decision that Article 5 of the modified Treaty of Brussels—which provides a security guarantee in case of attack on members—should not be applied between member-states of NATO and the WEU caused considerable irritation in Athens and has somewhat diminished the importance of WEU membership from Greece's point of view.

At the same time, the WEU's decision to invalidate Article 5 in case of a Greek-Turkish conflict has renewed Greek interest in the United States and NATO as the most credible deterrents against threats to Greece's security.[9] Some in Greece believe that NATO is the only effective institution that addresses Greek security concerns and can provide the country with a role in Southeastern Europe.[10] Greece considers the CSCE to be a useful forum for problem-solving in such areas as arms control and monitoring of human rights violations, but an unwieldy mechanism for collective security.

Relations with the United States have improved as a result of the conclusion of the defense cooperation agreement in July 1990, which regulates the operation of American bases and installations on Greek soil for the next eight years. Mitsotakis was the first Greek prime minister to visit Washington since 1964. Greece's naval support for the allied cause during the Gulf War aided the positive climate in Greek-American relations. Stressing the necessity of decisively opposing invaders, Greece also made its airspace and bases available to the Western coalition's forces. The island of Crete, in particular, was an important launching pad for U.S. operations in the Gulf.

A number of developments, however, could serve to undercut the recent improvement in relations. Greek officials fear that as the United States reduces its military installations in the eastern Mediterranean, it will draw closer to the non-EU members of NATO in the region, such as Turkey. In addition, American criticism of Greek policy toward the Muslim minority and the Slavic-speaking Greeks in Greek Thrace has caused irritation in Athens. Greek policymakers see such developments as indications that the United States is interested in enhancing its influence in the Balkans and Central Asia and that it regards Turkey as a useful partner in this endeavor.

Greek policymakers recognize that Greek membership in the EU, however, is no substitute for a security relationship with the United States. In the security area the United States is the most important actor in the Balkans and eastern Mediterranean. It can tilt the security balance in the region in a way that directly affects Greek

---

[9] "After strenuous diplomatic efforts, the Greeks were accepted as full members of the Western European Union at last year's summit. Yet, they were also asked to provide guarantees that they will never invoke some of the security provisions in this organization, a requirement at best contradictory and at worst downright insulting against a full EC member." Jonathan Eyal, "A Force for Good in a Cauldron of Turmoil," *The European* (September 3–6, 1992).

[10] See the article by the influential defense correspondent Costas Iordanides, "Greece and European Security," *I Kathimerini*, 13 November 1991.

interests as well as overall regional stability. At the same time, the EU is a long way from establishing its own credible system of collective defense.

Greece and the Balkans

The collapse of communism in Eastern Europe was not greeted with enthusiasm by many Balkan states. Albania's Stalinist regime initially resisted change, despite the mass exodus of its people to Greece and Italy. Serbia considered communism as the only tissue binding its different ethnic groups together. Romania's National Salvation Front, which won 66 percent of the popular vote in the May 1990 elections, included a number of high-ranking former Communist Party officials, including President Iliescu. Finally, Bulgaria's Socialist Party, which secured 47 percent of the vote in the June 1990 elections, was actually a modified version of the old ruling party.[11]

Given the rigid structures of the Warsaw Pact and the Soviet Union's fear that institutionalized Balkan cooperation could diminish bloc cohesion, Greece placed strong emphasis on bilateralism rather than multilateralism in its relations with the states in the Balkans. The first timid attempts at multilateral cooperation initiated by Premier Karamanlis in 1976 involved meetings of Balkan experts on such subjects as transport, communications, energy, commerce, and so forth, and left political issues aside. Papandreou broadened the agenda to include political subjects by reviving an old Romanian proposal for a regional nuclear-weapons-free-zone. Although expert deliberations on the question failed to make progress, the proposal gave the multilateral Balkan forum an important political dimension.[12]

With the change in Soviet policy initiated by Soviet leader Mikhail Gorbachev, the meeting of six Balkan foreign ministers in Belgrade in February 1988, dealing with confidence- and security-building measures and minority questions, heralded a new period of inter-Balkan relations. Balkan foreign ministers have met on several occasions since then to monitor progress on issues of common interest. The meeting of foreign ministers, held in Tirana during January 18–20, 1989, examined guidelines to govern relations between Balkan neighbors, while the meeting of experts in Bucharest, May 23–24, 1989, dealt with confidence- and security-building measures.[13]

Greece's bilateral relations with Bulgaria were institutionalized with the signing of the "Declaration of Friendship, Good Neighborliness and Cooperation" in September 1986. Despite criticism leveled against Greece for its rapprochement with Bulgaria, the declaration was actually the culmination of a long process of resolving

---

[11] Geoffrey Pridham, "Political Parties and Elections in the New Eastern European Democracies: Comparisons with the Southern European Experience," *Yearbook 1990* (Athens: Hellenic Foundation for Defense and Foreign Policy, 1991), 261–268.

[12] Evangelos Kofos, "Greece and the Balkans in the '70s and '80s," *Yearbook 1990* (Athens: Hellenic Foundation for Defense and Foreign Policy, 1991), 217–220.

[13] Ibid., 220–221.

old conflicts on territorial and ethnic issues and was motivated by both states' problematic relations with Ankara and Skopje. The gradual reduction of Soviet influence in the region contributed to Bulgaria's fear of isolation, while Greece wanted to secure its northern flank in case of conflict with Turkey.[14]

The advent of the Union of Democratic Forces (UDF) to power, however, led to a shift in Bulgaria's policy toward Turkey. The October 1991 elections resulted in a narrow victory by the UDF over the Socialists and made the Movement for Rights and Freedoms (MRF), the party representing the interests of the Turkish minority, the decisive factor in forming a government. This, along with U.S. leverage over Bulgaria, increased Turkey's role in Bulgarian affairs. The failure of a summit meeting to materialize between Greece, Serbia, and Bulgaria, originally scheduled to take place in Athens in September 1991, was widely considered to be the beginning of the shift in Bulgarian policy toward closer cooperation with the Former Yugoslav Republic of Macedonia (FYROM).

The most sensitive issue, however, between Greece and Bulgaria was the decision by the UDF government in January 1992 to recognize the Former Yugoslav Republic of Macedonia as an independent state with the name "Macedonia." Bulgarian Foreign Minister Stoyan Ganev made clear, however, that this recognition did not entail Bulgaria's recognition nor acceptance of the existence of a separate Macedonian nation. Thus, while the Bulgarians refuse to accept a separate Macedonian nation, they have opened lines of communication to Skopje that would allow Sofia to renew traditional claims on this disputed territory at a later date.

There is undoubtedly considerable invention in the formative myths of all nationalisms, but since its foundation in 1945 the Former Yugoslav Republic of Macedonia (FYROM) has exceeded the norm. By appropriating a geographical term that only in ancient times signified a political (but never an ethnic) entity, the FYROM has, in the Greek view, laid claim to a past that preceded the Slavic incursion into the Balkans by one thousand years. Since the end of communism in the republic, the government of Skopje has revived propaganda suggesting that it has irredentist aspirations on Greece's territory. Greek Macedonia, with an area of 34,177 square kilometers and a population of 2.1 million, is the largest of Greece's ten regions. Although no official statistics exist on the number of Greeks with Slavic linguistic and cultural affiliations, it is estimated that a few tens of thousands are of Slavic background, and these "generally regard themselves as Greek."[15]

While the threat to Greek security posed by Skopje is negligible, the sensitivities of the inhabitants of Greek Macedonia to any challenge to their identity are acute.

---

[14] F. Stephen Larrabee, "The Southern Periphery: Greece and Turkey," in *Problems of Balkan Security*, ed. Paul S. Shoup and George W. Hoffman (Washington, D.C.: Woodrow Wilson Center Press, 1990), 191: "Noteworthy in this regard has been the expansion of military ties, highlighted by the visit of Deputy Defense Minister and Chief of the Bulgarian General Staff, Atanas Semerdzhiev, to Athens in April 1988."

[15] Duncan M. Perry, "Macedonia: A Balkan Problem and A European Dilemma," *RFE/RL Research Report* 1, no. 25 (June 19, 1992): 36.

During World War II a significant part of northern Greece was annexed by Bulgarian forces and the inhabitants underwent forced assimilation. Furthermore, the periodic closure of the borders to traffic from Greece impedes the main land artery to the West through which 60 percent of total Greek exports is transported annually.

By August 1991 Yugoslavia had almost completely collapsed as an integral state. In the September 8, 1991, referendum in the Former Yugoslav Republic of Macedonia, the Slavic majority voted overwhelmingly for independence, but the Albanian minority (26 percent to 30 percent of the total population) signaled its preference for becoming an autonomous republic, which they proclaimed in April 1992.

Greek public opinion only gradually became aware of the significance of these developments. Initially, Prime Minister Mitsotakis displayed flexibility on the question of the emerging state's name.[16] Greece's main concern was that the new state-entity should not use the term "Macedonia" without signifying its geographic confines in order to exclude an implicit irredentist claim on its neighbors. Given the Former Yugoslav Republic of Macedonia's forty-five-year history of school indoctrination and maps that include both Bulgarian and Greek Macedonia, the Greeks considered such qualifications to be essential.

In its effort to block unqualified recognition of the Republic, on December 17, 1991, Greek Foreign Minister Antonis Samaras recognized Slovenia and Croatia, thus adhering to a common EC declaration establishing conditions for recognition, which included a ban on "territorial claims toward a neighboring Community State, hostile propaganda (and) the use of a denomination that implies territorial claims."[17]

Other Greek objections mainly concerned references in the preamble of the Skopjean Constitution to the founding manifesto of the Republic in 1944, which stressed "the demand to unite the whole of the Macedonian people around the claim for self-determination."[18] The amendments to the constitution, however, did not affect the preamble.

In the meantime, the controversy over the terms of recognition hit the Greek media with full force. With a little help from both rightist and leftist politicians, public opinion was inflamed by fears that Skopje would monopolize the term "Macedonia." Although Mitsotakis privately adopted a moderate position, his precarious majority in parliament (two seats) reduced his room to maneuver. When he sacked Samaras and assumed the duties of foreign minister himself in April 1992, he was obliged by domestic circumstances to maintain Samaras's basic position. On June 27, 1992, the EC Council of Ministers in Lisbon backed Greece's conditions for the recognition of the former Socialist Republic of Macedonia.

---

[16] Interview in *Eleftherotypia*, 19 November 1991.

[17] Declaration on Yugoslavia, Extraordinary EPC Ministerial Meeting, Brussels, December 16, 1991, EPC Press Release, p. 129/91.

[18] Reference in Yannis Valinakis, *Greece's Balkan Policy and the Macedonian Issue* (Ebenhausen: Stiftung Wissenschaft und Politik, April 1992), 27. See also John Zametica, "The Yugoslav Conflict," *Adelphi Paper* No. 270 (London: International Institute of Strategic Studies, 1992), 55, concerning an interview with IMRO leader Ljupe Georgievski expressing irredentism regarding Greek territory.

Ties between Greece and Albania have been expanded through a cross-border trade agreement signed in April 1988 and the termination of the state of war that had remained in force since World War II. A year before, Greece renounced its old claims to southern Albania. After the thaw during the Papandreou period, relations vacillated between carrot and stick politics. The fate of the Greek minority in Albania, which constituted the main obstacle in Greek-Albanian relations in the past, is still a contentious issue.[19]

The Albanian elections in March 1991 allowed the Socialists (formerly Communists) to retain power but the March 1992 elections gave the Democratic Party, headed by Sali Berisha, a clear mandate. The Greek minority was represented in the Albanian parliament by five deputies of the minority party "OMONIA" in 1991, but its deputies were reduced to two in 1992 and its name changed under government pressure to "Union for Human Rights." Greece responded to an amendment of the electoral law (February 1992) that constrained the rights of the Greek minority by criticizing the amendment within the CSCE.

The deterioration of economic and social conditions in Albania have resulted in a wave of emigration to Greece—emigration that, owing to the extended borders between the two states, is impossible to control. Some 300 thousand destitute people have crossed into Greece since 1991, including members of the Greek minority fleeing oppression. These refugees pose a major social and economic burden for Greece and have exacerbated Greece's already serious economic problems. Greek efforts to deport many of these refugees have led to growing strains in its relations with Albania.

With Romania, Greece has no serious outstanding problems. Without common borders and old feuds to settle, the two states share a cultural history that goes back to Ottoman times. After the overthrow of Ceausescu, Greece was one of the first states to aid Romania and continues to act as an intermediary between Romania and the EC and NATO.

Greek-Turkish Relations and Cyprus

Greece's main problems with Turkey stem from Turkey's aspiration to enhance its role as a regional military power. Paradoxically, Greece has a stake in Turkey's westernization because the process would tend to strengthen the latter's democratic institutions and minimize its assertiveness in its relations with its Western neighbors. Although Turkey's entry into the EU has been postponed, Greece could support Turkish entry in the future if the outstanding issues between the two states were resolved.

---

[19] Estimates of the size of the Greek minority vary. The Albanians claim that there are only forty thousand, while Greek estimates range as high as 400 thousand. The number probably lies somewhere in between the two estimates. For a discussion of the minority issue, see Larrabee, "Southern Periphery," p. 191; James Pettifer, "Albania's Way out of the Shadows," *The World Today* (April 1991): 55–57.

A settlement of Cyprus is the necessary catalyst for any improvement in Greek-Turkish relations. President Bush's initiative for a solution of the Cyprus question under the auspices of UN Secretary General Boutros Boutros-Ghali in the summer of 1991 contained the seeds of its own failure. Turkey's buoyant attitude after the Gulf War made it less disposed toward constructive negotiations. Encouraged by Ankara's tough line, the Turkish Cypriot leader Rauf Denktash withdrew from previously agreed-upon principles. In the secretary general's report of October 9, 1991 (paragraph 19), there was careful reference to Denktash's "new interpretations," which would alter the nature of any solution as envisaged under the 1977 and 1979 agreements.[20] The three questions that obstructed an understanding between the two sides were the territory that will be returned to the Greek Cypriots, the powers vested in the president and vice president by the Constitution, and Turkey's claim to unilateral intervention in the island.

Mitsotakis was criticized by the Greek press for agreeing to meet with the (then) Turkish Prime Minister Mesut Yilmaz in Paris in September 1991 on the eve of Turkish general elections. The meeting foundered on Turkey's demand that resolution of bilateral differences with Greece should precede discussions of the Cyprus issue and Greek insistence that the continental shelf is the only bilateral question to be considered. Greek officials generally believe that Turkey considers the present state of affairs in Cyprus advantageous to its interests and is, therefore, in no hurry to reach an agreement that would entail surrendering some of the gains from the 1974 invasion. In addition, Greece fears that Turkey wants to change the status quo in the Aegean.

A publication distributed to foreign correspondents by the General Secretariat of the Turkish Press following the 1991 parliamentary elections stimulated particular concern in Greece and reflects prevailing Turkish attitudes. In the publication, Greek islands of the Aegean Sea are marked as "Western Anatolian Islands."[21] The commentary by the author of the publication is even more disquieting: "It must also be remembered that the population of these islands, currently under Greek sovereignty, have never regarded themselves as Greeks."[22] Shortly before forming a coalition government with Erdal Inönü's Social Democratic party, the former Prime Minister Süleyman Demirel reiterated similar positions.

Prompted by the precarious state of affairs in the Balkans, however, Mitsotakis sought to improve relations with Ankara throughout the winter of 1991–1992. His attempt to revive the Davos summit with Prime Minister Demirel and promote the conclusion of a nonaggression pact failed to bear fruit because of the lack of progress on the Cyprus question. The reluctance of Turkish Cypriot leader Rauf Denktash to reach any agreement with his counterpart George Vasiliou on the basis of UN

---

[20] S. Efstathiadis, "Plus and Minus in the Cyprus Question," *To VIMA*, October 3, 1991. Also, "Ethnic Cleansing, Cypriot Style," *New York Times*, 5 September 1992.

[21] The Turkish Dossier, "*The Aegean Problem,* " *Turkish-Greek Relations* (Istanbul: International Affairs Agency, September 1991), 20, 21, 25.

[22] Ibid., 55.

General Secretary Boutros-Ghali's "set of ideas" during meetings in New York in August and September 1992 suggests that the Turkish government is not prepared to make substantial concessions and believes that time is on its side.

Greek Policy and the Yugoslav Crisis

Greek views on the crisis in the former Yugoslavia have not been affected by secessionist tendencies within its territory or any irredentist claims on others. The Muslim minority in Greek Thrace, even if its Turkish element was to be dominated entirely by the foreign policy priorities of Turkey, constitutes a small percentage of Greece's total population. Greece, however, has renounced its claims to southern Albania and has no irredentist designs in the region.

Greece has strong historical ties to Serbia. After having fought on the same side in two Balkan wars (1912–1913) and two world wars, the two states entered hostile camps with the rise of communist power in Yugoslavia. From the very beginning of the outbreak of the Yugoslav crisis, Greece supported a form of confederation in Yugoslavia that would guarantee the rights of the country's constituent parts and prevent the subsequent strife that could destabilize the region. Drawing on its strong historical ties with Serbia, Greece has tried to act as a credible interlocutor between Serbia and the EC and has sought to keep communications open with Serbia. Greek mediation was instrumental in freeing Bosnian President Alija Izetbegovic from Serbian captivity in Sarajevo during the spring of 1992. Greece also acted as a mediator between Ibrahim Rugova (leader of the Albanian Kosovars) and the Serbian government in Belgrade throughout the latter part of 1992 in an effort to find a peaceful solution to the impending crisis. In addition, Prime Minister Mitsotakis played a key role in brokering the Athens Agreement on Bosnia—later rejected by the Bosnian parliament—in May 1993.

Greece is particularly concerned about the growth of separatist tendencies in Kosovo, the Albanian part of Serbia. The secession of Kosovo could lead to its eventual annexation by Albania, which might also aspire to the western part of the former Republic of Macedonia with its sizable Albanian minority (26 percent). Such developments would threaten to alter the external boundaries of at least two Balkan states. Given that relations between Albania, Serbia, and Bulgaria are at a low ebb, any attempt to change external boundaries would undoubtedly lead to war between them. An enlarged Bulgaria that supported irredentism on the part of the former Yugoslav Republic of Macedonia or promoted irredentism in Bulgaria itself would constitute a serious concern for Greece.

The Ottoman Factor

The final element of potential destabilization and division in the Balkans could be the reemergence of the "Ottoman factor." Since the end of the Ottoman presence in the region, the Balkans had not witnessed a Turkish involvement in the affairs of indigenous Muslims until recently. The creation of modern Turkey was based on

Ataturk's principle of a secular state. Hence, links with Balkan Muslims on the basis of a common religious heritage did not play a strong role in Turkish policy.

After the collapse of communism in Eastern Europe, however, Turkey began to place greater emphasis in its policy on relations with the Turkic populations of the former Soviet Union and the Muslims of the Balkans. This development was given greater impetus by the gradual convergence of Islam and Turkish nationalism, a process that was facilitated by the late President Özal's advent to power. The reconciliation of nationalism and Islam after the forced separation attempted by Ataturk is based on the ideology elaborated by the most influential exponent of Turkish nationalism, Ziya Gökalp, during the first two decades of the twentieth century. According to Gökalp, the Turks partook of three traditions—those of the Turkish nation, the Islamic community, and Western civilization.[23] Whereas Ataturk considered the Islamic element incompatible with his own Western orientation, it is entirely possible that the present convergence of the two other elements of Gökalp's triad will ultimately impede the prospect of Turkey's entry into the Western community. Be that as it may, since 1989 Turkey has been making inroads into the Balkan peninsula via Islamic outposts. More than 5.5 million Muslims of Bulgarian, Turkish, Serbian, Croat, and Albanian ethnic origin reside in a geographic wedge that extends from the Black Sea to the Adriatic, separating Greece from its Slavic Christian neighbors. Turkey is trying to become the champion of the Balkan Muslims and extend its influence in the region in order to enhance its strategic importance in the post-Cold War era.

Rekindling the Islamic element, however, may prove dangerous in a region already torn by separatist movements. It could be extremely destabilizing in Albania with a population that is two-thirds Muslim and one-third Christian and in the former Socialist Republic of Macedonia whose population is more than 26 percent Muslim.

Prospects for the Future

Greek policy in the Balkans—and Greece's policy more generally—will depend on the policy pursued by the new Greek Prime Minister Andreas Papandreou. Papandreou's PASOK party won an impressive victory in the October 1993 elections, gaining 47 percent of the vote against 39.5 percent for Mitsotakis's New Democracy. This gives Papandreou a solid majority in parliament and provides him a free hand in both foreign and domestic policy.

Economic issues largely dominated the electoral campaign. Foreign policy played only a minor role. Mitsotakis paid the price for sticking to his tough—although necessary—austerity program, which provoked considerable dissatisfaction among the Greek electorate. In his inaugural address, however, Papandreou made clear that he intends to pursue an active foreign policy, particularly in the Balkans.

---

[23] Ziya Gökalp, "The Ideal of Nationalism," in *Nationalism in Asia and Africa,* ed. E. Kedourie (London: Weidenfeld and Nicholson, 1970), 89–206.

While Papandreou has said that he will not recognize the Former Yugoslav Republic of Macedonia (FYROM) as "Macedonia," Greece could act as the honest broker in the Balkans if it downplays the Macedonian issue. There is a general consensus among Greek parties that the cornerstone of Greek Balkan policy is the country's relative prosperity, democratic political system and membership in NATO and the EU. These factors act as a stabilizing influence in a region that threatens Greece with isolation from Western Europe, an increase of economic refugees (there are already more than 300,000 illegal Albanians in Greece), and potential military conflagration.

PASOK's return to power, moreover, coincides with the revitalization of the Socialist parties in Bulgaria and Albania. Given PASOK's good connections with Socialist parties in the region, PASOK may be willing to help Washington improve relations with both countries if Socialist parties come to power in these countries. This could help place Greek-U.S. relations on a firmer footing. Indeed, in his first few months in office Papandreou has consciously avoided the sharp anti-U.S. rhetoric that characterized his first term in office in the early 1980s.

The strong West European desire for a peace settlement in Bosnia may also work to Papandreou's advantage. Serbia will be key to any peace settlement and PASOK's good ties to the Socialist party in Serbia may prove useful in helping to broker a settlement. A settlement would also make it easier to get the sanctions against Serbia lifted, which have badly hurt Greek business. Papandreou, therefore, can be expected to push hard for an easing of the sanctions against Belgrade.

The new Greek government's top priority, however, will be the relations with the European Union. Greece assumed the EU presidency in January 1994. However, relations with its EU partners have been burdened by Greece's imposition of an embargo against the Former Yugoslav Republic of Macedonia in February 1994. Thus Papandreou will have to steer a careful course if he is to avoid Greece's further isolation within the EU.

VII

Turkey in the New International Security Environment

Graham E. Fuller

The extraordinary revolution and turmoil in global politics unleashed by Mikhail Gorbachev, culminating in the collapse of the Soviet Union and communism itself, have left few countries untouched. The republics of the former Soviet Union and Moscow's East European empire have been the most directly galvanized; other regions have been indirectly affected as fading Cold War paradigms create new policies and interrelationships. Turkey's geopolitical environment has been remarkably affected in this period, more so than at any time since the 1920s. These international changes, coupled with important change and reform inside Turkey, suggest that Turkey is undergoing a profound transition in its international relations of a sort scarcely imaginable a decade ago. While Turkey has been one of the more responsible and sober players in the region since the foundation of the Turkish republic over seventy years ago, predictions about Turkey's future security environment—Eastern Europe, the Balkans, the Aegean, Russia, the Caucasus, Central Asia, and the Middle East—are profoundly problematic.

Traditional Turkish Geopolitics

The collapse of empire—any empire—obviously involves wrenching change for the old metropole and its newly independent progeny. Old relationships must be refounded on new footings, where history often provides very little guide. As with the collapsing Soviet empire today, the collapse of the Ottoman Empire raised major new conceptual challenges for those charting Turkey's new regional politics. What were Turkish national interests to be in the new environments of post-World-War-I Russia, Europe, and the Middle East?

Turkey's foreign policy orientation since the founding of the Turkish republic has involved several key themes. In the early days of the republic, preservation of Turkey's territorial integrity was the dominant concern: conflict with Greece, Italy, Armenia, Russia, British Iraq, and French Syria involved the establishment of new borders. For Turkey's leaders, it was not merely a question of defense and security, but also the very definition of their new, truncated, post-Ottoman nation-state.

Security involved more than relations with neighbors. Relationships with the major imperial powers of the period also had a profound impact on the degree of acceptance that Turkey might enjoy in the new international environment. Turkey's place in the new post-World War I international order was carefully wrought, involving a whole series of new legal relationships that firmly established its position both in the region and the world. Unlike many other emerging radical nationalist states, Turkey had a remarkably high degree of respect for the international order and sought to work within its established instruments.

After World War II, the emergence of Soviet expansionism posed a new set of challenges to Turkey. Turkey's international orientation was fundamentally driven by the Soviet reality—down to the emergence of Gorbachev's *perestroika*. It is now evident how greatly the global character of the Cold War "corrupted" the "normal" character of international relations in the region. Today, as Russia struggles to grasp and reformulate the character of its "true" national interests, the national interests of other states are also all affected by that same process.

Turkey must now reassess not only its security needs in the new international environment, but also the possibility of at least partial reformulation of its national interests in the light of new circumstances. Reformulation of national interest is not, of course, an easy task. Far from being an objective process, the conceptualization of national interest involves often conflicting visions—political, economic, and cultural—of different partisan groups. Should Turkey be European or Muslim, associated with the capitalist or socialist world, friends of the First World or the Third, interested in narrowly conceived state interests, or a broader pan-Turkic vision?

The Domestic Element in Turkish Foreign Policy

Turkish politics had already begun to change well in advance of the Gorbachev revolution. The late President Turgut Özal, arguably one of the most influential political figures on the Turkish scene since Ataturk, helped effect a profound reorientation of Turkish domestic policies that have direct impact on Turkey's foreign policy as well. Although these new policies and developments evolved under the supervision of Özal, the basis for them had been slowly forming for a long time. Özal was the primary catalyst—and a remarkable, if controversial, one.

The first major area of change was the renewed move toward democracy in the wake of military intervention in 1980. The Turkish military has frequently during past decades intervened in internal politics by assuming power when the top military leadership concluded that the country was drifting toward anarchy. These political interventions have been very controversial within Turkey, and various motives have been attributed to the military interventionists. Whatever case may or may not be made for the wisdom of such military intervention, in practice democracy ultimately seems to have been strengthened and widened after each intervention, regardless of the laws passed in the immediate aftermath. Turkey has quite simply been growing more accustomed to the practice of democracy and the proliferation of political views. This gradual evolution in the direction of ever greater democracy, while far from complete, strengthens Turkey's standing among the nations of the world in which democracy is seen as a basic value.

Today, Turkish democracy, while incomplete, is leading to the development of a society more willing to consider a broader range of ideological issues, to debate long-forbidden issues such as communism, Islam, and the Kurdish issue in ways that will ultimately strengthen the nation. In a period when chaos will predictably be a major feature of political events in the Balkans and all over the former Soviet Union—not to mention the Middle East—the international system benefits from a nation whose stability and track record for international prudence is by and large impressive. (In this context, I would view the Cyprus issue as a major exception, where Turkey, rightly or wrongly, chose to move unilaterally rather than in conjunction with international instruments to influence the course of that crisis.)

The second, and perhaps even more radical, internal change in Turkey is in the economic sphere: the abandonment under Özal's direction of nearly seventy years of statist policies and a reversion to an open-market economy. These policies not only brought an extraordinary surge of growth to the economy, but lent it an international orientation that directly affects foreign policy. Turkey saw major new opportunities for markets in the Middle East, not only in Iran and Iraq during the Iran-Iraq war, but also in the Arabian peninsula and North Africa. The presence of economic interests in that area inevitably raised Turkish political consciousness toward Middle Eastern politics as well.

Turkey's new export-oriented policies sharply increase its interest not only in the Middle East, but in the developing economies of the Balkans, the Black Sea, and the new independent republics of the former Soviet Union. Most of all, it increases Turkish interest in Western Europe, where Ankara views the frustrating quest for integration in the EU to be an important foreign policy goal with major political implications. This opening of Turkish economic policies, partially akin to the process of *perestroika* in the Soviet Union or the *infitah* in Egypt, has still not run its course.

Turkey now possesses an international orientation unprecedented in its past. Whereas foreign policy—basically isolationist in character—had long been the exclusive preserve of a highly skilled and educated foreign policy elite, today Turkey's external economic interests serve to widen the base of foreign policy formulation and to interject newer elements of broader public opinion into the process. This process is still under way, and is resisted by the foreign policy professionals—as in all countries.

The popularization of foreign policy does not, of course, automatically lead to stability in the foreign policy process. Public opinion is usually far more fickle and nationalistic than the foreign policy establishment of any country; it is quite possible that the sobriety that has so long characterized Turkish foreign policy will be increasingly affected by other interests. These interests include economic and commercial goals that the business community might urge upon Turkish foreign policy; Islamic groups and sentiments that introduce an "Islamic factor" into Turkish foreign policy; and nationalist or pan-Turkic impulses that increase Turkish interest in the Turkic world to the East.

Lastly, in a world in which massive reevaluation of national interests is under way—starting in Russia and stretching to the United States at the end of the Cold War—Turkey may need to rethink the character of its national interests in ways not considered before. Here the democratic upsurge in Turkey will facilitate the process of policy reformulation. Already much of the revered Ataturkist tradition—so valuable and critical to the nation's survival in an earlier era of Turkish history—is now being reexamined. With a lessening of Ataturkist values—statism, isolationism, elitist paternalism, avoidance of Islamic and pan-Turkic ideological interests—factors such as nationalist or pan-Turkic and Islamic ideologies have greater room for influence. Neither of these ideological policies in themselves can be described as purely negative or positive: the value of such policies depends entirely on the wisdom with which they are implemented.

Under any circumstances, Turkish internal politics has been undergoing profound change in the last decade, coinciding with the Gorbachev revolution in the Soviet Union. In a way, the Özal era bore some resemblance to the Margaret Thatcher era in the United Kingdom: a period of remarkable change, radical new directions, of stimulating, creative, controversial, and provocative policies that wore out the electorate. In the end, these factors, coupled with rising inflation and nepotism around Özal's family, brought Özal's party to significant defeat in the elections of October 1991, leading to a new coalition government headed by veteran conservative politician Süleyman Demirel.

Demirel did not seek to dismantle any of the major changes introduced by Özal; indeed, they were not truly the issue so much as the style of Özal himself—and the growing disparity between rich and poor. The policies and principles of the Özal era have been firmly absorbed into the life of modern Turkey and are not likely to be repealed. Demirel did not shrink from dealing with the rapidly evolving Kurdish question that will have major impact on the internal policies of the future Turkish state.

Cooperation with the United States will remain a key feature of Turkey's policies, but expectations about the character of that relationship may move away from the heavily military-intelligence arena and into broadened economic and development ties. New issues emerging in the region are increasingly vital to Turkey itself, and gradually less vital to U.S. post-Cold War policies. U.S. influence over Turkey's foreign policies is, therefore, likely to diminish in the next decade, regardless of who comes to power. And the role of internal politics will now be more important than ever in formulating the Turkish national interest and the policies it pursues.

Turkey and Russia

Despite the stunning changes in the former Soviet Union that augur well for the future international role of Russia, the policies of Russia—the one country in the region theoretically capable of invading and taking over Turkey—will always be closely watched in Ankara. The history of Russian-Turkish relations over the centuries provides sufficient evidence of the importance of this massive political land mass to Turkey's north. And the new arms control agreements between NATO and the former Soviet Union are of less comfort to Turkey than to Western Europe. Major elements of the Russian armed forces have now moved east of the Urals, relieving pressure on the West, but arguably increasing potential pressure on Turkey. Turkey will, therefore, maintain a cautious vision of Russian power in the decades ahead, regardless of what progress is made in West European-Russian relations.

But the end of communist ideology and the emergence of "new thinking" in Soviet foreign policy suggests that Russia is now much less likely to threaten Turkey's territorial integrity. It also suggests that Moscow, too, now has far less reason to fear a strong Western presence in Turkey, and will be much less interested than it was in the 1970s in seeking to destabilize Turkey as a means of weakening NATO's power. In this sense, Turkey no longer represents any military threat to Moscow, either. And the Turkish Communist Party, in whatever form it may continue to exist, will no longer be seen as an instrument of foreign influence in internal Turkish politics.

The past Soviet threat to Turkey has not, however, had a purely negative impact upon Turkish interests. It was specifically this threat that enabled Turkey to develop much closer ties with Western Europe and the United States over the past forty years. From that point of view, some elements within the Turkish state may regret the diminution of the Soviet threat to the extent that it will weaken NATO and Turkey's special role within the alliance. For other more independent-minded elements, the lessening of the Soviet threat increases Turkish foreign policy options.

Even Turkey's strategic relationship with the former Soviet Union is now assuming a different character. Overnight Turkey's once contiguous borders with the Soviet Union are gone, having given way to relations with emerging independent states that will now serve as buffers between Russia and Turkey. All of these new entities or states-to-be are relatively small—Azerbaijan, Armenia, and Georgia—and, thus, present no direct military threat to Turkey. The potentially growing instability of many of these states, however, suggests new complications for Turkish interests and relations in the decades ahead. Georgia is in the midst of a brutal civil war, and contentious ethnic relations with its neighbors and its own minorities are likely to perpetuate turmoil. Armenia and Azerbaijan present far more serious problems for Turkey. The two new states are virtually in a state of war with each other over the issue of Nagorno-Karabakh, which is the Armenian enclave inside Azerbaijan. Passions and national sensitivities are running so high that the conflict has so far defied resolution. The emergence of the nationalist Azerbaijani Popular Front to power in mid-1992 further raised tensions as Azerbaijan openly appealed to Turkey to intervene on the side of their "Turkic brothers" in Azerbaijan. While Turkey has made great efforts to remain neutral in the quarrel, Armenian military action in the Karabakh area has raised popular emotions in Turkey in favor of Azerbaijan. Worse, it has virtually erased the very promising rapprochement in Turkish-Armenian relations in 1991 in which Erevan showed signs of realistic assessment of the need to get along with Turkey, and to which Ankara reciprocated. The longer the Karabakh conflict continues, the greater the stress it will impose upon Turkish-Armenian relations. Direct entry by Turkey into the conflict would have very serious repercussions on the area, and likely bring Turkey in conflict with Iran and even Russia.

The Azerbaijan problem also raises other extremely critical problems between Turkey and Iran. The nationalist government of Azerbaijan has openly called for the Azerbaijani population of Iran—perhaps some 10 to 15 million people—to break away from Iran and to unite with Azerbaijan. While the Azeris of Iran remain Iranians, or truly a Turkish people integrated into Persian culture, relations between Iran's Azeris and the republic of Azerbaijan will remain a source of major friction. Eventually, it could even result in the loss of as much as one-quarter of Iran's population and a huge section of northern Iran in a breakaway movement that would cripple Iran. Given Azerbaijan's attitude, Iran may look to Turkey as the moving force behind pan-Turkism in Azerbaijan. Turkish-Iranian relations thus face a very real prospect of serious deterioration for the first time since World War I—all brought about by Caucasian politics.

Far more than just the Caucasus is involved. Well to the east, the Muslim republics of Central Asia are all Turkic—with the exception of Tadjikistan. As these republics continue to develop their nationalist feelings, the importance of their Turkishness is likely to push them toward greater focus on Turkey. Turkey has always been the natural center of the Turkish world; Ankara may come to represent for many of these republics a more attractive alternative window to the West than Moscow. All of them are interested in attracting Turkish investment and trade, although they are pragmatically looking for help from whatever quarter it might come. The problems are not simple, in any case, because potentially the wholesale reorientation of economic relations of the entire region is involved, with the opening of the long-closed southern borders of Central Asia. What new patterns of economic and political relations will emerge across the swath of Central Asia and how will they involve Turkey? These new opportunities open dramatic new economic and strategic perspectives to Turkey's geopolitical interests.

All these startling new geopolitical metamorphoses will have unpredictable consequences on the nature of Russian-Turkish relations. Russia initially may have viewed Turkish influence in the Turkic republics of the former Soviet Union as a potentially benign and moderate force for secularism and restrained nationalism. Now that these republics are independent, Russia may view Turkey's influence, however moderate, as rival to Moscow's own desire for influence there. Under any circumstances, Turkey's relations with Russia are now vastly more important than at any time in modern history, because Turkey is likely to be so involved in the affairs of almost all states directly to the south of Russia. How cooperative or competitive those relations will be remains to be seen.

Yet, it has not been easy for the policymakers in Ankara, either, to consider developing special relations with the Muslim and Turkic areas of the former Soviet Union. The Ataturkist legacy expressly warned Turkey of the dangers of involvement in pan-Turkic or irredentist policies. Such advice made very good sense in the past in view of the Soviet Union's abilities to visit punishment upon Turkey for support of such provocative activities. Today, however, there is far less reason for Turkey to avoid close ties with these republics. Ankara will have to gauge the trade-offs involved in its relations with Russia at all times, and those trade-offs are not yet clear. On the one hand, if unfriendly relations should develop between the Central Asian republics and Russia, then Turkey's role in the area will be far less welcome to Moscow. On the other hand, closer Turkish-Central Asian economic ties could also work to Russia's benefit and open for it, too, a new gateway to the east and south.

The range of Turkey's potential ties extends yet farther east into China, where the large Turkic minority of Xinjiang province is in increasing contact with their fellow Turks across the Sino-Soviet border. Growing Turkic nationalism is likely to be viewed as an even greater danger in China than in the former Soviet Union, presenting in their minds a threat to the integrity of the multinational Chinese empire. Economic benefits could flow from these contacts, however; serious discussion is under way about rail links running from Beijing to Xinjiang, Kyrgyzstan, Uzbekistan, Turkmenistan, Tehran, and Istanbul—a de facto "Turanian line" that will certainly heighten cultural awareness and cultural contacts among all these Turkic areas.

It will be some time before Turkey moves toward a "Turkic"-oriented foreign policy. Ataturk's strong antipathy to ethnic adventurism is deeply imprinted upon Turkish statesmen. If Turkey finds, however, that many of its options for membership in the European Union (EU) are increasingly closed—as they now seem to be—Ankara may find advantage in broadening the vision of its foreign policy to include more Turkic-oriented policies. Some violation of the Ataturkist legacy has already occurred in this area with Turkish support for the Turkish Cypriots and the Turkish population of Bulgaria. Turkey has also expressed interest in the Turkmen population of northern Iraq, which brings it into conflict with Baghdad. It is not a far reach for Turkey to develop closer ties with Azerbaijan and even some of the Central Asian states. But at the same time, Turkey will not wish to jeopardize the important relations it has with Russia.

While the Ataturkist tradition is still strong in Turkey, it may be weakening in some respects as Turkey's internal situation continues to undergo profound change in the economic, political, and social spheres. Public opinion and the press tend to be more interested in the "external Turks" (*dis Turkler*) of the world than is the foreign ministry itself. If a more strongly nationalist movement were to come to power, the country could well adopt a bolder policy toward the external Turks. The character and consequences of those policies are largely unpredictable, but they will raise Turkey's profile and clout immeasurably in the east.

Turkey and the Balkans

Turkey is no stranger to the Balkans after so many centuries of Ottoman domination. In a sense, Turkey has never really had a chance to develop "normal" relations with most of the Balkan states since their integration into the Soviet empire over forty years ago. Indeed, for this same reason, Balkan politics themselves have not evolved "normally" during this period. Just as in the post-communist USSR, the post-communist era in the Balkans opens up new questions about the character of future relations among these states as they regain true independence after the long communist night. What will be the new lines of alliance among the various Balkan states?

One geopolitical fact is quite evident: Turkey will now be the strongest power in the Balkans, rivaled only by Ukraine and more distant Russia and Germany. The growing geopolitical power of Turkey will, therefore, affect emerging balances of power in the region.

Greek-Turkish enmity has long characterized the eastern flank of NATO. If anything, Greece will be more anxious about Turkey's growing population and rising economic and geopolitical influence. Such anxieties are likely to cast Greece into a search for Balkan allies to balance Turkish power. Independent Bulgaria could join Greece in the common perception that Turkey is the great power to be neutralized in the region; yet, Greece and Bulgaria are at odds over independent Macedonia. Will other Balkan states, therefore, see their interests as lying with Greece? Or will perhaps potential new enemies of Bulgaria and Greece—such as Albania—act on the basis that "the enemy of my enemy is my friend" and lean toward Turkey?

The collapse of Yugoslavia will powerfully affect the formation of other alliances in the Balkans. Serbia is clearly attempting to establish itself as the residual power within former Yugoslavia; its brutal efforts to control Herzegovina and the Muslim region of Bosnia with a stronger hand have deeply angered Turkey as well as the rest of the world. The Bosnian Muslims—living in a sea of Orthodox Slavs—now look to Turkey for support, at least on the moral level. The presidents of Bosnia and Albania privately visited Özal in Turkey in the summer of 1991. Clearly they see Ankara as a counterweight to pressures upon them. But would Turkey alter its historic determination to remain aloof from most pan-Islamic issues? Here again, a nationalist regime in Ankara in the future might view its interests differently and could opt to inject itself more closely into Balkan politics. Truly ethnic Turks reside almost exclusively in Bulgaria and Grecian Thrace; the remaining large Muslim populations of Albania and Bosnia are not Turks, but Turkish public opinion popularly considers them Turks and urges supporting them.

Turkey's preference to remain neutral in regional struggles, to avoid alliances other than with NATO, may well remain the basic constant of its Balkan policies in the future. If Greece and Serbia are already committed to an anti-Turkish posture, however, Turkey may have no choice but to gravitate toward other states more sympathetic to Turkey. That well may only be predominantly Muslim Albania and Bosnia—if it survives as an independent state. Serbian anti-Turkish instincts have always run deep. Belgrade is deeply suspicious of all former Yugoslav Muslims, and its relations with Orthodox Romania appear good. Slovenia and Croatia will inevitably be Western- and German-oriented. These states are not likely to look with any special sympathy upon Turkey except as a counter to Serbia. Thus, the Turkish role in the region raises questions. For Ankara, the wisest—and most traditional—course might be to avoid alliances of all kinds and to seek open relations with all Balkan states, especially as these states are in a position to affect Turkey's own future relations with the EU.

Turkey's role in the region will be further enhanced with the development of the Black Sea Economic Zone cooperation project, which was designed to link the interests of all the states of the Black Sea—Turkey, Bulgaria, Romania, Ukraine, Russia, and Georgia—with a few other regional states with interests there: Greece, Albania, Moldova, Armenia, and Azerbaijan (not Iran). The idea as first proposed by Turkey was to facilitate economic interchange by means of free trade among the Black Sea states, long isolated from one another by the politics of the Cold War. This broad approach to regional politics should enhance Turkey's position and provide greater benefits than would perhaps a more narrow, ethnically or religiously based policy in the Balkans. The organization has much to offer all its members; in the third "summit" in Istanbul in June 1992, its leaders signed an agreement formalizing the economic framework, while recognizing that ethnic rivalries in the area may hinder implementation of parts of the treaty for some time. The organization could well even evolve into a regional political forum to discuss those same political issues that affect the region. The ultimate complementarity or rivalry of its members' economic interests must be examined closely, however, before hypotheses can be drawn about the ultimate impact of economic factors on the politics of the area.

Balkan politics have been liberated far too recently to allow any firm judgments to be drawn about new interrelationships. As complex as Balkan politics have always been, they are now further complicated not only by a different kind of Russia, but by an independent Ukraine as well that has no geopolitical track record in the region whatsoever. Ukraine could well prove to be the state closest to Turkey in the entire Black Sea region.

Turkey and the Middle East

The impact of change in Soviet policy has reached the Middle East as well, sharply affecting the environment around Turkey. Initially, the oil boom of the 1970s, coupled with Turkey's shift toward an export economy in the early 1980s, brought Turkey into the Arab world even before the Gorbachev revolution. Turkish construction know-how was exported to the Arabian peninsula and Libya early in the 1980s. Then, the Iran-Iraq war also had a major impact on the Turkish economy as Turkey became the single largest trading partner for both Iran and Iraq, as a transit point and as a source of products to meet their heightened needs during the war. Turkey was already beginning to reorient its trade toward the Middle East.

The Persian Gulf War brought greater change to traditional Turkish foreign policy.

Whereas Ankara traditionally would have maintained strict neutrality toward conflict in the Middle East, on this occasion, Turkey, under the strong prodding of Özal, came down four-square on the side of the allies and the UN Security Council, committed its own troops to the conflict, and permitted Turkish airbases to be used by the allied forces in offensive air-strikes against Iraq. The Turkish press also indulged in discussions of the Turkmen minority in northern Iraq, suggesting a clear-cut Turkish interest in the welfare of Turks outside Turkey. A challenge had been laid to Iraq; Ankara did not shrink from hostile relations with Iraq given its interests in increasing Turkish leverage with the United States, NATO, and throughout the region.

The conflict with Iraq also unleashed the Kurdish issue anew. Ankara took a major step forward in granting Turkish Kurds the right to use the Kurdish language in public—and unofficially in publications. There is talk of greater reform in the Kurdish areas of Turkey. Most important, Turkey has now begun to recognize explicitly the existence of the Kurdish problem and to entertain discussion about how to cope with it. It is explosive, and eventually could threaten to push Turkey into a federal state—perhaps even partition.

Solution of the Kurdish problem in Turkey cannot be separated from the issue of the Kurds in Iraq and Iran. Undoubtedly, the Kurdish issue will be looming far larger in Turkish politics in the coming decade than in the previous ones. The issue will likewise involve Turkey in the internal affairs of both Iraq and Iran to the extent that the Kurdish problem is common to all three states. This Kurdish problem, the human rights problems that spring from it, and the sympathies many in the West have for the Kurds—all hurt Turkey's interests in the West and complicate its relations in the East as Arab states and others perpetuate suspicions toward Turkish intentions on the issue.

Turkey's status in the Middle East is also affected by the possible evolution of a new security regime in the Persian Gulf. With the continuing Western demand for secure oil supplies and the likelihood of the eventual collapse of the Gulf monarchies, security issues there will remain high on the international agenda. Turkey has always been considered a potentially important player in any effort to construct a broader Persian Gulf security system. Ankara's serious involvement in the Gulf War also suggests that important Turkish geopolitical interests will be affected. At this point, however, few in the Gulf area would welcome Turkish participation in a regional security arrangement. Turkey has for so long been identified with Western security interests that only the smaller Gulf sheikhdoms might welcome the balance that Turkey could bring. Most Arab states, including Egypt, want to keep Gulf security an Arab affair; Iraq would be strongly opposed, as is Iran. Thus, Turkish membership in any such security arrangement would probably come in the context of a broad regional organization supported by the United States.

In reality, the Middle East today is the most volatile region of the world, and an area where the de facto threat to Turkey is greater than ever before—even in comparison with the traditional threat from Russia. The proliferation of weapons places

Turkey well within range of the evolving missilery of many regional states while the region remains totally devoid of any kind of arms control—in conspicuous contrast to NATO's long-term dealings with the USSR. Weapons of mass destruction used against Turkey are no longer a purely theoretical threat; Turkey may well believe that it must move itself to develop such capabilities rather than depend on the uncertain guarantees of other Western powers that have already proven reluctant to back Turkey in regional conflict.

The emergence of new independent Turkic republics in the Soviet Union is likely to create additional frictions between Turkey and Iran. Both Turkey and Iran believe that they have "special ties" with Central Asia—Turkey because of Central Asia's Turkic character; Iran because of its centuries-long cultural domination and previous frequent political control of parts of that region. Rivalry for influence exists, although it is neither as volatile nor for as high stakes as in the Caucasus.

Turkey's future role in Arab politics remains uncertain. Basically, the Arab states continue to view Turkey with minor misgivings, based on Turkey's previous imperial role in the region and, more important, its membership in NATO and general support for Western interests. Can Turkey be "trusted" by the Arabs to be sensitive to the political aspirations of the Arab world? So far, their answer is negative.

Turkish relations with most Arab states have not been cordial during the Cold War, during which many important Arab states stood on the Soviet side of the struggle. The Arab-Israeli struggle further polarized the region. While Turkey has always supported the creation of a Palestinian state, it has also enjoyed fairly good, if low-key, relations with Israel.

If a comprehensive settlement to the Arab-Israeli settlement should emerge in the next few years, the face of Middle East politics will be further changed. The polarity of the confrontation with Israel will tend to give way to a less clearly unified body of interests among the Arab states. After a settlement with Israel, it will be more difficult for any Arab state to dictate what "Arabism" is or to demand Arab unity in the face of a major challenge. In an Arab world whose politics are more fractured, Turkey can more readily enter into closer political relations with other Arab states.

In short, the Middle East itself is undergoing major changes, some as an indirect result of the convulsions in the former Soviet Union. Turkey will face more new challenges, new openings, and new opportunities for influence than at any time over the past half century. Turkey may react slowly to these opportunities, but it is unlikely to ignore them. Will we see a new, broader formulation of Turkish national interests that might involve it more closely in regional competition? Eventually, that is possible, which is precisely the reason that the EU continues to entertain doubts about Turkish membership in the EU—because of anxiety about Turkish "involvement" in the Middle East that could prove complicating to the EU. Turkish policies for this reason will thus be closely scrutinized by European states. Turkey will have to decide how much it will allow the development of its other interests in the east to be held hostage to EU likes and dislikes. The Kurdish issue alone is likely to prove a serious point of friction between Turkey and Europe.

Turkey and Europe

Turkey's deepest foundations in Europe over the past forty years have been with NATO. NATO has served two functions. First, it has provided critical defense guarantees to Turkey against possible Soviet expansionism. While left-of-center elements in Turkey have questioned the degree of that Soviet threat, the saga of a Soviet republic in Iranian Azerbaijan during and after World War II and the Soviet invasion of Afghanistan made it difficult to argue that Soviet expansionism was an unrealistic threat. Second, the Soviet threat provided the major rationale for Turkish inclusion in the heart of West European security concerns. This association was valuable to Turkey because it anchored it in the eyes of the United States and Europe in the broader European context, which helped to fulfill a long and deeply held Turkish aspiration to be considered a European nation. Indeed, the collapse of the ideological mainspring of Soviet expansionism now raises questions about the depth and extent of Turkish involvement in European affairs.

The issue of Turkish membership in the European Community (now European Union) has long possessed its own particular complications relating to the compatibility of the Turkish economy with that of Western Europe. If Turkish membership in the EC was uncertain before the collapse of the Berlin Wall, the emergence of the East European states as independent entities today has vastly complicated the European economic and social equation: it is more difficult to gauge Turkey's role in the EU now when the "European status" of its East European neighbors is far from resolved.

If Turkey is not afforded EU status in the decade ahead, one of the powerful determinants of Turkey's economic development will be sharply affected. What then are the economic factors in Turkish national interest? Direct trade ties with the United States? With Eastern Europe? With the Black Sea states? With the independent states of the former Soviet Union, including Russia itself? Or with the Middle East? Where will the most effective sources of economic complementarity lie? Turkey's search for alternative trade ties is already prejudicing its case for full membership in the EU.

Turkish ties with Europe will continue to contain some element of a security relationship as long as NATO continues to exist. Even in the event that NATO atrophies, CSCE security relationships also involve significant Turkish cooperation. But major questions now arise in Europe's own view of its security arrangements. How broad will that concept of security be?

If turmoil in the former republics of the Soviet Union remains an active threat to European security, then Turkey, as a critical part of the NATO structure, will maintain an important position in regional security affairs. If there is a chance that a resurgent and expansionist Russia may yet emerge on the world scene, then Turkey's defense role is again vouchsafed. But Russia as a direct military threat to Europe seems unlikely in the next decade or so, given the death of the ideology that gave rise to the former Soviet challenge. Russia is likely to remain preoccupied in the future with internal problems of unity and the need to establish a firm economic foundation.

Today Western Europe is naturally asking the hard questions about Turkey. In crudest terms, how much should Western Europe interest itself in Turkey's future? What are the likely threats to Turkey today? How much are West European security interests affected by non-Soviet security threats to Turkey?

The Gulf War posed this question in a new and ambiguous way. Turkey's political activism and commitment to the United States, NATO, and the allied cause was appreciated, lending weight to Turkey's claim that it associates its own interests with Western interests. Yet, Turkey's very activism and the emergence of its own independent interests vis-à-vis Iraq also proved disquieting to states in Europe such as Germany that are concerned about the Turkish agenda in the region. Conversely, do the Turks not have a role serving as "middleman" to Western interests in trade and stability in Central Asia, as Ankara itself suggests? Or does a more activist Turkish role in the Middle East and the Muslim regions of Russia spell a Turkey that might drag Western Europe into conflicts in the Middle East that are of limited interest to Europe? The Soviet threat was very much part of the European security agenda, but Middle Eastern issues are less clearly so, especially when they include problems such as resurgent Kurdish nationalism within Turkey itself.

European "National Interests"

The question of Turkey's future security role in Europe will, therefore, depend primarily on Europe's own formulation of its long-term interests. How Eurocentric will the future EU be? Under the startlingly different world conditions now coming into existence, will the term "Europe" come to include all of Eastern Europe? All of the Balkans? Ukraine? Russia? Turkey—on more than an honorary basis?

Equally important will be Europe's evolving view of the Muslim world. The Muslim character of Turkey, despite its responsible international conduct over the past several decades, does remain a consideration in European thinking. Muslim societies tend to be viewed in the West as representing different styles and value systems than Western countries. How "European" will Turkey really be over the longer run? That will be an often unspoken issue on European minds in the next decade.

As former President Özal himself often pointed out, however, Europe should be interested in Turkey not in spite of its Muslim character, but precisely because of it. The chances are very good that nationalism and religion will become increasingly important factors in international politics in the next decade and the next century. The modern world, perhaps in reaction to the rampant internationalism and cultural homogenization that modern communications have brought us, seems to crave ever more deeply expressions of particularism, regionalism, and uniqueness of cultural identity. While international tensions on a global level are likely to recede, not to be polarized again as they were during the Cold War, local conflict will now be freer to rise. Local conflict is less dangerous, is no longer likely to spark global nuclear war between the superpowers, and may now even be of limited interest to most of the great powers of the world. Thus, local conflict will become more commonplace, and the search for expression of national identity will be an important characteristic of those conflicts, certainly in parts of Eastern Europe and perhaps even in parts of Western Europe.

If there is a danger of a polarizing factor in international politics that could again tend to divide the world into warring camps, it very likely could be a function of the old "north-south" conflict, or the "haves" versus the "have-nots." What would be even more disturbing would be the emergence of Islam as an ideological factor aligned on the side of the have-nots. Muslim countries are among the most intense in their search for a way to preserve their religious-cultural identities. It is important that Islam not be encouraged to move in the direction of supporting any kind of "North-South" confrontation.

It is in this area that the depth of the European political vision matters greatly. Will Europe seek to limit its political and economic unity to what are essentially the "Christian" nations of Europe? Will a de facto Christian versus Muslim political divide emerge, recreating a neo-Crusader mentality on the part of either Christians or Muslims? Turkey's role in Europe is of particular importance. The case for Turkish membership in Europe should indeed be strengthened by the very fact of its being Muslim. Turkish membership suggests a cultural diversity for Europe that will be of importance in European dealings with other Muslim nations. Turkey thus can serve as a bridge between the two cultures; it can strengthen its own commitment to European political values while seeking to preserve many of its own Muslim cultural values. If Turkey could play such a role, it would be an important model for the rest of the Muslim world as well.

European relations with Turkey are, of course, far from being the only intimate ties between Europe and the Muslim world. The development of a concept of a Mediterranean union of some kind immediately links all of Southern Europe with the Levant and North Africa. By any standard, North Africa is a neighbor of Europe; the relations across the Mediterranean are more significant for North Africa than are its horizontal relations across North Africa. The Turkish role in the EU thus becomes merely one facet of a potentially more complex concept of Europe and its periphery. Muslim migration to Western Europe, already well advanced, will require close political and economic links between Europe and the Muslim states of the region to enable this process of migration and integration to occur more gradually and smoothly. The integration of these Muslim states into Europe in some capacity will also play a major role in the secularization and democratization of that area of the world—helping establish a new and moderate form of Islamic civilization. If this cultural fusion cannot develop, and is instead blocked by deterring the integration of Muslim states into Europe, then harsh cultural confrontation is likely to emerge in the region in the next century. The question of Turkish membership in the EU embodies this choice.

Conclusion

We are experiencing a period of extraordinary international change. Turkey is one of those countries sitting in the eye of the hurricane as change swirls around it. Whereas for decades Turkey was at the tail end of Europe in geopolitical terms, today Turkey is at the center of a new geopolitical world of great importance and volatility. Turkey has basically been a source of considerable stability and predictability in past decades. Will Turkey continue along the same cautious course that has marked its past policies—defined by a Eurocentric focus, a neutrality toward most conflicts in the Middle East, and an avoidance of irredentist and revisionist policies as relates to most countries of the world? (Cyprus, Bulgaria, and Iraq show that Turkey has actually made significant exceptions in eschewing involvement in the affairs of the external Turks.) Or will Turkey also be affected by regional change and begin to explore new paths in the expression of its national character? Under more negative circumstances, for example, a more nationalist-chauvinist Turkey could emerge—championing the rights of all Turkic peoples everywhere. These trends fly in the face of Turkey's policies of the last seventy years, but they do exist, however modestly so far. The issue remains open. My guess is that Turkey will remain relatively cautious in pursuit of its foreign policy for many years to come in these new treacherous waters. But we will see a Turkey more interested in a role of influence and leadership among the external Turks, more interested in the economic benefits of ties with the Muslim states of the region, and perhaps more assertive of its goals in Europe. A more activist direction would seem the most likely for Turkey to pursue in the coming decades.

A change of policy need not imply a destabilizing policy. It suggests, however, that Turkey will not be able to be taken for granted, and that its own national interests will be more openly expressed, which would complicate the policies of the region as a whole. Turkey will figure more prominently in the politics of all the regions around it, with the possible exception of Western Europe.

PART 2

Regional Security Problems

VIII

The Strategic Environment in the Balkans and the Mediterranean

Ian O. Lesser

The strategic environment in the Balkans and the eastern Mediterranean has been strongly affected by the sweeping changes in international affairs over the past few years. The new prominence of Mediterranean security issues on the European and American security agenda, encouraged by events in the Balkans and the Middle East, is fast eroding the region's position on the strategic periphery. At the same time, the sense of increased security in Central and Northern Europe brought on by the political transformation in the east, the collapse of the Warsaw Pact, and the strategic contraction of the former Soviet Union, has hardly been mirrored in the Balkans where traditional antagonisms persist and flourish and political revolutions remain half-made. To these must be added a range of new concerns, many of which are a product of developments in the Middle East.

The thesis of this chapter is straightforward—that the Mediterranean, and above all the Balkans-eastern Mediterranean region, has emerged as a dominant center of risk in the new Europe. As such, it will demand the increasing attention of Europe and its institutions, and, by extension, the interest and involvement of the United States as a European power. Moreover, by virtue of history and geography, the region is linked to Middle Eastern as well as European security. The following discussion suggests some trends affecting the strategic environment, and considers alternative approaches to thinking about the region's role in security terms—that is, as an extension of the European security canvas; the "place where the Persian Gulf begins"; and as an area of strategic consequence in its own right.

Strategic Change in the Mediterranean and the Balkans: Some Trends

East-West Disengagement

Since 1945, developments in the Balkans and the Mediterranean, particularly those concerning NATO's southern region, have been viewed overwhelmingly in relation to the Cold War and the East-West strategic competition. Indeed, the Balkans and the eastern Mediterranean featured prominently in the early history of the Cold War.[1] Yet, with the exception of periodic crises, the general level of interest in regional security problems in the area never approached the consistent attention devoted to defense in Central Europe. The predominant role of nuclear forces in strategic thought throughout most of the postwar period tended to focus attention on the defense of "core" interests in Europe. This encouraged the neglect of security problems outside NATO's central region, and especially in Southern Europe where the perception of the Soviet threat was relatively distant and diffuse and security as a whole more conventional in character.[2] In the prevailing climate of political relaxation and military disengagement in Europe, the Atlantic alliance as a whole has perhaps come to resemble the traditional conception of its southern region. As security perceptions reflect a waning of the Soviet military threat, less reliance is placed on the nuclear aspects of deterrence, and regional concerns assume a more prominent place on national and institutional agendas.

In the immediate aftermath of the political revolutions in Eastern Europe, there was considerable concern that new opportunities and requirements in the east would absorb material and intellectual attention that might otherwise have been directed toward Southern Europe and the Mediterranean. In economic terms, these fears have not yet been realized. The limited ability of the reforming economies in Eastern Europe to absorb large-scale investment together with Western concerns about the character and pace of political change, particularly in the Balkans, have introduced an element of restraint that recent events in the former Soviet Union may only reinforce. Meanwhile, developments in the Adriatic and the Gulf have prevented, and indeed reversed, any diversion of strategic attention toward the east. Notwithstanding the costs imposed by participation in the Gulf coalition, this reversal of fortune has been most pronounced in the case of Turkey.

The end of the Cold War has already released numerous explosive ethnic tensions that have implications for security beyond national borders and beyond Europe's regions. The civil war in the former Yugoslavia, with all that it implies for the political evolution of the Balkans and Eastern Europe as a whole, provides the clearest example of what is at stake, even beyond the prospect of disastrous refugee flows. The disintegration of the former Soviet Union will directly affect the welfare and

---

[1] See, for example, Bruce R. Kuniholm, *The Origins of the Cold War in the Near East: Great Power Diplomacy in Iran, Turkey and Greece* (Princeton: Princeton University Press, 1980).

[2] See Diego Ruiz Palmer, "Paradigms Lost: A Retrospective Assessment of the NATO-Warsaw Pact Military Competition in the Alliance's Southern Region," *Comparative Strategy* 9 (1990).

security of the Black Sea region and could pose enormous dilemmas for Turkish policy toward the southern republics.

In the Middle East, the waning of the East-West competition has reduced the risk of superpower confrontation, but has also removed many of the superpower-imposed constraints on the behavior of regional actors. It is arguable that, under Cold War conditions, Moscow would never have "permitted" Iraq to invade Kuwait for fear of the escalatory risks involved. The central and eastern Mediterranean is home to important actors whose behavior may be shaped by the absence of traditional Cold War considerations—most notably Libya, Syria, Iraq, and Israel. Their actions, in turn, will influence the security environment facing Greece and Turkey.

If the revolution in East-West relations has increased the risk of conflict affecting the Balkans and the Mediterranean, it has also made possible various new initiatives for cooperation in a regional context. Prominent examples include the Italian-sponsored Central European Initiative (formerly Hexagonale Group), Balkan cooperation, and Turkey's proposal for economic and political cooperation in the Black Sea. In a broader sense, the CSCM (Conference on Security and Cooperation in the Mediterranean), in which Italy and Spain have been most active, is also a product of the new environment in which the demilitarization of East-West relations has given greater freedom of action to small and medium powers, encouraging the pursuit of regional initiatives. Notably, these initiatives, while reflecting a new interest in regionalism, emphasize the acceptance of existing frontiers. For Italy, Greece, and Turkey, these proposals are both useful vehicles for political activism and evidence of a desire for political reassurance in an uncertain security environment.

Europeanization and Its Limits

Across most of the countries that have traditionally constituted NATO's southern region (Portugal, Spain, Italy, Greece, and Turkey), attitudes toward foreign and security policy are increasingly European in character. One consequence of this trend has been a progressive decline in the distinctiveness of the southern region within the Atlantic alliance, and a convergence of security perceptions within Western Europe. To the extent that Europe as a whole worries less about Russian intentions and capabilities, and becomes more concerned with security and security-related problems emanating from the Mediterranean, this convergence is likely to be even more pronounced. The strategic implications of this trend are at least twofold.

First, bilateral patterns of cooperation with the United States will be affected by the growing importance of the transatlantic security discourse with the European Union, even in the absence of an operationally potent European defense organization. It is less and less thinkable, for example, that individual southern European countries will be willing to grant the United States the use of bases and overflight rights—or to contribute military forces of their own—for contingencies outside the NATO area if their EU partners are unwilling to do so. As the recent coalition experience in the Gulf demonstrated, the growing requirement for a European consensus on defense cooperation with the United States outside Europe does not preclude extensive cooperation, but will limit the United States' freedom of action in those cases where a clear convergence of interests does not exist. In sum, the era in which the United States could count on the assistance of one or two key allies in Southern Europe in conducting operations unpopular within the European Union as a whole has probably passed.

Second, Turkey, as a participant in neither the EU nor the WEU (and whose prospects for full membership in both organizations remain poor), is increasingly isolated from the process of Europeanization shaping the rest of NATO's southern region. To the extent that Turkey's postcontainment, post-Gulf War, strategic importance continues to be seen in Middle Eastern rather than European terms, Turkey's distinctiveness within the alliance will be reinforced. As the current situation suggests, the problem facing Turkey in the wake of the Cold War is less that of strategic neglect broadly defined with its political and economic consequences, but rather the narrower and more potent risk of exclusion from the European security equation and its effect on Turkey's relations with the West. As the EU moves to develop a common foreign and security policy, it will be more difficult for the Union to accept the additional burden of a direct exposure in the Middle East that Turkish membership in the EU or the WEU would impose.

An Expanding Security Canvas

The concept of Mediterranean security is expanding both geographically and functionally in a manner that will influence security perceptions in the Balkans and elsewhere. More precisely, the content of the security debate is growing, a phenomenon reflected in the NATO context by the notion of "an expanding southern region." The U.S. perception of the southern flank has never been limited to NATO's five southern allies and the direct threats to their security. Conflicts and crises in the Middle East and the Persian Gulf, including the problem of assuring access to oil supplies, have played a key role in U.S. strategy toward the Mediterranean. European, and particularly southern European, security interests in the south have traditionally been drawn along more limited lines.

In the emerging strategic environment there may well be a greater degree of convergence between Southern European and American perceptions with regard to the scope of Mediterranean security, as problems of stability and development in North Africa receive greater attention on a bilateral basis, within the EU, and in new initiatives on security and cooperation such as CSCM. With regard to the latter, there is a strong intellectual and practical rationale for defining the Mediterranean region in broad geographical terms, and expanding the definition of security to include social, economic, and political, as well as military factors.[3]

[3] "Non-papers" and other documents outlining national views on CSCM are assembled in *The Mediterranean and the Middle East After the War in the Gulf: The CSCM* (Rome: Ministry of Foreign Affairs, March 1991).

Character of Security in the Eastern Mediterranean

There will continue to be certain significant differences between the western and eastern Mediterranean in security terms. Without ignoring the existence of territorial issues such as the future of the Spanish enclaves in North Africa, and the problem of conventional and unconventional proliferation that spans the southern and eastern shores, the most pressing problems in the western and central Mediterranean are overwhelmingly political and economic in character. The demographic imbalance between a prosperous north and a poor south, and the resulting immigration pressure, is not a security problem in the direct sense, although friction over immigration policy could encourage a more general deterioration of north-south relations in the Mediterranean, thereby increasing the risk of conflict over other issues. By contrast, in the eastern Mediterranean, the potential for open conflict is much closer to the surface and the level of armament considerably greater. Even in the wake of the Cold War, the strategic stakes in the eastern Mediterranean will remain high, drawing the attention and involvement of the United States and, at lower but still significant levels, the successor entities of the former Soviet Union. The concentration of security risks in the eastern basin of the Mediterranean, including those flowing from the Arab-Israeli and Aegean disputes, friction between Turkey and its Middle Eastern neighbors, the use of the Suez Canal, and inter- and intrastate conflict in the Balkans, suggests that a Mediterranean approach to security and cooperation becomes more difficult as one moves east. Certainly, security initiatives in the eastern Mediterranean will be more demanding of the active involvement of extra-Mediterranean powers.

Migration

The movement of large numbers of people in response to violence or political and economic pressures is likely to be a persistent concern for Italy, Greece, and Turkey, particularly in the absence of rapid and positive change in Albania, Bulgaria, and Romania. The social and economic costs imposed by these movements have already contributed to a "reassessment" of national security in the Adriatic and Aegean regions. In historical terms, of course, economic migration and refugee flows have played a consistently important role in shaping the strategic environment in the eastern Mediterranean.[4] If one includes the problem of Kurdish refugees and the very large movements of ethnic Turks that might follow from further instability in the southern Soviet republics, it is clear that issues of migration will occupy a prominent place on the strategic agenda of policymakers and strategists around the region.

Continued refugee flows and prolonged lawlessness in the Adriatic region could impose considerable costs on Italy and Greece. The response may be a strategy of

---

[4] See, for example, the extensive treatment of population and migration issues in Fernand Braudel, *The Mediterranean and the Mediterranean World in the Age of Philip II* (New York: Harper and Row, 1972, first published 1949).

physical interdiction in the short term, or longer-term economic assistance to limit future migration, or both.[5] As separatist movements gather momentum in Macedonia and possibly elsewhere in the Balkans, the control of arms shipments may emerge as an even more pressing concern.

Communications and Resources as Strategic Issues

As a result of their position on the periphery of the European economic space, Greece and Turkey will have a strong stake in the maintenance of unimpeded transport across the Balkans and the Adriatic. The prolonged closure of the Yugoslav land link to the European market would be particularly troubling at a time when European economic integration is the focus of attention. Greater reliance on the maritime link across the Adriatic would raise new commercial issues and perhaps reinforce the commonality of strategic interest between Greece and Italy. Economic development in Eastern Europe, coupled with new regional initiatives in the former area of the Austro-Hungarian Empire, may also lead to a revival of Trieste as a link between Central Europe and the Mediterranean. As the Eastern European economies continue to move away from Russian sources of energy supply and toward reliance on the world oil market, such links will become even more important. The result will be new actors with a stake in the stability of the Adriatic and the Mediterranean.

The strategic environment in the Balkans and the eastern Mediterranean will also be shaped by resource and resource-related issues. Access to energy supplies, in particular those arriving via the Suez Canal and oil pipelines terminating in the Levant, will be a continuing source of European and U.S. interest in the region. Before the Gulf War, more than half of Europe's oil imports were obtained via the Mediterranean. The shipment of Iraqi oil through Turkish pipelines, halted as part of the program of economic sanctions following the invasion of Kuwait, will undoubtedly resume at some point. In the near term, the resumption of shipments will facilitate the payment of Iraqi reparations. Over the longer term, the desire to diversify the shipping routes for Gulf oil, avoiding an overreliance on Hormuz, is likely to reassert itself strongly.

The control over water resources will be an important dimension of the strategic environment ashore in the eastern Mediterranean, with potentially important implications for Turkey's relations with Iraq and Syria. As with oil, it is unlikely that water and other resource-related objectives will serve as causes of conflict in their own right—that is, in the absence of underlying regional ambitions and fears. In

---

[5] Greece absorbed perhaps 150 thousand migrants in 1990–1991, including thirty thousand Pontian Greeks from the Soviet Union, fifty thousand Albanians (perhaps half of whom are ethnic Greeks), and eight thousand Romanians. Marlise Simons, "Acharnai Journal," *New York Times*, 5 August 1991. In the third such exodus of 1991, at least eighteen thousand Albanians arrived in Italian Adriatic ports, resulting in the announcement of over $120 million in humanitarian and economic assistance to Albania from Italy and the EC. *Los Angeles Times*, 13 August 1991.

combination with wider territorial and political concerns, resource issues can exert a strong influence on national strategies and provide a spark for conflict.[6] This could also hold true for resource issues in the Aegean, as well as for fishing and environmental disputes elsewhere in the Mediterranean.[7]

Overall, an expanding definition of security in Europe as a whole is likely to result in increased attention to the Balkans and the Mediterranean for the simple reason that, in the absence of renewed East-West competition, many of the most prominent security and security-related problems will emanate from this region. An expanding security canvas may also suggest an expanded set of participants. To the extent that Germany begins to recast its defense policy to address risks outside Central Europe, and to support allied strategies outside the NATO area, the Mediterranean will be the first and most natural outlet. Indeed, a sizable portion of the German navy was deployed into the Mediterranean in support of NATO operations during the Gulf crisis.[8]

The Mediterranean as a Center of Security Concerns

The Mediterranean will be a center of residual military power even in the wake of conventional arms control agreements and unilateral reductions, as significant arsenals in the Maghreb and the Levant remain unaffected. To these must be added the U.S., former Soviet, and European naval and naval air forces that remain outside the Conventional Forces in Europe (CFE) framework. As a result, the link between European arms control and increased security is more ambiguous in the Mediterranean context, and perhaps least automatic in the Balkans. Countries around the region will be justifiably wary of future initiatives that might alter regional balances, particularly between Greece and Turkey, and among Turkey and its Middle Eastern neighbors. More broadly, the large and increasingly sophisticated arsenals along the southern and eastern shores of the Mediterranean suggest a future in which there will be a greater balance of military capability between north and south.[9] One consequence of this trend may be the growing significance of major nonlittoral states in regional deterrence after the Cold War.

---

[6] See Ian Lesser, *Resources and Strategy: Vital Materials in International Conflict, 1600-Present* (London: Macmillan and St. Martin's Press, 1989).

[7] See Giacomo Luciani, "The Mediterranean and the Energy Picture," and Gerald H. Blake, "Mediterranean Non-Energy Resources: Scope for Cooperation and Dangers of Conflict," in *The Mediterranean Region: Economic Interdependence and the Future of Society*, ed. G. Luciani (London: Croom Helm, 1984).

[8] The presence included seventeen vessels and 2,200 men. *Foreign Broadcast Information Service-West Europe Report*, February 19, 1991, p. 22. See also Jonathan T. Howe, "NATO and the Gulf Crisis," *Survival* (May/June 1991).

[9] Roberto Aliboni, *European Security Across the Mediterranean*, Chaillot Papers, no. 2 (Paris: Institute for Security Studies, 1991), p. 6; see also Laura Guazzone, "Threats from the South and the Security of Southern Europe" (Paper delivered at the Institute for Strategic and International Studies 10th Anniversary Conference, Lisbon, November 8–10, 1990), 13–15.

Some Consequences of the Gulf War

The experience of the Gulf War has reinforced existing concerns about the post-CFE military balance in the region. First, the war strengthened fears with regard to the proliferation of unconventional weapons—chemical, biological, and potentially nuclear—together with the means for their delivery at longer ranges. The continuing proliferation of conventional as well as unconventional arsenals, coupled with aircraft and ballistic missiles of increasing range, could transform the strategic environment in the Mediterranean, directly affecting the countries of the Balkans. Looking strictly at the Mediterranean littoral, Israel, Syria, Egypt, Libya, and Algeria all possess ballistic missiles of varying range and accuracy, and are seeking to acquire more capable systems.[10] In the absence of a parallel nuclear capability, these systems are unlikely to alter the outcome of potential conflicts around the Mediterranean (most of which are south-south, rather than north-south), but their presence may exert a strong influence on strategic calculations along the northern shore of the Mediterranean. In particular, the threat of retaliation against population centers in Southern Europe or Turkey could complicate decisions regarding intervention in the Middle East or the support for U.S. or allied operations outside Europe.

The recent threat of Libyan retaliation against targets in Spain and Italy in the event that bases in these countries are used to attack Libya suggests the possibility of more serious incidents on the pattern of the 1986 missile attack on the island of Lampedusa.[11] Crete, with its U.S. facilities, would be similarly vulnerable. The era of the "sanctuarization" of military facilities and population centers in Southern and Southeastern Europe in regional conflicts may be drawing to a close, which has important implications for relations across the Atlantic as well as the Mediterranean.[12] In some respects, of course, the Balkans has never been a sanctuary in relation to conflict in the Middle East, as the prevalence of international terrorist incidents in Italy and Greece suggests. Efforts to limit the proliferation of nuclear and ballistic missile technology as well as more prosaic weapons in North Africa and the Levant may well lead to demands for European, U.S. and Soviet naval and air reductions in the Mediterranean as a quid pro quo. Alternatively, countries in the southern and eastern Mediterranean may become less enthusiastic about regional arms control, preferring to develop their own defense capabilities unimpeded by restrictive regimes.

Second, and more broadly, the Gulf crisis encouraged a keen awareness of the linkage between events in the Middle East and attitudes and developments in North Africa. Although the worst fears of many Southern European observers proved

---

[10] See Janne E. Nolan, *The Trappings of Power: Ballistic Missiles in the Third World* (Washington: Brookings, 1991); Martin Navias, "Ballistic Missile Proliferation in the Third World," *Adelphi Paper* No. 252 (London: International Institute for Strategic Studies, 1990); and W. Seth Carus, *Ballistic Missiles in the Third World: Threat and Response* (Washington: Center for Strategic and International Studies, 1990).

[11] "Foreign Ministry Reacts to Al-Qadhafi Threats," *FBIS-West Europe Report*, July 29, 1991, p. 21.

[12] Guazzone, "Threats from the South," 13.

unfounded, the potential for a north-south confrontation across the Mediterranean sparked by future events in the Gulf or elsewhere in the Middle East cannot be ruled out. To the extent that Europe develops a more activist stance with regard to crises outside Europe, the risk of a strong reaction from North Africa will grow. So too, uncertainty about the political future of North Africa has given additional weight to existing southern European concerns with regard to proliferation. Southern European countries face the difficult task of bolstering deterrence in relation to risks from the south without encouraging the view, already widespread across the Mediterranean, that a militarization of north-south relations is emerging in the wake of the Cold War.

Third, the Turkish role in the Gulf coalition has resulted in growing Western attention to Turkey's position in the Middle East and the vulnerabilities and military modernization requirements flowing from this. The transfer of equipment "cascaded" to Turkey under CFE, together with expanded U.S. security assistance to Turkey, will help to address long-standing modernization needs, bolstering deterrence in the Middle East.[13] Meanwhile, this assistance will give rise to considerable anxiety in Greece and Bulgaria about the longer-term effects of Turkish defense improvement on the regional balance in the Balkans.[14] Much will depend on the context within which this strengthening of Turkish defense capability takes place. If accompanied by a new policy of Turkish activism in the Balkans, the effect on regional perceptions could be quite pronounced.

The United States and the Mediterranean

The level and character of the U.S. involvement in the Mediterranean will play an important part in shaping the strategic environment in the region over the next decade. This involvement is hardly new. The United States has been a Mediterranean power in at least a limited sense for almost 200 years, and its military presence is not simply a transitory phenomenon flowing from the requirements of the Cold War. As the East-West military competition in Europe wanes, the continued concentration of the U.S. presence in Central Europe would do little to respond to new security problems emanating from the Mediterranean, and might worsen the prospects for a continued U.S. presence in Europe, at whatever level, by raising German "singularization" concerns. In a period in which forces are being reduced across Europe, the essential question is not one of additional presence, but rather residual presence and its location.[15] If the Mediterranean is becoming more important to the

---

[13] Under NATO's Equipment Transfer Program, Turkey is to receive some 1,050 M-60 and Leopard tanks, 600 armored combat vehicles and 70 artillery pieces, as well as 40 F-4 fighters, attack helicopters and surface-to-air missiles. Greece will also be a substantial recipient of cascaded equipment, including 700 tanks, 150 armored combat vehicles, and 70 artillery pieces. *Jane's Defence Weekly*, July 6, 1991.

[14] See, for example, Yannis G. Valinakis, *Greece and the CFE Negotiations* (Ebenhausen: Stiftung Wissenschaft und Politik, June 1991), 23.

[15] The economic and strategic implications of a U.S. withdrawal from southern Europe are treated

security—broadly defined—of Europe as a whole, it is likely to become more important to the United States as a European power. In principle, this suggests that the U.S. military presence in and around the Mediterranean is likely to be the most durable dimension of its future presence in Europe.

Traditionally, the U.S. presence in NATO's southern region has served to promote the cohesion of a theater with diverse or even conflicting security interests, and to couple security across Europe's regions as well as across the Atlantic. In the wake of the Gulf War, there will be a further and important need to balance the European and Middle Eastern dimensions of Mediterranean strategy. The planned transfer of the 401st Tactical Fighter Wing to Crotone in Calabria will be relevant to security in both arenas, and a valuable hedge against reductions in naval presence as a result of economic stringency or, less likely, naval arms control. The base itself could facilitate the rapid deployment of forces to the eastern Mediterranean and the Middle East, and could support the sort of multilateral initiatives that are likely to be a central feature of future security arrangements in the Mediterranean (for example, a NATO rapid response force and a permanent naval force).[16]

Russian Interests and Behavior

The collapse of the former USSR and Russia's current economic weakness suggest a declining level of Russian military presence and activism beyond its immediate borders. A number of former republics will, however, retain a strong political and economic interest in access to the eastern Mediterranean. In the past years, roughly 30 percent of all Soviet imports and exports have flowed through the Black Sea. The former Soviet Union also made intensive use of the Suez Canal, with over one thousand transits each year.[17] There has been a marked expansion of Soviet—and more recently Russian—economic and political relations with Turkey in recent years. The Turkish proposal for economic cooperation in the Black Sea is a reflection of perceived political as well as economic benefits.[18] A leading economic role in the Black Sea is viewed in Ankara as enhancing Turkey's attractiveness to the EU. At a minimum, it could help to offset Turkey's position on the periphery of

---

in Jane M.O. Sharp, ed., *Europe After an American Withdrawal: Economic and Military Issues* (Oxford: Oxford University Press, 1990), in particular, the chapters by Athanassios G. Platias and Saadet Deger on Greece and Turkey.

[16] See Ian Lesser and Kevin Lewis, *Airpower and Security in NATO's Southern Region: Alternative Concepts for a USAF Facility at Crotone* (Santa Monica: RAND, 1991).

[17] A.P. Mikhailovsky, "The Mediterranean Sea: Security and Cooperation (Military Strategic Aspects)" (Paper delivered at the Madrid Complutense University Summer Seminar on Security and Cooperation in the Mediterranean, July 15, 1991).

[18] The volume of trade between Turkey and the Soviet Union has risen from $477 million in 1987 to roughly $1.9 billion in 1990. In 1989, this resulted in a Turkish trade surplus with the Soviet Union of over $100 million. The first meeting to discuss the Black Sea Economic Cooperation Region proposal was held in Ankara on December 19, 1990, with the participation of Turkish, Bulgarian, Romanian, and Soviet representatives. Subsequent meetings have been held in Bucharest

Europe. While Russia remains suspicious of Turkish long-term goals in Central Asia and the Caucasus, the prospect of a Turkish economic and political role in Azerbaijan and elsewhere in Central Asia may ultimately prove to be a relatively attractive alternative to the expansion of more radical Islamic influences.

Just as Western Europe begins to devote greater attention to problems emanating from the south, it is also likely that security perceptions in Moscow will be driven significantly by developments in the southern regions of the former Soviet Union and the areas beyond. Indeed, with the evaporation of the East-West competition, future Russian security interests are perhaps more likely to be oriented southward than westward. A reorientation of this sort would increase the importance of Central Asia, the Caucasus, and the Black Sea, and, by extension, the political, economic, and strategic significance of Turkey as a key actor in these regions.

Thinking about Strategy toward the Mediterranean and Southeastern Europe

Three broad approaches to thinking about the Mediterranean in strategic terms can be identified, each with specific implications for Southeastern Europe and the Balkans. They should be seen less as competing alternatives than as overlapping dimensions of the strategic environment.

The Mediterranean as an Extension of the European Security Environment

This view is, in many ways, the most traditional and NATO-centric. It focuses, above all, on the problems confronting the southern region countries, and defines developments around the Mediterranean in terms of their effect on the security of Europe and the nature of the transatlantic relationship. This approach is particularly attentive to the distinctive effects of conventional arms control in the center and south of Europe, and emphasizes the role of the U.S. presence in binding together security interests in the European center and south. The strategic environment, in this context, is characterized by a pronounced reorientation of European security concerns toward the south.

Within the Balkans, this approach argues for a less peripheral position for Greece within the Atlantic alliance. Should Turkey's strategic importance come to be seen, again, in European rather than Middle Eastern terms, Turkey would also benefit from this adjustment of European security interests. If Turkey remains outside Europe in a formal sense (that is, outside the EU and the WEU), and perhaps turns its attention to competing foreign and security policy interests in the Middle East, the Turkish border with Greece and Bulgaria could increasingly be seen as the political-

---

and Sofia, with a conference finalizing principles of cooperation held in Moscow on July 11–12, 1991. "Agreement Reached on Black Sea Economic Project," *FBIS-West Europe Report*, July 16, 1991, p. 42. See also, Sukru Elekdag, "Black Sea Economic Cooperation Region Project," unpublished paper, 1991.

military "fault line" between Europe and the Middle East.

Instability in the Adriatic and Aegean derives much of its strategic significance from the fact that conflict in these regions may have negative consequences for the political and economic evolution of Europe as a whole. The disintegration of the former Yugoslavia could encourage ethnic conflict and separatism elsewhere in Eastern Europe, as well as regional movements affecting Spain, Italy, and Greece. A new crisis in Greek-Turkish relations would probably ruin Turkey's already poor prospects for membership in the EU, but might also severely complicate Greece's integration in the European mainstream. In this context, Turkish membership in the EU might contribute to the prospects for crisis management in the Aegean by providing an additional institutional anchor for Greek-Turkish relations.

The Mediterranean as the Place Where the Persian Gulf Begins[19]

Recent events in the Middle East have reinforced the idea, always prominent in U.S. strategic thought, that the Mediterranean derives much of its strategic importance from its proximity to areas of crisis and potential conflict outside Europe. This approach tends to emphasize the economic and logistic dimensions of security, including the sea lines of communication for oil, access to the Suez Canal, and the role of bases and forces in the central and eastern Mediterranean in supporting operations beyond the littoral.

In this view, the Mediterranean and the Persian Gulf form a single geostrategic entity, with Turkey and Egypt (Suez) providing a continental and maritime bridge between Europe and the Middle East. Italy and Greece also occupy important positions on the logistical axis stretching from the Azores to the Gulf. Of the material needed to support the coalition operations in the Gulf during Operations Desert Shield and Desert Storm, 90 percent arrived via the Mediterranean.[20] If the United States and its European allies had been compelled to rely exclusively on the Indian Ocean route in deploying force to the Gulf, the capacity for rapid power projection would have been greatly reduced.[21]

From the narrower perspective of naval strategy and the maritime interests of the United States and Europe, it is likely that the free movement of ships between the Mediterranean and Persian Gulf and Indian Ocean regions will assume greater importance in the future. The essential factors in this regard will be the enduring requirement for a substantial presence in and around the Gulf, together with possible (budget-driven) reductions in naval forces in the Mediterranean. Even if the United States does not maintain a continuous carrier battle group presence in the Mediterranean (during the Gulf crisis, and for the first time in decades, there was a

---

[19] This formulation was originally suggested to the author by N. Bradford Dismukes; the theme is developed in "The Med. Remains Vital," in *U.S. Naval Institute Proceedings*, October 1991.

[20] Draft Interim Report of the Sub-Committee on the southern region, North Atlantic Assembly, 1991, p. 10.

[21] Jonathan T. Howe, "NATO and the Gulf Crisis," *Survival*, 33, no. 3 (May/June 1991): 247.

period in which there was no U.S. carrier group in the Mediterranean), very substantial U.S. and European forces will remain in the region. Under these conditions, however, the ability to shift forces between the Mediterranean and the Gulf via the Suez Canal will be a strategic imperative.

The tendency to view the Mediterranean, the Black Sea, and the Middle East as part of a single strategic complex is also evident in the Italian approach to CSCM, which has emphasized the interdependence of security interests from Gibraltar to Iran.[22] In addition to giving CSCM a broader and more visible political agenda, the definition of Mediterranean security in comprehensive terms reflects the perceived vulnerability of South European countries to developments in the greater Middle East.

The Mediterranean and Its Regions as Areas of Strategic Consequence in Their Own Right

Fernand Braudel's notion of the unity of the Mediterranean may be less persuasive in contemporary political and strategic terms, but there is undoubtedly a need to address regional security problems in the Mediterranean, including those in the Balkans, on their own terms; that is, in addition to their links with broader issues of European and Middle Eastern security. This approach has enjoyed a long tradition in Europe but is largely alien to American foreign and security policy, which, for good strategic reasons, has tended to view the Mediterranean as an extension of the European and Middle Eastern security environments.[23]

The Cold War encouraged the linkage of regional security concerns for purposes of deterrence and political reassurance. In this context, turmoil in Yugoslavia was dangerous largely because it invited Soviet intervention; conflict between Greece and Turkey in the Aegean corroded alliance cohesion and weakened deterrence and containment in the southern region. With the waning of the Soviet threat, the situation is quite different, and encourages the isolation rather than linkage of regional problems. Yugoslavia is one example; Europe's arm's-length approach to Turkey's Middle Eastern and internal security problems is another.

While the strategic contraction of the former Soviet Union has created the conditions for renewed political turmoil in the Balkans, it may also encourage the settlement of disputes elsewhere in the eastern Mediterranean. Leaving aside the prospects for an Arab-Israeli détente, which would greatly simplify Greek and Turkish relations with the Arab world, the experience of the Gulf War may yet open the way for a settlement of the Cyprus dispute. The emergence of the United States as a broker could change the balance of incentives in Athens and Ankara as both sides seek to assure themselves of a secure bilateral relationship with Washington in the

---

[22]Italian Non-Paper on CSCM, in *The Mediterranean and the Middle East After the War in the Gulf: The CSCM*, p. 118.

[23]See Ellen Laipson, "Thinking About the Mediterranean," *Mediterranean Quarterly* 1, no. 1 (Winter 1990): 63.

wake of the Gulf War.[24] Movement on the Cyprus problem could, in turn, pave the way for an overall improvement of Greek-Turkish relations that would serve the longer-term interests of both countries. In the absence of an active Soviet threat in Thrace, the EU and NATO may well prove less tolerant of the constraints imposed by difficult relations in the Aegean. As NATO seeks to develop rapid response forces, with a permanent naval component in the Mediterranean, the resolution of long-standing command and control disputes in the eastern Mediterranean will be essential. If Turkey does not progress beyond associate membership in the WEU, or if the WEU itself fails to develop an operational dimension, participation in such new NATO arrangements will be important both strategically and politically. Further incentives for moderation arise from Greek concerns about the reassertion of Turkey's strategic importance in the Middle East and its consequences, and Turkey's interest in promoting favorable perceptions as it presses for entry into the EU.

Greek opposition continues to serve as an impediment, not only to Turkish membership in the EU, but also to a significant deepening of relations at the current level. An optimistic assessment suggests that this situation may be changing for two reasons. First, there are tentative signs that both Athens and Ankara have recognized that institutional expressions of Greco-Turkish animosity may no longer serve the interests of either country in the post-Cold War environment. This observation applies to both NATO and the EU, and is reinforced by the perceived importance of being "members in good standing" at a time of strategic flux and economic stringency. Second, as NATO enters a period of uncertainty, the idea that Turkish involvement in the EU can serve to anchor and stabilize Greek-Turkish relations, already discussed in moderate circles, may gain wider currency. Ironically, as the incentives for Greek opposition to Turkey within the EU may be declining, there is a growing perception in Turkey that Europe as a whole tolerates and even fuels Greek-Turkish enmity as a pretext for holding Turkey at arm's length.[25]

Nonetheless, the prospects for Turkey's joining Europe in the institutional sense remain poor for reasons largely unrelated to Aegean problems. The Gulf experience has perhaps worsened the outlook for Turkish membership in both organizations by reinforcing the European perception that Turkey is an important *Middle Eastern* ally. As the EU seeks to develop a security dimension as part of the process of European integration, it will be increasingly unwilling to accept the additional burden of a direct exposure in the Middle East. So too, the likely broadening of the EU over the next decade will not necessarily improve the prospects for Turkey in Europe, but it will heighten the political and strategic implications of a negative response from Brussels.

The trend toward regional political and security initiatives around the Mediterranean, including Balkan cooperation, could promote stability in Greek-Turkish relations if the bilateral climate is supportive.[26] Under less favorable conditions, Greece

---

[24] See Maureen Dowd, "Bush Names the Next Challenge: Cyprus," *New York Times*, 19 July 1991.

[25] John Murray Brown, "Turkey Survey," *Financial Times*, 20 May 1991.

[26] The Greek government issued a proposal for disarmament along the borders between Greece,

and Bulgaria may be driven to more overt strategic cooperation as a means of countering Turkish power in the Balkans.[27] An essential point is that the prospects for cooperation and conflict between Greece and Turkey will turn critically on the overall evolution of relations between Turkey and the West. Turkish isolation from European initiatives, particularly on security matters, will worsen the prospects for crisis management in the Aegean.[28]

It is clear that the problems and potential responses posed by the ongoing crisis in the former Yugoslavia—and potential conflicts elsewhere in the Balkans—are of a fundamentally different character than those originating across the Mediterranean, in North Africa and the Middle East, or in the Aegean.[29] Unlike many of the other security concerns mentioned in this chapter, the United States has only a limited involvement in, and influence on, Balkan affairs (Greece and Turkey apart). In the Balkans, European influence predominates, and the EU enjoys wide prestige and legitimacy as an interlocutor. This is in direct contrast to the situation in the Levant, where the United States is the dominant external actor, and in the Aegean, where the United States is both an important actor and a common interlocutor. To the extent that Germany emerges as a dominant European power in Balkan affairs, this may also encourage more active German involvement in the Mediterranean.

Bridge or Barrier?

Finally, should the Balkans-Eastern Mediterranean region be considered a bridge linking Europe and the Middle East, or a barrier insulating Europe from risks emanating from the south and east? The legacy of Ottoman rule in the Balkans encourages a view of Southeastern Europe in which Greece and Bulgaria, in particular, form a strategic glacis on the European periphery. In the prevailing Turkish view, the notion of a glacis is also relevant, but here it is to be found on Turkey's Middle Eastern borders (and in a different context, the borders with the former Soviet Union). With regard to political and economic relations in the Middle East and around the Black Sea, the notion of a "bridge" has greater resonance. Ultimately, the issue of barrier versus bridge—and in the case of the former, where the "fault line" lies—is likely to depend, above all, on the overall evolution of Europe's relations with the Islamic world.

Bulgaria, and Turkey. Bulgaria expressed support for the proposal. Turkey considered and rejected it, wary of the fact that the proposal does not extend to the Aegean. See "Premier Announces Border Disarmament Proposal," statement by Prime Minister Mitsotakis of July 12, 1991, quoted in *FBIS-West Europe Report*, July 15, 1991, p. 37.

[27] See Paul Anastasi, "Greek-Bulgarian Tactics for Turkey," *New York Times*, 7 Feb. 1991.

[28] On the outlook for Greek-Turkish relations, see *Aegean Issues: Problems and Prospects* (Ankara: Foreign Policy Institute, 1989); James Brown, *Delicately Poised Allies: Greece and Turkey—Problems, Policy Choices and Mediterranean Security* (London: Brassey's, 1991); and Dimitri Constas, ed., *The Greek-Turkish Conflict in the 1990s: Domestic and External Influences* (New York: St. Martin's Press, 1991), with contributions by both Greek and Turkish authors.

[29] See Aliboni, *European Security Across the Mediterranean*, 3.

The question of bridge versus barrier also applies in a more limited sense to the issue of migration and its effect on security perceptions. Southern Europe is a conduit for migration from south to north, but as Europe's immigration policies tighten, these countries will increasingly be viewed as barriers. Indeed, this is already a common attitude on both sides of the Mediterranean.[30]

Overall Observations and Conclusions

In sum, the strategic environment in the Balkans and the eastern Mediterranean is being shaped by important trends emanating from Europe and the Middle East and affecting the role of the region in European and American security perceptions. The end of the Cold War, and the strategic contraction and subsequent disintegration of the Soviet Union, have encouraged the renewal of traditional antagonisms in the Balkans. These developments have also removed many of the superpower-imposed constraints influencing the behavior of regional actors in North Africa and the Middle East. Taken together with the problems of conventional and unconventional proliferation in the Mediterranean and the ambiguous effects of the CFE process on Southeastern Europe, the region emerges as a center of post-Cold War security risks.

The security canvas itself is expanding both geographically and functionally as Europe faces a host of security-related concerns, not the least of which is migration, arising from the Mediterranean. The result is likely to be a progressive redefinition of security interests in which the Mediterranean and Southeastern Europe will move from the strategic periphery to the center. As the region comes to play a more prominent role in European security perceptions, it will also become more important to the United States in defining a relevant residual presence in Europe. As a Middle Eastern as well as a European power, the United States will retain a strong interest in the Mediterranean as an economic and strategic conduit to the Gulf. Against these considerations must be set the uncertain evolution of the former Soviet Union, and the ability of events in the east to capture the strategic attention of the West.

The progressive Europeanization of NATO's southern allies in foreign and security policy terms will continue to transform the political and strategic landscape in the Mediterranean. Traditional patterns of cooperation with the United States will be particularly affected by this process. To the extent that Turkey remains outside this trend, with its strategic importance framed largely in Middle Eastern terms, the prospects for friction in the Aegean will grow.

Finally, the future strategic environment in the region will be determined, above all, by the character of relations between north and south in the Mediterranean and, even more broadly, between Islam and the West. The nature of this evolution will be critical in answering the fundamental question of whether the region will serve as a bridge or a barrier in strategic terms.

---

[30] As Michael Howard has noted, the southern European countries have long regarded the Mediterranean rather than the Elbe as the "real front line." Michael Howard, "The Springtime of Nations," *Foreign Affairs* 69, no. 1 (1989).

IX

Conventional Arms Control and Confidence-Building Measures

Thomas J. Hirschfeld

Although the Conventional Forces in Europe (CFE) and Confidence and Security Building Measures (CSBM) agreements of 1990 went far in making all European states feel more secure about the prospects of massive invasion, they did not directly address the regional aspects of European security. The Conference on Security and Cooperation in Europe (CSCE) negotiations, sometimes called Helsinki II, considered inter alia how to address regional issues, and especially those affecting the Balkans. Troubles in former Yugoslavia highlighted the need for such a regional focus.

The European arms control agreements of 1990 and their follow-on forums provide building blocks to further improve security for the Balkans. These building blocks include reduction and transparency measures in the agreements that diminished threatening arsenals and made military behavior more visible and predictable in virtually all European countries; the almost continentwide verification and inspection system; institutionalized dialogues; and opportunities to focus, exploit, and expand these measures to the advantage of the Balkan states through regional cooperation and through the Helsinki II follow-on negotiations. Several measures, some of them new and most of them modest, seem worth considering in the Helsinki II discussions. Taking advantage of these opportunities, however, may require more intense and long-lasting political cooperation among regional states than may be tolerable.

This chapter identifies the background to the Helsinki II discussions, including the achievements and shortcomings of the two Vienna agreements of 1990 agreed upon among the NATO and former Warsaw Treaty Organization members and among the now fifty-three CSCE members. It outlines the changing threat environment in Europe with particular reference to the problems of Southeastern Europe and the Balkans, followed by a description of a hypothetical but necessary political framework for organizing arms control efforts in this region. Against that background, particular arms control approaches and types of measures are then examined for their suitability to this region.

Background

It is a truism that arms control in Europe dealt with Western Europe's concern about massive Soviet invasion and surprise attack—problems of the past. This is not to denigrate the achievements of the two Vienna arms control negotiations: the Conventional Forces in Europe (CFE), and Confidence and Security Building Measures (CSBM) forums. On the contrary, there would be no addressing the security problems of the Balkans if the East-West confrontation that bedeviled the continent for over four decades had not been brought under control in Vienna.

Before the end of the Cold War, European arms control made sense as an enterprise to build confidence between members of two antagonistic alliances by increasing the transparency of military activities in Europe, and by adjusting force levels between them to parity. The CSBM talks achieved greater transparency from the Atlantic to the Urals for all CSCE partners. Between NATO and former Warsaw Treaty states, CFE provided more secure and stable force balances at lower levels, much reduced prospects of a surprise attack using forces in place, and circumscribed capacities for either side to initiate effective large-scale offensive action. These military benefits applied most particularly in the area that held the densest concentration of military forces between the two former blocs—what used to be the center region of Europe.

Yet, the end of the Cold War has exposed other problems, many of them problems of East Central Europe and the Balkans, which have been masked, suppressed, or deemphasized for most of the past half century. The CFE conventional force balance adjustments did not improve Southeastern Europe's regional military balances in any fundamental way.[1] If the CFE treaty ensures that NATO and former Warsaw Pact forces will be in balance for the first time since the late 1940s, it also assures that each of the subregional balances will be characterized by an imbalance of force, even after full CFE implementation. Nevertheless, even if the CFE treaty codifies that particular imbalance, it is a somewhat better relative balance than before CFE, in the sense that forces on what used to be Soviet territory are smaller.[2] It is also worth recalling that there are Balkan states other than present or former members of the two alliances. Several of these (the pieces of the former Yugoslavia and Albania) are unaffected by CFE and its provisions. One (Albania) has forces that

[1] See Yannis G. Valinakis, *Greece and the CFE Negotiations* (Ebenhausen: Stiftung Wissenschaft und Politik, June 1991), 22.

[2] Ivo H. Daalder, *The CFE Treaty: An Overview and an Assessment* (Baltimore: The Johns Hopkins Foreign Policy Institute, 1991), 23–24.

remain unconstrained and unobserved by the CSBMs agreed to concurrently in Vienna among the (then thirty-four) CSCE partners.

The CFE experience demonstrates the inherent difficulty of codifying European military balances through arms control outside the familiar East-West framework. The CFE treaty, the collapse of the Warsaw Pact, and the withdrawal of Soviet forces from Eastern Europe leave some East European states without collective security, but with national forces constrained by treaty with respect to their potential growth. Balkan states, especially those that are not NATO members, therefore, have a stake in an ongoing European security process, in the hope that some other collective arrangements can alleviate the remaining external security problems.

Some progress has been made beyond the CFE treaty. With the exception of Albania, all the states of the Balkans and all their European neighbors are parties to the December 1990 Vienna Agreement on Confidence and Security Building Measures. They thus already belong to a system that provides a high degree of transparency about military capabilities and activities in Europe west of the Ural mountains. Information about the structure, size, and location of national military forces is to be exchanged annually in detail and will be subject to inspection and evaluation. Also, all significant exercises, except alerts, will occur with advance notification.

Furthermore, the CSCE summit of 1990 in Paris called for a second Helsinki Conference, to establish "new negotiations on disarmament and confidence building" on the basis of a "more structured cooperation among all CSCE states on security matters." The present structure of fifty-three participants represents a deliberate departure from the East-West-oriented CFE framework of confrontational NATO-Warsaw Treaty states. It implies instead an attempt to devise measures that address the security of each of the fifty-three CSCE member states on some equitable national basis, still to be determined.

By the time Helsinki II opened in March 1992, the Warsaw Pact had disappeared. In a dramatic reversal, the USSR's former partners have, to varying degrees, attempted to move away from the former USSR by establishing closer ties with Western bodies. This is particularly true for the so-called northern tier states—Poland, the Czech Republic, Slovakia, and Hungary. As exposed neighbors of the former USSR with serious economic problems, these governments tend to favor further reductions, which would in the first instance involve former Soviet forces. Even if they do not fear an immediate Russian military invasion, they are concerned about the de facto establishment of some new buffer zone between East and West, and their future relegation to some Russian sphere of influence in such a zone.[3] NATO has so far kept Eastern Europe at arm's length. The establishment of the North Atlantic Cooperation Council (NACC) at the NATO summit in Rome in November 1991 has provided an institutionalized forum for the discussion of security issues directly affecting Eastern European countries, but the inclusion of the newly independent countries of Central Asia and Caucasus in the former USSR, together with

[3] "Central Europe: Adjusting to Reality," *Strategic Survey, 1990–1991* (London: International Institute for Strategic Studies, 1991), 159.

Slovenia, Croatia, and most recently Albania, has raised questions about how effective the NACC will be, since it now contains over thirty-five members.

This rather thin gruel highlights the security vacuum in East Central Europe and the Balkans, which may, however, not be permanent. Events, rather than deliberate policy, may determine the shape of future security arrangements. A first test of that proposition can be seen in the disintegration of the former Yugoslav federation. The experience of individual governments in managing the conflicting imperatives of reestablishing order, protecting human rights, preventing undue bloodshed and avoiding the dangers and expense of direct involvement have colored the positions individual governments took in Helsinki and the kinds of measures they suggested. What the Yugoslav experience demonstrates is the probability that internal upheavals will continue, and that European security forums must make continuing efforts to address them. These are, however, not the only possible threats to Europe as a whole and the Balkans in particular.

More fundamentally, the turmoil in the former USSR reduces the military threat in the short run, while increasing the possibility of conflict in the longer term. Russia's severe economic and social problems suggest that offensive external adventures in Europe are unlikely in the near future. Furthermore, the independence of the Baltic states and the reluctance of Ukraine and Moldova to join any collective defense arrangements with Russia implies the emergence of a band of diverse and not necessarily cooperative neighbors separating what is now Eastern Europe from what may still be a large and potentially powerful Russia. Similar populations on both sides of most Eastern European frontiers imply future disputes about territorial adjustments, both inside and outside former Soviet territory.

While Ukraine and Belarus, which previously had Soviet forces on their territory, agreed to abide by the CFE limits, Ukraine and Russia have recently pressed for a change in the CFE ceilings. Some East European states may also regard Helsinki II and its follow-on forums as opportunities to adjust adverse force balances imposed on them individually by CFE limitations that were negotiated in an overall East-West framework. In short, Helsinki II and its follow-on forums may be called on to renegotiate local balances between CSCE partners, their immediate European neighbors, and the newly independent republics of the former USSR, even if such calls fall on largely deaf ears. It seems doubtful that the larger Western parties to CFE agreements will be enthusiastic about renegotiating the CFE treaty balance, without some overriding immediate threat to the security of particular East European states.

For all these reasons, future measures agreed to in the Helsinki II framework should no longer be formulated directly or primarily with yesterday's familiar threat of Soviet invasion in mind. Instead, Helsinki II follow-on measures will need to establish, accommodate, ameliorate, or not impede national or collective arrangements looking toward a somewhat different set of dangers.

Organizing Security within a Political Framework

Writ large, arms control measures are contractual obligations between sovereign states. They perform the limited function of helping states and parties to agreements to assure each other, and thereby themselves, about the size, configuration, readiness, composition, movement, and location of potential adversary forces. Arms control agreements are hardest to negotiate, but perhaps most necessary between parties who distrust each other. Even if arms control eventually helps to alleviate distrust, it is no substitute for political arrangements between potential adversaries.

With respect to potential tensions in the Balkans, arms control is a limited instrument indeed. It has, for example, no demonstrable direct utility with respect to what may be the most significant class of potential problems: internal turmoil. At best, some arms control measures may help with the external aspects of internal problems. To be effective even for that purpose, an external political framework is necessary that will define and limit the legitimate interests and behavior of outside powers.

Limiting the behavior of outside powers is important to assure that internal conflict or local conflict in East Central Europe or the Balkans, should it break out, remains geographically confined. Although keeping conflict internal or local is an obvious desideratum (the worst alternative is having a local dispute grow into a general European war), local parties in dispute may have different views. Local parties have incentives to drag some external power in to avoid defeat. The attempts by Slovenia and Croatia to achieve external recognition (and thereby attract outside support to intimidate the government in Belgrade) constitute an obvious recent case.

Outside powers will, therefore, have to agree with each other and with the states of the Balkans not to act unilaterally, whether to act collectively, and if so, how. They would, in short, have to agree on measures limiting the involvement of outside powers. For Eastern Europe, that also means sharpening understanding about the identifiable differences between cross-border crimes that governments commit, and sufferings that governments inflict within their own frontiers. In other words, separate territorial and minority questions.

Separation is promoted by general CSCE principles under which all European states continue to recognize existing international borders while renouncing claims to territory not under national control. A further step toward separating these difficult issues is the creation within the CSCE of a high commissioner for national minorities. The high commissioner is appointed by the council and is able to draw on the resources of the Office for Democratic Institutions and Human Rights to promote early warning and action in cases where minority troubles threaten to provoke a crisis. This new structure should help reduce minority problems to human rights issues in which the international community has a legitimate, but limited, interest. Such a formula would neither support nor prejudice the legitimacy of internal independence movements. It would, nevertheless, remove the legal basis for a neighboring or other outside state to act in its own territorial interest in support of such a movement.[4] A modification of the Helsinki I formula in legally binding

---

[4]See Charles Cooper, Keith Crane, Thomas Hirschfeld, and James Steinberg, *Rethinking Security Arrangements in Europe*, N–3107 AF (Santa Monica: RAND, August 1990).

form, forbidding frontier changes except with the consent of the parties, and defining "parties" as CSCE member national governments, is one possible approach. This option would not, however, find favor with the many states' members, including the United States, that do not wish CSCE declarations to have formal legal status.

States outside the Balkans could also make individual or collective declarations with respect to particular events there, as they arise, such as negative security assurances. This could, for example, involve external powers agreeing not to use the territory or airspace of particular affected states for military purposes. Such an undertaking could be used to assure Russia that NATO had no plans to exploit disputes along the former Soviet border. Neither NATO nor any NATO country, however, could articulate such a principle as a general proposition without abrogating defensive obligations with respect to Greece and Turkey.

Any arms control or arms-control-related arrangements considered with respect to the Balkans must take extra-European factors into account. Turkey in particular is limited in the types of constraints on its own forces or territory that it can accept, by virtue of facing chronic and dangerous Middle Eastern problems. The CSCE process has acknowledged this factor by removing southeastern Turkey and Turkish forces there from the circumscription of CFE treaty obligations and CSBMs. Yet Greek observers have expressed concern about having significant parts of Anatolia outside the area of limitations and not subject to observation and inspection arrangements. This area, in the view of some Greek spokesmen, could serve as the venue for a Turkish force accretion directed at Greece, or at least for reinforcements directed at Cyprus. Cyprus aside, Greek concerns about an unconstrained area must be balanced against Turkish security requirements with respect to Turkey's eastern frontiers, as demonstrated in the Gulf War and its aftermath. It may be difficult to design, let alone negotiate, measures that meet Greek requirements, unless some more compelling relationship between Turkish buildup potential in eastern Anatolia and threats to the Greek metropole can be established analytically.

Arms Control Arrangements and Southeastern Europe

Arms control arrangements, including forums, classes of measures, and individual measures that already exist within the CSCE framework can be further expanded and adapted to the Balkans. Others can be extrapolated from existing arrangements for European security to the possible advantage of the Balkan states.

Exploit Existing Forums

The existing forums for discussion and resolution of European security problems have yet to be fully developed or usefully exploited. The two Vienna negotiations established follow-on forums for further limited negotiations, for continuing exchanges of information, to assure the implementation of the agreements and their verification systems to the satisfaction of all parties, and, if and where possible, for the resolution of disputes. Each forum represents opportunities to increase security in Southeastern Europe and the Balkans.

For instance, the limitations on manpower established within the framework of the CFE 1a negotiations could be extended to the non-CFE states in the Balkans. This would involve agreed limitations on the successor states of the former Yugoslavia and on Albania. A number of Balkan states, for instance, want constraints on the manpower of Serbia. These could be negotiated within the Forum for Security Cooperation (FSC), the successor to the CFE negotiations, which was mandated by the CSCE Ministerial in Rome in December 1993 to examine the issue of regional stability in Southeastern Europe.

Aerial inspections along the lines discussed in CFE could also serve as a model for future agreed adversary aerial inspections. Such inspections could be conducted in the Balkans between parties wishing to assure themselves of compliance with the CFE treaty. They could also serve as a model for any supplementary aerial inspection arrangements that Balkan states might agree to, such as the current "open skies" arrangements between Romania and Hungary.

The CFE participants also created a Joint Consultative Group (JCG), an institutionalized dialogue among CFE participants. This forum considers questions and complaints about compliance with the treaty and differences among the parties about interpretation of text. Beyond resolving technical questions and considering disputes arising from the way parties implement the treaty, the JCG is also empowered to adopt measures that enhance the effectiveness of the treaty, which suggests further negotiations in the CFE framework. CFE partners could, for example, run a watching brief on new types of military equipment being produced in or for Europe, or introduced into Europe, to see whether such equipment should be limited by agreement in any follow-on negotiations.

In addition, obligations already accepted among CFE participants could be broadened or adapted to all fifty-three CSCE members, in the service of a comprehensive European security system. An obvious candidate for expansion is the inspection system that assures compliance with the CFE treaty. In the Balkans, this would involve finding a formula for exposing Serb, Slovene, Croat, Macedonian, and Albanian forces to the same degree of observation as is required of the Russians, Turks, Bulgars, Romanians, and Greeks.

The most useful potential forum for the Balkans is the CSCE complex, especially its Conflict Prevention Center (CPC) and potentially the new Forum for Security Cooperation, which opened in Vienna on September 22, 1992. The CPC is authorized to give support to the implementation of CSBMs such as:

- a mechanism for consultation and cooperation regarding unusual military activities;
- annual exchanges of military information;
- a communications network;
- annual implementation assessment meetings; and
- cooperation regarding hazardous incidents of a military nature.

These tasks are listed without prejudice to other tasks concerning a procedure for conciliation of disputes, and broader tasks relating to dispute settlement.[5]

At the June 1991 meeting of CSCE foreign ministers in Berlin it was agreed that the CSCE should somehow be able to intervene in potentially explosive disputes in member countries. The USSR initially blocked proposals that would permit the CSCE to call members into emergency session. Apparently with the Baltic states in mind, the Soviet Union argued that affected member states would first have to determine for themselves if a particular issue is an internal one. If so, argued then Soviet Foreign Minister Alexander Bessmertnykh, it was outside the CSCE purview. On this point the Soviets were supported by Turkey, apparently out of concern that Greece would raise the Cyprus question.[6] Yet, in the debate that followed, CSCE partners modified the unanimity rule that has bedeviled action in the CSCE since the founding of that forum, at least with respect to emergency action. The parties have now agreed that a state concerned about a security matter can call an emergency meeting and have national representatives to the CSCE confer regardless of subject, at the instance of one member with the support of at least ten others. This rule was successfully invoked by Austria, in response to the Yugoslav crisis.[7] As currently interpreted by CSCE members, the rule imposes no limits on what may be discussed, although action requires approval by all members except the state(s) concerned—the "consensus-minus-one" principle, which was used to suspend the rump state of Yugoslavia from the CSCE decisionmaking process.

The CSBM negotiations conducted within the CSCE framework also provide for a Committee of Senior Officials, which can be convened by the chairman-in-office or eleven participating states under an emergency mechanism in "emergency situations" to assist the CSCE Council in reducing the risk of conflict.

Many CSCE partners, notably Germany and its East European neighbors, favor strengthening the CSCE, especially the role of the CPC. Chancellor Helmut Kohl, for example, has called the CPC the acid test of the effectiveness and credibility of the CSCE process. While the CPC played only a limited role in helping adjust disputes in the former Yugoslavia, states cite that failure as a reason for strengthening the CPC's role. Some Balkan states may find it in their interest to support a stronger CPC.

The UN's role also deserves mention before leaving the subject of how collective security arrangements may be used for the benefit of the Balkan countries. One area of potential UN action that may have some marginal utility for the Balkans is the prospective UN register of arms transfers. Britain, Japan, and the USSR have espoused the idea of the central recording of arms transfers. If arms transfers were centrally recorded at or near the time of purchase, the world community and individual governments could track which country, province, locality, or movement was

[5] See *Supplementary Document to Give Effect to Certain Provisions Contained in the Charter of Paris for a New Europe*, November 16, 1990, p. 4.

[6] Marc Fisher, "Soviets Block European Conflict Proposal," *Washington Post*, 20 June 1991.

[7] Theresa Hitchins, "CSCE Performance in Yugoslavia Crisis Draws Kudos," *Defense News*, 8 July 1991.

buying what, and could call both the buyer and the seller to account in some established forum, in public, and through diplomatic channels. Embarrassing transactions would have to be justified. Those hidden would face the danger of coming to light.

If such a registry system were operating effectively, Balkan governments involved in disputes could watch one another more accurately, and thereby avoid misperceptions about their respective buildups. More significant, governments might be able to monitor more effectively stockpiling of weapons and consumables by internal movements such as Kurds or Macedonians. How effective such observation might be depends in large measure on the content, timing, and stringency of the obligations to report, as well as on cooperation.

A global register under UN auspices does not exclude a European one established by the CSCE. Several states proposed such a register at Helsinki II. The CSCE has declared itself a "regional arrangement" under the UN as provided under Chapter VIII of the UN Charter, and could take the lead in establishing a regional register. For that matter, there is nothing to prevent such a central registry from being established for the Balkans. Presumably, multiple registries for different purposes and areas could check and complement each other. Had such registries been in place and operating perhaps a year before the Yugoslav crisis began, it might have inhibited some of the bloodshed. Registries might have caught at least some of the considerable transfers of Soviet weapons from Germany and East European weapons to Slovene and Croat organizations in 1990 and 1991.[8] However, the experience of the current crisis has made it clear that the establishment of such regimes will be a difficult process, particularly once crises have developed.

Finally, it is useful to recall in this context that in the 1990 CSBM agreement, the CSCE achieved consensus on common use of the UN military budget reporting instrument. Information forms in a standardized and, therefore, readily comparable detailed format are to be provided to all participating states no later than two months after a budget has been approved by national authorities. Participating states may query each other about the information provided, and states/parties are committed to "make every effort to answer such queries fully and promptly."[9]

Military budget discussions are useful in that they provide a calculation of comparable relative levels of expenditure over time that indicates increases or decreases in overall national defense efforts, and a proportional description of how defense money is spent. It is important to know, for example, whether expenditure increases reflect personnel pay raises or new generations of combat aircraft. As a legitimate subject of inquiry, anxiety-provoking aircraft purchases would presumably have to be justified by the purchaser to some of the potential target states.

---

[8] Peter Maass, "East Bloc's Cold War Arsenals Are Arming Ethnics," *Washington Post*, 8 July 1991.

[9] Articles (14), and (16), *Vienna Document 1990*, of the Negotiations on Confidence and Security Building Measures convened in Accordance with the Relevant Provisions of the Concluding Document of the Vienna Meeting of the Conference on Security and Cooperation in Europe.

Nevertheless, unlike the proposed central weapon registry that may help track weapon acquisitions by potential insurgents, budget reporting only addresses external security concerns. Yet, in combination, the two approaches suggest a new form of arms control where intended acquisitions of major systems require early reporting and discussion in a European context.[10] That kind of dialogue by its very existence could inhibit, delay, and reduce the variety and volume of actual purchases by all participating countries. By contributing to a slower rate and volume of change in the weapons holdings of European forces (and thereby reducing each country's need to react to change in neighboring countries), such a measure may especially interest countries of Eastern Europe who tend to be poorer than their northern and western neighbors.

Regional Collective Security

Generic arrangements—such as a "Balkan pact" where all regional states somehow agree to combine against outside invasion, respect each other's existing territorial integrity, agree to consult and cooperate in the event of trouble, or coordinate approaches to troubles inside the region or affecting it—are often prescribed. For example, on June 9, 1991, Romania's Defense Minister Constantin Spiroiu called for new "Inter-Balkan" political and security arrangements and a "Union of Central and Eastern Europe," which would, however, "not operate as a military alliance."[11] Such arrangements should obviously be encouraged. Yet, the content and effectiveness of individual measures count as much as the political framework. Practical measures are somewhat harder to derive because of the absence of a clear common antagonist, and because of past disputes between virtually all Balkan countries. Thus, the types of measures that are worth considering regionally are few, and many of them are flawed. Briefly, then, these are:

(A) ESTABLISH CLEARLY DEFENSIVE FORCE POSTURES

Defensive doctrine includes avowed self-restraint prior to attack, and no first-use of any military means. Other possible features include:

- common (and, therefore, predictable) mobilization procedures;
- mostly fixed prepared defenses on national territory along presumed enemy routes of advance;
- low levels of force readiness; and
- no heavy equipment or consumables stored forward.

The weightiest common argument against adopting an overall defensive force posture is that such a force posture inhibits counterattack, an often necessary tactical recourse in warfare. As with all suggested regional solutions, to be effective the extraregional states with whom regional states have potential disputes must

---

[10] The author is indebted to Ambassador Jack Maresca, the U.S. representative to CSCE, for this concept.

[11] Richard Norton-Taylor, "Britain to Train Romanian Army," *The Guardian,* 10 June 1991.

somehow be brought into line. In other words, forces in Hungary and Russia, for example, would necessarily have to adopt the same or suitably compensating defensive configurations as forces in the Balkans have with respect to each other.

Nevertheless, adopting some more defensive postures may make sense, regionally for the Balkans, and sometimes in combination with countries outside the region. These defenses might include the following:

Mutual pullbacks from frontier areas. This type of measure was advanced as a regional security suggestion by Greek Prime Minister Constantine Mitsotakis in July 1991. The fate of this proposal, so far, is a graphic illustration of the types of difficulties that tend to plague regional arms limitations in the Balkans. Briefly, he suggested the removal of CFE-treaty-limited items from Greek Thrace, European Turkey and a corresponding area of southern Bulgaria. The Bulgarian government was willing to discuss this proposal further. Turkey rejected the proposal outright, asserting instead that Turkish security could not be considered in pieces, and that the problem of Greek buildups in the Aegean also had to be included in these discussions.[12] In its conceptual form, mutual pullbacks mean agreement by all parties to withdraw forces, depots and other facilities, and units with particular weapons systems some agreed distance from national frontiers. Patrols could be conducted in the thinned-out zone on a regular basis by forces from the adjoining states, or by designated third parties. Distances from frontiers could presumably be adjusted to account for terrain or other differences. Although universal application is not excluded, states sharing particular frontiers could agree not to bother, or only to apply this provision in certain frontier areas. Choice about which frontiers to pull back from allows states to avoid the expense and difficulty of required compliance for particular frontiers (Turkey's security requirements with respect to its eastern and southern frontiers and its forces in Cyprus are clearly different from its requirements in the west, for example); and attempts to accommodate the paradox that, although not all frontiers are equally significant from a security standpoint, they nevertheless are best treated in similar fashion in treaty language about frontier security.

The fact that it is usually desirable to treat all partners to an agreement alike, or at least have the obligations that bind them read alike, should not be taken to mean that arrangements with specifically regional applications have no place in a CSCE arms control framework. On the contrary, it may be possible to devise local or regional obligations that bind particular CSCE partners, and then get agreement among the others to respect such obligations.

Force structure limits. The CFE agreements went far in circumscribing the heavy weapons holdings of national armed forces in Europe by establishing ceilings on

---

[12] See "Premier Announces Border Disarmament Proposal," and "Bulgaria Accepts Proposal," translated in *FBIS-WEU*-91-135, July 15, 1991, p. 37 and 38 respectively; also "Greek Demilitarization Proposal Rejected," in *FBIS-WEU*-91-138, July 18, 1991.

national holdings of battle tanks, artillery, armored combat vehicles, combat aircraft, and combat helicopters, and defined each of these weapons for treaty purposes for the first time. These weapons were chosen because they, and the units that contain them, are the main elements of forces that would be required to seize and hold territory in Europe. Although further cuts in these weapons within the Balkans are possible, such regional cuts would further aggravate the imbalance between the forces of these states and those of the successor states of the former USSR. However, the collapse of the USSR and the disintegration of Yugoslavia as an integral state has significantly changed the geo-strategic context for conventional arms control. In the future the main concern of many Balkan states is likely to be focused on the regional military balance within the former Yugoslavia—and within the Balkans as a whole—rather than on the old East-West balance that preoccupied negotiators during the CFE talks. Many of Serbia's neighbors, especially Bulgaria and Hungary, are worried about the size and capability of the Serbian army. They are likely to press for constraints and reductions on Serb equipment (especially tanks) and manpower. This could become a major issue in the Forum for Security Cooperation (FSC), the successor to the CFE negotiations, which was mandated at the Rome CSCE Ministerial (December 1993) to examine regional stability in Southeastern Europe. However, this issue is unlikely to receive serious attention until after the Bosnian conflict has been settled and Serbia has been readmitted to the CSCE.

In theory, it is also possible to abolish conscription. An end to conscription usually means an automatic reduction in the number of actual and potential personnel under arms: actual because regular personnel are usually more expensive to train and maintain than conscripts, and potential because of the smaller number of reserves generated by a smaller regular force. These factors in combination mean fewer trained men. Thus it becomes more difficult to generate the large forces that are needed to seize and hold terrain. The United States and Britain have found professional armies more effective and useful in modern war. Both countries appreciate the limited political constraints on employing professionals where necessary. Continental countries, on the other hand, value the political constraints that a citizen army is credited with imposing on governments, and especially on high commands. The former communist states of Eastern Europe may be caught between wishing to get rid of a party-oriented military system and the possible dangers of substituting a new professional military not strongly rooted in the general population or necessarily committed to democratic values.

Nonacquisition arrangements. It might be possible to agree regionally on the nonacquisition of particularly threatening or clearly destabilizing weapons systems. For example, it may not be too late to avoid acquisition of individually operated (or hand-held) antiaircraft missiles, or to acquire new generations of surface-to-surface missiles. Because hand-held antiaircraft missiles are favorites of irregular forces, governments may welcome an agreement not to acquire, transfer, or permit the transit of such systems. It might also be possible to affirm and refine regional undertakings made elsewhere about the nonacquisition of surface-to-surface missiles, nuclear, chemical and biological weapons, and inhumane weapons.

Nuclear-free zones. NFZs are the most familiar form of nonacquisition arrangements. Frequently propounded and seldom achieved (the Latin American nuclear-free zone established by the Treaty of Tlateloco is the only existing example), nuclear-free zones remain popular with governments of nonnuclear states that wish to remove actual or potential nuclear threats from neighboring countries, or that have disagreements with states that possess or host them. The end of the Cold War also ended much of the attraction that this idea may have had for the Balkans.

Residual interest in a Balkan nuclear-free zone as a contribution to nuclear stability in Europe may, therefore, be much reduced. In the past, Greece, Romania, and Bulgaria favored the establishment of such a zone, with mild support by Yugoslavia. Turkey strongly opposed the regional NFZ idea, making any nuclear withdrawals from the area contingent on a European solution to the problem. Ankara refused to attend the Balkan summit of 1984 until the NFZ idea was given a less prominent place on the agenda. Since then, the NFZ idea has figured rhetorically and occasionally in discussions, but without much emphasis in official discourse.[13]

(B) INCREASE DIALOGUE

In the planning leading up to Helsinki II, some governments, including the United States, suggested a permanent dialogue on security issues—where military subjects of all kinds could be raised by member states—in the belief that such discussions could generate new measures that would benefit Europe, either as a whole or regionally. Dialogues about military doctrine and other subjects among U.S., Soviet, NATO, and Warsaw Treaty military personnel, experts, and academics in the last few years of the Cold War yielded benefits for all parties. Aside from eroding simplistic, two-dimensional "enemy" images, such talks are said to foster a more sophisticated understanding of what concerns opponents, and about the reason armed forces acquire certain weapons or train and deploy in particular ways. Dialogue yields the double benefit of increased sophistication about the meaning of adversary force dispositions and greater confidence about the nature of adversary intentions. Furthermore, personal contacts established at such conferences can be pursued. Most participants appear to agree that there are benefits to this sort of dialogue for all sides, without being able either to specify exactly what they are or to quantify them.

If a Balkan security system or a southeastern CSCE caucus were developed, this procedure could provide a forum for fostering better relations between potential national antagonists. A promising start in this direction was made at the CSCE Ministerial in Rome (December 1993), which mandated the Forum for Security Cooperation (FCS), the successor to the CFE negotiations, to examine regional stability in Southeastern Europe. However, as noted earlier, discussions on arms control and regional security in the Balkans are not likely to make significant progress

---

[13] See F. Stephen Larrabee, "The Southern Periphery," in *Problems of Balkan Security: Southeastern Europe in the 1990s*, ed. Paul S. Shoup and George W. Hoffman (Washington, D.C.: Woodrow Wilson Center Press, 1990), 192–193.

until after a peace settlement in Bosnia has been achieved and Serbia has been readmitted to the CSCE.

"Hot lines"—dedicated and secure communication links between potential disputants at the highest level—are frequently suggested as a palliative for international difficulties. Their value lies in the presumed merit of allowing national leaders to deal directly with each other in emergencies, in a final effort to avoid conflict. The best known hot line—between Washington and Moscow—was established to inhibit intercontinental nuclear exchanges in a world where missile flight times took less than half an hour. The usefulness of hot lines in situations involving prospects of conventional war has been neither tested nor demonstrated. For risks of war in the Balkans, aside from the reliability and exclusivity of carefully maintained dedicated communications, there is no obvious advantage to hot lines over diplomatic dialogue—or, if political levels are required, direct telephone communications between leaders.

Hot lines may be of greater value in this region once conflict has begun and one party or another wishes to end it. In those circumstances, prearranged and reliable communications would be invaluable. But communications about conflict termination are better established between the prospective antagonists and a prearranged third party, than directly. The reason is that the mutual credibility of antagonists is low; and conflict termination requires a high degree of confidence in the reliability of the messenger, as well as in the content and nature of the message. One need only recall the Chinese warning of August 1950 about entering the Korean War if UN forces approached the Manchurian frontier, to understand the reason that verbal precision and reliable interlocutors are necessary. On that occasion, the Chinese sent an elliptical warning through the Indian UN delegate—a party the U.S. government distrusted. The message was, therefore, presumed to be self-serving propaganda and ignored.

In the Balkan context, prior agreement among potential disputants to remain in continuing contact with a European institution such as the CPC, or with a mutually agreed upon capital, could at a minimum provide a reliable channel for arranging cease-fires, or at least discussing them at the point where one party in dispute found that useful.

(c) Mutual Surveillance

In combination with CFE reductions, CSBMs will have reduced the risks of massive surprise attack to something close to the vanishing point. Thus, East European worries about enough warning of massive invasion from Russia or other neighbors may be somewhat reduced. It is the other class of military problems more peculiar to this region that remain unaffected—that is, dissident minorities and breakaway provinces—with unneighborly outsiders' support for either.

If there is a military threat, it might be infiltration of light forces or irregulars in support of dissidents, rather than cross-border operations of heavy forces. Therefore, governments could welcome more detailed oversight over remote regions on their own territory and that of their neighbors; and more control over outsiders' access to national territory. In short, governments might welcome better territorial surveillance.

An open skies agreement may succeed in exposing territory and military facilities in much of Europe between the Atlantic and the Urals and in all of Southeastern Europe (minus Albania and the former Yugoslavia) to adversary observation by air. Helsinki II may extend such agreed aerial observation to all of Europe. Hungary and Romania have already negotiated an open skies agreement of their own. Furthermore, Article XV of the CFE treaty calls on parties not to use concealment measures to impede verification of compliance "by national, or multinational technical means" (while allowing certain broad categories of concealment practices).

In other words, the future may bring an intercontinental aerial inspection regime; a European aerial inspection regime covering all European territory, keyed to the verification of CFE agreement compliance as expanded by Helsinki II; and the beginnings of some Europewide understanding about how much concealment from overhead (for example, satellite) observation is legitimate. If realized, these prospects could be building blocks for future regional cooperation among governments. Provided there is the political will, such arrangements might be exploited by additional measures in the Balkans, keyed to the special kinds of potential security problems noted above, such as:

- ad hoc open skies agreements among some or all Eastern European states, featuring common operation of observation aircraft (or permitted aerial adversary inspections). These could help parties in dispute assure themselves and each other about what may or may not be going on in remote areas; and
- overhead surveillance. As photographic resolution and radar imagery of commercially available satellite photography improve, governments may wish to contract with foreign owners of overhead systems for continuous coverage of particular areas.

Conclusions

It is tempting to suggest that the Cold War was somehow a historical pause between more familiar or natural-seeming patterns, such as the periods before and just after World War I. As then, today the anticipated threats to peace and order in the Balkans are the collapse of empires, and the actual or potential outbreak of ethnic or religious conflicts between mutually uncongenial populations forced to coexist within borders imposed by outsiders.

Yet, the world of the 1990s is different from the world of the 1890s or the 1920s. Regional outbreaks of violence now seem less likely to escalate into continental ones. Then, disturbing foreign events eventually appeared as newsprint for the literate minority in dominant countries. Governments could maneuver around ignorant, and often unconcerned, general publics. Today, global events are visible to virtually all when they happen, if not exactly as they happen. Then, a weak or disintegrating state was a temptation for rival powers to impose their influence. Today, even if instability in the Balkans is a pervasive and unpleasant prospect, states outside this region may not regard most conflicts there as of concern sufficient to justify the use of force—not if large, long-term, bloody, or expensive involvement is the price of interference. Governments outside the region may find it more congenial to rely initially on economic measures or on partial military steps. Thereafter, they may choose to confine participation in foreign military operations to limited collective action for that high proportion of potential cases where no compelling and publicly plausible national interest can be identified.

In short, attracting and involving stronger outside support may no longer be easy for antagonists within this region. Instead, states or other parties within the Balkans may need to resolve their own conflicts, or rely on arrangements with regional or broader international mechanisms to reduce the dangers of conflict, or to limit conflict should it break out. Among such arrangements, norms and procedures that separate minority questions from territorial issues are among the most important. Such procedures could render illegitimate and, therefore, perhaps more difficult the most dangerous threats to this region—territorial claims justified by the dissatisfaction of dissident minorities in would-be breakaway provinces.

Were such norms in place, information exchanges, inspection and surveillance systems, and limits on force size, location, and readiness could help convince governments that are traditional antagonists about the more benign intentions of neighbors. So might agreed limits on weapons acquisitions and transfers. Yet, to be effective, all these measures require continuing detailed and open dialogues among past and potential antagonists about subjects that affect their security. Also needed is a high degree of reliable cooperation among governments within the region, so that any actually agreed arms control or confidence-building measures work as anticipated. Continuing dialogue and cooperation is necessary to assure that measures intended to build confidence do not, instead, merely provoke anxiety.

X

Balkan Cooperation: Realities and Prospects

Radovan Vukadinovic

The long history of Balkan relations has been marked for centuries by alternating periods of peace and sudden tumbles into the abyss of war. The terms "balkanization" and "Balkan powder keg" faithfully reflect features of the Balkan landscape and relations between Balkan states.[1] Now the Cold War has ended East-West bloc divisions. In this new situation, the key question is whether the end of the Cold War has increased or diminished the prospects for Balkan cooperation.

One can readily understand that it is much easier to analyze the Balkan wars, conflicts, disputes, and misunderstandings than the forms and content of Balkan cooperation. The relatively modest literature on modern political trends in the Balkans focuses mainly on analyses of those conflicts, the possible strategic activities of the great powers or the Balkan states, the impact of earlier bloc policies and general appraisals of the place that the Balkans occupy in the political strategy of the superpowers.[2]

The Quest for Balkan Cooperation

To appreciate current prospects for regional cooperation, it may be useful briefly to review past efforts to foster cooperation in the Balkans.

After World War I, many smaller European countries found themselves in uncer-

---

[1] Ranko Petkovic, *Balkan: Niti "bure baruta" niti "zona aira"* (Zagreb: Globus, 1977), 31.

[2] See Paul S. Shoup and George W. Hoffman, eds., *Problems of Balkan Security: Southeastern Europe in the 1990s* (Washington, D.C.: Woodrow Wilson Center Press, 1990), and David Carlton and Carlo Schaerf, eds., *South-Eastern Europe after Tito: A Powder Keg for the 1980s?* (London: The Macmillan Press, 1983).

tain political vacuums on the continent. Soon after the end of the war, attempts were made to create new alliances aimed at strengthening their respective positions. Fearing a restoration of the Hapsburg dynasty in Hungary, Czechoslovakia and Yugoslavia concluded the Little Entente, later signed by Romania.[3] When Romania joined, the Little Entente was extended to include Bulgaria, so that the three Balkan states were linked up by a certain degree of political cooperation.

The clauses of the treaty guaranteed the security of existing frontiers and mutual assistance in the event of an unprovoked attack. In mid-February 1923 in Geneva, a pact was signed formalizing the organization of the Little Entente and establishing a standing council of foreign ministers, an economic council and standing secretariat.

Although the Little Entente came into being because its members sought self-protection, the actual motive for the action was the effort by France to preserve the provisions of the Peace of Versailles. At the same time, France hoped the Little Entente would constitute a bulwark against growing German and Italian ambitions. In practice, however, the Little Entente never engaged in any major activities and its last meeting was convened in Bled, Yugoslavia, just before the collapse of Czechoslovakia in August 1938.

The Balkan Entente, modeled on the Little Entente, came into being in 1934 and was encouraged by fear of German and Italian aspirations in the Balkans. Once again Balkan and French policies were in accord, as both sought to preserve the status quo in the Balkans and check the growing strength of fascist forces.

Unlike the Little Entente, however, which was mainly of a political nature, the Balkan Entente was charged with organizing Balkan defense. Its members—Yugoslavia, Bulgaria, and Greece—pledged to promote closer political, economic, and cultural ties.

However, the Balkan Entente came into being too late. Internal and external factors were already undermining its main objectives. The growth of fascist forces in some Balkan countries could no longer be checked, and the entire Versailles peace order was crumbling. Germany and Italy dealt the final blow to the short-lived alliance.

The Balkan countries emerged from World War II with differing characteristics. Some—Yugoslavia, Albania, Greece—had actively fought among the ranks of the antifascist forces; Romania and Bulgaria had sided with the fascists; Turkey had remained neutral.[4] Meanwhile, the new political-strategic pattern in Europe was directly reflected in new divisions in the Balkans. There, the interests of the big powers were in collision, as were two competing sociopolitical structures.

At this time the idea of a Balkan Federation came to life among the countries of the so-called peoples' democracies. Yugoslavia and Bulgaria, and later Albania,

[3] The treaty between Yugoslavia and Czechoslovakia was signed on August 1, 1920; between Romania and Czechoslovakia on April 23, 1921, and between Yugoslavia and Romania on June 7, 1921.

[4] See Cedonir Popov, *Od Versaillesa do Danziga* (Belgrad: Prosreta, 1976).

strove for stronger political, military, and economic positions and closer links with the Soviet Union. Bulgaria, headed by communist leader Georgi Dimitrov, hoped the Balkan Federation would definitely do away with the animosities and conflicts of the past, and enable the country to forget the role it had played in the last war. There was some hesitation on the part of Yugoslavia, which believed the time was not yet ripe for a federation, and which was also suspicious of Stalin's intentions.[5] Furthermore, Yugoslavia had its own problems establishing new relations within the new federation. From the outset Stalin feared that he might be unable to control the Balkan Federation.

Vacillations regarding a Balkan Federation were cut short by a shift in Soviet policy. Stalin gave up his earlier idea of creating a number of federations in Eastern Europe and determined that bilateral relationships between the USSR and the "peoples' democracies" would be best.[6] When the Cominform Resolution was published in 1948, Bulgaria was the leading light in the anti-Yugoslav campaign, while the other Balkan "peoples' democracies" joined wholeheartedly in the policy of condemning and "excommunicating" Yugoslavia. This definitively ended the idea of a Balkan Federation becoming the supreme form of regional cooperation.

The idea of a Balkan Federation was also the first and most pronounced attempt to merge Bulgaria and Yugoslavia into a single state, the prototype of continuing integration. Differences over the speed at which this integration should take place, however, as well as the Soviet political and ideological onslaught on Yugoslavia, made it impossible to realize this plan.

Under these new circumstances, Yugoslavia needed Western support against its former allies in the "peoples' democracies." New efforts were made to rally the other Balkan states. The Treaty of Friendship and Cooperation between Greece and Turkey was concluded on February 28, 1953, in Ankara. It was valid for a period of five years and referred in particular to Article 51 of the UN Charter, dealing with the right to individual and collective self-defense. Under the treaty, the respective Balkan states pledged to strengthen defense and security measures, cooperate in preserving peace, and hold regular consultations among their foreign ministers. The treaty also provided for direct consultations between the chiefs-of-staff to discuss any threats to peace and measures to be taken in the event of an unprovoked attack.

Apart from these security provisions, stress was also placed on the general strengthening of economic, technical, and cultural ties. The three countries pledged to resolve their disputes peacefully and to refrain from joining any treaties jeopardizing the interests of the others. Considering the ongoing Cold War and East-West bloc divisions, the alliance of the three Balkan countries was highly important, as it was open to any other country in the region.[7] Indeed, Yugoslav authors considered the Balkan Pact to be the first applied form of "peaceful coexistence."

[5] See Tito's explanation, *Borba*, 28 Apr. 1950.

[6] According to Vladimir Dedijer, Stalin envisaged forming three federations in Eastern Europe: Polish-Czechoslovak, Romanian-Hungarian, and Bulgarian-Yugoslavian. Vladimir Dedijer, *Staljinova izgubljena bitka* (Sarajevo: Svjetlost, 1968), 132.

[7] Ljubomir Radovanovic, *Nesvrstanost* (Belgrade: Rad, 1973), 72.

The treaty on political cooperation and mutual international aid between Yugoslavia, Greece, and Turkey, valid for a period of twenty years, was signed on August 9, 1954, in Bled. The treaty stressed the peaceful resolution of conflicts and banned any use of force. Each of the members pledged support and arms aid in the event of aggression against one of the signatories. Should one of the members be at war, the form of aid would be determined by consultation. This latter provision was highly significant. It created the possibility that Greece and Turkey, as NATO members, might be involved in a conflict that Yugoslavia would not wish to join.

In many ways the Balkan Pact was a unique international agreement. Its signatories were three Balkan countries, one of which had opted for a nonaligned policy coupled with building socialism, while the two others were active NATO members and committed to the values of the capitalist world. Some students of international relations consider this example of cooperation—initiated several years before the emergence of Khrushchev's concept of peaceful coexistence between capitalism and socialism—as proof that peaceful cooperation could, indeed, be realized between countries with different sociopolitical regimes.

One should not forget, however, that all three of these countries were exposed to the Soviet threat. Expelled from the Cominform, under pressure of an economic blockade and exposed to military provocations, Yugoslavia sought outside support without raising the question of joining NATO. Greece, which had been through a bloody civil war and still feared continuing upheavals, and Turkey, with its extensive border with the Soviet Union and membership in NATO, were both ideal Yugoslav allies. Under the so-called southern NATO wing, Yugoslavia was able to find Balkan allies.

NATO strategists were satisfied that Yugoslavia's alliance with Turkey and Greece had virtually linked up NATO's southern wing, without raising the issue of Yugoslavia's joining the alliance as a full member. But views differed. Some Western policymakers considered Yugoslavia's association with two NATO members to be sufficient and believed that Yugoslavia had been brought under the protection of the Western alliance.[8] Others held the view that Yugoslavia still was not to be fully trusted, and that NATO policy was endangering the treaty's vital interests.

East European and Soviet propaganda branded the Balkan Pact as evidence of Yugoslavia's "betrayal" of socialism and an example of what the so-called independence of a one-time socialist country might lead to.[9] Soviet commentators clearly

---

[8] The Greek author Stratis Sorneritis wrote that the defense pact concluded by the three countries, only thanks to the Yugoslav stand, retained its strictly Balkan character despite efforts to include it in NATO's military and political mechanism. See *Review of International Affairs*, no. 129–130 (August 15–September 15, 1955), pp. 4–5.

[9] The "price" for Western aid, and partially possible NATO agreement for Greece and Turkey to enter into a defensive alliance with Yugoslavia, was paid: Yugoslavia stopped its aid to the partisans in the Greek civil war, the question of Trieste was settled, and no more territorial claims were made on Austria. Walter R. Roberts, "U.S.-Yugoslav Relations—An Historical Appraisal," in *Problems of Balkan Security: Southeastern Europe in the 1990s,* ed. Paul S. Shoup and George W. Hoffman (Washington, D.C.: Woodrow Wilson Center Press, 1990), 37.

considered that Yugoslavia was joining NATO through the back door.

The Treaty on Friendship and Cooperation, and the Treaty on Alliance, Political Cooperation and International Aid, and finally the founding of the Balkan Consultative Assembly, laid sound foundations for cooperation between the three Balkan states. However, just when the structure was completed, the whole issue was shelved.

There are two reasons that the Balkan Pact never really came into its own. The first is the timing of the conclusion of the pact. Faced with the Cold War, the Korean War, and Balkan East-West divisions, the three countries wholeheartedly sought to create an alliance designed to link up three different states that were also expected to cope with certain open questions in their other bilateral relationships. After the death of Stalin in 1953, the Soviet Union began to show a willingness to restore relations with Yugoslavia, and the issue of reconciliation with Moscow gradually acquired a priority in Yugoslav foreign policy. After the Belgrade meeting between Khrushchev and Tito in 1955 and the Moscow Declaration of 1956, relations between the USSR and Yugoslavia were normalized and Yugoslavia no longer felt seriously threatened by the Soviet Union. As a result, the Yugoslav side was no longer interested in promoting trilateral Balkan cooperation. Meanwhile, Yugoslavia was busily engaged in working toward a new goal: rallying the nonaligned countries. To this, one should add the first signs that the Cold War was waning—a fact that put Yugoslavia's security in a completely new light.

Neither Greece nor Turkey, however, had any special reason to advance the Balkan Pact.[10] Their dispute over Cyprus, relegated to second place during the Cold War, flared up again, making any trilateral Balkan cooperation impossible.

Despite these changed circumstances, all three countries agreed not to rescind the Balkan Pact, but quietly to shelve it.

This sophisticated structure of Balkan relations, containing political, military, and economic components, which was designed to pave the way for better tripartite cooperation, illustrated once again that the Balkan countries find it difficult to build their cooperation arrangements on the basis of their own interests and needs. Once France had been a major external factor; later the Soviet Union briefly played this role; and during the Cold War, the common fear of the danger from the East induced the three Balkan states to seek security in an alliance. As soon as external conditions changed, however, the alliance virtually ceased to exist.

The Idea of the Balkans as a Nuclear-free Zone

In 1957, Romanian Prime Minister Chivu Stoica launched a plan for transforming the Balkans into a nuclear-free zone. This prompted, in various parts of the Balkans, a series of discussions, conferences, and meetings of heads of state to debate the elimination of atomic weapons and chemical warfare.[11]

---

[10] See Andrew Wilson, "The Aegean Dispute," *Adelphi Papers No. 144* (London: International Institute for Strategic Studies, 1979–1980).

[11] Radovan Vukadinovic, "Possibility for Balkan Denuclearization," *The Korean Journal of Interna-*

Initially, the entire idea was derived from the USSR's wish to eliminate American nuclear weapons from Turkey and Greece. In time, however, the concept acquired a different outline. Romania's initiative was later supported and further elaborated by Bulgaria, while in the early 1980s, Greece, under Prime Minister Andreas Papandreou, joined the campaign. Although each of the Balkan countries hoped to further its foreign policy goals by developing the idea of a nuclear-free zone, this unrealized long-term political proposal did produce some positive results.

The efforts to eliminate the nuclear threat, applauded by most of the Balkan countries, gave rise to a broad-based movement of political and societal forces that launched a campaign under the watchword "eliminate nuclear weapons" while simultaneously seeking to attain other aims. The sponsors of this extensive campaign, however, could hardly have believed that the results of the then popular European plans (Rapacki, Unden, Gomulka, Palmo) would pave the way for dealing with far more important and vital issues.[12]

The Romanians, trying to achieve a more independent stand, embraced the original Soviet initiative on denuclearization as their own, hoping that it would promote a special role for Romania. At a certain moment, Bulgaria did much the same, striving to display broader interest in a more independent approach in foreign policy generally. Bulgaria saw the issue as a useful way to take some initiative of its own in the Balkans (Zhivkov proposed to denuclearize the Balkans in 1981, for example). Support for the proposal was also a defense against possible Soviet pressure to deploy SS-20 missiles on Bulgarian territory. For both Balkan countries, the idea—especially in the 1980s—had a special meaning owing to the general antinuclear sentiment in Europe at the time generated by the acrimonious debate over the deployment of U.S. medium-range missiles in Europe.

Greece initially opposed nuclear-free zone proposals in the 1950s and 1960s to maintain solidarity with its NATO partners. But in the 1980s under Prime Minister Andreas Papandreou, who sought to exploit the issue for domestic purposes (to appease his Left wing and because it allowed him to portray himself as a champion of détente in the Balkans), denuclearization became a very important priority in Greek foreign policy. In particular, it gave Papandreou the chance to raise the issue of U.S. military bases in Greece.

Turkey was strongly opposed to the idea of establishing such a zone in the Balkans. Its opposition came from the special notion of Greek-Turkish relations, distrust of the Warsaw Pact members, and the fact that nuclear weapons were stationed at American bases in Turkey. Turkey also wished to be a loyal member of NATO and a strong ally of the United States.

---

tional Studies XX, no. 3 (Fall 1989): 405–421. Athanasios Platias and R. J. Rydell, "International Security Regimes: The Case of a Balkan Nuclear-Free Zone," in *South Eastern Europe after Tito: A Powder Keg for the 1980s?* ed. David Carlton and Carlo Schaerf (London: The Macmillan Press, 1983), 105–131.

[12] For more details, see Radovan Vukadinovic, *Zone bez nuklearnog oruzja* (Zagreb: Liber, 1979).

At the time, when Balkan relations started to improve (the first conference of ministers for foreign affairs in Belgrade in 1988), there was clearly no consensus on the issue. At one time, there were vague plans for establishing such a zone without Turkey, or rather without that country's Asian part. Then followed proposals to expand the zone to include Hungary and Austria. All this clearly showed that all the plans for setting up a nuclear-free zone were only one part of extensive discussions to resolve other problems in a more comprehensive view of the overall Balkan situation.

Yugoslav statements to the effect that Yugoslavia was in favor of such a zone, that in principle Yugoslavia supported all plans in the direction of disarmament, that the country itself was the largest nuclear-free zone in the Balkans, and that it was not aligned with any of the blocs, nonetheless were couched in a tone of restraint. Yugoslavia, jealously guarding its independent foreign policy, feared the formation of any zone and the emergence of any situation involving the acceptance of pledges on the part of the nuclear superpowers. This appeared to be too high a price to pay in Yugoslav eyes.

Yugoslav policy correctly appraised the need to join in this plan, however, as a possible way of calming relations in the Balkans and even developing some kind of cooperation. At a time when the leaders of Greece, Bulgaria, and Romania were engaged in a series of meetings, Yugoslavia gradually realized that it should promote good relations with its neighbors. Its diplomats paved the way for Balkan cooperation, combining the development of cooperation with steps toward the creation of an atom-free zone in the Balkans. Mutual cooperation in the Balkans was considered a sound basis for eventual denuclearization, which could be discussed in the more distant future.

After the Greek election in April 1990, the new Greek government under Prime Minister Constantine Mitsotakis dropped Papandreou's antinuclear stand and rejoined the NATO consensus on nuclear weapons. This move resulted partly from the need to accept the doctrine of nuclear deterrence as a condition for entry into the West European Union.

Bulgaria and Romania, faced with new international developments and internal changes, also dropped the idea of denuclearization. As a result of domestic turmoil throughout the region and the disintegration of Yugoslavia, the entire idea lost its international and regional importance. The only concrete meaning denuclearization could have in Greek-Turkish relations was the removal of offensive weapons from border areas, which Mitsotakis proposed in July 1991. This proposal came too suddenly and without adequate preparation, however; and partly because of this, Turkey refused to start discussion on the proposal.

Pan-Balkan Cooperation

The international reputation of the Balkans as an eternal scene of strife and the most backward part of Europe, economically and culturally, could only be disproved by comprehensive Balkan cooperation and the inclusion of the states concerned in Europe's economic and scientific integration. Balkan statesmen realized this when they decided, after the 1975 meeting in Helsinki, to embark on a quest for new, joint Balkan activities.

The new atmosphere in Europe, the policy of détente, and the first convocation of a meeting of Balkan heads of state in the history of the Balkans (Albanian leader Enver Hoxha was absent), tended to enhance the momentum toward greater cooperation. The idea of a nuclear-free zone remained as a permanent link in all discussions, while other concrete proposals were offered suggesting ways to strengthen Balkan ties.

The first meeting of Balkan experts, convened in Athens in 1976, dealt with issues of economic and technical cooperation. It identified as many as 162 fields in which Balkan cooperation would be possible, including especially agriculture, trade, economic relations, energy, health services, communications, and environmental protection.

The Athens meeting marked the beginning of a series of discussions on ways and means to promote closer cooperation in the Balkans. Any serious student of these meetings and their achievements will see that in practice there was actually no appreciable progress. One should not forget, however, that when the talks on cooperation first began, bloc divisions were still much in evidence and bloc restrictions did much to hamper cooperation between various Balkan countries. Furthermore, as possible forms of cooperation were enumerated, the idea emerged that, despite all their differences and divisions, the Balkan states coexisted in a region both Mediterranean and Middle European, extending along the reaches of the Danube, meaning that the Balkans inevitably must share the destiny of Europe. All the turbulent events that shook the artificial frontiers of Europe made themselves felt in the Balkans, and the foreign ministers of the region, impressed by the possibility (later reality) of change, took up discussions on possible Balkan cooperation with new enthusiasm.

The key event for all future activities was the first meeting of foreign ministers of Balkan states, convened in Belgrade in 1988. The attendance of the Albanian foreign minister was a historic event.[13] In fact, this was the first meeting at such a level in Balkan history, which in itself marked a step forward in pan-Balkan cooperation.

Extensive discussions over whether or not cooperation should be the only subject—setting aside other open problems in the Balkans (frontiers and minorities)—preceded the meeting. In the end, pragmatic views prevailed. The deliberate postponement of disputed issues that had impaired successful dialogue did not, however, mean that these questions had been shelved. They were simply put on the back burner, owing to the ministers' conviction that the development of extensive Balkan cooperation would result in new, better relationships if the most controversial issues that had perennially divided the nations of the region were initially excluded from the discussions.

This approach proved to be completely justified. The first meeting in Belgrade

---

[13] Documents from the Belgrade Foreign Ministerial Meeting. See *Review of International Affairs*, Belgrade, no. 910 (1988).

was followed by many other meetings of experts and foreign ministers. Despite the political and social changes in most of the Balkan countries, all the countries continued to show an interest in pan-Balkan issues.

As regionalism gained momentum in Europe, this trend found an even stronger echo in the Balkans. There can be no more national ivory towers, no splendid isolation of the poor. Nor was it the intention of the Balkan leaders to use regional cooperation to create an exclusive club to defend themselves against Europe nor to compensate for not being able (with the exception of Greece) to enter the European Community (renamed European Union).

Regional cooperation in the Balkans is regarded as the foundation upon which to transcend the legacy of the past and accelerate development, and equally, as evidence that political initiatives have matured in the Balkans. The Balkan initiatives have intrinsic value and enable these countries to show Europe that they can eventually catch up with the latter's development.

The new picture of Balkan cooperation was created under the influence of the changes sweeping over Europe. The first meeting of Balkan foreign ministers in Belgrade was marked by messages from Ceausescu and Zhivkov, the predominating political vision of Papandreou, and the newly enthroned Ramiz Alia, as well as by the still functioning state presidency of Yugoslavia. By the time of the second foreign ministerial meeting in Tirana in 1990, however, the situation had changed significantly. The host country, Albania, was in the throes of major internal changes that were to end forty years of socialist rule, as had already happened in Bulgaria and Romania. In Greece, Papandreou was no longer prime minister; and in Yugoslavia, divisions and conflicts were rife. Only Turkey maintained a certain continuity of political views and actions.

The fact that despite all these changes all Balkan countries were represented at the meeting and that cooperation was raised to an even higher level is noteworthy. The foreign ministers submitted over sixty proposals at their regular sessions and in various meetings.[14] Bulgaria suggested that Balkan cooperation be institutionalized, and it was finally decided that ministerial meetings would be convened regularly every year. This was a hopeful sign that, under the newly created conditions, the Balkans were moving to strengthen mutual cooperation.[15]

The ministers did not dwell excessively on issues still dividing the Balkan countries. They stressed, however, that in the new European circumstances everything should be done to prevent a resurgence of territorial, minority, ethnic, cultural, or religious disputes. Such a trend, argued Bulgarian Foreign Minister Ljuben Gotsev, might result in the "renewed Balkanization of our relations and not in the acceptance of joint European values and institutions, something we all desire."[16]

---

[14] Ranko Petkovic, "Meeting of Balkan Foreign Ministers in Tirana," *Review of International Affairs*, Belgrade, no. 744 (1990): 7.

[15] Documents from the Foreign Ministerial Meeting in Tirana. See *Review of International Affairs*, Belgrade, no. 975 (1990): 8–26.

[16] Ibid., 9.

The minority question has always been the touchiest and most serious problem in the Balkans and has consistently thwarted efforts to establish bilateral or regional cooperation. Collective and individual minority rights that are protected by the UN Charter, the Helsinki Act and other international documents have now been adopted as standards in the Balkans as well. Balkan representatives have argued that the two issues of minorities and territories should be strictly separated. In keeping with international and European agreements, they have stressed that there must be strict respect for the territorial integrity of every Balkan state.[17]

The fields in which already existing cooperation should be continued have been clearly noted (trade, traffic, industry, tourism, scientific-technical cooperation, energy, agriculture, hydro-engineering, ecology, health, culture, information). A proposal has been suggested to establish an Athens-based scientific institute for economic cooperation in the Balkans, to create a Balkan bank for development, and build a Balkan Forum that would rally all institutions engaged in the advancement of Balkan cooperation.

The breakup of Yugoslavia, however, has created a new situation in the Balkans. As long as the war in Yugoslavia rages, serious implementation of the decisions taken at the recent high-level Balkan meetings is unlikely. Every Balkan country is now watching the deepening of the crises, hoping that they will not further rupture the fragile stability of the region.

Prospective Balkan Cooperation

Although of short duration, efforts at Balkan cooperation to date have shown that such cooperation is possible and useful. Bilateral contacts have paved the way for multilateral cooperation in the interests of every Balkan country's progress.

The economic advantages of cooperation are evident. The development of foreign trade relations in this region enables countries to make rational cuts in transportation costs; international cooperation enables them to produce on economies of scale, the market is larger, and better use is made of raw materials and energy. All these advantages are a result of geographical proximity, complementary economies, and the mutual dependence in traffic and communications in the Balkan region.[18]

Economic cooperation among the Balkan countries never acquired major significance. If one considers trade between the various Balkan countries, it is clear that mutual exchange is on a modest scale. According to Organization for Economic Cooperation and Development (OECD) data, Yugoslavia's share in Greek imports is a mere 1.2 percent, Romania's only 0.5 percent, and Bulgaria's 1.1 percent. In Yugoslavia's total imports from neighboring Balkan states, Romania's share is 1.4 percent, Bulgaria's 0.9 percent and Greece's 0.6 percent; Turkey comes last with only 0.2 percent.[19] At present, specialization and cooperation are hardly worth men-

---

[17] For stand on minorities, see Joint Statement of Ministers. On this very sensitive topic, see Christopher Cviic, *Remaking the Balkans* (London: Pinter Publishers, 1991).

[18] Edita Stojic Imamovic, "Mogucnosti unapredenja multilateralne balkanske suradnje u medunarodnim odnosima," in *Balkan krajem 80-tih* (Belgrade: Marksisticki Center, 1987), 210.

[19] Ibid., 211.

tioning, although efforts are being made in this direction, particularly between some Bulgarian enterprises and partners in Greece and Turkey. The highest forms of production cooperation have been recorded in the joint Yugoslav-Romanian construction of the power stations Djerdap I and II, as well as in military production.

There are several reasons for this state of affairs. These countries' economic development levels, industrialization, and technological standards are far behind those of other European countries.[20] These are not the only reasons, however. Their earlier policies and the desire to develop trade with more industrialized countries led them in different directions that ignored the potential of Balkan cooperation. Now, faced with the difficulties in joining the European Union, economic disintegration in the East, and the collapse of Yugoslavia's nonaligned policy, the Balkan countries must adopt a different view of the Balkans as a potential region of cooperation.

Extensive European regionalization and the many new forms of European cooperation (Baltic, Black Sea, Danubian, Alpen-Adria, Central European Initiative) clearly confirm that this is the road to more rapid development. Regional cooperation is seen as paving the way for these countries to eventually enter the EU.

Turkey is emerging as an important new actor in the southern part of Europe. Turkey not only boasts a vigorous growth rate, it is developing ties to the economies of its less well-developed neighbors. One part of Turkish activities centers on the former Soviet republics in Central Asia, while the other is focused on the Balkans. This very new regional power—some Turks now say that Turkey has its own foreign policy for the first time in the postwar period—is ready to invest abroad. Balkan countries, particularly Albania and Bulgaria, Serbia, and the new republic of Macedonia, are looking to Turkey for economic assistance and capital investment. Turkey was the first country to recognize all four former Yugoslav republics (Slovenia, Croatia, Bosnia-Herzegovina, and Macedonia). Turkish political circles are studying with particular concern the situation of Muslims in the former Yugoslavia. With its economic power and enhanced political influence in the region, Turkey can be expected to try to isolate Serbia and cultivate special relations with Bosnia-Herzegovina, Macedonia, and Albania. In doing this, Turkey is more and more returning to the Balkans. Hoping to embrace former Soviet Central Asian republics, but also Russia and Ukraine in closer regional cooperation, Turkey has recently begun to promote the idea of a Black Sea Economic Zone. All Black Sea countries have been invited to join in creating a customs union and in developing closer economic cooperation. In part this scheme appears designed to isolate Greece. It is also part of the wider American approach to the south, in which Turkey is considered pivotal.

Despite the efforts of the EU to keep some form of cooperation open among former Yugoslav republics, owing to the war in Croatia and Bosnia, it would be unrealistic to expect broader forms of cooperation to develop in the near future. Former Balkan divisions and antagonisms also make prospects for wider cooperation between the southern Slav countries of Serbia, Montenegro, Bulgaria, and Mace-

[20] Ibid., 212.

donia very difficult. The only form of cooperation likely to develop is between Serbia and Montenegro, but event this cooperation has begun to disintegrate lately, as more and more Montenegrins have begun to question the value of close association with Serbia, which has led to Montenegro's progressive isolation and impoverishment.

The fact that none of the Balkan countries really stands a chance of joining the EU before the end of the century will have its effect on Balkan economic cooperation. Furthermore, with the disintegration of old patterns of socialist socioeconomic relations, there are now completely new possibilities for quicker and easier action on the part of interested partners. Slovenia, Croatia, Bosnia, and Macedonia, for instance, are members of the Central European Initiative (formerly Hexagonale).

In view of the earlier forms that cooperation has taken in the region, and of the various suggestions of working groups studying Balkan cooperation, economic cooperation is not the only kind of cooperation that is open. There are extensive possibilities in other fields as well. Environmental-protection issues have long extended beyond national frontiers. This problem can be solved in the Balkans only by multilateral action. The steps taken to clean up the environment along the Danube and the Mediterranean, where pollution has reached disastrous proportions in some countries, could be applied in the Balkans as well.

Cooperation in health services, veterinary science, energy, hydro-engineering, traffic, communications, and agriculture will enable all the Balkan countries to establish closer links. The more rational use of resources will help them to resolve their particular and common problems. The disappearance of earlier ideological and political barriers now has created opportunities for a concrete approach to multilateral projects, all of which may strengthen possibilities for joint Balkan actions. New forms of local border traffic and the abolition of visas will facilitate large-scale contacts among the citizens of Balkan states.

Possibilities in tourism are also extensive. Despite numerous similarities in regional sites, the Balkan states should not so much compete with one another as strive to develop joint tourism plans on a comprehensive scale. The geographic variety of the Balkans could attract many visitors from Europe and North America who will find in this cultural microcosm the traces of many ancient civilizations.

Cultural cooperation in the Balkans has a sound tradition. Better relations in the Balkans will further encourage such activities.[21] The same applies to sports, which have a long tradition in Balkan history.

Intensified international cooperation in the Balkans—and with a widening circle of participants—would be the best way for cooperation gradually to overshadow earlier animosities, misunderstanding, hatred, and enmity, so that in the newly created circumstances of peaceful neighborly relations, it will be easier to cope with all disputed issues. But all of this will depend on the political situation, which, at the moment, is not favorable for the promotion of cooperation.

---

[21] See Milena Milanovic, "Kulturna suradnja izmedu Jugoslavije i balkanskih zemalja, posebno u knjizevnosti," in *Balkan krajem 80-tih* (Belgrade: Marksisticki Center, 1987), 269–286.

The Balkans and Europe

The disintegration of the once monolithic socialist system has ended the past socioeconomic order in the Balkans. The four former socialist states in the Balkans are seeking to cope with the new situation, but face great difficulties. All of them regard "joining Europe" as the only way out of their political and economic problems. The former Yugoslavia, Albania, Bulgaria, and Romania, all of which face the collapse of their economic structures, see closer ties to Europe as the only means of survival during the years ahead. For different reasons Turkey too is seeking admission to the EU. Turkey has always faithfully supported NATO, but its West European allies apparently do not think that Turkey is ready for membership in the EU.

Aware of the critical Balkan situation, the EU has continued to maintain its stringent criteria for the admission of new members. The same applies for the countries of Central and Eastern Europe—the so-called Visegrad countries: Hungary, Poland, the Czech Republic, and Slovakia—which are likewise seeking admission.

In both cases, these groups of countries are expected to first prove that they have developed a vigorous multiparty political system, that they are developing market economies, and, finally, that they have ensured consistent respect for human and minority rights. With the possible exception of Slovenia, the former socialist countries in the Balkans all have had considerable difficulty in proving that they have met these conditions. The creation of a democratic multiparty political system is only in an embryonic stage in these countries. In their economies, they are vacillating between the law of the market and a new state-controlled order. As far as human rights are concerned, none of the former socialist countries in the Balkans has a spotless record. To this list of weaknesses one must add the shaky economies of all of these countries. They will require massive aid before they can hope to be anywhere near eligible for membership in the European Union.

Consequently, the problems of the Balkan countries are still quite remote for planners in Brussels. Indeed, the Visegrad countries stand a much better chance of being admitted to the EU—perhaps by the turn of the century—than do the former communist states of the Balkans.

The Balkan political landscape today strongly resembles the one that existed in Europe just before World War I. One can see the potential German and Italian sway in the western part of the region, a rather weak Russian position in Serbia and Montenegro, growing Turkish interests in Macedonia and Bosnia-Herzegovina, as well as unrest in Kosovo—all fertile ground for increasing instability.

Will the pieces of former Yugoslavia be swallowed up by these conflicting interests? Will a new war flare up in the Balkans? What will remain, for example, of Macedonia? Will Turkish interests be sufficient to ensure its existence? Will there be a Muslim uprising? And will war break out between the Serbs and the Albanians?

Some analysts of the Yugoslav crisis stress that it is certainly not in Europe's interest to have such an unsettled region on its borders or to countenance new

Balkanization that would result in a situation similar to that in Lebanon.[22] It is not only a question of maintaining north-south communications in Europe, or of who will pay Yugoslavia's debts.

The issue is far more complex and might well give rise to many new disputes and confrontations. It is clear that there are numerous contested issues among all the Balkan countries (territorial, minorities) and that one crisis may well set off others. It is but one step from the Greco-Turkish dispute over Cyprus to a possible Serbian-Albanian war, growing claims on Macedonia, Bulgarian-Serbian disputes, and the new bitter conflict between Serbs and Croats.

When in late 1991 there was a call for European crisis management in Yugoslavia, Europe turned a deaf ear.[23] As the crisis has gained momentum, good services and observer missions have become a reality. One might say that Balkan issues have been thrust on Europe. Unless it wishes to see the Balkans and pieces of the former Yugoslavia become a second Lebanon, Europe will be unable to avoid more direct and stronger engagement in the Balkans.[24]

The disintegration of Yugoslavia confirms that the Balkan countries have no alternative but to join European institutions and the movement toward European integration. Now that links are stronger between all countries, especially in Europe, the Balkans cannot remain outside Europe. Balkan cooperation is not an end in itself, but only a means to join Europe as soon and as easily as possible. The acceptance of European norms may result in the European way of life being brought to this region. Some of the Balkan protagonists seem to realize this today. The question is how to achieve this goal as quickly and painlessly as possible.

---

[22] Yugoslavia's internal development and foreign policy are soundly described in Christopher Cviic, "The Background and Implications of the Domestic Scene in Yugoslavia," and Zachary T. Irwin, "Yugoslavia's Foreign Policy and Southeastern Europe," in Shoup and Hoffman, *Problems of Balkan Security*, pp. 89–124 and 151–175.

[23] Ranko Petkovic, *Anatomy of the Yugoslav Crisis*, CSS Papers, No. 6, Belgrade Center for Strategic Studies; Radovan Vukadinovic, *The Breakup of Yugoslavia: Threats and Challenges* (The Hague: Clingendael Institute, 1992).

[24] Radovan Vukadinovic, *La fin de la Yougoslavia et l'instabilité balkanique* (Paris: Foundation nationale des sciences politiques, 1991), 40.

PART 3

The Role of External Actors and Institutions

XI

Washington, Moscow, and the Balkans: Strategic Retreat or Reengagement?

F. Stephen Larrabee

The Balkans have traditionally been a source of instability and rivalry in European politics. During the Cold War, the region emerged as a major focal point of strategic rivalry between the United States and the Soviet Union.[1] Then, as now, Yugoslavia acted as a catalyst for the involvement of both superpowers in the region and later served as an important strategic buffer separating the two opposing blocs.

The end of the Cold War has shattered the bipolar division of the Balkans into blocs and unleashed a tumultuous process of change in the region. As in the early postwar period, developments in the Balkans are forcing the United States and Russia to redefine their interests in the region and the world more broadly. This process could have far-reaching implications for the role that each plays, not only in the Balkans, but also in the world at large in the post-Cold War era.

This chapter examines the interests of the United States and the USSR (and later Russia as a successor state to the USSR) in the Balkans. The first part of the chapter focuses on the evolution of these interests during the Cold War. Subsequent sections analyze the impact of the end of the Cold War on these interests and how these interests may evolve in the future. Is the end of the Cold War likely to lead to strategic disengagement or "strategic reengagement" by the United States and Russia? What are the driving forces behind their policies? How is each power likely to define its interests in the region in the future?

[1] For a detailed discussion, see F. Stephen Larrabee, "Balkan Security," *Adelphi Papers*, No. 135 (London: The International Institute for Strategic Studies, 1976).

The Cold War and the Balkans

Current U.S. and Russian policy in the Balkans must be seen against the background of the Cold War. Attitudes and policies formed during the Cold War directly shaped the approach that each power adopted toward the region after the collapse of the Berlin Wall. Indeed, the tendency of the United States to see the unfolding crisis in Yugoslavia largely from a Cold War perspective was one of the main factors inhibiting a more forward-looking and enlightened policy toward Yugoslavia in the early stages of the conflict.

U.S. and Soviet involvement in the Balkans during the early postwar period was a direct product of the Cold War. Prior to 1945, the United States had no strong indigenous interests in the Balkans. The region had never been a major focal point for U.S. policy. American interest emerged principally as a by-product of Washington's overall interest in preventing the Soviet Union's domination of Europe. This interest, however, did not manifest itself immediately. Rather, it grew gradually with the intensification of the Cold War and the growing perception of the need to counter Soviet moves in Eastern Europe and Iran.

The withdrawal of British power from the Mediterranean in early 1947 faced the United States with a major strategic choice—whether to replace the British as the major power in the area, or risk the possible extension of communism farther south into the eastern Mediterranean. Aid to Greece and Turkey was seen by the Truman administration as essential to forestall a possible collapse of the two governments. In order to obtain congressional support for the assistance to Greece and Turkey, however, President Truman consciously portrayed the aid as a part of a larger struggle between "two ways of life" and a broader policy designed "to support free peoples, who are resisting attempted subjugation by armed minorities or by outside pressures."[2]

The clear implication was that if the United States did not assist Greece and Turkey, they would fall under Soviet domination.[3] Actually, however, the Soviet Union had done very little to assist the communist rebels in Greece. A Soviet military mission did not arrive in Greece until 1943. Once in Greece, the mission maintained a low profile; its main task appears to have been to dampen the hopes of the communist-led resistance forces that they could expect much Soviet support or assistance.

---

[2] On the background to the formation of the Truman Doctrine, see in particular Joseph Jones, *The Fifteen Weeks: February 21 to June 5, 1946* (New York: Viking, 1955); Bruce R. Kuniholm, *The Origins of the Cold War in the Near East* (Princeton: Princeton University Press, 1980); and John Gaddis, *The United States and the Origins of the Cold War 1941–1947* (New York: Columbia University Press, 1972). Also Gaddis's insightful article, "Reconsiderations: Was the Truman Doctrine the Real Turning Point?" *Foreign Affairs* 52 (1974): 386–402.

[3] The situation of the two countries, however, was quite different. Greece faced a civil war; Turkey, however, faced no such imminent threat. As one U.S. observer aptly put it at the time, Turkey "was slipped into the oven with Greece because that seemed the surest way to cook a tough bird." See Jones, *The Fifteen Weeks,* 163.

Stalin never really trusted the Greek communists and did not believe they had much chance of success.[4] He feared that they might provoke U.S. military intervention in an area where Moscow had limited control and that lay outside its primary sphere of influence. Hence, he pursued a cautious policy, discouraging the guerrillas on several key occasions from resorting to force. He also delayed sending aid a number of times, seriously crippling the effort by the Greek communists to overthrow the government in Athens.[5]

Stalin's rather cautious approach to the Greek civil war was dictated by two concerns in particular—his desire not to unnecessarily provoke U.S. intervention, and his concern about Tito's increasingly independent behavior. Actually, it was the Yugoslavs, not the Soviets, who were fueling the fires of the Greek civil war. Stalin feared that a successful Greek civil war would increase Tito's power and make him even more difficult to control. Hence, in 1948 he insisted that the insurgency in Greece had to "fold up."[6]

Stalin opposed Bulgarian communist leader Georgi Dimitrov's proposal in 1947 for a Balkan federation between Yugoslavia and Bulgaria for the same reason. He feared that it would be dominated by Yugoslavia and increase Tito's power and stature. Stalin's main aim was to see pliant communist regimes installed in the Balkans that would subordinate their narrow parochial interests to the larger interests of Soviet foreign policy. Hence, he mistrusted both the Greek communists and Tito, whom he regarded as far too independent to be a useful tool of Soviet foreign policy interests.

The Truman Doctrine provided the political basis for increased U.S. involvement in the Balkans and a gradual expansion of U.S. ties to Greece and Turkey. Both countries eagerly sought U.S. protection against the Soviet Union. The United States, however, was initially cautious about including the two countries in a Western collective defense network and only acceded to their entry into NATO after the outbreak of the Korean War.[7]

The Stalin-Tito break in 1948 provided new opportunities, which America quickly seized, for U.S. efforts to contain Soviet expansionism. The decision to render economic and military assistance to Yugoslavia in its struggle against Moscow was purely pragmatic and dictated by realpolitik. Tito was an ardent communist, but he

---

[4] In February 1947 he told a high-level Yugoslav delegation headed by Tito that the Greek uprising had "no chance of success at all" and "must be stopped." Milovan Djilas, *Conversations with Stalin* (New York: Harcourt, Brace and World, 1962), 182.

[5] For an excellent analysis of various shifts in Soviet policy during the early postwar period, see Peter J. Stavrakis, *Moscow and Greek Communism 1944–1949* (Ithaca: Cornell University Press, 1989).

[6] Djilas, *Conversations with Stalin,* 181.

[7] For the background to Greece's entry into NATO, see Theodore Couloumbis, *Greek Political Reaction to American and NATO Influences* (New Haven: Yale University Press, 1967). For Turkey, see George Harris, *The Troubled Alliance: Turkish-American Problems in Historical Perspective* (Washington D.C.: American Enterprise Institute, 1972), 1–46; and George McGhee, *The U.S.-Turkish-Middle East Connection* (London: Macmillan, 1990).

opposed Moscow's effort to expand its influence in the Balkans, which, in the final analysis, was the decisive factor conditioning U.S. policy.

American assistance to Yugoslavia did not turn Yugoslavia into a full-fledged ally, but it ensured that Yugoslavia did not fall back into the Soviet camp. It also contributed to a reduction of tensions with Greece and the formation of the Balkan Pact, signed by Greece, Turkey, and Yugoslavia in Bled (Yugoslavia) in 1954. The pact was largely a dead letter by the time it was signed, but it underscored the degree to which the Balkans had essentially divided along bloc lines by the mid 1950s.

East-West Détente and the Erosion of "Tight Bipolarity"

In the 1960s and 1970s the "tight bipolarity" that had characterized East-West relations in the early postwar period began to dissipate. Centrifugal forces, spurred in particular by the more relaxed East-West atmosphere, began to erode the ability of both superpowers to maintain cohesion within their respective alliances in the Balkans.

The impact was first felt within the Warsaw Pact. Albania's defection to the Chinese camp in 1961 was followed by the emergence of a more autonomous policy on the part of Romania after 1964. The conflict with Romania began as a disagreement over the division of labor within Comecon, but it gradually expanded to encompass a whole range of issues—ties to China, relations with West Germany, reform of the Warsaw Pact, the Middle East, and détente in Europe. Romania adopted a position on all these issues that significantly differed from that of Moscow. Thus, by the mid 1960s, only Bulgaria could be considered firmly in the Soviet camp.

The growing polycentrism within the Soviet bloc in the 1960s prompted a shift in U.S. policy. As the signs of change in Eastern Europe proliferated, the United States abandoned the effort to "roll back" Soviet power and instead emphasized a policy of "peaceful engagement" or "bridgebuilding" in Eastern Europe.[8] The prime goal of the new policy was to exploit the increasing diversity within Eastern Europe and encourage a broad process of East-West reconciliation designed to alter gradually the East-West status quo in the West's favor.

Romania was one of the principal focal points of this new policy. President Nixon's visit to Romania in 1969—the first visit of a U.S. president to Eastern Europe in the postwar period—symbolized the Nixon administration's effort to exploit the new fluidity in East-West relations and to encourage Bucharest's increasingly independent path. In 1975 Romania was awarded most-favored-nation (MFN) status, another important sign of Washington's desire to encourage Ceausescu's deviation.

As with U.S. policy toward Yugoslavia after 1948, the U.S. effort to cultivate Romania after 1968 was essentially an act of realpolitik. It was not that Washington either approved of or was oblivious to Romania's poor human rights record, but this was seen as less important than the fact that Ceausescu was willing to thumb his

---

[8] On the conceptual origins of the policy of "peaceful engagement" see Zbigniew Brzezinski, *Alternative to Partition* (New York: Praeger, 1965).

nose at Moscow on many foreign policy issues, thus making it difficult for Moscow to maintain cohesion within the Warsaw Pact. By the late 1970s, however, Ceausescu's megalomania and repressive domestic policies had become so blatant that the United States gradually began to distance itself from Romania, and relations with Bucharest began to cool.

The United States also continued to voice strong support for Yugoslavia's independence and territorial integrity. Yugoslavia's nonaligned position was considered an important bulwark against the expansion of Soviet influence in the Balkans. Concern about the possibility that Moscow might seek to exploit any instability in Yugoslavia in the wake of Tito's death led the Carter administration to consider resuming arms sales to Yugoslavia.[9] But public revelation of the fact embarrassed the Yugoslavs and put a damper on the move before it could be consummated.

Albania's strong anti-Soviet policy, however, did not lead to an improvement in relations with the United States. On the contrary, Albania found "U.S. imperialism" as reprehensible as Moscow's, and attacked the United States and the USSR with equal vehemence. Tentative overtures by Washington in the mid-1970s to explore Tirana's interest in improving relations were curtly rebuffed, and relations remained essentially nonexistent until the early 1990s.

Thus, by the end of the 1970s, Moscow's position in the Balkans had seriously eroded. Yugoslavia and Albania had escaped from the Soviet orbit, while Romania was a member of the Warsaw Pact in name only. Only Bulgaria could be counted firmly in the Soviet camp.

NATO's Crumbling Southern Flank

The same forces, however, that undermined Soviet hegemony in the Balkans also contributed to an erosion of cohesion within the southern flank of NATO. During the Cold War, both Greece and Turkey subordinated their national interests to the dictates of the NATO alliance, which provided an indispensable shield against any possible Soviet threat. As the sense of immediate threat receded, however, both countries began to give greater weight to national considerations in their policies.

These differences bubbled to the surface in 1963–1964 over Cyprus. The 1963–1964 Cyprus crisis highlighted the differing perspectives of the various actors. For Greece and Turkey, important national interests with deep historical roots were at stake. For the United States, Cyprus was mainly a strategic problem. Washington's main concern was to prevent Moscow from exploiting the crisis to its political advantage; the rights and wrongs of the conflict were of secondary, if not tertiary, importance.

The crisis precipitated a sharp deterioration of U.S. relations with both Greece and Turkey. President Johnson's threat, contained in a letter to Turkish President Ismet Inonu, to cut off aid to Turkey if Ankara invaded Cyprus, unleashed a wave of

---

[9] Bernard Weintraub, "U.S. to Sell Arms to Yugoslavia and Wider Military Cooperation," *New York Times,* 14 Oct. 1977.

public indignation, and prompted Turkey to undertake a reassessment of its foreign policy and reduce its reliance on the United States.[10] In the aftermath of the crisis, Ankara began to diversify its foreign policy, forging closer ties to both Moscow and the Arab countries of the Middle East.[11] Turkey also became guarded about allowing the United States to use Turkish facilities.

Relations with Greece were further exacerbated by the 1967 coup by a group of U.S.-trained military officers. Although there is little evidence that the United States actually engineered the coup, it did little to prevent it. Moreover, the Nixon administration's cozy relationship with the Greek colonels reinforced the impression that the United States, largely for strategic reasons, tacitly supported the dictatorship. The United States, in effect, found itself facing a major dilemma—moral considerations dictated that it condemn the dictatorship; strategic interests, however, dictated that it "get along" with the colonels. In the end, strategic considerations won out—a fact that came back to haunt the United States when the colonels' dictatorship collapsed in the wake of the Cyprus debacle in July 1974.

The 1974 Cyprus crisis contributed to a further erosion of alliance solidarity in the southern region.[12] In contrast to 1964, the United States proved unable to prevent a Turkish invasion of the island. With the decline of the Soviet threat, neither Greece nor Turkey was willing to put alliance solidarity automatically ahead of what each perceived as vital national interests. Meanwhile, the threat of possible Soviet intervention—which had helped to deter Turkey in 1964—had lost much of its credibility and could no longer be used as an effective instrument to ensure alliance solidarity and compliance with U.S. policy preferences.

In the aftermath of the Cyprus crisis, U.S. relations with Turkey seriously deteriorated. The imposition of the arms embargo by the U.S. Congress in February 1975 was seen by Ankara as an unwarranted slap at a loyal ally and provoked a marked cooling in relations. In retaliation, Ankara shut down four important intelligence-gathering networks, which remained closed until the embargo was lifted in 1978 by the Carter administration. Activities at Incirlik airbase and other facilities were also curtailed.

Relations improved somewhat after the lifting of the embargo in 1978 by the Carter administration. In 1982, after difficult negotiations, the Reagan administration succeeded in signing an important Co-location Operation Base Agreement with Ankara, which provided for the expansion and modernization of ten airfields in Turkey.[13] The modernization of the airfields brought U.S. and NATO fighters within

---

[10] The Johnson letter is reprinted along with Inonu's reply in the *Middle Eastern Journal* 20, no. 3 (1966): 386–393.

[11] For a detailed discussion, see Udo Steinbach, *Grundlagen und Ansätze einer Neuorientierung der türkischen Aussenpolitik* (Ebenhausen: Stiftung Wissenschaft und Politik, January 1973). Also Harris, *The Troubled Alliance,* 105–124.

[12] For an excellent discussion of U.S. policy during the 1974 crisis, see Lawrence Stern, "Bitter Lessons: How We Failed in Cyprus," *Foreign Policy* (Summer 1975): 34–78.

[13] For details, see Bruce R. Kuniholm, "Rhetoric and Reality in the Aegean: U.S. Policy Options Toward Greece and Turkey," *SAIS Review* (Winter-Spring 1986): 137–157.

closer striking distance of the Persian Gulf. Turkish officials, however, were quick to emphasize that the bases were to be used only for NATO contingencies, and that their use was subject to Turkish approval.

The 1974 Cyprus crisis also had a strong impact on U.S.-Greek relations. The inability of the United States to prevent the Turkish invasion and the perception of a U.S. "tilt" toward Turkey in the crisis unleashed a wave of anti-Americanism and anti-NATO feelings. Under strong pressure from public opinion, Prime Minister Constantine Karamanlis, who had been called back from his Paris exile to take over the reins of power in the midst of the crisis, was forced to temporarily withdraw Greece from the military structure of NATO. (Greece quietly rejoined the military wing in 1980 after public indignation had abated.)

These moves were part of a larger reorientation of Greek policy that was designed to reduce Greece's reliance on the United States and strengthen its ties to Europe. The cornerstone of this policy was the decision to accelerate Greece's entry into the EC which Karamanlis regarded as an important guarantee against his country backsliding into dictatorship. Moreover, by tying Greece more tightly to Europe, membership in the EC gave Greece a new point of reference, thus allowing it to reduce its dependency on the United States.

In the aftermath of the crisis, Greek security perceptions also underwent a marked shift. Greek concern about a "threat from the North" (the Warsaw Pact) diminished and was replaced by a growing preoccupation with the "threat from the East" (Turkey). In January 1985, the Papandreou government formally announced a shift in Greece's military doctrine designed to reflect the new threat perception. The announcement of the "new doctrine," however, was largely for public consumption. It essentially institutionalized changes that had already taken place in Greek defense policy since the 1974 Cyprus crisis.[14]

The Cyprus crisis also exacerbated Greek-Turkish differences over the Aegean.[15] These bilateral disputes tended to spill over into NATO and erode alliance cohesion on the southern flank. Under the Rogers Agreement, which provided for Greece's reentry into NATO, a new allied air force command (Seventh AFAF) was to be established in Larissa in northern Greece. The Larissa headquarters, however, was never opened because of differences with Turkey over air command responsibilities. Greece also repeatedly canceled its participation in NATO exercises in protest over the exclusion of the island of Lemnos on the grounds that this policy represented tacit support of the Turkish position in the Aegean.[16]

---

[14] See Thanos Veremis, "Greece and NATO: Continuity and Change," in *NATO's Southern Allies: Internal and External Challenges,* ed. John Chipman (London: Routledge, 1988), 271–272.

[15] A detailed discussion of these disputes is beyond the scope of this chapter. For a comprehensive analysis, see Andrew Wilson, "The Aegean Dispute," *Adelphi Papers,* No. 155 (London: International Institute for Strategic Studies, Winter 1979–1980).

[16] For a good discussion of NATO command and control problems caused by the Greek-Turkish dispute see Robert McDonald, "Alliance Problems in the Eastern Mediterranean—Greece, Turkey and Cyprus, Part II," *Adelphi Papers,* No. 229, 72–89. Also Veremis, "Greece and NATO," 267–278.

The advent to power of Andreas Papandreou's Pan-Hellenic Socialist Movement (PASOK) in 1981 added new strains to an already wobbly relationship. Papandreou's vitriolic anti-American rhetoric, as well as his flirtation with Third World radicals and lax attitude toward terrorism, were a source of constant irritation to American officials. Papandreou also demonstratively departed from NATO positions on key issues such as the deployment of U.S. intermediate-range missiles in Europe (INF), the Soviet shooting down of the KAL airliner, and Western sanctions imposed on Poland.[17]

Papandreou was careful, however, not to allow relations with Washington to deteriorate too far nor to take actions that might irrevocably jeopardize ties to the United States. He never withdrew from NATO—primarily because he recognized that Greece would be even more vulnerable outside than inside NATO. Nor, despite his many threats, did he close the U.S. bases in Greece. A new base agreement was concluded in 1983 that gave the United States continued use of the most important bases. Moreover, Greece's growing economic problems and need for Western economic assistance led Papandreou to tone down his anti-American rhetoric after his reelection in 1985. Still, relations remained cool, and Greece was regarded more as a nuisance than a reliable ally.

The Soviet Union, however, was unable to exploit these strains for its own advantage. Moscow's relations with Turkey were damaged by the invasion of Afghanistan, which heightened Turkish concern about Soviet intentions in the Persian Gulf and induced Ankara to seek closer military cooperation with the United States.[18] Meanwhile, Moscow made surprisingly little effort to court Greece, despite Papandreou's strident anti-American rhetoric, principally from fear of further damaging relations with Turkey, which remained far more important from the Soviet point of view.

The Yugoslav Crisis and the End of the Cold War

The Yugoslav crisis in 1991–1992 was the first post-Cold War crisis. It highlighted the changing nature of the security challenge in Europe after the end of the Cold War. Both Washington and Moscow were slow to comprehend the nature of this change—in part because they were preoccupied with other issues—the United States with the Gulf War, and the USSR with its own internal problems. Hence, both misjudged the seriousness of the crisis and failed to appreciate its wider implications for European security.

The United States viewed the brewing crisis in Yugoslavia largely from a Cold War perspective. During the Cold War, Yugoslavia had been a pawn in the larger

[17] For a detailed discussion of Papandreou's policy, see F. Stephen Larrabee, "Greece for the Greeks," *Foreign Policy* (Winter 1981): 158–174, and John C. Loulis, "Papandreou's Foreign Policy," *Foreign Affairs* (Winter 1984/85): 375–391. See also Thanos Veremis's discussion of Papandreou's policy in this volume.

[18] The Co-location Operation Base Agreement, signed with the United States in 1982, was one of the direct results of this closer military cooperation.

strategic competition for influence between Moscow and Washington. It acted as a balancing wheel and strategic buffer in the region. Each side feared that any change in Yugoslavia's nonaligned position would upset the strategic balance in the region. Hence, each side sought to ensure that Yugoslavia did not drift into the other camp, thereby upsetting the regional balance.

The main U.S. goal during the Cold War was to prevent Yugoslavia from falling under Soviet influence, which it feared might occur if Yugoslavia disintegrated. Once the USSR collapsed, however, U.S. concern about Yugoslavia significantly diminished because a breakup of Yugoslavia no longer risked triggering Soviet military intervention. Washington initially regarded the crisis as a "tribal war" or "local conflict," with little strategic significance and failed to foresee the broader implications of the conflict for European security and stability.

In addition, when the Yugoslav crisis first broke out, the Bush administration's attention was focused on other issues—the Gulf War, the breakup of the Soviet Union, and German unification. Thus, despite clear warnings from the CIA that Yugoslavia was about to break up, the United States did not give the crisis the high-level policy attention it deserved.[19] Again, however, this was partly because the conflict was seen primarily as a "local conflict," and its larger implications were ignored or underestimated.

The administration's preoccupation with the disintegration of the USSR influenced its perception of the problem. American policymakers worried that any encouragement of separatist trends in Slovenia and Croatia would have a ripple effect elsewhere in Eastern Europe and the USSR, encouraging a host of separatist and irredentist movements from the Baltics to Bessarabia. As a result, the United States continued to insist on preserving Yugoslavia's unity long after Yugoslavia as an integral state had effectively ceased to exist.[20]

Indeed, strong support from the United States for maintaining Yugoslavia's integrity may well have indirectly (and unintentionally) contributed to the escalation of the conflict by encouraging Serbian leader Slobodan Milosevic and the leadership of the Yugoslav army (JNA) to believe that the United States would not oppose the army's intervention to hold the country together, as long as this was done quickly and with a minimal loss of life.

---

[19] The U.S. response to the Yugoslav crisis bears marked similarity to the U.S. handling of the 1974 Cyprus crisis. In both instances, the United States had clear advance warning of a potential crisis, but mid-level officials could not get high-level officials to focus on the impending crisis because they were preoccupied with other issues, particularly Watergate and the Middle East. On this point, see in particular Stern, "Bitter Lessons: How We Failed in Cyprus," 34–78.

[20] During Secretary of State James Baker's visit to Belgrade in mid-June 1991—a week before the outbreak of conflict between Slovenia and the Yugoslav federal army—the United States still insisted that Yugoslav unity had to be preserved. See David Hoffman, "Baker Urges Yugoslavs to Keep Unity," *Washington Post*, 22 June 1991; David Binder, "United Yugoslavia Goal of U.S. Policy," *New York Times,* 1 July 1991; "Baker Backing for United Yugoslavia," *Financial Times,* 22–23 June 1991.

Even when fighting broke out in Slovenia in June 1991, the United States continued to see the conflict as a "local conflict" with no broad geo-political significance. The Bush administration viewed the conflict largely as a "European problem," which was best left to the Europeans to handle since, in the administration's view, it involved no broad strategic U.S. interests.[21] It thus encouraged the European Community—since renamed the European Union—to take the lead in managing the issue. Only when the EU mediation failed did the United States become actively engaged in the conflict diplomatically. By then, however, it was too late: the conflict had already burgeoned into a major international crisis with far-reaching political and strategic consequences.

The Clinton administration initially seemed inclined to take a more interventionist stand on Bosnia than the Bush administration. But President Clinton was unable to get allied support for his preferred options—air strikes and lifting the arms embargo against the Bosnians—and he was unwilling to intervene unilaterally. He thus was forced to "redefine" the problem. Having initially implied that vital U.S. interests were at stake, the administration then backtracked, arguing that the United States had no vital stake in the conflict. In response to European pressure, however, it did send 300 ground soldiers to Macedonia. The exact purpose of this force, however, was unclear, since it was obviously too small to serve as an effective fighting force. Indeed, it appeared to confirm the worst fears of many critics and military leaders—that the administration was being dragged incrementally into the conflict "through the backdoor" without either a clear concept or a strategic objective.

Bosnia, moreover, has provoked strong fissures within the alliance. Divergences between the United States and its European allies have surfaced over a number of issues: (1) the shape of the peace plan; (2) sanctions; (3) lifting the arms embargo; (4) air strikes; and (5) peacekeeping and U.S. diplomatic engagement in facilitating a negotiated settlement.[22] Indeed, the crisis has raised serious doubts in Europe about President Clinton's resolve and capacity for leadership. Thus, how well he manages the crisis in the future could have a major impact on the future of transatlantic relations as well as relations with Russia.

While it is still too soon to make a definitive judgment about the impact of the Bosnian crisis on the alliance and on U.S. policy, several lessons can be drawn from the U.S. handling of the crisis so far. The first is the need for early diplomatic intervention. Had the United States and its allies initially taken the crisis more seriously and moved to head it off, much of the later violence might have been avoided.

The second lesson is that timely U.S. leadership is still important. The time may come when the Europeans may be able to manage such crises alone, but, as the failure of EU mediation efforts underscored, that day has not yet arrived. U.S.

---

[21] See Bush's interview with Carola Kaps, "Bush sieht in der Bewältigung der Krise in Jugoslawien zunächst eine Aufgabe der Europäer," *Frankfurter Allgemeine Zeitung*, 10 July 1991.

[22] For details, see F. Stephen Larrabee, "The Yugoslav Crisis and U.S.-European Relations," *Chaillot Papers* (Paris: WEU Institute for Security Studies, forthcoming).

leadership still remains indispensable, even if the United States cannot always persuade its allies to accept its views.

Third, a credible military threat is an indispensable element of any effective diplomacy. From the outset, Serbian leader Slobodan Milosevic knew that he faced little risk of military retaliation, and that there was little likelihood that the United States would intervene. Thus, he had little incentive to negotiate seriously—and he didn't.

Shifting Russian Interests in the Balkans

The end of the Cold War has also had a major impact on Russian interests in the Balkans. The collapse of communism has deprived Moscow of a foothold in the area. Bulgaria, once Moscow's strongest ally in the region, is increasingly looking westward and has shown little interest in developing strong security ties to Russia. As a result, Russian influence in Bulgaria has dwindled significantly. Albania is also looking increasingly to the West and shows little interest in close ties to Moscow. Relations with Romania remain cool as a result of Moscow's support for the separatist movement in the self-proclaimed "Trans-Dniestrian Republic."

It is thus tempting to see Russia as no longer an important factor in the Balkans. Such an assessment, however, would be premature. While initially Moscow seemed less interested in the Balkans and less capable of playing a role there—witness its rather low-key profile in the early stages of the Yugoslav conflict—since mid 1992 it has begun to play a more active role in the region. The pro-Western policy pursued by Foreign Minister Andrei Kozyrev has come under increasing attack by conservatives and nationalists, who have accused Kozyrev of betraying Serbia, a traditional Russian ally.[23] As a result, Russia has begun to pursue a more "balanced" policy in the Yugoslav conflict and has emerged as one of the most important defenders of Serb interests behind the scenes.

This support may pay important dividends in the long run. Indeed, Serbia could become an important Russian ally. The two countries have strong historic and cultural ties. Moreover, there is a strong coincidence of political and strategic interests between the two Slavic states that goes beyond religion or history. Serbia needs Russia to break out of its political isolation, while close ties to Serbia allow Russia to maintain a foothold in the Balkans. Moreover, any settlement in Bosnia is likely to need Russian acquiescence, ensuring that Russian interests will be considered in any eventual settlement.

The growing Russian involvement in Georgia and Moldova—especially the latter—also reflects Moscow's desire to remain a player in the surrounding region, as does Moscow's recent effort to mend fences with Greece. The communiqué issued at the end of Yeltsin's visit to Athens in July 1993 stressed the strong cultural,

[23] See, in particular, the article by Evgeni Ambartsumov, head of the Committee on International Affairs and Foreign Economic Ties of the Russian Supreme Soviet, *Izvestiya,* 29 June 1992. For a detailed discussion, see Suzanne Crow, "Reading Moscow's Policies Toward the Rump Yugoslavia," *RFE/RL Research Report* (November 6, 1992): 13–19.

religious, and historical ties between the two countries.[24] These interests extend far beyond a commitment to Orthodoxy, however, and have an important strategic dimension. Both countries share a common concern to contain Turkey, and both see close ties to Serbia as an important means of accomplishing this. Hence, an informal Athens-Belgrade-Moscow axis could eventually emerge, designed to block Turkish (and German) penetration of the Balkans.

The emergence of a security vacuum in the Balkans could, moreover, lead to an intensification of geo-political rivalry between Turkey and Russia and the possible emergence of a "new Eastern question." The collapse of the Ottoman Empire led to the withdrawal of Turkey from the Balkans, and thereafter Turkey adopted a low profile in the Balkans, especially in the postwar period.

However, with the end of the Cold War, Turkey has begun to pursue a more active policy in the Balkans. Ties to Bulgaria and Albania have been strengthened, especially in the defense area. Ankara has also been active within the Islamic world in drumming up support for Bosnia. In May 1992, Turkey joined Iran and Algeria in calling for a special meeting of the foreign ministers of the Organization of the Islamic Conference to discuss the situation. And in early 1994 Turkish Prime Minister Tansu Ciller and Pakistani Prime Minister Benazir Bhutto made a highly publicized visit to Sarajevo to dramatize the plight of the Bosnian Muslims in the besieged city.

At the same time, the disintegration of the Soviet Union has opened new opportunities for the expansion of Turkish influence in Central Asia and the Caucasus. Many of these countries look to Turkey, a secular Muslim state with an expanding market economy, as a model for their own development. While Turkey has been relatively cautious about exploiting these new opportunities presented by the collapse of communism in Central Asia and the Caucasus, Ankara's expanding ties to the Muslim countries in these regions have made Moscow very nervous and sparked a new, albeit muted, struggle for influence in the region.

The danger is that this growing geo-strategic rivalry between Russia and Turkey in Central Asia and the Caucasus could be transposed to the Balkans, where both countries have strong historic interests. Turkey has already made important inroads in Bulgaria, Albania, Macedonia and Bosnia. This has begun to worry Greek officials, who have expressed increasing concern about the emergence of a "Muslim arc" on Greece's northern border. Serbia has expressed similar concerns. These concerns could lead both countries, especially Serbia, to forge closer ties to Moscow in order to block the expansion of Turkish influence in the Balkans, sparking the type of geo-political rivalry between Russia and Turkey that characterized Balkan politics in the late nineteenth century.

U.S. Policy toward Greece and Turkey after the Cold War

At the same time, the end of the Cold War is likely to have a significant impact on

[24] Didier Kunz, "La Grèce et la Russie affirment leurs positions communes dans les Balkans," *Le Monde*, 3 July 1993.

U.S. relations with Greece and Turkey. During the Cold War both countries were regarded as important barriers against the expansion of Soviet influence in the Mediterranean and as a means of tying down large numbers of Soviet troops that otherwise might have been used in Central Europe had a conflict broken out there. Both countries also provided important bases and intelligence facilities directed against the Soviet Union.[25]

The end of the Cold War and collapse of the Soviet Union, however, have reduced the importance of both allies—though not in equal measure. Meanwhile, growing instability in the Persian Gulf has increased U.S. concerns about the security threats that may emanate from this region. Hence, in the future, U.S. interests in the eastern Mediterranean are likely to be dictated less by concerns about any residual Russian threat to Europe than by the role that bases and facilities in the region may play in Middle East and Persian Gulf contingencies. At the same time, "out of area" issues are likely to become an increasingly important part of the security dialogue with both countries, especially Turkey.

In the coming decade, Greek and U.S. interests may increasingly diverge. The U.S. bases in Greece have become less vital now that the Soviet threat has disappeared. In addition, Greece's ties to Europe have become more important. Greece's entry into the EC (now EU) has contributed to a gradual "Europeanization" of its foreign policy—a trend that is visible elsewhere in the southern region as well (with the exception of Turkey).[26] Today, Greece looks increasingly to Brussels rather than to Washington, which is a major change from a decade ago.

The end of the Cold War seems likely to reinforce this trend. The elimination of the Soviet military threat and the collapse of communism in Eastern Europe diminishes the importance of the U.S. military guarantee for Greece. Meanwhile, Greece's need to stay in step with its EU allies on defense issues is likely to intensify the trend toward the "Europeanization" of its foreign and defense policy. This does not preclude bilateral cooperation with the United States, but it will limit American freedom of action on those issues in which there is not a clear convergence of interests.

Developments in the Balkans, moreover, could create new strains in relations with the United States. The growing turmoil in the Balkans since 1989, especially the disintegration of Yugoslavia, has led to a "renationalization"—and, to some extent, a "re-Balkanization"—of Greek policy. As the turmoil in the Balkans has spread, Greece has revived its traditional ties to Serbia to counterbalance Turkey and contain the Former Yugoslav Republic of Macedonia. As a result, Greek policy has increasingly diverged from that of the Western allies, including the United States. Greece has opposed the use of force against Serbia and maintained close ties to Belgrade, which it sees as a bulwark against the expansion of Turkish influence in the region. Greek objections over the name of the newly independent Former

---

[25] For a good discussion of the strategic importance of these bases and facilities, see John Chipman, *NATO's Southern Allies: Internal and External Challenges* (London: Routledge, 1988), especially chapter 1.

[26] See Ian O. Lesser, "The United States and the Mediterranean After the Cold War," *Yearbook 1990* (Athens: The Hellenic Foundation for Defense and Foreign Policy, 1991), 230.

Yugoslav Republic of Macedonia have paralyzed EU policy and put Athens at odds with its European Union partners as well as the United States.

The renationalization of Greek policy is likely to be even more pronounced as a result of the Greek elections in October 1993, which returned former Prime Minister Andreas Papandreou to power. While Papandreou is unlikely to engage in the type of Washington-bashing that characterized his policy during the early 1980s, he is likely to be a more difficult partner than Prime Minister Mitsotakis was. Papandreou's party has traditionally had close ties to the socialists in Serbia. Thus, Greece may be unwilling to go along with future efforts to isolate Belgrade and could even undercut the sanctions against Serbia, either openly or by not enforcing them vigorously. It may also block efforts by the EU to provide much-needed economic assistance to Macedonia. Indeed, a de facto Athens-Belgrade alliance could emerge in the Balkans—perhaps supported by Moscow—as a means of countering Turkey's expanding influence in the area. Greece and Serbia may also collude to keep Macedonia weak and prevent an increase in Bulgarian influence there.

U.S. ties to Turkey could also prove to be an increasing source of tension with Athens. The United States has traditionally tried to maintain an awkward balance in its relations with Greece and Turkey—often with little success.[27] With the end of the Cold War, however, the United States may feel less constrained to maintain this balance. This could lead to a strengthening of ties to Turkey, especially in the military area. Greece, for instance, has shown great anxiety about U.S. plans to "cascade" military equipment withdrawn under the CFE treaty to Turkey.

While Turkey no longer is important as a bulwark against Soviet expansion (the main U.S. interest during the Cold War), its strategic importance in the Persian Gulf and Central Asia—where Turkey has strong economic and political ties—has increased. The Gulf War underscored Turkey's critical importance in any Persian Gulf contingencies. Turkish approval for the use of its military airbases gave the United States an important military advantage, allowing it to strike targets in Iraq from two directions at the same time. The redeployment of 100 thousand Turkish troops along the Iraqi border also forced Iraq to redeploy a substantial number of troops to the north that otherwise would have been used to defend Kuwait. In addition, Turkey's closure of the Mosul pipeline, which carries 54 percent of Iraq's oil, significantly contributed to the success of the economic sanctions.

President Özal clearly hoped to leverage his support for the United States in the Gulf War into developing a "new strategic relationship" with Washington. The prospects for this were always somewhat dubious. Bush's defeat, and Özal's death in April 1993, made them even more so. As Ian Lesser has noted, the window for expanded defense cooperation has probably closed—if, indeed, it was ever really open.[28] The imperatives that drove U.S.-Turkish military assistance, above all the

---

[27] For a good discussion of this delicate balancing act and its dilemmas, see Theodore A. Couloumbis, *The United States, Greece and Turkey* (New York: Praeger, 1983).

[28] See Lesser, *Bridge or Barrier: Turkey and the West After the Cold War*, RAND, R-4204-AF/A, 1992, p. 34.

Soviet threat, have disappeared. In addition, support for foreign assistance is diminishing in Congress. Thus, while Turkey will probably remain one of the top recipients of U.S. security assistance, the overall amount is likely to decline and be increasingly in the form of credits rather than grant aid, as had been the case in the past.

In addition, Ankara is likely to remain cautious about allowing the United States to use its facilities for "out of area" contingencies. Turkey has strong economic and political interests in the Middle East and it is unlikely to risk jeopardizing these interests—as its reserved attitude toward the deployment of a multinational "rapid reaction force" near Silopi on the Iraqi border underscores. Moreover, the Turkish government is under strong domestic pressure to end the deployment of the allied troops stationed in southern Anatolia to provide humanitarian assistance to the Kurdish refugees under Operation Provide Comfort. While the mandate was extended in the summer of 1993, the deployment continues to be a sensitive issue in U.S.-Turkish bilateral relations as well as Turkish domestic politics. Many Turks fear that U.S. support for the Kurds in northern Iraq will create pressures for the establishment of an independent Kurdish state and exacerbate separatist pressures among the Kurds in Turkey.

Indeed, the Kurdish issue could become an increasing irritant in U.S.-Turkish bilateral relations. The Turkish military has long pressed for a tougher policy toward the Kurds and, with Özal's death, their influence on Turkish policy is likely to increase. However, a more repressive policy toward the Kurds could lead to tensions with the Clinton administration, which has made human rights one of the key elements of its foreign policy, as well as with the U.S. Congress.

These interests will have to be balanced against Turkey's growing strategic importance in the Persian Gulf, the Balkans, and Central Asia, where the United States also has important interests. In all these areas, Turkey's role is likely to be increasingly important. Turkey serves as a successful model of a secular, democratic state for the countries of Central Asia, and it can play an important role as "bridge" to these countries. A Turkey in disarray, however, increasingly beset by domestic turmoil and economic disorder, and feeling abandoned by the West, could be a source of tension. Hence, Washington will have to be sensitive to Turkey's domestic environment as it seeks to work out a new relationship with Ankara in the post-Cold War period. Moreover, pressing Turkey too hard to become a "Western outpost" or "Trojan horse" in Central Asia could backfire, intensifying Russian suspicions and fueling pan-Turkish sentiment—currently not strong—thereby weakening Turkey's ties to the West over the long run.

Prospects for the Future

Future U.S. and Russian policy in the Balkans are likely to be heavily influenced by developments in the former Yugoslavia, especially Bosnia. Indeed, the Bosnian crisis could prove to be a watershed. Both the United States and Russia are being forced by the crisis to redefine their national interests, not just in the Balkans, but in the world more generally. At the same time, both powers, albeit for different reasons, find themselves being dragged back into the Balkans.

The Yugoslav conflict has sparked a major debate in the United States about U.S. interests in the post-Cold War era. In effect, two major schools of thought have emerged. On the one side are the "neo-Wilsonians," who argue that failure to take stronger—albeit limited—military action against Serbia makes a mockery of U.S. calls for a "new world order" and risks encouraging further aggression.[29] On the other side are the "neo-realists," who maintain that the United States has no vital interests in Yugoslavia and should not get involved militarily.[30]

The debate on Yugoslavia, moreover, has intersected with, and given greater impetus to, a larger debate within the U.S. political and military elite about the use of American military power in the post-Cold War era. While some parts of the State Department have argued for a more active American policy in Yugoslavia, including the selective use of U.S. air power, the U.S. military has been strongly opposed to the use of U.S. military forces in Yugoslavia, fearing that Yugoslavia could become a "slippery slope" that will drag the United States into a protracted—and essentially "unwinnable"—civil war. General Colin Powell, former head of the Joint Chiefs of Staff, was particularly outspoken on this issue, arguing that, unless victory can be achieved quickly and decisively, U.S. military forces should not be committed.[31]

The "Powell Doctrine," however, is essentially an "all or nothing" strategy that leaves the United States very few options for dealing with the type of conflicts the United States and its allies are increasingly likely to face in the post-Cold War world. It is heavily influenced by the successful U.S. prosecution of the Gulf War as well as U.S. experience in Vietnam and Lebanon. The Gulf War, however, is unlikely to be repeated, at least not in Europe. As Uwe Nerlich points out in his contribution to this volume, rather than exemplifying the dominant type of future aggression, the outcome of the war is likely to be a powerful deterrent against a similar conflict breaking out in the future.

In short, the Gulf War scenario is misleading and not an accurate guide to policy—at least not for Europe and the Balkans. The type of conflicts that will arise in the Balkans and elsewhere in Eastern Europe in the future are more likely to resemble

---

[29] See, for instance, George Kenney, "Blueprint for a Wider War," *New York Times*, 30 September 1992. Kenney was Yugoslav desk officer in the State Department. He resigned in late August 1992 to protest U.S. policy. See also Don M. Snider, "Stop Serbia; Bomb Serbia," *New York Times*, 13 October 1992, and Jim Hoagland, "August Guns: How Sarajevo Will Reshape U.S. Strategy," *Washington Post*, 19 August 1992.

[30] See Christopher Layne, "Is America Marching to Folly Once Again?" *Los Angeles Times*, 9 August 1992, and by the same author, "Tragedy in the Balkans. So What?" *New York Times*, 29 May 1992. Also, Benjamin Schwarz, "Leave the Little Wars Alone," *Los Angeles Times*, 8 June 1992; Ronald Steel, "Let Them Sink," *The New Republic* (November 2, 1992): 15–16.

[31] See Michael Gordon, "Powell Delivers a Resounding No on Using Limited Force in Bosnia," *New York Times*, 28 Sept. 1992. Also, Colin Powell, "Why Generals Get Nervous," *New York Times*, 8 Oct. 1992.

the conflict in Yugoslavia than the one in Iraq. Thus, the United States and its allies must give more thought to how military power can be used to achieve limited objectives in conflicts where the end goal may not be "decisive victory" in the traditional military sense.

At the same time, Western security structures, above all NATO, need to be reshaped to deal with these new "Yugoslav-like" conflicts. Unless NATO proves capable of meeting the new challenges posed by the end of the Cold War, it is likely to become marginalized and increasingly irrelevant.[32] Today, these conflicts are largely outside the traditional NATO area; therefore, the real issue is whether NATO remains an alliance of last resort against an armed attack against member-states or whether it assumes new crisis management functions.

Future U.S. policy in the Balkans, therefore, is likely to increasingly hinge on the nature and pace of the transformation of NATO as well as on the domestic developments in the United States. America's European allies are likely to tie their willingness to send peacekeeping forces to Bosnia to the size and level of U.S. peace-keeping forces. President Clinton initially promised to send 25 thousand peacekeeping troops to enforce a Bosnian peace settlement. But it may be increasingly difficult to muster congressional and public support for such a large peacekeeping operation in the post-Somalia and post-Haiti climate in the United States.

Failure of the United States to live up to its commitment would have serious implications, not only for the enforcement of a peace settlement in Bosnia, but on U.S.-European relations more broadly. If the United States does not send peacekeeping troops or substantially reduces its original commitment, many Europeans are likely to perceive this as a signal of diminished U.S. commitment to Europe. This could spark intensified efforts to create a European defense force independent of NATO and/or lead to a renationalization of European defense policy.

At the same time, the United States will have to find a way to bring Russia into the peace process without giving it a veto right over NATO's freedom of action in the Bosnian conflict. The Russian effort to broker a cease-fire in March 1994 underscores that Russia remains an important factor in the Balkans, especially vis-à-vis the Serbs. No lasting peace is likely in Bosnia unless Russia supports it. The creation of a "Contact Group" composed of the United States, the European Union, Russia and the UN, established in April 1994, may help to bring Russia more closely into the peace process and diminish Russian concerns about the lack of consultation and fears of diplomatic marginalization, which were the main driving forces behind the March 1994 Russian initiative.

Ultimately, however, it is the U.S. role that will be the most critical. The course of the Yugoslav conflict has demonstrated time and again that U.S. engagement and leadership are indispensable to any long-term resolution of the conflict and the restoration of stability and security in the Balkans as a whole. Only the United States has the military muscle and military assets to provide a credible military threat that

[32] See Ronald D. Asmus, Richard Kugler and F. Stephen Larrabee, "Building a New NATO," *Foreign Affairs* (September/October 1993): 2–14.

can undergird effective diplomacy and bring about a negotiated settlement. The real question—the one on which Balkan security and the future of the transatlantic relationship ultimately is likely to rest—is whether it has the political will and diplomatic skill or not. Indeed, Bosnia could prove to be a major watershed in U.S.-European relations.

XII

The European Community and the Balkans

Loukas Tsoukalis

The Balkans today are little more than a geographical definition and a historical legacy derived from the period of the Ottoman Empire. Conflict in the region during the nineteenth and the early part of the twentieth centuries had been directly linked to the progressive disintegration of the old empire and the arrangement of frontiers for the new nation-states. It had been fueled by the new forces of nationalism, the irredentist claims, and the ethnic tensions that characterized large parts of the area. The relative stability that ensued, especially during the Cold War, now appears to be threatened once more.

The region consists of countries that are very different in terms of size, economic development, politics, culture, and religion. Political differences have become, of course, less pronounced since the collapse of communist regimes in those countries that had been under the Soviet sphere of influence since the end of World War II. More than four decades of such influence, however, have left large scars that are unlikely to disappear soon.

Because of those differences as well as the Cold War line that formerly divided the countries of this region, bilateral contacts, whether economic, political or cultural, have been extremely limited until recently. All countries previously have looked for privileged partners outside the region, and they are likely to continue doing so, even though bilateral and multilateral contacts among neighboring countries may be strengthened in the near future.

The Balkans include one member country of the European Community (renamed European Union). Greece became an associate member of the EC in 1961 and a full member twenty years later. The Balkans also include two prospective members currently holding associate status. Turkey applied for membership in 1987 and Cyprus in 1990. Both are considered "orphans of Europe," a term coined by then

EC Commission President Jacques Delors to refer to those European countries that had remained outside Europe's main economic blocs. Political reality in Europe, however, has changed radically since President Delors first used this term. Virtually all the countries of the European Free Trade Area (EFTA), the old rival organization in Western Europe, are now knocking at the door of the EU, while the countries of Eastern Europe have also joined the ranks of "orphans" since liberating themselves from their oppressive Soviet father. They include the Balkan countries that have recently emerged from a long period of communist rule.

There are numerous actual and potential conflicts in the region that can be the source of major instability. The Greek-Turkish dispute has old, historical roots. It has survived despite the fact that both countries found themselves on the same side of the old Iron Curtain (or is it partly because of that?), and it has acquired a bigger and more dangerous dimension since the Turkish invasion of Cyprus in 1974 and the continued Turkish occupation of a large part of the island. The breakdown of the old political order in Eastern Europe, welcome though it undoubtedly is, has created a totally new situation in the Balkans. Countries such as Albania, Bulgaria, and Romania will have to experience a painful transition to a market economy and parliamentary democracy, with serious risks of internal instability for countries that have precious little experience of either. Because of historical legacies, irredentism that has been lurking in the background, and the existence of ethnic minorities, internal instability risks spilling across national frontiers. The disintegration of the former Yugoslavia constitutes the worst-case scenario for what could happen elsewhere.

EC/EU Interests in the Area

The EC (now EU) is an unusual animal in the international zoo in which nation-states coexist with an ever increasing number of intergovernmental and transnational organizations. It is still qualitatively different from traditional sovereign actors, even though important powers have been already transferred from its constituent units to the center, and more are expected to move in the same direction in the near future, especially after the ratification of the Maastricht treaty. It has little in common, however, with organizations such as NATO, which is basically an intergovernmental alliance, and the CSCE, which is much less.

The latest phase of integration in the EC, which started in the second half of the 1980s and has been largely associated with the completion of the internal market, has brought the EC into the new areas of economic regulation inside national boundaries and into services and factors of production.[1] The dramatic transformation of the economic and political climate in Western Europe has led to a continuous expansion of the EC agenda, which has eventually included the creation of new redistributive instruments, some hesitant steps in terms of social policy, and, more

[1] Loukas Tsoukalis, *The New European Economy: The Politics and Economics of Integration,* Second Revised Edition (Oxford: Oxford University Press, 1993).

recently, the renewed attempts to establish an economic and monetary union and a political union.

The revitalization of European economies in the late 1980s, with the return of high growth and the creation of many new jobs, went hand in hand with a major restructuring of industry; and, unlike earlier periods, this restructuring was no longer confined within national boundaries. Political initiatives had a noticeable effect on market expectations, thus creating a favorable environment for investment as well as the further expansion and deepening of regional integration.

The deceleration of economic growth in more recent years may suggest that this virtuous circle had by then come to an end. The strong skepticism with which European public opinion has reacted to the Maastricht treaty, of which economic and monetary union and a common foreign and defense policy are the most important parts, can be taken as a further indication of the change of climate. It is, indeed, possible that we have already reached the end of another phase in European integration, although it is still too early to pronounce a clear judgment. The process of integration has always been characterized by fits and starts, and this may be just a temporary shift to a smaller gear and a lower speed.

The emerging European system is characterized by a rapidly increasing mobility of goods, services, and factors of production; it is also characterized by a high degree of decentralization of political power. Historical experience suggests that there is a strong element of spillover between different areas of economic policy as well as between economics and politics. There are good reasons to expect in the future a further transfer of powers to the center.

A similar observation can be made with respect to the role of the Community as an international actor. In view of the relative weakness of the European political system compared with its sheer economic weight, the Community has often tried to use available economic instruments for political objectives. There has also been a discrepancy between its ambitions and the expectations of other countries about the Community's role on the one hand and its ability to deliver the goods on the other. These may be seen as the frustrations of an economic giant who remained for years a political dwarf.

The EC started basically as an incomplete customs union, which meant that the common external tariff constituted the building block of its fledgling international role. With the gradual deepening of integration, new common instruments have been created, while there has also been a shift in the division of external policy competences from national to EC institutions. The deepening of integration has included incursions, hesitant in the beginning, into the area of high politics—even though the distinction between low and high politics is sometimes highly misleading (being essentially a product of the Cold War). European Political Cooperation (EPC), which aims at the coordination of the foreign policies of member countries, still operates on an intergovernmental basis—that is, unlike decisionmaking in the field of economics.[2] The demarcation line between the two, however, has become

[2] Alfred Pijpers, et al., *European Political Cooperation in the 1980s: A Common Foreign Policy for Western Europe?* (Dordrecht: Nijhoff, 1988).

increasingly blurred over the years, while EPC has acquired greater importance. Recent developments in Central and Eastern Europe have played the role of catalyst in this respect. The implementation of the Maastricht treaty should further accelerate this process.

While the EC of Twelve remains a predominantly economic organization, although gradually acquiring some of the traits of a federal political system, its actual economic interests in the Balkans are marginal. This is true of both trade and foreign investment. It is significant that among the countries of the region, only Turkey (and former Yugoslavia as a whole) account for more than 1 percent of overall trade in goods between the Community of Twelve and the rest of the world (that is, excluding intra-EC trade). The actual figures have always been below 2 percent. The picture is not much different with respect to foreign investment, even though Turkey stands out, in relative terms, as a recipient of European investment.

The limited economic importance of those countries for the Twelve can be explained in terms of the closed nature of the former centrally planned economies, the small size of most countries, and the low level of economic development. The progressive integration of Balkan economies in the international economic system and the medium- and long-term potential for growth for all the countries of the region should bring about closer economic ties with the EC. Starting from such a low base, however, it is highly unlikely that economics will constitute in the near future the main driving force for a stronger EC role in the region.

As one might expect, the economic relationship between the EC and the different countries in the region is highly unequal. What is marginal for the EC represents a substantial part of total foreign economic exchange for those countries. Trade and investment flows between the Twelve and the Balkan countries are expected to grow rapidly over the next few years, subject to the balance-of-payments constraint of the latter countries. Trade statistics since 1989 clearly indicate that by far the biggest part of the growth of trade for every East European country, including the Balkans, has been owing to an increase of trade with the EC. There is every reason to expect that, for most of those countries, trade with the EC as a percentage of total trade will rapidly converge toward the figure of 60 percent or above, which is about the average for the other non-EC European countries.

If EC economic interests in the region are still small, security and political interests no doubt exist. They are linked to the responsibilities and interests of the only important regional power left in Europe. The Community sees the danger of instability in its immediate neighborhood, and it can only be seriously concerned about the wider consequences if the source of instability remains unchecked. The most immediate and tangible consequence of a failure of the economic and political experiments in the former communist countries would be an invasion of refugees into the countries of the EC. To some extent, this has already started to happen. What used to be for many years the main fear of Western Europeans, namely an invasion of Soviet armies, has been replaced by the fear of invasion of economic refugees from the East.

Undoubtedly, when talking about EC interests in the region, some generalization is unavoidable. The war in the former Yugoslavia has brought the Balkans back on the mental map of most West Europeans—a place it had ceased to occupy for many years. This applies to all members of the Community, although geography and history also determine the relative interests of member countries. Italy and Greece are naturally more directly concerned with developments in the Balkans than countries such as Belgium and Denmark. It is, therefore, not surprising that Greece and Italy have been actively promoting economic and political cooperation between the EC and the former communist countries of the Balkans. This cooperation should include financial assistance and the conclusion of bilateral agreements. The interests of Greece and Italy are both economic and political. They are also the countries that will suffer the most from any major upheaval in the region. The large numbers of Albanian refugees in both Italy and Greece provide only one manifestation of the kind of problems that may lie ahead.

For Greece, there is another very important dimension—namely, transport routes that connect it with the rest of the EC and which, inevitably, go through other Balkan countries. Greece has already paid a heavy economic price for the civil war in Yugoslavia (estimated at approximately 1.5 billion U.S. dollars for 1991), because it has had to divert road transport for its imports and exports through alternative and more costly routes, and also because it has lost tourist receipts since visitors from the north no longer have been able to come to Greece by land.

Geographical contiguity is certainly not the decisive factor behind Germany's active interest and policy in the region. Historical reasons are part of the explanation. By far the most important factor, however, is the sheer economic and political weight of Germany, especially after reunification and the radical change of the political map of Central and Eastern Europe.

Association Agreements and the Magnet of Membership

Because of the predominantly economic nature of the EC, trade and aid have been the policy instruments most frequently used in its relations with the rest of the world. The EC has gradually built a so-called "pyramid of privilege" in its trade and financial relations with third countries, based on different kinds of preferential and nonpreferential agreements.[3] Among the countries of Southeastern Europe, Cyprus and Turkey, strange bedfellows in many ways, have long been near the top of the pyramid because of their association agreements with the EC. The Balkan countries, however, as former members of Comecon, until recently had suffered from the opposite problems. They are expected to climb, in a short period of time, from the bottom to the top of the pyramid, along with the other countries of Central and Eastern Europe.

Association agreements will provide the climbing gear. Negotiations for signing

---

[3] R. C. Hine, *The Political Economy of International Trade*, Second Edition (Brighton: Harvester Wheatsheaf, 1985).

such agreements with Czechoslovakia, Hungary, and Poland were concluded in December 1991 and with Bulgaria and Romania in late 1992. As for Albania, it will first have to experience a more limited trade and cooperation agreement before proceeding to the higher stage of association.

With respect to trade, the new association agreements are intended to create a free trade area within a period of ten years, with a shorter timetable of liberalization on the EC side. Yet, a distinction is made between "general industrial goods" and "sensitive" sectors, such as agricultural products, steel, coal and textiles, where EC liberalization will be slower or more limited. These are, however, the sectors where the Community's partners have some comparative advantage. Another difficult issue of contention between the two sides has been the free movement of workers. Despite strong pressures from the other side, the EC has made virtually no concessions in this area. The persistence of high rates of unemployment in the Community and growing social resistance to immigrants, combined with the strong migratory pressures from the former communist countries, hardly allowed any room for flexibility. The association agreements also contain provisions for technical and economic cooperation and the approximation of laws in many areas. Last but not least, the political dialogue between the two sides is institutionalized, the "European vocation" of the associated countries explicitly recognized. This means that the associated countries are treated as potential members of the EC, although no specific date is mentioned for their entry.

The role of the EC has not been limited to the signing of association agreements. Trying to help the transition of Eastern European countries to democratic, pluralist regimes and market economies, the EC has provided technical assistance through the Aid for Economic Reconstruction of Poland and Hungary (PHARE) program which, starting with Poland and Hungary, has been gradually extended to all the countries of the region, including the Balkan countries. Economic loans are also provided through the European Investment Bank. On the other hand, the EC Commission has acted as the coordinator of bilateral economic aid provided by the Organization for Economic Cooperation and Development (OECD) countries, the so-called G–24; and the community has been a catalyst for establishing the European Bank for Reconstruction and Development (EBRD) which concentrates its lending to the private sector in East European countries. Until now, by far the biggest part of economic aid to Eastern Europe has come from the EC, either in the form of multilateral aid or bilaterally by member countries, and most notably Germany. EC governments have insisted on keeping control of the purse strings and the result has been an uneasy compromise between them and the Brussels executive in regard to formulating and implementing policy toward Eastern Europe.

The economic and political importance of the Europe agreements for countries struggling to secure a place for themselves as latecomers in the world of liberal democracies and market economies should not be underestimated. Outlets to EC markets will be absolutely crucial for their economic development; hence, the importance of trade liberalization measures, as well as technical and financial aid, especially during the first difficult years of transition to a market economy.

The political dimension is no less important. The association agreements are considered to be a major step leading to full membership in the EC. What can be the future for European countries on the periphery of a powerful economic bloc, such as the EC, which acquires more and more the characteristics of a pre-federal system? This is even more valid today, since the superpower in the East has already collapsed and the other one in the West seems increasingly inclined, for economic and other reasons, to leave the management of intra-European affairs to the Europeans themselves. Membership in the EC constitutes the single most important foreign policy objective of countries such as Hungary and Poland, not to mention Lithuania. The same becomes increasingly true of the former communist countries of the Balkans, which should have wider implications for their general foreign policy orientation. Membership in the EC is generally considered to be an important means of strengthening political stability and parliamentary democracy in those countries.

Thus, the provision for regular bilateral consultations with the EC and the EC's recognition of their "European vocation" are extremely valuable elements in the association agreements for the Eastern countries. The prospect of EC membership, especially if it is not written *ad calendas Graecas*, can also produce immediate economic benefits for the associated countries by adding considerably to their attraction as foreign investment locations.

The Community's policy toward those countries, however, will not be without problems. To put it differently, satisfying the immediate and long-term demands of East European countries will imply certain costs for EC members, and some of those costs will be far from insignificant. Trade liberalization is easier said than done. What do those countries want to export? Generally speaking, the answer is export of goods that are already in surplus in EC markets and for which export outlets are already difficult to find. They include agricultural products, textiles and clothing, and sometimes steel. Increased import penetration by the East European countries, and the Balkans in particular, will require further adjustment inside the EC. In political terms, the Community will have to persuade or simply buy off domestic producers to make room for Bulgarian wine and Romanian textiles. This will not always be easy, especially in sectors that are already in crisis. Free-trade arguments are not always convincing in the political marketplace.

In EC negotiations with developing countries (in many respects, East European countries can be included in this category), there has usually been some kind of a tradeoff between trade and aid, which has produced the familiar north-south division inside the Community. The economically more developed countries have always expressed a preference for trade liberalization—not so much for ideological reasons, but because the burden of adjustment should be expected to fall mainly upon the weaker members whose export specialization is closer to that of developing countries. Naturally enough, the less developed members of the Community have been more keen on aid that would be paid mainly by the others. This story is likely to be repeated in the search for a new economic relationship with East European countries.

Another difficult economic and political choice must be made by the Community between Eastern Europe and developing countries in regard to both trade concessions and aid. The Third World expects to pay at least part of the price for trade preferences and capital outflows to Eastern Europe—and with very little enthusiasm, it should be added. Historical and cultural ties, together with geographical contiguity and security considerations, explain the reason that West European countries have shown a certain largesse toward their Eastern brethren, which they had refused to show all along toward countries of the Third World—including those countries that had enjoyed privileged relations with the former colonial home country.

Association agreements in the past have contained provisions with respect to the movement of labor. Major problems have already arisen over Turkey's association agreement, which have led to only a very partial implementation of the measures envisaged. The very issue of the free movement of labor makes German and other EC negotiators shiver with trepidation. Virtually all EC countries, including traditional exporters of labor such as Italy and Greece, have become in recent years large recipients of foreign labor, most of it illegal. Given the political and social problems created by the presence of large numbers of immigrants in several West European countries and the concomitant rise of racism, important concessions from the EC in this area are unlikely. Yet, the pressures will persist, both from the east and the south.

The biggest problem of all for the EC will be enlargement itself. The increasing number of candidates for membership raises the awkward question of boundaries. Only European countries have the right to apply, but is there a consensus about which country is European and which is not? After all, traditional geographical boundaries do not always conveniently coincide with political ones. The answer to this question would largely determine whether Turkey is considered more European than Russia and Ukraine or vice versa. Some ambiguity as regards the ultimate frontier of Europe to the east, since all the other frontiers have been clearly demarcated by nature, is likely to persist. Ambiguity is very often a necessary ingredient of a successful policy.

If the boundaries of Europe are still somewhat ambiguous, the criteria for eligibility for EC membership are more clearly defined.[4] They start with the ability and willingness of candidates to adopt the *acquis communautaire* (the whole body of EC legislation), after a relatively short transitional period. This should also include the aims set out by the Maastricht treaty in terms of Economic and Monetary Union (EMU) and the two new pillars of the European Union—namely, foreign and security policy and cooperation in the fields of justice and home affairs. There is sometimes talk of the need for an explicit acceptance by candidates of the *finalité politique* of the Community, although there is hardly a consensus among existing members as to what precisely this term is supposed to mean. Democratic institutions and the respect of human rights are also essential conditions, which are now explicitly mentioned in Article F of the Common Provisions of the new treaty.

---

[4] Anna Michalski and Helen Wallace, *The European Community: The Challenge of Enlargement* (London: Chatham House Discussion Paper, 1992).

At the time of writing, seven applications were already waiting at the table of the EC Council of Ministers, and the number could increase further in the future. Turkey applied in 1987; it was followed by Austria in 1989, Cyprus and Malta in 1990; and then came the other EFTA candidates, namely Sweden (1991), Finland and Switzerland (1992). Norway has also applied. The further enlargement of the Community is expected to take place in different waves, and the EC must decide which countries will be included in the first wave, what, if anything, should be done with those who may have to remain in the waiting-room for much longer, and what kind of internal policy and institutional reforms may be required in a Community with more members. The old dilemma between deepening and enlargement has cropped up again. And, having made an exception for the very special case of East Germany, the Twelve have so far insisted on further deepening as a precondition for a new enlargement. Thus, the establishment of the internal market and the completion of the ratification process of the Maastricht treaty have been considered as the starting point of negotiations with the first group of candidates.

The issue of deepening and enlargement is likely to dominate intra-EC discussions for several years to come. Despite their mounting pressures to obtain an early entry ticket, one may hazard the guess that East European countries will not be able to join the EC ranks before the turn of the century. The waiting period for the countries of the Balkans may prove even longer, not only because of domestic political and economic conditions in those countries but also because of the lack of powerful sponsors inside the EC.

Association agreements and political recognition will constitute the central pieces of a carrot and stick policy that the Community should be expected to pursue in the Balkans and more widely to promote political and economic reform as well as peace and stability in the region. In its role as a stabilizer, the Community will have to rely heavily on those instruments. They will be powerful instruments, although not always sufficiently powerful to prevent trouble. The former Yugoslavia, and many other cases in the past, have shown that the threat of external sanctions is not always a sufficient incentive for peacemaking.

The EC has become closely involved in the intra-Yugoslav conflict in a peacemaking capacity, although with very limited success until now. For many observers, the continuation of the war in the former Yugoslavia and the inability of the EC to act successfully as a mediator and peacekeeper is yet another proof of the Community's weakness as a political power. But can solutions always be imposed from outside? Assuming that the EC already had its own army, does this mean that it should be sent to fight in a country where there is a civil war? A peacekeeping role would have been a totally different affair, but this would have required the agreement of all the main parties concerned. It is arguable, however, that the main blame lies elsewhere—namely, in the premature recognition by the EC of constituent republics without the necessary preconditions. This policy, which did not take sufficient account of the ethnic complexity of several of those republics and the historical sensitivities of the people there, may have precipitated the war and the disintegration of the former Yugoslavia.

The very existence of the EC and the prospect of membership in the future could strengthen the centrifugal forces inside existing nation-states; and this problem will not necessarily be limited to Central and East European countries. The existence of a large supranational entity in Europe makes the economic and political viability of relatively small units (be they Slovenia or Slovakia tomorrow) more credible—that is, on the assumption that they can secure political recognition and access to EC markets and financial resources and eventually full membership. Therefore, as the problem of ethnic tribalism in some European countries grows, the attitude adopted by the Community can prove decisive.

The Old Problem of Greece, Turkey, and Cyprus

Greece has been a full member of the Community since 1981, having gone beforehand through a long transitional period as the first associate member of the EEC of Six. The first years of membership proved difficult, owing to a combination of such different factors as the deep economic recession in Western Europe during the early 1980s, the weak economic structures of Greece, which was largely unprepared for the shock of liberalization implied by accession to the EC, and last, but not least, the policies pursued by the Socialist Party in power. Confused *tiersmondiste* ideas, coupled with a strong attachment to protectionist policies and heavy state intervention in the domestic economy, proved, not surprisingly, incompatible with EC membership and also increasingly out-of-step with political and economic reality in Europe. It is worth noting that the policies pursued by PASOK in Greece were radically different from those pursued by socialist parties in countries such as France and Spain. The result was considerable friction with the other EC partners and much delay in the process of adjustment to EC membership. Greece had a weak economic performance for most of the 1980s, and it proved unable to benefit from the "Euro-euphoria" and the economic boom associated largely with the establishment of the internal market in the EC.

Attitudes have, however, changed radically in recent years. Greek Socialists have discovered, although belatedly, the advantages of EC membership and the market economy. Opinion polls indicate that the Greek public is now one of the most European-oriented in the Community, with large majorities in favor of further deepening of the process of integration. Greece now pursues federalist goals inside the Community. However, such goals are not always easy to reconcile with the present economic weakness of the country. This has been particularly evident in the context of negotiations leading to Economic and Monetary Union. In this respect, the objective of an ever closer union in Europe, which makes perfect sense for a small country that finds itself in a difficult neighborhood, needed to be reconciled with the fear of being relegated to the second division, if the Community were to decide to move swiftly toward a complete Economic and Monetary Union. Thus, Greece's negotiating position has sometimes required a difficult balancing act.

Geographically being part of the Balkans, Greece has a strong political, strategic, and potentially also economic interest in the region. As a member of the EC, it favors close Community involvement there, looking toward a stabilizing EC role. It could potentially play the role of a spokesman for the Balkans inside the Community and the forward outpost of the EC in the region, following perhaps the example of Denmark vis-à-vis the other Scandinavian countries. To a limited degree, this has already started to happen, although Greece's small size and economic weakness impose their own limitations. An important additional complication has been created with respect to the sensitive issue of the recognition, and under which name, of the former Yugoslav Republic of Macedonia. Greece is, after all, much more directly affected by developments in the former Yugoslavia than any other EC country, and relatively recent memories of war in the region still linger on. Economically weak and sometimes a difficult partner inside the Community, Greece is, however, by far the most prosperous and politically most stable of all the countries in the Balkans. After all, prosperity and stability are very relative concepts.

Turkey has a long and rather turbulent history of institutional relations with the Community, and in 1987 it applied for accession. Membership in the club constitutes a primary political objective for Turkey for both economic and political reasons. Turkey is, of course, a big fish for the EC to swallow and digest. Despite the impressive rates of growth it has experienced in recent years, Turkey is still closer, in terms of economic structures, to many developing countries than to the advanced industrialized countries of the West. On the basis of purchasing power parities, the per capita income in Turkey is approximately 60 percent of that of the poorest member of the Twelve. Economic factors, together with a large and rapidly expanding population, and strong cultural and religious differences from the rest of Western Europe (and, indeed, most of Europe as a whole), have all combined to temper any enthusiasm that may have been exhibited about Turkey's early accession to the Community. The strategic importance of the country, however, its membership in NATO, and its long-standing institutional relations with the Community make an outright rejection of Turkey's "European vocation" almost impossible; hence, the enormous difficulties experienced by the Community in providing a clear answer to Turkey.

Greece has often been presented as the main obstacle to Turkey's accession. In this respect, a distinction must be made between Turkish long-term aspirations concerning EC membership and the improvement of bilateral relations in the context of the existing association agreement. Greece has a strong interest in Turkey's European orientation. The last thing that Greece should want is an Islamic neighbor with its back turned to the West. Thus, in the medium and long term and assuming that, in the meantime, there is some progress toward resolving bilateral problems, Turkey may find in Greece a potential ally and supporter of its European policy. The main objections to eventual EC accession would most likely originate from the other members as soon as the convenient Greek smokescreen, behind which the other countries have been hiding for years, were removed.

As for the short term, it is true that the development of EC-Turkish relations has been directly linked to the bilateral disputes between Greece and Turkey and especially the resolution of the Cyprus problem. It is interesting that the Community itself has so far played a very subdued role as a mediator in this area. One important reason must be that Turkey has always preferred the good services of the United States, sometimes strenuously resisting any EC intervention. At the same time, several members of the Community have found it convenient to leave this hot issue to the Americans to deal with. With the increasing role of the EC in intra-European affairs, this restraint may no longer be possible.

The small size of Cyprus and its relatively high level of economic development should present few problems with respect to its application for EC membership. Short of a political resolution of the internal problem, however, it may be difficult to envisage EC membership extended to a divided island; or should the two be part of the same package deal?

Conclusions

Let us draw some tentative conclusions regarding the role that the EC is expected to play in the Balkans and Southeastern Europe more generally. Our main argument is that the Community constitutes at present the only important and solid part of the European architecture. Its importance has grown immensely in recent years as a result of the rapid acceleration of the process of regional integration and the spectacular developments in Central and Eastern Europe. It should be expected to play more and more the role of a regional power and a stabilizer in a part of the old continent where economic weakness, political instability and ethnic heterogeneity can produce an explosive mixture. Although as a "civilian power" its instruments are still mainly economic, its ability to influence events is far from negligible; and it has been growing with time, as it tried to meet the expectations of other European countries.

The expanding presence of the EC should also become increasingly evident in the Balkans, where the Community should be expected to assume the role of the main external power. In the pursuit of regional stability, close cooperation between the EC and the United States will be absolutely crucial, and this can also take place in the context of NATO and the CSCE. Yet, under normal circumstances, the EC should be expected to occupy the place of the driver, with the United States adopting a supporting role. Normal circumstances are meant to imply that there is no major conflagration in the area, in which case military power may become crucial, thus bringing other external actors near the center of the stage. Judging from the escalation of conflict in the former Yugoslavia, such a development cannot be excluded altogether.

The United States is likely to place relatively more emphasis on its relations with Turkey. The development of this "privileged relationship," however, will, in turn, depend on the Community's response to Turkey's amorous advances and indirectly on the "troubled partnership" between Greece and Turkey.

The EC, also, will have to reconcile in the next few years the objective of further internal integration with its responsibilities as a regional and also as a global power. Economic adjustment, stronger financial powers, and more effective central institutions will be the necessary preconditions for the EC to play its role as a stabilizer in the region. Its success in this respect will, of course, also depend on its internal unity and its ability to extend and strengthen cooperation in the fields of foreign policy and security.

The apparent lack of enthusiasm shown by a large part of European public opinion with respect to the Maastricht treaty, which provides the framework for the post-1992 phase of integration, is directly linked to the adverse economic environment prevailing at the time and the crisis of governance manifesting itself in several national political systems. Yet, it has also confirmed some of the weaknesses of European integration—the gap between the economic and the political dimension, not only in terms of institutions but also in terms of the political discourse and popular perceptions; and the technocratic and often incomprehensible (to the public) nature of European agreements, themselves the product of delicate compromises between member governments. A prolonged crisis inside the EC, as a result of those developments, would seriously impair its ability to act as a stabilizing force in its neighborhood; but that is, of course, far from inevitable.

XIII

The Response of International Institutions to the Yugoslavia Conflict: Implications and Lessons

James B. Steinberg

On June 25, 1991, the Yugoslav Republics of Slovenia and Croatia declared their independence, triggering Europe's first serious military conflict of the post-Cold War era. Two years later, tens of thousands were dead, millions were forced to leave their homes, scores of cities lay in ruins and bitter fighting continued among Serbs, Croats, and Muslims in the former Yugoslav republic of Bosnia-Herzegovina.

The Yugoslav war was the first test of how well Europe's political institutions, freed from East-West divisions, would cope with ethnic and national conflict. Writing in the *Frankfurter Allgemeine Zeitung*, Günther Gillessen offered this judgment:

> First . . . the CSCE conflict regulation machinery was reduced to ridicule. . . . Then the European Community's political authority was destroyed. Third, the UN Security Council, the decisionmaking center of the United Nations, was damaged, with Europe and the secretary-general disagreeing over the fighting. One major international institution after another has shown signs of wear and tear as a result of the fighting.[1]

One suspects that only the demands of journalistic brevity spared other European institutions, including NATO and the West European Union, from this harsh indict-

[1] "Europe confronted with a moral dilemma in the Balkans," *Frankfurter Allgemeine Zeitung*, 10 Aug. 1992 (translation from *The German Tribune*, 14 Aug. 1992, p. 1).

ment. Nor was Gillessen alone. Throughout the region and the world, the international community's apparent helplessness as Yugoslavia burned fueled public skepticism at hopes for a more peaceful continent built around a more united Europe.

Only days before the conflict began, Europe had celebrated the latest step on the road to constructing what was to be a cornerstone of the new "peace order"—an institutionalized CSCE, holding its first council (foreign ministers) meeting, approving a new procedure for responding to crises. During the eighteen months before the June 19–20, 1991, CSCE Council meeting, European leaders had engaged in a virtual frenzy of institution-building activity. Their efforts ranged widely: adopting the Paris (CSCE) Charter in November 1990; launching two European Community intergovernmental conferences on Economic and Monetary Union (EMU) and Economic and Political Union (EPU) in December 1990, leading to the December 1991 Maastricht treaty; new steps to institutionalize the WEU as the expression of a European defense identity; and an ongoing reform of NATO's strategy, force structure, and relationships with its former adversaries in the Warsaw Pact. On the broader international level, the UN's response to Iraq's invasion of Kuwait in August 1990, culminating in the multinational, UN-sanctioned Desert Storm, marked a new phase in that organization's role in international peacemaking, followed by the multinational effort to assist Iraqi Kurds—Operation Provide Comfort.

This chapter reviews the activities of the international institutions during the Yugoslav conflict in an effort to understand what happened and why, offers some lessons learned, and suggests changes that could improve the response in future crises.

Background

The history of Yugoslavia's dissolution is deeply tied to its founding. It was a multiethnic, multireligious nation created in the wake of World War I and was held together for three decades after World War II by Marshal Tito's unique blend of nationalism and communism.

With Tito's death in 1980, the institutional structure of a rotating federal presidency among the country's six republics helped deepen the fissures among the federation's principal ethnic and religious groups (Serbs, Croats, Slovenes, and Muslims) and loosen the various republics' ties to the center. Ambitious politicians, such as Serbia's Slobodan Milosevic and Croatia's Franjo Tudjman, seized on historical grievances to achieve power, filling the vacuum left by the collapse of the ruling League of Yugoslav Communists (LYC) and furthering the divisions and suspicions among the republics. Fears of Serbian dominance fueled the movement toward greater autonomy by Croatia and Slovenia.

After months of futile negotiations to turn Yugoslavia into a loose confederation, first Slovenia (in December 1990) and then Croatia (in May 1991) voted for independence. As the two republics moved closer to a formal split with the federation, both individual nations and European institutions appealed for a peaceful settlement. In the weeks before the crisis quickened, the CSCE debated Yugoslavia at its

Berlin council meeting.[2] The EC dispatched Commission President Jacques Delors to Belgrade.[3] Secretary of State James Baker also visited Yugoslavia following the CSCE meeting.[4] But the preliminary efforts to head off the crisis were primarily rhetorical and unsuccessful.

The crisis in Yugoslavia exploded when the governments of Slovenia and Croatia decided to declare independence from the Yugoslav federation on June 25, 1991. The initial confrontation centered around Slovenia, which sought to assert control of its international border crossings, and led to armed clashes with the federal army. These actions raised alarm throughout Europe and set in motion a series of efforts by various European institutions to defuse the crisis.

The international community's effort to resolve the Yugoslav crisis has fallen into five elements. The first effort was directed at ending the fighting in Slovenia (June 25–July 8, 1991). The second focused on the EC's attempt to maintain peace and broker a political settlement in Croatia (July–September 1991). The third began with the EC's initial decision to turn to the UN Security Council and ended with the decision to deploy UN peacekeepers in Croatia (September 1991–March 1992). The fourth centers around efforts to end the fighting and broker a political settlement in Bosnia-Herzegovina following that republic's referendum on independence (March 1992–present). Finally, the international community has sought to head off the danger that the conflict would spill over into Macedonia or beyond.

The actions of the European institutions during this crisis were shaped by the viewpoints of their constituent members.[5] Each country came to the crisis with its own blend of historical, cultural, and political (domestic and international) considerations, which colored its preferred response. Initially, virtually all European countries supported efforts to keep Yugoslavia together in some form. They foresaw that disintegration was likely to precipitate violence, and feared that the precedent of Yugoslavia's dissolution might encourage the forces of fragmentation and national-

[2] During the Berlin CSCE Council meeting on June 20, the foreign ministers had agreed to support the "democratic development, unity and territorial integrity" of Yugoslavia and called on the parties to "redouble their efforts to resolve their differences peacefully through negotiations." *Guardian*, 28 June 1991, p. 28.

[3] The EC gave its first indication of the difficult policy line the Community would seek to walk: Luxembourg's Foreign Minister Jacques Poos (whose country held the EC presidency) stated that the EC would not recognize the unilateral declaration of independence by Slovenia or Croatia, but Dutch Foreign Minister Hans Van den Broek (the Netherlands would succeed to the EC presidency on July 1) also warned that the EC would not support the Yugoslav federation "at any price." Agence France Presse, June 28, 1991 (FBIS-WEU-91-125, June 28, 1991, p. 1).

[4] Baker said: "We support the democratization, protection of human rights, territorial integrity, and preservation of the unity of Yugoslavia." *Tanjug*, June 21, 1991 (FBIS-EEU-91-121, June 24, 1991, p. 37). He also said that the United States would not recognize Slovenia's independence unless it was achieved through dialogue with the other republics and central government. *International Herald Tribune*, 22–23 June 1991, p. 1.

[5] The United States is a "European" country for the purpose of this discussion by virtue of its membership in the CSCE and NATO, as well as its more general involvement in European security affairs.

ism elsewhere in Europe—both in the Soviet Union and in the West.

As the process unfolded, however, different points of view began to emerge. The first step toward a more sympathetic approach to Slovenian and Croatian independence came in Germany, where a number of Christian Democrat (CDU) Bundestag members called for a policy more supportive of Slovenia and Croatia. In a strongly worded statement, the chairman of the CDU stated:

> We won our unity through the right to self-determination. If we Germans think everything else in Europe can stay just as it was, if we follow a status quo policy and do not recognize the right to self-determination in Slovenia and Croatia, then we have no moral or political credibility. We should start a movement in the EC to lead to such recognition.[6]

German sympathy for Slovenia and Croatia was buttressed by cultural and religious ties to that part of Yugoslavia that belonged to the Hapsburg Empire and was predominately Catholic (in contrast to the Eastern Orthodox Serbs). Similar concerns generated sympathy in Austria and in Italy.

By contrast, France, the United Kingdom, Spain, and Greece appeared most determined to hold Yugoslavia together. Commentators suggested a number of reasons for this reluctance to support Croatian and Slovenian independence: fears that it would inflame separatist movements in their own countries (Basques and Catalans in Spain, Corsicans in France, Northern Ireland in the United Kingdom); concern that dissolving Yugoslavia would set a precedent throughout Eastern Europe and the Soviet Union; and, in the case of France, its historical ties to Serbia. Greece was the strongest supporter of maintaining the federal state, driven by its fear of a potential conflict with an independent Macedonia and Greece's strengthening political alliance with Serbia.

Yugoslavia's former communist neighbors faced a complex situation, with Hungary and Albania concerned about human rights abuses of their ethnic nationals in Vojvodina and Kosovo, respectively. Albania's concerns were shared by other Muslim countries, especially Turkey, which has close links with Bosnia's large Muslim population. Romania and Bulgaria were interested in maintaining good relations with the West, but had cultural, religious, and historical ties with Serbia.

The conflict posed a difficult dilemma for Russia. The crisis began when the Soviet Union still existed. President Gorbachev was one of the strongest advocates of preserving Yugoslavia's unity, primarily out of concern for the implications of Yugoslavia's dissolution on his own multiethnic nation. After the Soviet Union collapsed at the end of 1991, Russia's policy was driven by three factors: historical ties to Serbia dating from Serbia's conflicts with the Hapsburg and the Ottoman empires; a desire to avoid an obstructionist role in such international organizations as the CSCE and UN; and an interest in promoting peaceful dispute-resolution mecha-

[6] *Guardian*, 2 July 1991, p. 8. These criticisms were echoed by senior Social Democrat (SPD) spokesmen after a hasty trip to Yugoslavia. *Frankfurt Allgemeine Zeitung*, 2 June 1991.

nisms that might be applied to ethnic and national conflicts on Russia's borders (for example, the conflict between Armenia and Azerbaijan over Nagorno-Karabakh) or even within the Russian Republic itself. Over time, Russia's approach to the Yugoslav conflict became entangled in the internal political struggle between Yeltsin and his nationalist critics, who accused him of blindly following an anti-Serb policy to please the West, at the expense of Russia's own interests.

During the Cold War era, the United States took a particular interest in maintaining Yugoslavia's stability, fearing that conflict in Yugoslavia could lead to a dangerous East-West confrontation. As communism collapsed in Eastern Europe, the United States continued to support keeping Yugoslavia together, out of concern that a fragmented Yugoslavia would serve as a precedent for the USSR. Meanwhile, the United States began to express more vocally its support for human rights and democracy along with unity.[7]

After Secretary Baker's last-ditch effort to stave off Slovenia's and Croatia's independence, the United States retreated from the policy foreground, content to let Europeans, especially the EC, lead. This reticence proceeded from a rethinking of the nature of U.S. interests in the post-Cold War world and doubts that the American public would support significant U.S. military involvement. Not until the spring of 1992 did the United States take a more active role, under growing public pressure in the face of graphic media coverage of the suffering in Bosnia.

The Initial Response—From the Declarations of Independence to the Brioni Accord (June 25–July 8, 1991)

European leaders reacted quickly to the outbreak of violence, pursuing two parallel tracks—the CSCE and the EC. As the crisis began to unfold, Austria notified Belgrade on June 27 of its concern over "unusual military activity" in Yugoslavia, triggering a requirement that Yugoslavia clarify its intentions through the Conflict Prevention Center in Vienna.[8] Meanwhile, the European Council (EC heads of state and government) agreed on June 29 to send the "troika" (foreign ministers from Italy, Luxembourg, and the Netherlands)[9] on a mediating mission to Yugoslavia.[10]

---

[7] In October 1990, the administration described its policy: "The United States supports unity, democratic change, respect for human rights and market reform in Yugoslavia." Although the administration said that it would oppose the use of force to block democratic change in Yugoslavia, it placed its emphasis on democracy as a means to sustain unity: "We believe that democracy is the only enduring basis for a united, prosperous, voluntary Yugoslav union."

[8] This requirement was established by the Stockholm Confidence and Security Building Measures Agreement (CSBMs) as further amended in the Paris CSCE Charter, Article 17.

[9] The EC's troika consists of the foreign minister of the country holding the EC presidency, as well as the ministers from the immediate past and succeeding presidency nations (with the presidency rotating every six months in alphabetical order). The troika changed to Luxembourg, Netherlands, and Portugal on July 1, as the Netherlands assumed the presidency.

[10] Germany and Italy took the lead in pushing for EC action. The speed of the EC's response was

They also decided to support Austria's request to convene the CSCE emergency mechanism and to freeze aid to Yugoslavia unless there was an immediate cessation of violence. As the troika departed for Belgrade, the EC called on Slovenia to suspend its declaration of independence and proposed a cease-fire.

The overnight mission to Belgrade and Zagreb produced the EC's first success—an agreement to suspend hostilities and a three-month moratorium on Slovenia's and Croatia's move toward independence. It was hailed by senior European officials as a sign of the community's political coming of age: "This is the hour of Europe," said Luxembourg's Foreign Minister Jacques Poos. "From our point of view, it is a good sign for the future of political union." "When a situation becomes delicate, the Community is able to act as a political entity," said Italian Foreign Minister Gianni de Michelis. Slovenia called on the EC to send observers to monitor the terms of the agreement.

Meanwhile, the CSCE began to consider what actions it might take. Representatives to the Conflict Prevention Center (CPC) met in Vienna on July 1.[11] Two days later, representatives of thirty-five CSCE nations met in Prague (the seat of the CSCE secretariat) pursuant to the new CSCE emergency mechanism.[12] At the Prague meeting, the CSCE officials reached agreement on two diplomatic missions. The first, "a good offices" mission, would seek to promote a dialogue among the parties "in consultation and agreement with the Yugoslav authorities."[13] The CSCE also approved the idea of sending observers to monitor the cease-fire, with the arrangements to be implemented by the EC (leaving open the possibility of enlarging the observer group to include other CSCE states).

In response to the CSCE's endorsement of an EC-arranged observer mission, the EC began to lay the groundwork for a group of civilian observers to monitor the cease-fire. The EC foreign ministers also agreed to embargo arms shipments to Yugoslavia and to suspend EC aid. The ministers also held out the prospect of recognizing Slovenia and Croatia should the violence continue.

---

facilitated by an EC meeting fortuitously scheduled to take place in Luxembourg beginning on Friday, June 28.

[11] *The Times*, 1 July 1991, p. 8. The CSCE's involvement was further complicated by the fact that Yugoslavia itself held the chair of the Conflict Prevention Center (though Germany chaired the Prague-based political directors' group in charge of the crisis mechanism). Since it was directly implicated, Yugoslavia was obliged to pass the chair to Albania, next in line but only recently admitted to the CSCE, and which has its own problems with Yugoslavia in connection with Kosovo and other Muslim enclaves.

[12] Vienna Österreich Radio Eins, June 30, 1991 (FBIS-WEU-91-126, July 1, 1991, p. 2). Under the emergency mechanism, Yugoslavia had forty-eight hours after the official request to provide an explanation of its actions, after which time an emergency meeting would be convened (if supported by the initial requestor plus twelve other CSCE nations).

In the end, Austria and the EC Twelve were joined by the United States, Czechoslovakia, and Sweden in requesting the CSCE senior officials meeting. *Guardian*, 2 July 1991, p. 8.

[13] *Guardian*, 4 July 1991, p. 9; *Le Monde*, 5 July 1991, p. 5. The Soviet Union initially resisted the idea of CSCE involvement but eventually accepted it so long as it was with the consent of the Yugoslav government. *Guardian*, 5 July 1991, p. 8.

On July 7–8, the troika met with representatives of the central government, Serbia, Slovenia, and Croatia, on the Adriatic island of Brioni and hammered out a "Common Declaration on the Peaceful Resolution of the Yugoslav Crisis," in which Slovenia and Croatia agreed to suspend their declarations of independence for three months while the parties sought a political settlement. All sides agreed to refrain from unilateral acts, especially acts of violence. In an annex, the declaration called for dispatching thirty to fifty EC observers to Slovenia and "if possible" to Croatia to monitor its implementation.[14]

The EC Struggles to Maintain Peace (July 8–September 19, 1991)

The second phase of the conflict was dominated by the EC's effort to broker a political settlement and to use unarmed observers to help monitor a cease-fire until negotiations bore fruit. During this phase the CSCE primarily served to endorse and further legitimate EC actions. On several occasions during this phase, the WEU considered possible uses of force to achieve a halt to the fighting, but no action was taken. NATO and the UN stayed in the background.

On July 10, the EC foreign ministers met and endorsed the decision to send thirty to fifty observers to Yugoslavia "to stabilize the cease-fire and to monitor the suspension of the implementation of the declarations of independence."[15] The ministers rejected Germany's suggestion to include observers from other CSCE countries; Van den Broek said that broader participation in the observer force would be acceptable only if Yugoslavia requested it.[16]

Initially, the observers were sent to Slovenia, but after the Yugoslav government's decision to withdraw federal forces from Slovenia (accepting de facto Slovenia's independence), attention shifted to Croatia. Although the Brioni Declaration contemplated the possibility of extending the observer mission to Croatia, there was confusion over what role the observers could play in Croatia, and federal Yugoslav authorities resisted the effort to extend the mandate.[17]

As fighting in Croatia escalated, the EC foreign ministers met again on July 29 in Brussels, joined, at the EC's invitation, by representatives from the Yugoslav federal presidency and the Yugoslav prime minister and foreign minister. Van den

[14] *Le Monde*, 10 July 1991, p. 3.

[15] Each nation chose its own participants (the group also included representatives from the EC Commission), generally drawn from the ranks of diplomats, retired military, or, in some cases, military officers in civilian clothes. At the strong insistence of the United Kingdom, the observers were not permitted to carry any weapons, even for self-defense. The United Kingdom also insisted that the funding for the effort come from national governments, not EC funds. *Le Figaro*, 11 July 1991, p. 3.

[16] The ministers also created a task force of senior officials from the Twelve to assist in the negotiations contemplated by the Brioni Declaration. Agence France Presse, July 10, 1991 (FBIS-WEU-91-133, July 11, 1991, p. 1).

[17] The head of the EC observer group initially suggested that Croatia was "not part of the Mandate." *The London Times*, 17 July 1991, p. 10.

Broek tabled a proposal for joint Croatian/federal patrols to implement a cease-fire, but he and British Foreign Secretary Hurd opposed France's suggestion that the EC send a "peacekeeping" force, perhaps under WEU auspices.[18] The ministers decided to extend the observer mission to Croatia, to increase the number of observers to 300 plus 300 support personnel (and to permit participation by other CSCE nations), and to send the troika back to Yugoslavia.

But EC-sponsored mediation in early August met resistance, both from Serbia and from pro-Serbian forces in Croatia who refused to allow EC observers to enter contested areas. On August 8, the CSCE met again in Prague and decided (with Yugoslavia's agreement) to send some 200 to 500 additional observers (from Czechoslovakia, Poland, Sweden, and Canada, as well as the EC countries) to help monitor the truce in Croatia. Yugoslavia vetoed a British proposal backed by the EC to convene a peace conference, although the CSCE did call for some form of negotiations to begin by August 15.[19]

With the CSCE route to a peace conference blocked by Yugoslavia's veto, the EC itself turned its attention to trying to organize a peace conference. After preliminary discussions in Yugoslavia, France tabled a proposal, endorsed on August 27 by the EC foreign ministers and supported by the United States, for an EC-sponsored peace conference coupled with the appointment of a panel of five experts drawn from the heads of the constitutional courts of EC states (two to be named by Yugoslavia and three by the EC) to arbitrate the dispute. The EC threatened comprehensive economic sanctions against Serbia if it rejected the EC's latest peace moves.[20] The conference finally convened on September 7, chaired by former NATO Secretary General Lord Carrington, even though fighting continued in Croatia.[21]

Lord Carrington's initial efforts centered around establishing a cease-fire. As the fighting continued through early September, the Dutch foreign minister, with the support of France, Germany, and Italy, proposed that the EC send a "lightly armed"

---

[18] The WEU secretary general broached the idea of sending a group of several hundred lightly armed observers in mid-July, on the grounds that they would be safer and more effective than unarmed EC observers. *The London Times*, 27 July 1991, p. 9, and 30 July 1991, p. 9. WEU ministers discussed the idea on August 7, but took no action in the face of reservations by the U.K., Denmark, Portugal, Spain, and Germany.

[19] *Independent*, 10 Aug. 1991, p. 8; *Le Monde*, 17 Aug. 1991, p. 4.

[20] Agence France Presse, Aug. 28, 1991 (FBIS-WEU-91-167, Aug. 28, 1991, p. 2). The EC action marked the first time that Serbia was so clearly singled out as the cause of the continued fighting. Both Germany and Italy threatened to recognize Slovenia and Croatia, if Serbia did not agree to the cease-fire and peace conference. *Financial Times*, 4 Sept. 1991.

[21] The twelve EC foreign ministers, plus the Yugoslav prime minister and the presidents of the six Yugoslav republics, took part in the opening session. Two working groups were formed: One was tasked with examining future constitutional arrangements; the second, was concerned with minority rights. A third group, on economic relations between the Yugoslav republics, was created in late September. *Le Monde*, 28 Sept. 1991, p. 3. Judge Robert Badinter of France was appointed to head the arbitration panel, along with the heads of the Italian, German, Spanish, and Belgian constitutional courts. *Financial Times*, 4 Sept. 1991.

contingent to Yugoslavia under the WEU's aegis, an idea renewed after the parties reached a new cease-fire agreement on September 17. The United Kingdom agreed to support a proposal for the WEU to develop contingency plans for deploying peacekeeping forces in the event a lasting cease-fire could be arranged, but it opposed armed intervention.[22] In a meeting on September 19, the EC foreign ministers declined to endorse the idea of an armed peacekeeping force in the face of continued fighting in Yugoslavia, and Lord Carrington suspended his peacemaking efforts that same day.[23]

Throughout the early stages of the crisis, NATO maintained a low profile. On June 27, a NATO spokesman stated that NATO was "greatly concerned about the deterioration of the situation," and indicated that NATO was "following the situation closely."[24] NATO's reluctance to become involved was attributable in part to the United States' inclination to allow Europeans to take the lead. The *Financial Times* quoted one U.S. official: "After all, it's not our problem, it's a European problem."[25]

During the summer, NATO's Political Committee continued to meet, primarily as a forum for exchanging views and as a channel between the United States and the NATO members that belong to the EC. There was no visible indication that NATO discussed playing a military role or initiating contingency planning at that stage.

In the first months of the conflict, the UN also maintained a low profile. Secretary General Pérez de Cuéllar seemed at pains to stress that the crisis was an internal matter that the Yugoslavs should resolve on their own. He specifically rejected the idea of sending UN observers in response to any request by Slovenia on the grounds that "Slovenia is not an independent UN member."[26] That view was echoed by the U.S. ambassador to the UN, Thomas Pickering, who stated that "the UN has no role in Yugoslavia" unless the EC and CSCE efforts fail.[27]

Europe Turns to the United Nations (September 1991–March 1992)

The third phase of international involvement in the conflict featured an expanded

---

[22] *Guardian*, 16 Sept. 1991, p. 6; *Wall Street Journal*, 17 Sept. 1991, p. 13; *The Times*, 18 Sept. 1991, p. 1. Several sources reported that the WEU ministers were considering a force as large as thirty thousand peacekeepers. *Guardian*, 18 Sept. 1991, p. 6.

[23] *New York Times*, 20 Sept. 1991, p. 6. However, the EC did ask the WEU to prepare a list of options for peacekeeping. In its September 30 meeting, the WEU defense ministers offered four options: (1) logistical and technical assistance for the unarmed observers; (2) armed bodyguards; (3) a light peacekeeping force (five thousand to six thousand troops); and (4) a full peacekeeping force (twenty-five thousand to thirty-five thousand troops). *Independent*, 1 Oct. 1991, p. 10; *Financial Times*, 1 Oct. 1991.

[24] Agence France Presse, June 27, 1991 (FBIS-WEU-91-125, June 28, 1991, p. 1).

[25] *Financial Times*, 29–30 June 1991, p. 3.

[26] *Der Spiegel*, July 1, 1991 (FBIS-WEU-91-127, July 2, 1991, p. 2).

[27] *Washington Post*, 4 July 1991, p. 19.

role for the United Nations as the international community followed a two-track approach: the UN for peacekeeping and the EC leading the efforts to find a political settlement.

Even before the EC decision on September 19 to suspend peacemaking efforts, Austria formally called on the UN Security Council to take the lead in organizing a peacekeeping force, an idea picked up by both France and Germany.[28] France, in its capacity as chair of the Security Council for September, proposed that the UN establish an emergency force under Chapter 7 of the UN charter and impose an arms embargo.[29] The Security Council agreed to an arms embargo on September 25 but did not include any provisions for enforcement.[30]

EC peacemaking efforts resumed in the wake of the UN action, in an effort to reach agreement before the October 7 expiration of Slovenia's and Croatia's suspension of their declarations of independence. The effort appeared to bear fruit with Serbia's agreement to respect Croatia's right to independence within existing borders in return for giving Serbs in Croatia special protected status, but fighting continued, even in the face of an EC threat to cut off its trade and cooperation agreement with Yugoslavia and to seek a worldwide trade embargo. Soviet President Gorbachev initiated his own effort to halt the conflict, effectively abandoning the earlier Soviet posture of noninvolvement, but Slovenia and Croatia began to implement their declarations of independence. A brief truce (the eighth since the fighting began) on the night of October 7 led the EC to delay its threatened economic sanctions to allow further peacemaking efforts, and the parties reached an agreement in principle in the Hague for the withdrawal of Yugoslav army troops from Croatia, raising hopes that at last a breakthrough was at hand.[31]

During this period, the UN began its first direct involvement, when on October 8, UN Secretary General Pérez de Cuéllar appointed former U.S. Secretary of State Cyrus Vance as his personal envoy to Yugoslavia. After Vance's return, the secre-

---

[28] Austrian ORF Television, Sept. 17, 1991 (FBIS-WEU-91-180, Sept. 17, 1991, p. 3). At the time, Austria was sitting as a rotating member of the Security Council. *Guardian,* 19 Sept. 1991, p. 8. Genscher argued that the UN was the appropriate body because "according to international law, the WEU would only have been able to become active with the unanimous agreement of all affected parties." By contrast, "only the UN Security Council can make decisions that are binding for all." *Der Standard*, Sept. 24, 1991, p. 2 (FBIS-WEU-91-185, Sept. 24, 1991, p. 7).

[29] *Le Monde*, 24 and 26 Sept. 1991. The French cited the precedent of UN Resolution 688, which authorized intervention in Iraq to protect the Kurds.

[30] *Le Monde*, 27 Sept. 1991, p. 1. Resolution 713 also endorsed the EC's efforts to halt the fighting and invited the UN secretary general to confer with the Yugoslav government and report back to the Security Council. The unanimous vote in favor of the resolution was achieved after France agreed to eliminate its call for an emergency force, an idea opposed by Britain. China and many of the nonaligned nations agreed to support the resolution only after the Yugoslav government itself indicated that it was not opposed.

[31] *Independent*, 11 Oct. 1991. The EC established a December 10, 1991, deadline for the parties to reach a peace agreement. In the event the parties failed to reach agreement by that time, the EC indicated that it would consider recognizing Slovenia and Croatia.

tary general prepared a report to the Security Council, calling the fighting in Yugoslavia a threat to international peace and stability, which set the stage for further UN action.[32]

The EC-sponsored peace conference reconvened on October 18. Van den Broek and Carrington unveiled a comprehensive constitutional plan calling for a loose association among the republics, with a few central institutions, including a council of ministers, court of justice, and parliament, modeled to some extent on the EC itself. The plan would retain the existing republic borders.[33] The United States and the Soviet Union issued a joint communiqué in support of the EC's efforts. Slovenia, Croatia, Bosnia, Macedonia, and Montenegro (until this point firmly allied with Serbia) accepted the plan, but Serbia (joined by the head of the JNA, the Yugoslav army) rejected it on the grounds that it would abolish Yugoslavia and fail to provide autonomy for Serbs living in Croatia. Serbian President Slobodan Milosevic also objected to provisions of the EC plan that would restore autonomous status to Kosovo and Vojvodina. The Community announced that it would impose trade sanctions against any republic that refused to agree to the plan by November 5, 1991.[34]

Meeting in conjunction with the NATO summit in Rome, the EC heads of state and government agreed on November 8 to impose sanctions against Yugoslavia, including abrogating the trade and cooperation agreement, reapplying limits on Yugoslav textile imports, and repealing other trade preferences. The leaders agreed to adopt compensatory measures to aid those republics that agreed to the EC peace plan, and to ask the Security Council to impose an oil embargo. The NATO summit endorsed the EC efforts.[35]

The collapse of the EC peace plan, and the need for UN support to impose effective trade sanctions against Serbia, refocused attention on the United Nations. Both Croatia and the Serbian-dominated rump presidency appealed to the UN to send in peacekeeping forces: Croatia asked for forces to be stationed at the borders between the republics, while the federal presidency urged that the UN place its troops between the forces then in conflict (in effect, at least temporarily marking Serbian territorial gains). The United Kingdom introduced a draft resolution in the Security Council calling for an oil embargo against any of the Yugoslav parties that refused to halt the fighting, while Lord Carrington, joined by Vance and UN Under Secretary General for Peacekeeping Goulding, traveled to Belgrade in a final effort to

---

[32] *Guardian,* 29 Oct. 1991, p. 1.

[33] *Independent*, 18 Oct. 1991, p. 1. See also *Yugoslav Survey,* XXXII, no. 3 (1991): 87–96.

[34] *Guardian*, 29 Oct. 1991. The EC received legal advice that it could act immediately to suspend its trade and cooperation agreement with Yugoslavia, paving the way for selective sanctions against individual republics, even without formally recognizing the republics as independent states. The plan also called for a UN-imposed oil embargo in the event no agreement was reached. *Financial Times*, 5 Nov. 1991, p. 19.

[35] *Independent*, 9 Nov. 1991, p. 12; *The Times*, 9 Nov. 1991, p. 20. On December 2, the EC voted to restore aid and trade privileges to Slovenia, Croatia, Bosnia, and Macedonia, leaving only Serbia and Montenegro subject to the November 8 sanctions.

achieve a cease-fire that would set the stage for sending in peacekeepers, under either UN or EC/WEU auspices.[36] At a November 18 WEU meeting, the United Kingdom, France, and Italy indicated a willingness to deploy naval vessels in support of providing humanitarian aid to or evacuation of civilians caught up in the fighting.[37]

On November 23, Vance negotiated a new cease-fire (the first with direct UN involvement) and offered a compromise plan on deploying UN peacekeepers and, after overcoming considerable resistance from nonaligned members, the Security Council adopted Resolution 721, urging the secretary general to present "an early recommendation" for a peacekeeping force if the conflicting parties actually observed the latest truce agreement.[38]

Meanwhile, German leaders repeated warnings that Germany would move forward to recognize Slovenia and Croatia by December 25 if an agreement was not reached by the EC-imposed December 10 deadline, and their position received support from Italy's prime minister. Pérez de Cuéllar and Carrington, supported by the United States and the United Kingdom, strongly opposed the German proposal on the grounds that it would exacerbate the conflict. Several EC leaders, including French Foreign Minister Roland Dumas, argued that unilateral German action was inconsistent with the recently concluded Maastricht agreement strengthening the EC's common foreign and security policy.

Germany remained insistent, however, and on December 17, the EC foreign ministers reluctantly agreed to recognize Croatia and Slovenia (as well as any of the other four republics that sought recognition by December 23) on January 15, 1992, if, based on the judgment of the Badinter panel, they met certain criteria—protection of individual and minority rights and the rule of law, democratic processes, and a commitment not to change internal borders by force.[39] Chancellor Kohl called the decision "a great triumph for German foreign policy."[40] Serbia denounced the proposal as a violation of the UN Charter.[41] Although Germany agreed to respect the EC's decision not to extend formal recognition before the arbitration panel could report (and in any event, not before January 15, 1992), it began to implement informal ties immediately after the EC meeting.[42] In addition, German Foreign Minister

---

[36] *Independent*, 14 Nov. 1991, p. 1; *Guardian*, 16 Nov. 1991. France led the effort to gain Security Council support for peacekeeping forces in the event of a cease-fire and an agreement to separate forces.

[37] *Guardian*, 19 Nov. 1991, p. 10.

[38] *Guardian*, 28 Nov. 1991, pp. 12 and 23.

[39] See "Declaration on the 'Guidelines on the Recognition of New States in Eastern Europe and in the Soviet Union,' " and "Declaration on Yugoslavia," Dec. 17, 1991, reprinted in *Yugoslav Survey*, XXXII, no. 4 (1991): 4–5.

[40] *Washington Post*, 18 December 1991, p. A25.

[41] *The Times*, 18 Dec. 1991, p. 9.

[42] Thus Germany announced on December 17 its intention to recognize Slovenia and Croatia, effective January 15, and immediately announced a package of economic aid to Croatia. *Washington Post*, 20 Dec. 1991, p. A39.

Hans Dietricht Genscher made clear that Germany intended to recognize Slovenia and Croatia regardless of the conclusions of the Badinter panel.[43]

The Badinter panel finally completed its work on the eve of the January 15 deadline. It gave only Slovenia and Macedonia a "clean bill of health," while expressing reservations about Croatia's commitment to protect the rights of the Serb minority. The panel conditioned recognition of Bosnia-Herzegovina on a clearer "expression of the will" of the population for independence, perhaps through a referendum.[44] Notwithstanding these reservations, the EC unanimously agreed to recognize Slovenia and Croatia on January 15, deferring action on the other two applications.[45] While a number of other countries followed the EC move, the United States declined to act, indicating that it would wait until a peace settlement was reached.[46]

In a mission to Yugoslavia at the beginning of 1992, UN envoy Vance brokered a new cease-fire, and won Serbian and Croatian acceptance of the UN plan to deploy ten thousand peacekeeping troops in Croatia.[47] As the fighting continued, the UN secretary general sought approval for deploying fifty UN military observers but deferred seeking Security Council endorsement for sending the main peacekeeping force until the agreed cease-fire actually took hold.[48] At Vance's request, the EC agreed to assign its 200 Yugoslav observers to monitor the new cease-fire agreement.[49] Over the next several weeks, the cease-fire broadly held, although the shoot-

[43] *Washington Post*, 11 Jan. 1992, p. A14. The EC agreement on recognition was formally limited to recognition by the EC itself, although most members believed that individual EC countries should follow the lead of the Community as a whole. Genscher stated that the Badinter panel report "was not a condition for implementing the decision to recognize." Ibid.

[44] The Badinter panel concluded that Macedonia met the EC's criteria on human rights and democracy. But the EC deferred endorsing recognition based on Greece's fears that Macedonia would assert territorial claims. The texts of the Arbitration Commission opinions can be found in *Yugoslav Survey,* XXXIII, no. 1 (1992): 121–134.

[45] The EC justified its decision to recognize Croatia based on Croatia's "fresh guarantees" (after the Badinter panel's work was completed) to respect human rights. France and the United Kingdom announced their intention to delay actually exchanging ambassadors with Croatia until Croatia demonstrated its willingness to carry out this commitment. *Washington Post*, 16 Jan. 1992, p. A21.

[46] *New York Times*, 16 Jan. 1992, p. A6.

[47] *The Times, 2* Jan. 1992, p. 1. The UN plan called for deploying the peacekeepers in twenty-two contested sectors of Croatia and the withdrawal of the Yugoslav army from Croatia—a compromise between Serbia's position (which proposed deploying peacekeepers along the actual line of fighting between Serbian nationalist and Croatian forces, thus recognizing de facto Serbian territorial gains in Croatia) and Croatia's approach (that the UN should place its forces along the formal Serbia-Croatia border).

[48] The monitors, drawn from UN peacekeeping forces in the Middle East, arrived on January 14, with bases in Zagreb and Belgrade. Their mission was to serve as liaison with the parties to the conflict. *Financial Times*, 15 Jan. 1992, p. 1. The original group of UN monitors included representatives from eighteen countries, including Russia, France, and the United Kingdom. *The Times*, 9 Jan. 1992, p. 7, and 15 Jan. 1992, p. 7. This marked the first time that Russian/Soviet forces had participated in UN peacekeeping operations.

[49] *New York Times,* 6 Jan. 1992, p. 1.

ing down of a helicopter carrying EC monitors by a Yugoslav air force jet on January 7 (which led to suspending the EC monitoring mission) imperiled the peacemaking efforts.

Despite some continued fighting, on February 12, Vance recommended to the UN secretary general that the UN begin to deploy some twelve thousand to thirteen thousand peacekeepers, after Croatian President Tudjman provided new assurances that his government would cooperate with the effort.[50] The Security Council endorsed the proposal (Resolution 743) on February 14.[51] The plan authorized deployment of peacekeepers (the UN Protection Force or UNPROFOR) for one year, the second largest peacekeeping force ever authorized by the UN.[52] Their role was to supervise the cease-fire, the withdrawal of the JNA, and the demobilization of paramilitary forces in four UN "protected areas" (UNPAs), and to facilitate the return of displaced residents. Forces from approximately thirty nations began to deploy on March 8, under the command of Indian Lt. Gen. Satish Nambiar, with the Bosnian capital of Sarajevo as the headquarters. A UN official called the decision to deploy a "calculated risk," given the danger that peacekeepers could become caught in renewed fighting, which was justified in view of the danger that a failure to act would exacerbate the conflict and lead to its spread throughout the rest of Yugoslavia.

The actual deployment was beset by delays and controversies.[53] There were some skirmishes in the protected areas and especially in areas with large Serb populations outside the protected areas near sectors North and South (the so-called "pink zones"). The government of Croatia complained that UN forces were failing to assure the resettlement of displaced Croatians, and the disarming of militias encountered a number of problems. There has been sporadic fighting, including a Croatian offensive to secure the Maslenica bridge in January 1993. Although the agreement that formed the basis for the UN deployment was never fully carried out, UNPROFOR did dampen the conflict somewhat between Croats and Serbs in Croatia, and Croatia has agreed to extend the mandate of UNPROFOR.

The Conflict Spreads to Bosnia (March 1992—Present)

Phase four focused on Bosnia. In addition to continuing the two-track EC-UN

---

[50] *New York Times*, 13 Feb. 1991, p. 1. After the EC's decision to recognize Croatia in January, President Tudjman appeared to backtrack from his earlier acceptance of the UN plan. In a letter to Vance, Tudjman stated that he "fully accepts all the terms of reference of the [UN] peace plan."

[51] Resolution 743 was not adopted under Chapter VII of the Charter, at India's insistence that such a move would represent an impermissible interference in a country's internal affairs.

[52] While the UN normally authorizes forces for six-month periods, the decision to give the Yugoslav peacekeeping force a one-year mandate was designed to reassure the Serb minority in Croatia that their rights would be protected pending a political settlement to the conflict.

[53] Although the intial deployment began in March, it was not until April 7 that the Security Council authorized full deployment of UNPROFOR (Resolution 749), which called for completing deployment according to the secretary-general's report S/23777, by May 15. In fact, UNPROFOR did not assume its full responsibilities in Sector East until May 15; Sector West until June 20.

approach, a new set of issues appeared on the international community's agenda—humanitarian relief, human rights and refugee management, and enforcement of economic sanctions. Nations also discussed a more direct military role, but time and again declined to act.

Pursuant to the Badinter panel recommendation, the government of Bosnia scheduled a referendum on independence for February 29–March 1. As the date approached, the EC launched an effort to reach a political settlement among Bosnia's ethnic groups, convening a meeting in Lisbon on February 21 that led to an agreement among Bosnia's three principal factions to respect the existing borders of the republic. In the referendum, approximately 90 percent of Bosnia's voters approved independence. Approximately 60 percent of eligible voters participated; Serbs (who make up nearly one-third of the population of Bosnia) boycotted the vote. Shortly thereafter, conflict among the three ethnic communities began to break out.

On April 6, the EC foreign ministers decided to recognize Bosnia.[54] The next day, the United States extended recognition to three republics, Slovenia, Croatia, and Bosnia.[55] On April 7, the Security Council adopted Resolution 749, calling on the parties in Bosnia to cooperate with on-going EC efforts to mediate the conflict, and on April 10 the Security Council adopted a presidential statement requesting the secretary general to send Vance to Bosnia.

As ethnic conflict escalated in Bosnia, the EC gave Serbia an April 29 deadline to halt its military support for Serb nationals in Bosnia, under threat of additional diplomatic penalties, and the CSCE scheduled a meeting for the same day to discuss suspending Yugoslavia's (that is, Serbia's) membership. In addition, Western countries threatened to cut off Yugoslavia's membership in the IMF. It briefly appeared that Serbia had bowed to international pressure when, on April 27, the leaders of Serbia and Montenegro announced a new constitution for Yugoslavia, territorially limited to those two republics, and agreed to accept the independence of the four breakaway republics.

---

[54] *New York Times,* 7 Apr. 1992, p. A3. The EC ministers agreed to delay implementing the decision for one day to permit simultaneous recognition with the United States. At the same time, they agreed to restore trade preferences to Serbia, if Serbia agreed to respect the nonviolability of borders, open airspace, and withdraw legal claims to Serbian enclaves in Croatia. *Financial Times*, 7 Apr. 1992, p. 2.

[55] Both the EC and the United States deferred action on Macedonia's appeal for recognition in the hopes that negotiations would resolve Greece's continued objection to recognizing Macedonia. Greece objected to the republic's use of the name "Macedonia," which Greece claims rightfully belongs to Greek heritage, and it also accused the republic of harboring territorial designs on parts of Greece. Several countries in the region had already recognized Macedonia, including Bulgaria and Turkey.

Slovenia, Croatia, and Bosnia-Herzegovina were admitted to the UN General Assembly on May 22. On September 22 the UN General Assembly voted to deny the self-proclaimed successor state "Yugoslavia" the Yugoslav seat in the UN, forcing Serbia and Montenegro to apply anew for UN membership, but requiring the UN to act on any new application by the end of the current General Assembly session in mid-December. The Security Resolution that paved the way for General Assembly action was adopted 12–0 with China, India, and Zimbabwe abstaining.

Violence continued to spread through Bosnia, however, and on May 6 the EC withdrew its monitoring mission, following the killing of one of its monitors. There was growing interest in extending the UN peacekeeping mandate to that republic. The foreign ministers of France, Germany, and Poland, as well as the government of Bosnia called on the UN to act, but the UN secretary general demurred. In his May 12 report (S/23900) to the Security Council, he argued that the on-going fighting precluded deploying peacekeepers, that an intervention force was impractical, and suggested that the EC might be the appropriate organization to send peacekeepers in any event. He placed the principal blame for the fighting on Serbian paramilitary forces and the JNA.

In response, the Security Council adopted Resolution 752 on May 15, calling for the end of outside interference in Bosnia, and the withdrawal of the JNA and Croatian army, as well as the disbanding of paramilitary forces. The Security Council also called for the first time for an end to forcible expulsions ("ethnic cleansing") and for noninterference with humanitarian relief operations (including safe and secure access to airports). The Security Council also asked the secretary general to keep the option of UN peacekeepers for Bosnia under review.[56]

Despite the resolution, fighting continued to block delivery of humanitarian aid, and on May 26, Boutros-Ghali submitted a report to the Security Council (S/24000) outlining two options: "protection through agreements binding all armed factions" or "armed protection of UN forces." Under strong prodding from the United States, on May 30 the Security Council voted mandatory economic sanctions against Serbia and Montenegro (Resolution 757), terming the situation in Bosnia a "threat to international peace and security," invoking Chapter VII of the UN Charter.[57] Several weeks later, first the WEU, then NATO offered at the CSCE summit to send naval forces to the Adriatic Sea to monitor the embargo.[58] They were followed several

---

[56] The fact that Bosnia's Muslims were the principal victims of the fighting served to mobilize broad segments of the international community. The Ministerial Meeting of the Non-Aligned Countries, held on May 14–15, called for respecting the territorial integrity of Bosnia, and on May 18, the secretary general of the Organization of the Islamic Conference sent a letter to the UN secretary general urging Chapter VII measures to respond to "Serbian aggression against Bosnia." *Yugoslav Survey*, 33, no. 2 (1992): 73.

[57] The resolution bans the import or transshipment of commodities and products from Serbia and Montenegro, and the export of goods (other than medical supplies and foodstuffs) to those republics. The resolution also froze payments and credits to Serbia and Montenegro, cut off landing and overflight rights, and barred their participation in sporting events, scientific and technical cooperation, and cultural exchanges.

[58] The WEU force consisted of ships from Italy, France, Spain, and Portugal and German patrol aircraft, while the NATO contingent was drawn from the Standing Naval Force Mediterranean, which includes ships from the United States, Germany, Italy, Greece, Turkey, the Netherlands, Spain, and the United Kingdom. Both were under Italian command, and both were limited to monitoring, rather than enforcing, the embargo. NATO also supplied AWACs aircraft to assist in the operation. At its meeting, the WEU also agreed to take steps to consider opening a land corridor to Sarajevo. *The Times*, 11 July 1992. The German deployment caused considerable domestic controversy: the

weeks later by civilian inspectors who were sent to the borders of neighboring countries to monitor compliance with the embargo on overland routes and on the Danube.[59] Over the summer the embargo grew progressively tighter, inflation in Serbia skyrocketed, gasoline was strictly rationed, and shortages of raw materials and parts shut down many industrial plants. The availability of hydroelectric energy and adequate food supplies, however, coupled with continued smuggling, allowed Serbia to struggle on. Nonetheless, all Western countries continued to reject direct military involvement as requested by the Bosnian government.

In an attempt to assure the delivery of humanitarian aid to Sarajevo, the UN in early June brokered an agreement between the Bosnian government and Serbian forces to place the Sarajevo airport under UNPROFOR control. The Security Council agreed in principle to extend UNPROFOR's mandate to supervise the withdrawal of heavy military equipment from around the airport and assume control of the airport with an additional eleven hundred UN troops (Resolution 758, June 8, 1992). But the impasse at the airport was not broken until President Mitterrand's surprise visit to Sarajevo on June 28, following an EC summit in Lisbon.[60]

The Mitterrand-inspired cease-fire did not last long, however, and pressure increased to authorize the use of force to assure the delivery of humanitarian supplies to the remaining government-controlled enclaves in Bosnia. This effort was spurred on by the public disclosure of Serb detention camps in Bosnia. Meanwhile, the United Nations High Commissioner for Refugees convened an international conference in late July to seek additional financial support for relief operations and greater willingness to accept refugees.[61] On July 20, EC foreign ministers voted to seek Yugoslavia's expulsion from the United Nations and other international organizations.

After considerable internal debate, the Security Council, at U.S. prodding, on August 13 adopted Resolution 770, which "called upon all states to take nationally or through regional agencies or arrangements all measures necessary to facilitate in coordination with the United Nations the delivery of humanitarian aid."[62] But there was little consensus on how to implement this provision. NATO's military staff

---

opposition SPD claimed that it violated the German Basic Law and brought a challenge in the German constitutional court.

[59] The CSCE summit also decided to send observers to Kosovo, Vojvodina, and the Sandjak to monitor Serbia's compliance with human rights guarantees and continued Yugoslavia's suspension from the CSCE until October 14. *Financial Times*, 9 July 1992.

[60] The EC meeting followed a meeting of the WEU on June 26, which considered a range of military options, especially those directed at enforcing the embargo. The leaders of the G–7 agreed on July 7 that the Security Council should take steps "not excluding military means" to assure delivery of humanitarian aid.

[61] *Washington Post*, 30 July 1992, p. A22.

[62] The United Kingdom and France were more reluctant to use force, preferring to strengthen the UN force in Bosnia to protect convoys. UN officials worried about the further politicization of the UN troops, which already were under attack from both Bosnian and Serb forces. *New York Times*, 8 and 9 Aug. 1992. China, India, and Zimbabwe abstained.

initially drew up a plan that would require about 100 thousand troops, but it was rejected by political leaders, and a far more modest proposal for approximately six thousand troops drawn from NATO countries but under UN rather than NATO command (but paid for by the contributing countries) was adopted instead. France offered to send an additional eleven hundred troops while the United Kingdom overcame its initial reluctance and offered eighteen hundred to enforce the delivery of humanitarian aid, which eventually became known as UNPROFOR II.[63] Canada and Spain also provided troops, with support elements from Denmark, Belgium, the Netherlands, and Portugal. Meanwhile, the UN Human Rights Commission also agreed to take up the question of human rights abuses in Bosnia, appointing former Polish Prime Minister Tadeusz Mazowiecki as special investigator; and on October 6, the UN agreed to set up a war crimes tribunal.[64]

During this period, tensions began to surface between the two principal avenues of international action: the UN and the EC. In mid-July, EC mediator Lord Carrington brokered a cease-fire in Bosnia that called for placing heavy weaponry under UN supervision, without consulting UN officials concerning their willingness to take on that role. The Security Council in turn, at the request of the British ambassador, endorsed the proposal without seeking the secretary general's views, which provoked a stern response from Boutros-Ghali, who also suggested that the Security Council was paying undue attention to the problems of Europe while ignoring crises in the developing world, such as Somalia.[65] Boutros-Ghali also expressed concern that growing Western military involvement would jeopardize the safety of UN peacekeepers in Croatia and Bosnia. France began to push to involve the UN in the EC-sponsored peace conference, on the grounds that the United States and Russia could put additional pressure on the parties to come to an agreement. Britain, holding the presidency of the EC, initially resisted, but in early August agreed to host a joint EC-UN conference on August 26–28. On the eve of the conference, Lord Carrington resigned as EC mediator. He was succeeded by Lord Owen, the former leader of the United Kingdom's Social Democrat Party.[66]

At the London conference, the parties in Bosnia agreed to more intensive, ongoing talks in Geneva beginning September 3, based on an agreed "Statement of Principles," including nonrecognition of territorial gains achieved by force, unconditional release of civilian detainees, and protection of minority rights.[67] The parties

---

[63] The Security Council authorized the action on September 14, 1992. China, India, and Zimbabwe abstained.

[64] In his August 31 report, Mazowiecki called for stationing UN observers in ethnically tense areas in Serbia (Kosovo, Vojvodina, the Sandzak) to prevent the spread of fighting. *New York Times*, 1 Sept. 1992, p. 1.

[65] *New York Times*, 24 July 1992, p. A3, and 3 Aug. 1992, p. A1.

[66] Vance continued to serve as the UN mediator until he was replaced by Norway's Foreign Minister Thorvald Stoltenberg in the spring of 1993.

[67] The conference was attended by the heads of the six former Yugoslav republics plus the president and prime minister of the self-declared Yugoslavia, foreign ministers of the EC states, United States, Russia, Japan, China, Turkey, Canada, Switzerland, Saudi Arabia, and the former Yugoslavia's

agreed to a ban on military flights, international monitoring of the Serbia-Bosnia border, tougher sanctions enforcement, and full cooperation in permitting the delivery of humanitarian relief. They established six working groups (on Bosnia, ethnic and minority issues, legal implications of the successor states to Yugoslavia, humanitarian relief, economic issues and confidence-building measures), three to be chaired by the EC, and three by the UN. Serb leaders in Bosnia also unilaterally pledged to place their heavy equipment under UN supervision. Taken together, the UN and EC described their approach as a "three-pronged strategy"—political negotiations, humanitarian relief, and confidence-building.

But Serbia and Serb forces failed to observe their pledge to end military flights, and on October 9 the Security Council voted to ban military flights over Bosnia, although not until March 31, 1993, did it authorize military measures to enforce the ban, to be implemented under NATO operational control.[68] The Security Council also voted in October to create a War Crimes Commission, which was formally established in February 1993.

On January 2, 1993, Vance and Owen presented their plan to divide Bosnia into ten largely autonomous districts, with a weak central government. Each of Bosnia's principal ethnic groups would dominate three of the proposed districts (although the districts would not necessarily be ethnically pure) while Sarajevo, the tenth district, would be placed under joint control. The United Nations would play an extensive role in assuring freedom of movement among the districts, guaranteeing the integrity of the judicial system and providing peacekeepers to assure order.

Although the plan would have required Bosnian Serbs to relinquish some of the territory gained in the fighting, the Bosnian government as well as the Bosnian Serbs resisted the plan. The EC foreign ministers enthusiastically embraced the proposal, but the newly elected Clinton administration remained lukewarm.[69] After extensive pressure, including arm-twisting by Serbian President Milosevic, the Bosnian Serb leader Radovan Karadzic reluctantly agreed to the plan in a meeting in Athens in early May, and NATO prepared to send a large peacekeeping force to help implement it.[70] But Karadzic was repudiated by the parliament of the self-

---

neighbors (Albania, Austria, Bulgaria, Hungary, Romania), as well as representatives from the CSCE, EC Commission, International Red Cross, and the Organization of the Islamic Conference. Representatives of Bosnia Serbs and Croats, Kosovo Albanians, and Vojvodina Hungarians attended as observers. For the text of speeches and concluding documents, see *Yugoslav Survey,* XXXIII, no. 3 (1992): 19–55.

[68] See *New York Times,* 3 Apr. 1993, p. 5. The operation was directed by the commander of NATO's 5th Allied Tactical Air Force, including aircraft from the United States, France, and the Netherlands (later joined by Turkey), but under the overall political control of the Security Council. See *Washington Post,* 9 Apr. 1993, p. 1.

[69] See *New York Times,* 4 Feb. 1993, p. 1.

[70] *Washington Post,* 4 May 1993, p. 1. The UN secretary general insisted, however, that while NATO would have "operational and tactical control," the UN would retain "overall strategic and political control" and would wear blue helmets identifying them as a UN force. *Washington Post,* 5 May 1993, p. 24.

proclaimed Serbian Republic of Bosnia, and the continued fighting ultimately rendered the Vance-Owen proposal obsolete.

With the failure of Vance-Owen, the United States briefly floated a proposal to lift the arms embargo against the Bosnian government and use air strikes to protect Bosnian Muslim positions until the arms could be delivered.[71] The U.S. proposal met strong opposition in Europe, especially among countries with troops in Bosnia. Instead, the international community fell back on an idea developed by France, with the support of Russia, Britain, Spain, and, ultimately, the United States, for establishing six "safe areas." Foreign ministers developed the so-called Washington Joint Action Plan in meetings held in the U.S. capital on the weekend of May 21–23 and the Security Council implemented it by a 13–0 vote (Pakistan and Venezuela abstaining) on June 4, 1993. Although the resolution contemplated sending additional troops to guard the safe areas, few countries were prepared to contribute. The resolution also authorized air strikes to protect the UN forces should they come under attack.

But the UN action failed to halt the Bosnian Serbs' continued advance on Sarajevo, and at the prompting of the United States, NATO and the UN devised a plan for direct attacks on Bosnian Serb forces should they refuse to lift the siege of Sarajevo.

Responding to the Danger of Spillover

As the fighting continued in Bosnia through much of 1992, the international community became increasingly concerned by the danger that the conflict could spill over into the heavily Albanian Muslim province of Kosovo or into Macedonia, and ultimately widen to include the former Yugoslavia's neighbors as well as Turkey, which had historical and religious connections to the Muslims in Bosnia, Kosovo, and Macedonia. Reports that Serbia had begun "ethnic cleansing" of Hungarians in Vojvodina prompted similar fears of wider international involvement.

In July 1992, the CSCE decided to send monitors to Vojvodina, Kosovo, and the Sandzak (another heavily Muslim area of Serbia) as well as Macedonia. On December 11, the Security Council authorized the preventive deployment of peacekeepers in Macedonia, at the request of the Macedonian government. The initial deployment of 700 Scandinavian peacekeepers (under the overall command of the UN Force Command of UNPROFOR) was augmented by 300 U.S. troops in July 1993.

In late December 1992, President Bush reportedly warned Milosevic that the United States would use military force against Serbia "in the event of conflict caused by Serbian action."[72] After months of wrangling, Greece accepted a proposal to permit Macedonia's UN membership under the interim name "Former Yugoslav

[71] Earlier, in March 1993, the Clinton administration had slightly expanded U.S. involvement in the Bosnia humanitarian relief operation when it began a series of air drops to deliver food and medical supplies to isolated parts of Muslim-controlled eastern Bosnia.

[72] *Times*, 29 Dec. 1992, p. 1.

Republic of Macedonia," pending further UN/EC arbitration, and Macedonia joined the UN on April 7, 1993.

Lessons from the Yugoslav Crisis for International Institutions

Although the international community had devoted considerable time and attention to the conflict, it could point to little concrete success. A UN peacekeeping force of unprecedented size and scope was charged with trying to keep the peace in Croatia, assuring humanitarian relief in Bosnia, and preventing the conflict from spreading to Macedonia. The UN and EC jointly were trying to broker a political settlement in Geneva. Meanwhile, the WEU and NATO monitored economic sanctions in the Adriatic, and (nominally) enforced a no-fly zone over Bosnia.[73] Finally, the CSCE was monitoring the human rights situation in ethnic minority communities within Serbia. In light of the many harsh judgments currently being expressed about the performance of international organizations in the face of the crisis, it is timely to try to understand what happened and why, what worked and what didn't, in the international community's response.

The Characteristics of the Yugoslavia Conflict

The outbreak of internal conflict in Yugoslavia was the first European security crisis in the post-Cold War era. For several reasons, the conflict has posed a difficult test for European political and security institutions:

(1) THE CONFLICT WAS PRIMARILY INTERNAL.

Although the conflict produced large numbers of refugees, some of whom fled to neighboring countries, and intermittent border problems arose as a result of Yugoslav military activities, there was little danger during the first months that military conflict would spread across international borders.[74] This fact posed problems for many of the relevant political institutions. For NATO, the dispute was "out-of-area" and, therefore, outside the ambit of NATO's military response under Articles V and VI of the Washington treaty. The WEU faced a similar problem: although the Brussels treaty contains no geographical constraints similar to NATO's Articles V and VI, few believed that the conflict posed a substantial military threat to its members' security.

The CSCE's role was complicated by the constraints imposed on intervening in a

---

[73] In June 1993, NATO and the WEU agreed to merge the two Adriatic operations, under the joint political control of the WEU and NATO councils, but under the sole operational control of NATO's SACEUR.

[74] The prospect of transborder involvement was raised during the flurry of diplomatic activity in early August, as some voiced fears that Germany, Italy, or other European countries might intervene in Yugoslavia to protect their nationals from the escalating violence. *New York Times*, 8 Aug. 1991, p. A3.

member nation's internal affairs without its consent, a point the USSR insisted on when it agreed to the new emergency crisis mechanism. Similar constraints seriously hampered UN involvement, especially in the early stages of the conflict; neutral and nonaligned countries (including China, with its Security Council veto) were reluctant to support UN involvement in what they saw as an internal dispute.

The situation evolved considerably over the course of the crisis. The UN in particular became increasingly active in four dimensions— peacekeeping, economic sanctions, humanitarian and refugee relief, and human rights. The CSCE sent monitors into Serbia to check on human rights. Both NATO and the WEU deployed forces to monitor and later enforce the economic embargo; they were also to become more involved in supporting the peacekeeping and humanitarian relief activities implemented by the UN. NATO not only assumed operational control over the Bosnia no-fly zone enforcement, but also was tapped to plan and operate the complex operation for enforcing Vance-Owen. To some extent, this growing involvement was facilitated by the international recognition of Slovenia, Croatia, and Bosnia, which converted the crisis into an international conflict more subject to traditional action by international organizations.

The crisis clearly expanded the range of permissible internal intervention, but international institutions are still feeling their way cautiously in uncharted territory. Inspired by the humanitarian operation in support of the Kurds in northern Iraq (Operation Provide Comfort), they broke new ground in involvement in internal conflict, while shying away from direct military involvement.

(2) THE DISPUTE PITTED THE PRINCIPLE OF SELF-DETERMINATION AGAINST THE IDEA OF INVIOLABLE NATIONAL BORDERS.

The conflict raised a delicate and sometimes embarrassing dilemma for European nations: the inherent tension between support for the principle of self-determination and the belief in preserving the international territorial status quo. Since the Helsinki Final Act of 1975, the foundations of European stability had been built on the principle that international borders should not be altered through the use of force and that any alteration should be voluntary. At the same time, the democratic revolutions of 1989–1990 heightened European awareness of the importance of self-determination, a principle also enshrined in the Helsinki accord and the Paris CSCE Charter. Serbia's unwillingness to negotiate constitutional change or to accept Slovenia's and Croatia's independence put these two principles in conflict.

Each of the European nations had a different approach to balancing these conflicting interests. For Germany, the problem was particularly acute. Having just achieved unity on the basis of the German Democratic Republic citizens' right to determine their own destiny, the German government found it increasingly awkward to turn its back on the claims of Slovenia and Croatia to do the same. Historical, cultural, and religious ties further enhanced German (and Austrian) public sympathy for the Slovenian and Croatian cause.

The European nations facing their own national separatist movements (Spain, France, Czechoslovakia, the USSR, and the United Kingdom) feared that hasty support for independence could have repercussions at home. As a result, they tended to support efforts to maintain Yugoslavia's political integrity. This concern was greatest in the USSR. Soviet President Mikhail Gorbachev stated: "We are looking for ways to resolve the problem by peaceful means, respecting the peoples of Yugoslavia but proceeding from the premise that we favor Yugoslavia's integrity and are committed to the inviolability of borders." He added that if nations failed to respect this principle, "developments in Europe will be out of hand."[75]

Italy was torn between two conflicting interests. It offered public sympathy for the plight of neighboring Slovenia and Croatia, while facing its own problems of internal cohesion (a separatist movement in Alto-Adige and a broader political tide for greater regional autonomy, centered in Lombardy).

These differences in perspective could be seen throughout the deliberations of both the EC and the CSCE; the more homogeneous EC had somewhat greater success in achieving consensus than the more diverse CSCE. The EC resolved its qualms by advancing the notion that "internal boundaries" should not be changed by force, thus providing a rationale for recognizing Slovenia and Croatia, and later Bosnia, but not the self-proclaimed Serb republics of Krajina and Bosnia.[76] The decision to recognize, however, was affected more by the desire to preserve unity at the time of the Maastricht summit than a shared belief in the wisdom of the course; and others, especially at the UN, blame the EC's decision to recognize for triggering the conflict in Bosnia. Moreover, the EC's commitment to its own approach was belied by its unwillingness to move forward on recognizing Macedonia, primarily because of concern for the political consequences in Greece.

(3) MOST INSTITUTIONS WERE NEW OR IN THE PROCESS OF EVOLUTION.

In many respects, the crisis in Yugoslavia was "premature"; it caught Europe in the act of self-redefinition. The most dramatic case is the CSCE. Less than one week after the CSCE foreign ministers agreed to an emergency-response mechanism, the CSCE was put through its first trial by fire.

For the European Community, the process of foreign policy cooperation dates back to the creation of European Political Cooperation (EPC) in 1970. But the Twelve were in the throes of debating whether to strengthen foreign policy cooperation through a common foreign and security policy (in the context of the ongoing intergovernmental conference on political union). The crisis in Yugoslavia often complicated the political union discussions, as the overtaxed machinery of the EC presidency tried to cope simultaneously with the two formidable challenges. The

[75] *Los Angeles Times*, 10 July 1991, p. A6.

[76] Van den Broek stated, "It is not acceptable that *internal* or international borders be changed unilaterally by force." *New York Times*, 8 Aug. 1991, p. A3 (emphasis added). See also the Badinter Commission Opinion, Number 2. *Yugoslav Survey*, XXXIII, no. 1 (1992): 122. Whether the international community is prepared to accept this as a principle of international law, and to draw the appropriate consequences (including a right to intervene to guarantee what had heretofore been viewed as essentially administrative demarcations) is unclear.

WEU was embroiled in a debate over two alternatives for its future: as an independent West European military organization operating in conjunction with the EC, or as a strengthened European pillar under the NATO umbrella.

NATO, too, was in the midst of redefinition. With the London Declaration, it had moved away from its near-exclusive preoccupation with the Soviet/Warsaw Pact threat, but the NATO strategy review (the new "strategic concept" was finally adopted in November 1991) failed to resolve NATO's operational role in managing conflict in Eastern Europe. The UN, fresh from its successful involvement in the Persian Gulf conflict, had ambitions to play a larger part in international stability but it remained unclear how the Gulf experience might apply to crises such as Yugoslavia.

The conflict clearly accelerated the adaptive process for most of the key institutions. The UN broke new substantive ground in the justifications adopted for action, and began to elaborate new mechanisms beyond traditional peacekeeping for UN involvement. The CSCE took several important steps, including the decision to authorize action based on "consensus minus one" rather than full unanimity; deciding to become a regional organization under Chapter VIII of the UN Charter; expanding protection of minority groups through a new high commissioner for national minorities; and agreeing to undertake peacekeeping in appropriate circumstances.[77] NATO and the WEU both agreed to offer peacekeeping forces to the UN or CSCE on a case-by-case basis, thus expanding the scope of their potential operations, and the WEU moved toward a more permanent institutional footing with the decision to establish a planning staff and procedures for identifying forces for WEU contingencies. The EC tried to enhance its role in security and defense through the decisions made at Maastricht in December 1991 to establish a common foreign and security policy and an organic link between the EC and the WEU.

As a result, it is likely that the international institutions would respond somewhat more effectively today to the outbreak of a Yugoslavia-style conflict than they did at that early stage of post-Cold War Europe. But, as discussed below, further evolution is necessary and, in any event, there are limits to what institutions can do.

(4) The international community believed its response to the crisis would set important precedents for future ethnic and national conflict in Europe.

Precisely because Yugoslavia was the first post-Cold War crisis, the international community has been preoccupied with the precedent-setting consequences of its actions. The simultaneous breakup of the Soviet Union and the ongoing internal dispute in Czechoslovakia over that country's future as a single nation caused many to worry about the consequences of any action (or inaction) in Yugoslavia for future conflicts. The international community's response was continually tempered by fears that it might live to regret actions that seemed appropriate to Yugoslavia but destabilizing elsewhere.

Initially, the fear of setting a precedent tended to support inaction, but, as the

---

[77] Conference on Security and Cooperation in Europe, *The Challenges of Change*, Helsinki, July 1992 (hereafter *The Challenges of Change*).

conflict dragged on, proponents of greater international activism began to argue that failure to intervene might encourage others to believe that they could use force to settle ethnic and national questions without fear of international response. Thus, the precedent-setting implications of the conflict and the international community's role remain central elements of the debate.

(5) THE CONFLICT EXPOSED THE DIVERGENT GEO-POLITICAL ORIENTATIONS OF EUROPEAN NATIONS.

The Yugoslav crisis had its most direct external impact on Yugoslavia's neighbor states — Austria, Hungary, Albania, Romania, Bulgaria, and Greece — who faced the greatest danger from the conflict's spread and the growing numbers of refugees. Their interest was further shaped by the complex history of the Balkans and ancient alliances with elements of Yugoslavia's population based on culture, religion, ethnicity, and geography. Italy, too, shared some of the same connections.

Germany's sympathies were clear, but posed an acute dilemma. Historical bonds between Germany, and Slovenia, and Croatia remained strong; many Germans (and Austrians) continued to refer to Ljubljana and Zagreb by their German names Laibach and Agram, dating back to the Austro-Hungarian Empire. Economic ties were extensive, and there was deep emotional support, especially in Bavaria, for the cause of independence, fueled by ties of Catholic loyalty.[78] At the same time, German activism in favor of independence created a certain unrest among other European states; there was even some dark muttering about Germany's ambitions to create a German zone of influence through the region.[79]

France, too, had geo-political ties to the region. These, however, pointed in the opposite direction—a historical alignment with Serbia in its earlier conflicts with Germany.[80]

All of the EC countries had their natural political and cultural inclinations tempered by their commitment (in varying degrees) to a common EC line toward the crisis. This problem was particularly acute for Germany, where public sentiment for Slovenia and Croatia was strong; yet, Germany held itself out as a leading champion for a strengthened EC common foreign and security policy. For this reason, the German government was forced to walk a fine line, embedding rhetorical support

---

[78] In the fiery language of one German commentator: "The Croats are among the columns of the Catholic global church." Johann Georg Reissmueller, "Abandoned by the Nations," *Frankfurter Allgemeine Zeitung*, Nov. 16, 1991, p. 1 (FBIS-WEU-91-233, Dec. 4, 1991, p. 8).

[79] "L'Allemagne, puissance protectrice des Slovenes et des Croates," *Le Monde*, 4 July 1991, p. 4. Skeptics also pointed to the alliance between Germany and the Croatian fascist government during World War II.

German officials were highly sensitive to this concern. One remarked, "The very idea of Germany, or Austria or Italy being involved in [a European military intervention] is politically impossible. History forbids it." *Guardian Weekly*, 28 July 1991, p. 7.

[80] A French reporter asked the French foreign minister: "Why is France reluctant to name the aggressor in the fighting? Is France still the Serbs' protector?" Dumas acknowledged: "France and Serbia have had preferential ties in the past." *Liberation*, 6 Dec. 1991, p. 18.

for self-determination in the self-imposed policy constraint of needing to act collectively.[81]

(6) THE LEADING ACTORS OF THE COLD WAR ERA TOOK A BACK SEAT.

The Cold War era in Europe was dominated by the two superpowers, who gave policy direction to their allies and whose confrontation indirectly helped to suppress smaller conflicts in Europe, out of fear that they would escalate into an East-West confrontation. The decision by both the United States and the USSR to remain relatively aloof from the conflict in Yugoslavia during the early stages in some ways contributed to the outbreak of violence, because the parties were emboldened to risk military confrontation without triggering a massive conflagration. Meanwhile, the relative absence of the superpowers gave other European nations and institutions freedom to maneuver, but they faced a difficult problem of forging consensus in the absence of a single dominant policy-making voice. It seems clear that the more active U.S. role beginning in April–May 1992 finally enabled the UN to move forward on a number of fronts, including economic sanctions and humanitarian relief backed by the threat of force. Similar U.S. activism galvanized adopting the no-fly zone. Although President Clinton hinted at a more assertive U.S. role, his decision to rule out sending U.S. ground troops and insistence on multinational action limited the efficacy of U.S. leadership.

Taken together, these six factors posed difficult challenges for the political/security institutions' efforts to achieve a peaceful resolution to the crises in Yugoslavia. Yet, there is little reason to believe that this situation is unique. Many, if not all, of these factors are likely to be present in future European crises. For this reason, the successes and failures have profound implications for the evolution of European security institutions.

Lessons Learned: Some General Conclusions

The developments in the Yugoslav conflict suggest five general lessons on the role of security institutions in Europe's future.

(1) THE LIMITED WILLINGNESS TO USE OUTSIDE MILITARY FORCE IN RESOLVING ETHNIC CONFLICT, ESPECIALLY INTERNAL CONFLICT.

Throughout the Cold War, the balance of military forces and the threat of military response to aggression played a key role in maintaining European stability. Yet, in the Yugoslav situation, no nation seriously advocated military intervention, and even the deployment of peacekeeping forces proved controversial.

There were several reasons behind this diffidence. None of the nations had a legal

[81] Austria faced a similar problem. With its application for EC membership pending, Chancellor Vranitzky was eager to demonstrate Austria's willingness to coordinate with the EC, notwithstanding the very strong domestic pressure (even within the governing coalition) for moving forward independently to recognize Slovenia and Croatia.

or political commitment to come to the aid of the warring factions; none considered their supreme national interests sufficiently threatened by the victory of one side or the other to warrant the risk of casualties or long-term political entanglement in Yugoslavia's conflict.[82] They also worried that military intervention would set a precedent for future ethnic and national conflicts.

The international community also doubted the efficacy of military intervention. Although a major commitment of forces might bring a temporary halt to the fighting, it was uncertain whether this would contribute to an underlying political settlement that would restore stability to a disintegrating Yugoslavia.[83] The United Kingdom's involvement with ongoing civil strife in Northern Ireland proved a powerful lesson and was frequently cited by European leaders during their deliberations.

During the course of the crisis, there was growing enthusiasm for deploying peacekeeping forces, driven by the continued failure of diplomatic efforts and economic sanctions. Initially, the international community backed away from sending forces unless the parties could reach a reasonably durable cease-fire. Over time, more nations came to accept the idea that deploying peacekeeping forces could help bring about a cease-fire. The UN decision to deploy in Croatia in February 1992 was a compromise between these two views—a cease-fire was nominally in place, but fragile. The decision to expand the UN force in Bosnia was another development down this road, since there was no reliable cease-fire when UN forces moved into Sarajevo airport, and the humanitarian mission of UNPROFOR II is not predicated on the parties' consent. Finally, the decision to impose a no-fly zone might have represented a further step toward nonconsensual use of force; however, notwithstanding explicit UN authorization, NATO forces seemed unwilling to act, despite rather blatant violations of the Security Council resolution.

Because significant military force was never used, it is impossible to conclude definitively that force would actually be ineffective. There is certainly reason to believe that a concerted military effort directed against the Yugoslav army (to deny it the use of airpower, for example) might have hampered or even halted the military

[82] The two partial exceptions were Austria and Italy, both of which sent military forces to their borders with Yugoslavia when fighting broke out between Slovenia and the Yugoslav army. *New York Times*, 1 July 1991, p. 6; Rome RAI Radio, July 7, 1991 (FBIS-WEU-91-131, July 9, 1991, p. 20). As the plight of Bosnia's Muslims worsened, several Islamic nations, especially Turkey, pressed for a more active international role and there have been reports of Iranian arms shipments to Bosnia, but none has shown an inclination to act unilaterally.

[83] When asked about the prospect of European military forces intervening in crises such as Yugoslavia, Italian Foreign Minister de Michelis stated: "I do not think this would be a suitable instrument in the event of a civil war and armed clashes; there is no military solution. We cannot anticipate the presence of military troops that might be able to stay in power for a long time with legal means. We must find a political solution." *Wiener Zeitung*, Aug. 1, 1991 (FBIS-WEU-91-148, Aug. 1, 1991, p. 13). Similarly, on several occasions President Bush referred to the conflict as a quagmire, and the Chairman of the Chiefs of Staff General Colin Powell warned about the risks of military intervention. "Why Generals Get Nervous," *New York Times*, 8 Oct. 1992, p. A21.

actions of the Serbian-led forces. Many believe that the shelling of Dubrovnik could have been avoided by an international show of naval force. The intensity of the intracommunal fighting between Serb and Croat partisans in Croatia, however, and later among Serbs, Croats, and Muslims in Bosnia suggests that some fighting would likely continue even with outside military intervention.

The most important consequence of this conclusion is for NATO. Although it is difficult to dispute NATO's value in protecting its members against aggression, the crises in Yugoslavia underscores the limits (political as well as practical) of NATO's utility as a military organization in responding to future security challenges that do not directly threaten member nations' security. Prompted by the crises in Yugoslavia, NATO agreed to accept the idea of becoming involved out-of-area as a peace-keeping arm of the UN and the CSCE, but putting even this into practice proved difficult. NATO did deploy naval forces to the Adriatic to monitor UN sanctions, and eventually engaged in limited enforcement actions. Similarly, NATO nations agreed to provide forces to assist in humanitarian relief operations, but under UN rather than NATO command. Finally, NATO assumed operational control of the no-fly operation. It remains an open question, however, whether NATO's ongoing adaptation will lead it to develop an operationally relevant role for the crises in Europe's future; the air strikes conducted under UN mandate in April 1994 mark a major departure in NATO's role in the postwar period and could presage a deeper involvment of NATO—and the United States—in the Bosnian conflict. Yet if the air strikes prove unsuccessful in promoting a peace settlement, NATO's image and credibility could be seriously tarnished.

The experience in Yugoslavia has similar implications for the future development of the WEU as an operational military organization. Although the WEU does not face the same treaty-based limitations as NATO, many of the same political and practical considerations would apply.

(2) THE IMPORTANCE AND LIMITS OF ECONOMIC LEVERAGE (CARROT AND STICK).

Precisely because the use of military force seemed unavailing, the existence of economic levers became a crucial factor in determining the relative importance of outside actors. On the negative side, the limited trade and aid ties between Yugoslavia and the United States contributed to keeping the United States on the sidelines. By contrast, the EC and its member nations had extensive economic relations with Yugoslavia, which provided them with a variety of tools in seeking to influence the outcome of the dispute.[84]

These tools were available against all sides of the dispute. Before the outbreak of the conflict, the EC (which at that time focused its efforts on slowing the breakaway republics' drive to independence) made clear that membership in the EC (with its

[84] The Yugoslav crisis thus differs from the Gulf War, where the military dimension predominated and Europeans, lacking the institutional means for collective response, were forced to take a back seat to U.S. leadership. However, the availability of economic sanctions (imposed by the EC at the outset of the Gulf crisis) assured that the Community could play some role.

attendant economic benefits) was unlikely to follow a declaration of independence.[85] Once the focus shifted to halting the military actions of the Serbian-led central government, the EC moved to consider sanctions, beginning with suspending economic aid and an arms embargo. Then, as the situation in Croatia deteriorated, it adopted the most potent weapon—trade and financial sanctions. The EC also offered the central government incentives in the form of a new economic assistance package, in the event that the parties reached a peaceful political settlement.

The logic of economic sanctions led beyond the EC, however, because to be effective, sanctions must be universal. Thus, the UN was brought in first to impose an arms embargo, and later a more comprehensive set of economic sanctions against Serbia and Montenegro.

It is difficult to judge the efficacy of the various economic measures imposed during the conflict. Clearly, the threat of withholding EC membership did little to slow the movement for independence in Slovenia and Croatia. Similarly, the arms embargo was, at least initially, primarily symbolic, since black market sources remained available. Over time, however, many, including the newly elected Clinton administration, came to believe that the arms embargo was counterproductive, favoring Serb forces in both Croatia and Bosnia, who not only had the backing of the JNA, but also access to its military stockpiles to arm Serb militias. The threat of trade sanctions during the fall of 1991 may have had a tactical impact on the parties, but each cease-fire was soon broken, notwithstanding EC threats. One can only speculate about whether an earlier decision to impose comprehensive economic sanctions, such as those adopted by the UN in May 1992, might have averted or limited the violence. The sanctions certainly have had a very serious impact on the Serb economy, but it is unclear whether the hardship is simply stiffening Serbian resolve and playing into the hands of Serb hardliners and Milosevic.[86] The efficacy of sanctions in this case is further complicated by the political and logistical problems of enforcement and the difficulty of applying differential sanctions against "offending" republics where the economies of the various republics are, to some degree, integrated.[87]

Nonetheless, it seems clear that the availability of economic measures contrib-

---

[85] According to Daniel Gros of the Centre for European Policy Studies, Slovenia and Croatia conduct about two-thirds of their trade with EC countries. *Financial Times,* 8 July 1991, p. 11.

[86] Yugoslavia's prime minister, Milan Panic, had appealed to the international community to lift the sanctions to strengthen his hand in his ongoing power struggle with Milosevic. Despite Western hints that Panic's election might begin the process of restoring trade with Serbia, he was overwhelmingly defeated in the December 1992 Serbian elections.

[87] Slovenia and Croatia argued that across-the-board sanctions had a disproportionate impact on them, since 60 percent of all of Yugoslavia's exports to the EC came from those two republics. Agence France Presse, Nov. 19, 1991 (FBIS-WEU-91-224, Nov. 20, 1991, p. 1). For the most part, employing sanctions was relatively painless economically for the EC, because the percentage of the EC's trade that involves Yugoslavia is quite small and Yugoslavia is not the source of any critical commodity (such as oil). But for at least one EC member, Greece, the economic impact is proportionately far more important. Athens has applied to the EC for assistance to compensate for the economic loss.

uted to the predominant role played first by the EC and later the UN. In the future, economic leverage seems likely to play an increasingly important role in responding to future threats to stability, although the efficacy of those measures remains in doubt.

(3) THE NEED FOR INSTITUTIONAL FORA FOR COLLECTIVE DECISIONMAKING AND THE LIMITS OF CONSENSUS.

The divergent interests of outside actors, and the lack of a single, generally accepted policy leader, might well have led to chaos in responding to the crisis in Yugoslavia. Instead, structured fora facilitated both dialogue and compromise in forging an agreed-upon response to the conflict.

Germany's response to the crisis is particularly instructive in this respect. It seems clear that had it not been for the EC decisionmaking procedures and Germany's commitment to developing a common policy, Germany would have acted much sooner to recognize Slovenia and Croatia. When Germany finally concluded that further delay was unacceptable, the rest of the Community (in some cases reluctantly) fell into line rather than risk divergent responses.[88]

As the conflict resolution efforts turned toward the UN in 1992, the pressure to develop a consensus helped contribute to Russia's willingness to join in political and economic measures, and to the nonobstructionist path of abstention chosen by China and India, notwithstanding their fears over the precedent being set. It also helped to promote compliance with economic sanctions by Serbia's neighbors, such as Greece and Romania, who had economic incentives to ignore or subvert the embargo.

That said, the consensus within the various institutions tended toward a "least common denominator" response. It was relatively easy to agree to condemn the violence and urge a cease-fire, but much harder to implement common courses of action. The EC had difficulty with simple steps such as suspending aid; more controversial measures, such as deploying peacekeeping forces, proved highly contentious, and the other eleven EC members labored long to overcome Greece's resistance to recognizing Macedonia. Both the UN and the CSCE faced similar daunting problems, and the broad spectrum of opinions and interests limited their ability to respond. The specific strengths and limits of these institutions (and possible avenues for improvement) are discussed in greater detail below.

(4) THE NEED FOR EARLY INTERVENTION AND THE IMPORTANCE OF PRO-ACTIVE POLICY.

Commentators have harshly criticized both individual governments and political institutions for failing to act early and effectively to head off the outbreak of violence in Yugoslavia. To a large extent, the institutions functioned primarily as a

[88] Italy's decision to withdraw its offer of passage through Italian territory for Yugoslav army forces trapped in Slovenia, in the face of EC opposition, is another example of the impact of collective decisionmaking.

bucket brigade to put out the fire, instead of helping to prevent it in the first place.[89]

The slowness to react cannot be attributed to lack of forewarning. In the autumn of 1990, the CIA warned of the likely breakup of Yugoslavia and the probability that it would lead to violent conflict. Similarly, many observers predicted that Bosnia would become the focus of ethnic fighting following its move to independence, yet no preventive measures were taken.

To some extent, this was a problem of substantive policy, rather than institutional functioning. Most governments (in vain, as it turned out) hoped to keep Yugoslavia together by focusing on their support for a federal or confederal solution; they underestimated both the breakaway republics' determination to achieve independence and Serbia's willingness to use force to prevent it.

The institutions' ineffectiveness before the outbreak of violence, however, also reflects institutional limitations—a tendency, when members hold divergent views, to avoid confronting difficult problems until absolutely necessary. This limitation deeply complicated effective intervention. Crisis response and management mechanisms are presently insufficient to permit early action; improving early warning and consultation must be a focus of future development (this point is developed further for the EC and CSCE below).[90]

(5) THE VALUE AND RISKS OF MULTIPLE INSTITUTIONS WITH OVERLAPPING RESPONSIBILITIES, AND THE NEED TO COORDINATE THEIR EFFORTS.

The response to the crisis in Yugoslavia was highly improvisational. It was difficult to foresee which of the many potential institutional actors might be most effective, and the nations' initial instinct was to activate all of them, in the hope that one or more might hold the key.

This, in the end, proved a strength of the emerging European security architecture. Although many nations continue to stress the importance of NATO as a pillar of stability, in this event NATO was unwilling (and perhaps unable) to play a major role.[91] After the first tentative probing, the CSCE moved to the sidelines, but it was an important forum to engage the Soviet Union in developing a common viewpoint (particularly in view of the historical links between Serbia and the USSR, and the Soviet Union's concern over the implications of any precedent for its own internal problems). The CSCE also was an important forum for the countries of Eastern Europe, which, by reason of geographical proximity and their own internal ethnic conflicts, felt no small stake in the agreed response. Finally, the CSCE offered a

[89] See, for example, Lawrence Freedman, "Yugoslavia Provides Lesson in the Art of the Possible," *The Independent*, 3 July 1991, p. 19.

[90] NATO, too, has recognized the importance of crisis prevention and crisis management in its new strategic concept. See The Rome Declaration, ¶4, and "The Alliance's New Strategic Concept," Press Communiqué S–1(91)85, Nov. 7, 1991, ¶32–33. UN Secretary General Boutros-Ghali has also proposed strengthening the UN's ability to respond to various crises with measures such as shared intelligence and preventive deployments. See *Agenda for Peace*.

[91] Had the United States chosen to play a more active role, or if the Europeans had favored military intervention, it is conceivable that NATO would have been more involved.

mechanism for inserting human rights observers into Kosovo and Vojvodina.

While the EC quickly emerged as the first among equals, the EC ministers frequently sought support from the broader international community—through the CSCE, with the United States through consultations in NATO, and, in the later stages, through the UN Security Council to achieve both broader legitimacy and more effective means. Although few favored a military response, the existence of the WEU provided the EC an option for considering military involvement and NATO itself came to play a supportive role in helping to organize humanitarian relief, monitoring the economic sanctions, and planning for more extensive military operations.

The UN Security Council's emergence as an important locus for consultation and decisionmaking in the Yugoslav crisis came as something of a surprise, given the heretofore limited role the UN had played in European security. There are several reasons for this development. First, the end of the East-West confrontation in Europe freed the Security Council from the almost inevitable use of the veto in matters of European security. Second, many of the key political forces in Germany—the SPD, and, to some extent, the Free Democrats (FDP)—prefer acting under UN rather than EC auspices (particularly in the event of deploying peacekeeping forces).[92] Third, the UN was a vehicle for associating the United States and the Soviet Union (later Russia) with the mediation effort. Although the CSCE offered the same opportunity, its prestige and operational experience still trail those of the UN. Fourth, broad-scale economic sanctions required broader international support. Finally, by mid-autumn 1991, the EC's own efforts seemed exhausted. There was simply no other place to turn.

The use of multiple institutions occasionally threatened to confuse and overwhelm the process of trying to forge an effective policy, particularly at the early stages of the conflict. At times, the collective response resembled a three-(or four- or five-) ring circus, as government representatives met simultaneously in several fora searching for an agreed-on policy. Lines of communication and divisions of responsibility repeatedly threatened to break down between the EC and the UN, leading to a confrontation between the EC and the UN secretary general in the summer of 1992. Coordination resulted primarily from the presence of the EC nations in all the principal institutions, and the de facto acceptance of the EC as the lead institution. The problem might well have been more acute had U.S. or Soviet (Russian) interests been more directly implicated (as in a dispute involving a NATO member, or one of the USSR's, or Russia's neighbors), which might have led to greater divergence among the various institutions.

The experience of the Yugoslav crisis, and the ongoing process of institutional definition, may eventually lead to a more explicit division of labor between institutions. In particular, there is a clear need to sort out the relative division of responsibilities between the UN and regional organizations (as contemplated by Chapter VIII of the UN Charter) and to decide the relative responsibility of the broad

---

[92] This is true even though virtually all German politicians opposed German participation in a Yugoslav peacekeeping force, regardless of the sponsoring organization.

regional organization, the CSCE, and such subgroupings as the EC, NATO, and WEU. But the flexibility offered by overlapping jurisdictions is, in itself, an asset; it extended the range of options for the international community.

Lessons Learned: The EC and CSCE

The crisis in Yugoslavia also presents important lessons for the individual security organizations.

THE EUROPEAN COMMUNITY.

Beyond a doubt, the EC's involvement in Yugoslavia marked a watershed for Community foreign policy. Analysts, the press, and politicians have harshly criticized the EC's performance; EC leaders, in turn, have pointed to the limited development of the EC's foreign policy-making capabilities and suggest that the EC's efforts have had a positive impact.[93] Even at this stage, it is possible to draw some important conclusions.

The crisis marked a new focus on the EC's role in European security policy. While the EC nations' leaders may have differed among themselves on the appropriate course of action, all agreed the Community should become involved. The initial response was facilitated by the timely coincidence of the European Council meeting in Luxembourg on June 28, but there is little doubt that the foreign ministers would have swung into action in any event.

Equally significant, there was a clear commitment to try to reach a common approach before any unilateral action. This was especially important given the divergent viewpoints and interests of the EC members; despite considerable domestic political pressure, the EC governments held fast to their attempt to develop a common line. The habits of consultation and cooperation built up over twenty years through EPC seemed deeply ingrained in EC governments' foreign policy-making processes.

The EC's response was handicapped by the need to achieve consensus, but it is unclear whether moving to decisionmaking by the majority would influence the

[93] In response to the charge that the EC failed in Yugoslavia, de Michelis observed: "Despite everything, the European Community succeeded in a few weeks in organizing a peace conference [with] a complete plan for a solution of the crisis which was accepted by five republics out of six. . . .And we also succeeded in sending observers, which for Europe is something absolutely new . . . . [W]ithout the observers many more would be killed. . . . Further, the idea of the embargo was affirmed . . . and with the winter coming, could have the effect of bending Serbia." *La Repubblica*, 27–28 Oct. 1991, p. 15 (FBIS-WEU-91-223, Nov. 19, 1991, p. 28). According to Dumas: "If each West European country had acted separately, we would have created the situation which existed at the beginning of the century, before 1914. . . . The Community prevented that possibility. But it did not have enough unity to take more effective action. . . . Europe must be given what it lacks." *Liberation*, 6 Dec. 1991, pp. 17–18.

outcome. A key issue in the intergovernmental conference on political union was extending qualified majority voting to the EC's foreign policy arm to implement a more effective common policy. The Community (renamed the European Union) has now proposed taking a very limited step in this direction.[94] Although there is no doubt that the need to develop a consensus under existing EPC practices contributed to the tentative nature of the EC's response, it is unlikely that majority voting would have altered the outcome. The importance of the issues at stake in Yugoslavia made it unlikely that the Community would try to impose a common response on a strongly recalcitrant member (even if majority voting were available). Conversely, the pressures on Community members with divergent views to compromise are sufficiently strong in most cases to help lead to a consensus even without the formalities of majority voting. While majority voting might have made a difference on matters of implementation (for example, whether the observers could carry personal firearms for self-protection), most of the implementing decisions were reached with relatively little controversy.

The EC's response would benefit from an ongoing, institutional foreign policy "arm." The crisis in Yugoslavia demonstrated the limitations of the troika approach to conducting joint foreign policy. The troika's shifting composition (especially the need to rotate the troika's membership in the first week of the crisis) not only raised questions about "who speaks for Europe" but also brought into play a complex problem of coordinating national foreign policy bureaucracies (the principal staff support for the troika). The problem is compounded when the smaller EC nations make up the troika, as was the case for much of the crisis in Yugoslavia.

The EC Commission's low-key yet effective assistance to the troika eased some of these problems and points the way to a more effective solution. While Maastricht made clear that the EC will continue to make key foreign policy decisions on an intergovernmental basis for the foreseeable future, there is a clear need for the Community to evolve some form of "foreign ministry" that could both staff the intergovernmental process and implement its decisions. The agreement at Maastricht to create a small foreign policy secretariat is but a small step in this direction. Community governments are unlikely to accept an EC foreign minister with stature equal to national foreign ministers, but they should be prepared to delegate to the commission (in the person of the commission president, or a specially designated vice president for foreign policy) a clearer and more extensive role in representing the joint or common Community foreign policy.[95]

---

[94] At Maastricht, the twelve nations agreed to allow majority voting for some implementing decisions on foreign policy, but only if there is a previous unanimous vote authorizing majority decisions.

[95] The continued separation of EC "foreign policy" activities from the commission's responsibilities for external affairs under the Rome Treaty was maintained at Maastricht. Even within the "separate pillars" approach agreed at Maastricht, however, the Community could "dual-hat" the commission president to act under the two distinct treaty regimes.

The EC must improve its ability to anticipate and act early in response to emerging foreign policy crises. The weakness of the Community's foreign policy apparatus is particularly glaring in formulating joint policy before a crisis becomes acute. Although the EPC consultation network has facilitated routine policy dialogue among member states, most contingency planning occurs at the national level, and foreign ministers in EPC rarely address policy questions unless they are thrust upon them.

Developing a "Community" foreign policy staff could facilitate anticipatory policy development. This staff would be charged with monitoring potential sources of instability and formulating policy options for ministers on a Community-wide basis, to assure that tomorrow's crises, as well as today's, are subject to collective deliberation.

The EC needs the means to mount collective military action, at a minimum, for peacekeeping purposes. The issue of a "defense identity" for Europe was one of the most hotly contested issues in the intergovernmental conference on political union. While many accept the desirability of more concerted military action outside Europe, the role of a possible "European" defense force in Europe is more controversial.

For the core problem of defending NATO member states' security, a strong case can be made for preserving NATO's central role (at least as long as the United States remains committed to its obligations under Article V of the Washington Treaty). But the problem of conflict "in Europe" yet "out-of-area" reveals a glaring hole in the military component of European security. For crises in Eastern Europe, NATO military intervention may be inappropriate or unacceptable to many of NATO's own member states. In some cases, the United States may choose not to become involved, and might prefer that Europeans act on their own.

This leaves three possibilities: the CSCE, the UN or the WEU. The broad scope of CSCE's membership, and the relatively informal nature of CSCE's processes, make it difficult to envision a CSCE-organized military force in the near term (although the CSCE has stated that it is prepared to provide the political framework for peacekeeping efforts).[96] The UN is more promising for peacekeeping or "peacemaking" missions, given its previous experience, and there is growing interest in strengthening the UN's military capability. There is still considerable opposition, however, to intervening in cases of internal conflict, and, even in cases that come more clearly under the UN Charter (such as the Iraqi invasion of Kuwait), the UN, at least thus far, has limited its role to authorizing action, instead of organizing military forces under its leadership. In addition, the UN secretary general has made clear that for political, administrative, and financial reasons, he would prefer to see regional organizations shoulder the principal burden.

The WEU, therefore, seems the natural locus for contingency planning and organizing on-call forces, both for peacekeeping and more active military operations.

[96] See *The Challenges of Change*, "Helsinki Summit Declaration," paragraph 20 and "Helsinki Decisions," Ch. III paragraphs 17–51.

Such a force would be available to act at the behest of either the Community alone or other international institutions (the CSCE or the UN).

Whether this force is associated with the EC or a "stand alone" WEU seems less important, since the WEU membership is a subset of the Community and would, therefore, follow the same policy direction adopted by the Community. Moreover, the WEU maintains close links with the United States through NATO, thus facilitating joint U.S.-European action, if appropriate. The WEU's recent decisions at Maastricht and Petersberg may help pave the way toward a more useful WEU military role in the future.[97]

As noted above, military force may be irrelevant to many of the likely crises that Europe will face in the future. But the menu of European responses would be enriched by quickly available trained forces accustomed to working together and supported by competent planning before the outbreak of conflict.

THE CSCE.

The CSCE is in its formative stages as a European security institution. The crisis in Yugoslavia demonstrated that, despite the requirement of consensus and the limits on interfering in a nation's internal affairs, the CSCE's institutional components (the emergency mechanism and the Conflict Prevention Center) have already emerged as relevant actors in the European security landscape. The CSCE has much to learn from Yugoslavia, however.

The CSCE's most valuable role is as a forum for dialogue. As a forum that convenes all European nations in addition to the United States and Canada, the CSCE has a unique ability to foster dialogue over emerging crises. In the case of Yugoslavia, the CSCE proved particularly useful in providing a platform for the nations to call Yugoslavia to account for its actions and to involve the Soviet Union and Eastern Europe in developing agreed-upon policy. Although it is possible to enhance the CSCE's ability to act (see below), it is important not to sacrifice this valuable function in an attempt to make the CSCE more effective.

In particular, a premature effort to move the CSCE away from consensus decision making could prove counterproductive.[98] The CSCE is a place where all European nations plus the United States and Canada can have their views considered without fear of being outvoted; majority voting or some kind of CSCE Security Council could cause states involved in a conflict to walk away from the CSCE entirely. The CSCE has already taken some steps to limit the gridlock caused by the consensus requirement, especially the decision to allow action by "consensus minus

---

[97] See "Declaration on the Role of the Western European Union and Its Relations with the European Union and with the Atlantic Alliance," Maastricht, Dec. 10, 1991, and Western European Union's Council of Ministers, "Petersberg Declaration," Bonn, June 19, 1992.

[98] For a more extensive discussion of the CSCE's evolution and its future role in European security, see James B. Steinberg, *Integration and Security in an All-European Order*, RAND, P–7733, 1991.

one" and the option of suspending or even expelling member states that fail to comply with their CSCE obligations. While some stronger form of nonconsensus decision making may make sense in the future, that time has not yet arrived.[99]

The CSCE can enhance European stability by extending its role in norm setting. One of the most difficult problems posed by the crisis in Yugoslavia is the tension between stability based on existing borders and noninterference in internal affairs, on the one hand, and the broad commitment to the principle of self-determination, on the other. This conflict is present in Europe's international constitutions: the Helsinki Final Act, and the Paris Charter.

The CSCE could contribute to a more stable Europe by developing clearer norms governing the conflict between these principles. Although each case is ultimately unique, and states' deep political interests are often at stake, more concrete guarantees of minority group rights, local autonomy, and even criteria for peaceful secession could constrain governments' behavior, or, at a minimum, give institutions and concerned outside parties a clearer mandate for acting in support of the agreed-upon norms. This effort will prove contentious, but it could contribute to dealing with endemic problems of nationality and ethnicity. The decision to establish a High Commissioner on National Minorities is a step in this direction.

CSCE institutions should be streamlined by merging the emergency mechanism with the Conflict Prevention Center and enhancing the role of the CPC as a mediator. The parallel activities of the CSCE senior officials in Prague and the CPC in Vienna contribute little except an element of confusion. The dispersal of CSCE institutions serves an important symbolic purpose in rewarding states that had contributed to CSCE's new role, but these considerations are outweighed by the need to streamline CSCE functioning. The CSCE risks repeating, on the level of the Fifty-three, the European Parliament's comic commuting between Brussels, Strasbourg, and the staff headquarters in Luxembourg.

At the same time, the CSCE's structure should be strengthened. Germany's role as chair of the senior officials group in Prague illustrates several problems. On the one hand, Germany's activism, its strong support for the CSCE, and its competent foreign ministry enhanced the CSCE's effectiveness; what might have happened if Malta held the chair? On the other hand, Germany's chairmanship also raised concerns; its relatively unique perspective resulting from its close association with Slovenia and Croatia led some to argue that Germany was using the CSCE for its own purposes.

The Helsinki review conference in July 1992 took some steps to deal with these problems, by establishing a troika of the immediate past and succeeding chairmen

---

[99] In the Rome Communiqué, paragraph 14, the NATO heads of state suggested giving consideration "to develop further the CSCE's capability to safeguard, *through peaceful means*, human rights, democracy and the rule of law in cases of clear, gross and uncorrected violations of relevant CSCE commitments, *if necessary in the absence of the consent of the state concerned*" (emphasis added).

to assist the chairman-in-office, as well as "ad hoc steering groups" to support the chair in specific crises.[100] The CSCE heads of state also agreed to strengthen mediation through such devices as fact-finding and rapporteur missions. But these steps, while welcome, do not solve the multiple institution problem, and still rely heavily on the chairman-in-office or the Committee of Senior Officials. More is needed.

Part of the answer is to enhance the role and stature of the CSCE secretary general, which is a step the CSCE has initiated with the appointment of German diplomat Wilhelm Hoeynck as the organization's first real security general in May 1993, and to consolidate the secretary general's activities with those of the CPC. The history of international institutions shows the limits of secretary generalships (consider the case of NATO and the UN), but, in a situation where the member states might use the CSCE's good offices to broker a political solution (as in Yugoslavia), a well-respected, well-staffed leader with no encumbering political ties or responsibilities could prove valuable.[101]

Lessons Learned: NATO

The Yugoslavia conflict has had a significant impact on NATO and its members' perception of NATO's role in the post-Cold War world. Initially, NATO members were deeply reluctant to involve NATO as an institution. Eventually, however, they began to ask, "If NATO is irrelevant to the Yugoslavia conflict, what role does NATO serve in the post-Cold War world?" As Western involvement became more military and operationally complex, leaders turned increasingly to NATO because NATO has unique military capabilities and institutionally NATO offered the best way to assure U.S. involvement alongside Europe.

By mid-1993, NATO had taken several key steps toward becoming the UN's direct military arm. NATO was not only directly responsible for sanctions and no-fly-zone enforcement, but the UN also turned to NATO for contingency planning in connection with enforcing the Vance-Owen plan and protecting the UN forces charged with guaranteeing the Bosnian safe areas. In addition, the activities in former Yugoslavia provided an important impetus to the evolution of the newly created North Atlantic Cooperation Council (NACC), especially in coordinating peacekeeping activities (including planning, training, and doctrine) between NATO and non-NATO members in Europe.[102] NATO must take additional steps, however, to maintain its relevance and efficacy in future Yugoslavia-type conflicts.

---

[100] *Challenges of Change*, Ch. 1.

[101] The Rome Communiqué also makes a number of suggestions in this regard. In particular, it calls for strengthening and making more flexible the means available to the CPC, steps to assure the "complementarity among CSCE activities in the security field," and allowing the Committee of Senior Officials to "acquire greater operational capacity." These proposals would go partway to correct the deficiencies identified above.

[102] The NACC includes all sixteen NATO members plus the former members of the Warsaw Pact (including the states that formerly made up the USSR). NATO heads of state created the NACC at the Rome NATO summit in November 1991.

NATO must adapt its military forces, training, and doctrine to the new sources of instability. At the Rome summit, NATO leaders adopted a new strategic concept, moving away from NATO's long-standing static approach to defending Western Europe against a massive Warsaw Pact, in favor of more flexible forces. But the Rome approach predates NATO's decision to act as a peacekeeper and is still primarily focused on collective defense rather than conflict prevention and crisis management outside the NATO area. In particular, NATO's new Rapid Reaction Force is not optimized for the most likely contingencies facing NATO members.

NATO should move promptly to build on the evolution started by the Rome strategic concept, to develop forces trained, equipped, and configured for peacemaking and peacekeeping activities outside NATO's borders. This effort should build on the lessons learned by Europe's preeminent peacekeepers, the Nordic countries and Austria, as well as Canada, but must include sufficient military capability to handle the more dangerous military environments faced by "peacemakers." Rapid response, mobility, and flexibility are the most crucial elements, along with reliable command, control, communications, and intelligence (C^3I).

NACC peacekeeping activities should expand to include other CSCE members likely to contribute to European peacekeeping efforts. It is ironic that the non-NATO nations with the most experience in peacekeeping—Finland, Sweden, and Austria—are outside the framework that seeks to coordinate the operational side of peacekeeping activities between NATO and its neighbors. While Finland is an NACC observer, and Sweden and Austria are participating as trainers in NACC peacekeeping programs, a more formal association is needed.

Further, contingency planning involving non-NATO members should also be formalized, by creating a peacekeeping planning staff associated with NATO's planners (SHAPE) but outside the formal NATO integrated military structure. Liaison officers from all CSCE should participate on a continuing basis. This will allow prompt and timely action, even though nations will not have made a previous commitment to participate in a given contingency.

NATO should develop more formal institutional links with the CSCE and UN. The experience in Yugoslavia suggests that in the future, although NATO may have operational control over many aspects of peacekeeping and peacemaking operations, political authority will rest in whole or in part with either the CSCE or the UN. There are numerous reasons for this sometimes cumbersome arrangement, including France's reluctance to extend NATO's competence and to come too close to NATO's integrated military command, the continued debate in Germany over when and under what auspices the Bundeswehr may act out of area, and the need to involve non-NATO states in the political control over quasi-military operations. Meanwhile, the political decisionmakers in New York and Vienna lack the benefit of detailed military planning that is so important to crafting an appropriate mandate for military operations or to conducting effective oversight. These two political institutions must draw on NATO's expertise both before actions are authorized and while they are continuing, even if (as suggested below) the UN in particular beefs up its own capabilities.

Lessons Learned: The UN

The conflict in the former Yugoslavia has also had a significant impact on the UN, although the lessons from Yugoslavia must be seen in the context of a truly extraordinary period in the UN's history: an explosion of missions and roles that, as of June 1993, led the UN to deploy more than seventy thousand peacekeepers (including more than twenty thousand in the former Yugoslavia) across four continents. To do full justice to the "lessons learned" requires far more extensive discussion than is possible here, but a few notable issues stand out.

The UN must come to grips with the consequences of Article VII "enforcement" actions. For most of its history, the Security Council predicated UN involvement on the consent of the parties: so-called Chapter VI actions.[103] The most notable exception was Korea, where blue-helmeted troops responded to North Korea's invasion of the South under Security Council mandate. The reason for this limitation was both political and prudential. Politically, the Cold War conflict made it difficult to avoid a veto by one of the Permanent Five, unless the UN's involvement had the parties' consent. Prudentially, many felt that the UN should protect its legitimacy and effectiveness in brokering solutions by remaining "neutral"—a judgment reinforced by the scarring experience of the Congo, when the UN became more directly involved on the side of one of the parties to the conflict.

With the end of the Cold War, the political barriers to Article VII actions have lifted somewhat; even China, with strong reservations about UN interference in internal conflicts, has on the whole preferred to abstain rather than block action when the other permanent members have agreed, as the Yugoslavia experience amply demonstrates. In the former Yugoslavia, however, UN commanders have been reluctant to use Article VII powers, even when the operations are conducted under a mandate authorizing force. The resolutions authorizing both the humanitarian relief operations and the Bosnian no-fly-zone enforcement in principle grant UN commanders authority to use force in connection with their mission, but usually they have preferred to use suasion and negotiation rather than force (other than in extreme instances of self-defense).

As a consequence, the UN's credibility is in jeopardy. On the one hand, the Security Council authorizes the use of "all measures necessary" to assure delivery of humanitarian relief, yet allows Serbs (and occasionally other forces) to block convoys. On the other hand, acting under "consent" in Croatia, UN forces refuse to use force to implement the parties' own agreement. UN troops are viewed as enemies by all sides, yet powerless to accomplish their mission.

Two different options are open. First, the UN could return to its earlier practice,

---

[103] For a summary of UN peacekeeping activities through 1992, see William J. Durch, ed., *The Evolution of UN Peacekeeping* (New York: St. Martin's Press, 1993).

intervening only with the parties' consent, and maintain its role as impartial broker. Alternatively, the UN could accept its broader role that requires making judgments about who is responsible for threatening peace and security, and prepare to take decisive measures in support. There is merit in both approaches, but if the members of the Security Council want to reduce the risk that interested outside actors will take matters into their own hands (with the risk of widening the conflict), a more active UN role (operating where appropriate through regional institutions) in "enforcement" seems the wiser course.

This does not mean that the UN must act in all cases. Resources are limited, and frequently it is doubtful whether military intervention, even if sizable and determined, can achieve the objective. What seems clear, however, is that once the UN becomes involved, it must be prepared to take the actions needed to achieve its goals.

The UN must substantially improve its ability to plan, conduct, support, and finance large-scale peacekeeping/peacemaking activities. There is a burgeoning literature on reforming the UN, especially with respect to streamlining and enhancing the conduct of peacekeeping activities.[104] If, as suggested above, the UN is to continue to play a role in enforcement, reform is imperative. Although Canadian General Lewis MacKenzie's lament about the unavailability of UN officials on nights and weekends is somewhat unfair to the headquarters staff, undoubtedly the resources in New York are inadequate and poorly organized. In response to Yugoslavia, Somalia, and other operations, the UN has established a "situation room" to monitor ongoing operations; it is also improving its planning and information collection capabilities. The reorganization of the Secretariat to split off peacekeeping and political operations is another useful reform.

There are cogent political and operational arguments why the UN should not have its own military force.[105] If the UN is to rely on nations to provide forces on a case by case basis, however, competent permanent staff must be available to mobilize national resources quickly and effectively and plan their use. The UN must radically overhaul its archaic method of supplying and equipping UN forces in a way that will meet commanders' real operational requirements on a timely basis, and the UN must have adequate financial reserves to meet unanticipated needs.

Lessons Learned: Balkan Stability and New European Security Order

The nature of the security issues that may erupt in the Balkan region will pose a

[104] See, for example, Thomas G. Weiss, "New Challenges for UN Military Operations: Implementing the Agenda for Peace," *The Washington Quarterly* (Spring 1993); Indar Jit Rikhye, *Strengthening UN Peacekeeping: New Challenges and Proposals* (Washington: U.S. Institute of Peace, Oct. 1992); Durch, *The Evolution of UN Peacekeeping*.

[105] For the argument in favor of a UN force, see Brian Urquhart, "For a UN Volunteer Military Force," *New York Review of Books*, 24 June 1993. For responses to Urquhart's proposal, see the letter of Robert Oakley, McGeorge Bundy, Sadruddin Aga Khan, Olusegum Obasanjo, Anthony Parsons, and Marion Donhoff, *New York Review of Books*, 15 July 1993.

severe test for all relevant European security organizations. Some will involve internal ethnic disputes, others potentially more dangerous cross-border conflicts. In the latter case, the stakes in preventing or containing conflict will be even higher than thus far experienced in the crisis in Yugoslavia, yet cross-border conflicts may prove even more difficult for institutions that depend on a high degree of consensus.

Consider, for example, a potential conflict involving Turkey and Greece. For institutions that contain both members, such as NATO and the CSCE, there are few tools, other than moral suasion, available (witness NATO's relative ineffectiveness in resolving past Greek-Turkish conflicts). Institutions that contain only one of the parties (such as the EC) could face even greater barriers to action other than unilateral support of the member country. It is difficult to act in an evenhanded manner when one of the parties to the conflict has a veto over policy.[106]

This suggests several conclusions. First, it is important not to overestimate the ability of any of these institutions to respond effectively to new outbreaks of violence in the Balkan region. Although they will certainly seek to play a role, as they have in Yugoslavia, there is no guarantee that their involvement will be decisive nor that they will be prepared to take effective action.

The second point is the importance of early intervention. The most effective time for consensus fora such as CSCE to become involved is before the simmering conflicts explode, when mediation and dialogue are most likely to produce political solutions. The concrete steps identified above to strengthen the EC and CSCE can help in this process.[107]

Finally, the European institutions may prove most effective in their long-term role of integrating states into a broader political, economic, and security framework. Just as the EC has helped end long-standing rivalries between member states, so, too, should the habit of cooperation and the elaboration of ties among the European states help to constrain the outbreak of conflict. The EC (now EU) has the most to offer in this regard because of the extensive economic as well as political relations among its members; but CSCE also has an economic component, and all Balkan nations belong to CSCE, while for most Balkan nations, membership in the EC remains in the distant future, if at all. The involvement of several Balkan countries in NACC, too, is part of this integrative process; although full NATO membership for most, if not all, seems remote, leaving open the prospect in principle could also contribute to constraining states' resorting to force in resolving conflicts.

---

[106] This partially explains many WEU member countries' reluctance to admit Greece as a member. Under the compromise agreed at Maastricht (in the face of Greece's threat to veto the political union treaty unless the WEU offered it full membership), Greece will become a member of the WEU, but Turkey will be allowed to become an associate member "in a way which will give [it] the possibility to participate fully in the activities of WEU." WEU Maastricht Declaration. In addition, WEU members will not be allowed to invoke the Brussels Treaty against a NATO member.

[107] In their July 1992 agreement, the CSCE leaders specifically identified improved early warning as a key objective.

XIV

Balkan Security in the European Post-Cold War Environment: Challenges and Policy Choices for the West

Uwe Nerlich

Ever since the retreat and contraction of the Ottoman Empire, the Balkan peninsula has been viewed as a political entity, and, as its identity emerged, its uniqueness was visible throughout Europe.[1] It differed in particular from the continent's other two southern peninsulas—the Italian and the Iberian. The ethnic, cultural, and religious diversities of the Balkans were a source of unruliness that the Ottoman Empire failed to manage, and, ultimately, no pattern of stable statehood resurfaced as the empire contracted. The assertive responses of the Balkan peoples, however, were shaped by the strong force of nationalism that prevailed in Europe during the mid-nineteenth century. While the fluidity of the regional state system and the checkered population pattern throughout much of the peninsula rendered nation-state formation more difficult than in most other European regions, however, the new entity in Southeastern Europe began to attract the interest of the major European powers. Germany, Russia, France, Great Britain, Italy, and Turkey continued to be involved in the region, as did Austria for several crucial decades and the United States after the late 1940s.[2] They increasingly saw the balance of power on the continent

[1] Ironically, this new entity was labeled with a Turkish word while the Ottoman Empire was withdrawing from this very region.

[2] The American engagement in Turkey and Greece became manifest in the Assistance Bill of April 3, 1947. See *Legislative Origins of the Truman Doctrine.* Hearings held in Executive Session before the Committee on Foreign Relations, United States Senate, 80th Congress, First Session, on

affected by how the Balkan states would be delineated, which European powers they would select as allies, and upon which of the major powers the various Balkan states would be dependent.

Balkan security, therefore, became uniquely regional in terms of the peninsula's inherent difficulties in establishing domestic regimes. Yet, although regional affairs have been proverbially termed "balkanization," state formation in large measure turned controversial over issues of centralism versus federalism. Meanwhile, the Balkan peninsula remained uniquely fragmented as a result of how its constituent parts were drawn into competing coalitions within Europe. As a result, patterns of interaction have developed between regional tensions, conflicts on the peninsula, and great-power rivalries.

Key events underscore the dynamics of this interaction. The assassination of Arch-Duke Franz Ferdinand in Sarajevo on June 28, 1914, was as much the catalyst for an unprecedented continental war for which all of Europe had long been prepared, as it was a regional outcome foreshadowed by the Balkan Wars and resulting from forces that were released by the contraction of the Ottoman Empire.[3] Although it is too early to assess the nature of the interaction in the current Yugoslav crisis, it is obvious that the Yugoslav conflict was driven by forces in the region released after the breakup of the Soviet empire in Eastern Europe—a structure of which it really was not even a part. If today, unlike in 1914, major European powers abstain from intervention, they nevertheless differ over how best to resolve the crisis in ways that very much reflect familiar historical patterns. They relate more to the perceived positions of major players in the European security game than directly to the specific requirements of a regional settlement.

During the early stages of the conflict the chief concern was the precedent that any stand on a settlement might create for the USSR.[4] As the USSR dissolved and the new united Germany was seen to cast longer shadows, the emphasis shifted. The increasing cruelty of the war negated, and thus undermined, all rules of conduct the European nations had elaborated to ensure peace and security on the continent, such as the Paris Charter of November 1990 and the second Helsinki Conference. While failure to cope with the initial stages of the war was universal, even if for

---

S. 938. *Historical Series* (Washington, D.C., 1973). The involvement in Yugoslavia was stepped up after the Korean War. See Beatrice Heuser, *Western Containment Policies in the Cold War. The Yugoslav Case 1948–1953* (London: Routledge, 1989), especially p. 184. The military rationale for American assistance notwithstanding, support for Yugoslavia also met with massive criticism from military leaders, including the former chairman of the Joint Chiefs of Staff, Nathan N. Twining. See Twining, *Neither Liberty nor Safety. A Hard Look at U.S. Military Policy and Strategy* (New York: Holt, Rinehart and Winston, 1966), 278.

[3] For a brilliant critique of the familiar breakdown-of-control argument about the outbreak of World War I, see Marc Trachtenberg, *History and Strategy* (Princeton: Princeton University Press, 1991), especially chapter 2, "The Coming of the First World War: A Reassessment."

[4] In a slightly bizarre manner Great Britain and Spain had additional interests in avoiding creating a precedent, although the problem they both face is not self-determination but violent minority assertiveness, that is, terrorism.

divergent reasons, disagreement about how to stop a war that was increasingly self-destructive and had long ceased to be an internal matter centered on Germany.[5]

Germany (with approximately 400 thousand Croatians on its territory) was the most strongly committed to the European security regime that, emphasizing gradual transfers of sovereignty and growing commitments to cooperative structures, had just proven sufficiently stable to handle the unification of Germany and the dissolution of the communist empire without unleashing intervention by the vast Soviet military machine. Yet, the same regime tended to be undermined by Western indifference to the first European war since 1945. Germany's efforts to create stakes for both sides in a settlement of the conflict were widely viewed as a sign of new German assertiveness. In the United States, where opposition to the recognition of individual Yugoslav republics was particularly strong, the German drive for recognition of Slovenia and Croatia was seen as a German "declaration of independence (after '45 years on America's leash') that immediately weakens American leverage in Europe and hence in the world."[6]

This left the United States in a dilemma. Alienating Germany over this issue would have reduced American leverage in Europe even further—almost as much as an outright effort to build a coalition with France and Britain to diminish Germany's role—a policy that would lack continental partners, be grossly counterproductive, and fail to solve any problems in the crisis regions. While the power most likely to be nervous over a growing German role, France was above all perplexed by the uncomfortable realization that the preservation of much of its global and regional influence depends on its cooperation with Germany. Yet, while this resulted in a more concerted effort, France "also failed to suppress nationalist impulses that it insists must be held in check within Germany."[7] Great Britain was most openly outraged over Germany's alleged muscle-flexing—even if only for domestic consumption. Prime Minister John Major called for a summit of the members of the UN Security Council as a tailored countermove after the EC compromise on the

---

[5] Instant support for the unity of Yugoslavia came from all sides—the United States, the EC, Germany, and others—and in no case was it associated with a warning against the use of military force. Predictably, this invited precisely the outbreak of military conflict in this "tinderbox of ethnic hostilities" (Richard H. Ullman, *Securing Europe* [Princeton: Princeton University Press, 1991], 28). The Western cure (most outspokenly in Austria and subsequently in Germany) of threatening Serbia with recognition of Slovenia and Croatia in case military force continued to be employed was bound to turn this into a two-sided military conflict where both sides felt encouraged by the political (in addition to material) support from Western countries. Thus, a dynamic of conflict was created that was almost inevitably complicated by the way local minorities became nearly independent players.

[6] Roland Evans/Robert Novak, "Germany's Europe," *Washington Post*, 20 Dec. 1991, p. A27. However, unlike many other American officials and observers, Evans and Novak use this to criticize the Bush administration rather than Germany: "Bush and Baker have seemed locked in the dream of rebuilding the lost past, from the salvage of a centralized power in what used to be the Soviet Union to the holding together of a palpably artificial Yugoslavia whose cement the last half century has been communist arms." For a more systematic critique of this American line see Henry Kissinger, "What Kind of New World Order?" *Washington Post*, 3 Dec. 1991, p. A21.

[7] Ibid.

recognition of "new states in Eastern Europe and the Soviet Union"[8] into which it saw itself pressured by Germany. Because Germany was not a member of the UN Security Council, not consulting Germany on this summit served no other purpose but to engage in confrontational diplomacy. The German side was by and large sufficiently prudent to disregard this as posturing for domestic consumption.

The fact that much of this foreign policy—at least on the part of European countries—is driven by domestic impulses does not diminish the controversy, but rather underscores its depth. If governments think that they cater to domestic audiences through their actions concerning recognition or, more important, the way they portray the German role in this context, this demonstrates not only the need for future efforts to create a common foreign policy among members of the European Community (renamed European Union), but also the growing obstacles facing such efforts. This is best illustrated by the dilemmas European actors are unwillingly creating for themselves. As the country most committed to integration and most eager to reassure partners to reinforce their cooperative spirit, Germany has given priority to self-determination at the expense of integration in Yugoslavia and against the preferences of its key partners. France, however, with all its biases in favor of nationalism, has favored—at least until very recently—the preservation of an artificial federal structure in Yugoslavia. Yet, France compromised with Germany on recognition, thus reinforcing the effort to forge a common foreign policy that it is so anxious to see free of German domination.

This controversy explains more about the general European situation than about the Balkans, but there are historic reasons why it developed in the Balkans rather than the Baltic states or the former USSR. Yet, although old patterns of interaction resurface more openly, it is also important to see how different the present situation is from earlier contingencies like 1914.[9] In 1914 a Balkan incident ignited a war in Europe by unleashing a process of rapid horizontal escalation. In 1991 the first war in Europe since 1945 turned into military self-encapsulation rather than escalation, although for much of the last two decades, the disintegration of Yugoslavia was precisely one of the few contingencies that NATO considered would be likely to

[8] Guidelines for the Recognition of New States in Eastern Europe and the Soviet Union, Resolution of the EC Ministerial Council, December 16, 1991, in *Bulletin des Presse und Informationsamt der Bundeszegierung* (Bonn, December 17, 1991): 1173.

[9] Historically, the pattern of Balkan-European interactions is by no means confined to the role played by Germany. This is particularly evident during the period when Germany played no role whatsoever in the Balkans—namely, during the early 1950s. See Beatrice Heuser's account of "friendly relations between the Western powers (that is, Great Britain, France, and the United States) and Yugoslavia, rivalry among the Western powers," in Beatrice Heuser, *Western Containment,* in particular p. 198f. British and French preferences for prolonging support for a central Yugoslav government have been replays of how both countries tended to handle the Yugoslav situation after the Stalin-Tito break—"masterly inactivity," as Beatrice Heuser has termed it. Both Britain and France had clearly opted for a "stand-offish" policy at the time, one which Bevin spelled out most forcefully: it is advisable "not to do anything ourselves with regard to Yugoslavia—let the Communists quarrel among themselves." Bevin's dispatch No. 936 to Washington, June 30, 1948, is quoted in Heuser, *Western Containment*, 46.

initiate an East-West confrontation (as a result of Soviet support for Serbia—a danger that was conspicuously absent in 1991).

What caused a major row in Europe—in addition to the problem of avoiding precedents—requiring a more active policy by external powers was that the European security system, which had successfully served to channel the disappearance of Soviet rule throughout most of Eastern Europe without provoking the use of Soviet military power, appeared to be in jeopardy precisely because it offered little else but indifference as an improvised means of arbitration. With similar conflicts in Europe looming in the future, unchecked violent nationalism as displayed during the Yugoslav conflict is likely to reinforce nationalism throughout the whole of Europe—simply as a result of the failure of multinational structures to provide solutions. Encapsulation rather than some mandated military containment of the Yugoslav conflict may result from a combination of the weakness of European powers—the United States is included here—and the functioning of those institutionalized constraints that have developed in recent decades. But the absence of more forceful action by major powers and existing security organizations tends to diminish even further the deterrent that the Serbs and Croatians have already disregarded. The longer the war lasts—leaving aside the other conflicts that could follow—the more diminished is the scope for a European security system sufficient to cope with future challenges in and to Europe.[10]

The main challenge the Yugoslav conflict poses, therefore, is its potential to undermine existing security structures in Europe, risking a repetition of current failures in crisis management. This suggests that the Balkan situation, with all its

---

[10] As Richard Ullman has observed, politics and war are about stakes. In the case of the aggression against Kuwait, the stakes were obvious, and twenty-eight nations interfered—with a UN mandate—in a hybrid coalition. The Serbo-Croatian war occurred in Europe with the most complex and elaborate security system known, and the perceived absence of stakes signals that preservation of the existing rules of conduct is not considered a high stake.

To that extent, the wider implications of that war not only relate to the limitations of existing security organizations, but also to the nature of the commitments of major powers engaged in European security. This is most noticeable in the case of the United States—not only in view of its leading role during Desert Storm, but also in view of the U.S. démarche of February 21, 1991, on "NATO Strategy Review—Security Identity and Related Issues" and the subsequent support for Great Britain's conservative stand on how to reshape the Atlantic alliance to secure useful roles for future contingencies.

Interactions during 1991 may also shed new light on how limited the utility of existing security organizations may have been in real conflict in the first place. For example, Germany was rightly blamed for questioning security guarantees to Turkey in the Iraq war. In this context, however, the following statement deserves scrutiny: "I hope you will understand that your NATO allies have not yet had a chance to consider whether they have an obligation to protect Turkey against the Soviet Union if Turkey takes a step which results in Soviet interventions without the full consent and understanding of its NATO allies." The contingency was not Kuwait, but Cyprus, and the statement was not Count Lambsdorff's, but President Lyndon Johnson's letter to Prime Minister Inonu, June 5, 1964 (reprinted in *Middle East Journal* 20, no. 3 [1966]: 387). It is not readily apparent that the American case in 1964 was stronger than the German one in 1991, unhelpful as Johnson's letter may

potential for violent conflict, may actually provide a pretext for continuing familiar European rivalries, but tends to be less central and less likely to trigger large-scale conflict than it would have in previous circumstances. This, too, is a post-Cold War lesson. At the same time, however, although much political and diplomatic shortsightedness may have figured on all sides during this war, the recurrence of patterns of interaction does not mean that Europe has returned to traditional power games. In fact, the moves here considered disturbing on the part of the major powers were largely inspired by two factors. First, there was a preoccupation with the vastly more crucial European and, indeed, global problem of how to manage the transition from the former USSR to a viable successor arrangement—a process that provides ample evidence of how dominant new patterns of cooperation have become in Europe and beyond. Second, there is the very progress of European community-building itself.

While the development of a common European foreign and defense policy is partially overshadowed by divergencies between European governments over how to respond to the Serbo-Croatian crisis, this very crisis—more than any diplomatic bargaining on the way to Maastricht—has turned the EC, now the EU, into a major security player. Not only has the EC/EU become the most important stabilizer of socioeconomic conditions in Eastern Europe and the new Commonwealth—which is the key to crisis prevention in these problem-ridden areas—but it is also the main force in all the international efforts to bring the war to an end and engage the conflicting parties in some peace process. It is the key player in any process leading toward a political settlement, and it was the key also to engaging the United Nations successfully in the negotiation and enforcement of the Serbo-Croatian armistice. Both the role for the EC and the resultant engagement of the United Nations in a European conflict are unprecedented. The EC requires UN support to ensure the effectiveness of trade sanctions and embargoes. Together, these two means and processes suggest a promising pattern that will profit from experience and certainly enhance future crisis management efforts. In this perspective one may add that less prudent rivalries among major actors unfolded largely in response to progress toward collective crisis management, particularly on the part of the EC.

In the aftermath of the Cold War and the dissolution of the USSR, conflict could have arisen in other critical areas, but it has not thus far, except within narrow confines. Not surprisingly, the first European war since 1945 occurred on the Balkan peninsula, with its numerous opportunities for conflict. War was initiated where conflict was most imminent. The Serbo-Croatian friction was the one most likely to develop into open conflict, although it might have been avoided through more vigorous crisis diplomacy by the international community. This is so, not only because of traditional conflict patterns and the forces behind these, but also because of the centrality of the issue of statehood.

---

have been. That presidential letter, combined with the American handling of the Jupiter issue, had a lasting impact on Turkish-American relations and contributed to Turkey's effort to diversify its foreign policy in the wake of the Cyprus crisis.

There is another feature of the Balkan region that tends to shape regional-European interactions in many ways. Few regions are similarly diversified in ethnic, cultural, and religious terms, and few have faced similarly tough problems of state formation as the Balkan countries have since the nineteenth century. Patterns of governance, dominance, migration, suppression, and even genocide have changed time and again on the peninsula. Yet, after the controversial and stable settlements following World War I embodied in the Paris agreements, the one thing that has remained essentially unchanged is the state system on the Balkan peninsula. By and large all Balkan states have thus far "retained their statehood and most of their territory."[11] Until 1991 this has even been true of Yugoslavia—a state "with seven neighbors, six republics, five minorities, four languages, three religions, two alphabets and one army."[12]

During the continued interactions between the Balkans and Europe at large, this feature has survived not only the turbulent changes on the peninsula, but even more dramatic changes throughout Europe. One aspect of the current Yugoslav crisis is precisely that several major powers remained committed to the most artificial creation of the Paris peacemakers—the Yugoslav state. Paradoxical as this may seem, the Balkan state system thus has been a continuing feature in regional-European interactions for more than seventy years. This holds true for the post-World War I situation, the years of rising German totalitarian dominance, World War II with its German occupation, Stalin's postwar drives into the Balkan peninsula, and the era of bipolarity up to 1991.

Patterns of interpenetration and alignment with external powers have changed regularly, and so have local responses. Throughout the decades of the European division, the Balkan peninsula was once again uniquely fragmented, and the European divide was far from being as clearly defined in the Balkans as in other European regions. Indeed, the divisions that were waterproof followed essentially different lines in the Balkans than in Central Europe.

The modes of self-assertiveness also tended to be different. Greece and Turkey became members of NATO. Greece is the only EC member and joined the WEU in 1992. Unlike Northern Europe, some Balkan states remained under Soviet domination until 1990, and some sought room to maneuver by balancing commitments in the East-West context. Sweden remained outside NATO and thus reserved leverage to protect Finland—the so-called Nordic balance. In many ways Yugoslavia's search for a "third way" was inspired by similar considerations. While Yugoslavia remained communist, it stayed outside the Soviet orbit and sought material support and protection from the West—camouflaging both sides of its policy by its active policy of nonalignment.[13] Subregional arrangements were also sought in ways

[11] James F. Brown, "The East European Setting," in *Eroding Empire: Western Relations with Eastern Europe,* ed. Lincoln Gordon (Washington, D.C.: The Brookings Institution, 1987), 8.

[12] Heinz Vetschera, "Faktoren in der Fehleinschätzung entstehender Krisen: Das Beispiel Jugoslawien," unpublished manuscript (Ebenhausen: Stiftung Wissenschaft und Politik, 1991), p. 296.

[13] This was initially pursued in a European setting, in particular through the Balkan Treaty with

sensitive to the confrontational pattern—special zonal arrangements (in particular "nuclear-free zones") in one direction and selective cooperative alignments (such as the more recent Central European Initiative) in the other. In different ways there may be new utility for subregional arrangements in the post-Cold War era.

What is profoundly new is that the domestic situation in the Balkan countries is changing along with the European map. Balkan security is undergoing profound changes on all levels—domestically, on the regional interstate level, with statehood increasingly affected for the first time since 1919; on the level of external relations with major powers in the European context (with the USSR dissolved, the United States retreating, West European states engaged in a process of community-building, and Japan appearing on the horizon); and on the level of multinational institutions—the CSCE, NATO, and the EU—all of which are in search of some future new role.[14]

Balkan countries thus share much of the transitional uncertainty facing the northern half of the globe. There is no country that finds itself in a stable framework for designing its future international policies, nor is there a country that can shield its domestic affairs from the currents of international change that have followed the Soviet Union's collapse. But the Balkans also have the unique task of redefining in some cases their very statehood—and in all cases their regional interstate system—on a peninsula with a growing potential for conflict, yet with diminishing strategic relevance, as suggested by the "masterly inactivity" of the West in the face of the Serbo-Croatian war.

The region's peculiar importance for security policy is affected because it is considered distant and its affairs less critical than developments in Central and Eastern Europe. It, therefore, offers the choice between indifference and interventionism in the interest of preserving a European security order that is worth preserving, but thus far does not provide the legitimacy and the means for peace enforcement. Partly for that reason, the main thrust of current European security policy, namely economic and political stabilization, is likely to affect the Balkans less directly and effectively than the Commonwealth of Independent States (CIS) and Central and Eastern Europe—transferable resources are limited, and Western priorities are obvious. Yet, the only viable future for the Balkan countries rests with their capacity to engage in cooperative relations with the EU, which requires that they meet certain minimum standards. Today some of the Balkan countries hardly meet the EU conditions for the recognition of new states, let alone closer cooperative relations.

The future security options of the Balkan countries will thus require subregional cooperation as a precondition for gradual integration into the European system (for

---

Greece and Turkey (and open to Italy). Only later and primarily because European partners for a third way were lacking, Yugoslavia turned to Third World countries (Belgrade Conference of 1961). See Heuser, *Western Containment*, 205–207.

[14] As Henry Kissinger has observed, "For the first time in two centuries, Eastern Europe, the Baltics and the Balkans would be insulated from Russian military pressure" (*The International Herald Tribune,* 13 Jan. 1992, p. 5).

example, the Visegrad grouping). Meanwhile, however, these countries must define a viable kind of regional-European interaction for the future—one that reinforces rather than weakens the more general trends in the Atlantic and Eurasian world. To that extent, mapping out options for Balkan security requires a look not only at internal conflict, but also at the forces driving current structural developments in the Northern Hemisphere—political change as well as changes in military power.

Integration versus Renationalization—The Dynamics of Political Change

Colossal failures take time to create. Well over two thousand years ago at the harbor of Rhodes, a proclaimed "world wonder" was built that was to become the proverbial "colossal" failure. An earthquake destroyed what had lasted for only fifty-six years. Today, the world is facing the implications of another earthquake of enormous social and political dimensions that ended what had been envisaged as a transformation of mankind but which actually became the most colossal failure in history—Soviet rule. It lasted for approximately seventy-four years.

It had been the origin and prime mover of the most systematic and universal confrontational order in the life of nations. Conversely, the unraveling of that imperial structure—especially after the summer of 1989—displayed a rather logical sequential structure. It undid an unprecedented military confrontation that was robust, although NATO had faced a maturing Soviet invasion capability combined with the means to suppress its nuclear response. It undid the German division, although even German governments had sometimes assumed that the unification issue had been put to rest. It undid the Soviet rule in the East European Warsaw Pact countries, although consolidating the belt of "people's republics" had been a priority of Soviet European policy for decades. It thus undid the European division, although the possibility of a Russian relapse remains. All this happened without any Soviet military intervention in spite of overwhelming Soviet military power. During the seventy-four hours of the coup in August 1991, even the shadows of suppressive restoration disappeared. With the military confrontation already gone, now the political competition, which had been the source of tension since the late 1940s, and, in many ways, since 1917, was vanishing. Although the process had been initiated in the center—in Moscow—the crumbling began at the periphery—literally at barbed wires surrounding that structure. Yet, the cataclysmic end occurred again at the very center.

This process of unraveling destroyed what former Soviet Foreign Minister Eduard Shevardnadze has called a "horrible stability," thereby unleashing passions and forces with obvious destructive potential that had hardly figured in the international order after 1945. To paraphrase what a great nineteenth-century European has said about absolutism, totalitarianism "violated and tortured nationalities for so long that nationalities now turn to nationalism, however much that may contradict the prevailing trends that are geared toward internationalism. It is both plausible and justified that suppressed and dismembered nations stand up to get their nationality recognized again."[15]

Meanwhile, new circumstances obviously have been created through civilization, in particular infrastructure, distribution, and communication, as well as through political innovation, especially economical interdependence, internationalism, and political integration. They will continue to influence international affairs even in those areas where traditional conflict patterns are now resurfacing. Some of these circumstances—most noticeably the United Nations—are acquiring at long last the importance that had been envisaged for them at their beginning.

Today, we are witnessing two countervailing trends—one "back to the future," guided by revived fears and prebipolarity concepts of conflict and order, the other "forward toward unlocked opportunities," informed by postbipolarity views on limited sovereignty and cooperative order.[16] Reconciling these megatrends is the raison d'être of future political competition over international order. They will combine with two traditional tendencies that will acquire special relevance during the current phase of profound reconstruction—one will preserve patterns that appeared advantageous in recent decades, the other will require fresh looks, imagination, and initiative. There will be continuity and change, but at issue is the prudent resulting mix.

Momentous change has already altered the European political map. While most of the post-1917 and post-1945 structures that had been imposed for decades have been undone, the dynamic of change is still strong. Yet, the objectives now are different. In the former GDR, in the Central and East European states, and most recently in the former USSR, a process of reform and reconstitution is under way. Outcomes are uncertain, but one trend is toward developing cooperative structures. Since the collapse of the Soviet putsch on August 21, 1991, this reconstruction is clearly gathering momentum, though its outcome is uncertain. Reforms in Central and East European states are no longer overshadowed by the dangers of relapse in the former USSR. The removal of potentially imminent threats of totalitarian restoration does not by itself resolve the enormous problems of economic and social reform, but it does remove major obstacles on the road to reconstruction, and it provides reforms with the air of freedom that can encourage initiative and synergism and outside support.

The prudent approach toward reconstituting an aggregate of sovereign republics—though not in terms of what has been constituted as the Commonwealth of Independent States—certainly fits into the overall development and reinforces the dominant trend toward an increasingly cooperative constellation involving the United States, Western Europe, the CIS, Eastern Europe and Japan. This is a zone characterized by increasing interdependence, transfer of sovereignty, self-restraint, and political interaction. The stability of this emerging constellation is far from given,

[15] Constantin Frantz, "Die Überwindung des Nationalismus," in *Der Föderalismus als universale Idee,* ed. Ilse Hartmann (Berlin: Oswald Arnold, 1948), 343f.

[16] See John J. Mearsheimer, "Back to the Future. Instability in Europe after the Cold War," *International Security* 15, no. 1 (Summer 1990): 5–56.

and its scope and limits tend to be fluid. Short of major blunders or relapses, however, this new "Silk Road"—as Eduard Shevardnadze has called this Eurasian-North American belt[17]—will be the dominant international structure. The two major conglomerates on the Eurasian land mass will develop toward unprecedented constitutional patterns—mixed systems or aggregates with some central authority cum constituent parts that can command loyalty.[18]

Unlike currently propagated formulas such as "from Vancouver to Vladivostok," this constellation embraces all major actors as well as the main forces of integration and disintegration. Institutional arrangements, however, do not yet fully reflect this basic reality of today's international predicament, nor do prevailing definitions of the national interests of the major powers consider it in the spirit of building a durable international order. For example, the increasing role of the G-7 in building international order does not compensate for excluding Japan from the cooperative framework "from Vancouver to Vladivostok," and American policies of keeping regional security frameworks separated may eventually tend to weaken American internationalism itself. Yet, the increasing cooperation of northern industrial centers and increasing societal interactions within the new Silk Road constellation will largely determine future global outcomes.

There do exist conceivable variations on this pattern as a result of national assertiveness, the failure of reforms, new challenges from outside, unilateral action, or trends toward regionalism that would turn this constellation into a more disjunctive, if not competitive or chaotic, environment, or else create an international viscosity that would absorb the current dynamics of change.

The prime task of the governments active throughout this constellation is to reinforce trends toward restraint, interdependence, the transfer of sovereignty (where this serves common purposes) and the stabilization of cooperative structures. Yet, as former President Bush has stated, this belongs to the "hard work of freedom."[19] Among the various risks and challenges are some of a military-security nature. The most important of these relate to nonmilitary conditions of security, in particular the success of reforms in Eastern Europe and the CIS. Western-tailored support thus has an important security dimension. Failure could eventually lead to strategic vacua, if not to the eventual reconstitution of a hostile strategic environment.

The Changing Nature of Military Power

Given the dominance of military power in the postwar order, as well as the near

[17] Eduard Shevardnadze, *Die Zukunft gehört der Freiheit* (Hamburg: Rowohlt, 1990), 285.

[18] To label the West European or new Soviet unions "federation" may confuse rather than clarify the issues, because, as Robert Bowie and Carl J. Friedrich have pointed out in a classic study on federalism, any historically known federation is sui generis, and the two emerging ones undoubtedly are. Robert R. Bowie and Carl J. Friedrich, eds., *Studies on Federalism* (Boston: Brown and Little, 1954). We still need to understand them on their own, as the quarrel over "F-words" preceding the Maastricht summit suggests.

[19] State of the Union Address, January 29, 1991.

irrelevance of a vast military machinery during an unprecedented change of political relationships it was designed to prevent, there are profound reasons to rethink the role of military power. It was already increasingly ambivalent under conditions of cooperative security relationships. Yet, as Pierre Hassner observed a quarter of a century ago, once the political transformation of a divided Europe comes to an end, political attention will be drawn to a new and surprisingly unexplored problem area—the problem of security.[20] While stabilizing these conditions to secure political evolution and prevent crises and conflict has necessarily turned into a matter of economic, social, and political efforts, the danger of military conflict has become more real—in a manner most European nations had considered to have disappeared into the shadows of history. The Gulf War happened outside the European security system that has developed over several decades. It proved to be a manageable contingency. The Yugoslav conflict occurred in a European heartland, and European security policies and arrangements turned out to be painfully inadequate.

Before taking a closer look at what kind of challenge the Yugoslav conflict poses to Europe and beyond, and what kinds of responses tend to be needed in future contingencies of this type, it may be prudent to draw some lessons from recent experience.

- Until the late 1980s any of the major changes that have taken place within the former Soviet orbit would have been expected to trigger large-scale employment of military forces with grave risks for East-West security. Instead the world is witnessing since 1989 a new "tradition of non-use" of Russian military power (to paraphrase Tom Schelling's formula).
- Iraq has been a Soviet ally with treaty links. And in many NATO exercises of the past, a Yugoslav breakup scenario has been the assumed origin of a major conflict between the USSR and NATO following Soviet intervention on behalf of Serbia. Instead, the world has seen Soviet strategic cooperation with the United States on Iraq (although with an inclination to capitalize on Western preoccupation in a dual crisis—just as in the Hungary-Suez conflicts in 1956), and Soviet interest in Yugoslavia was mainly restricted to avoiding a possible precedent for the Soviet Union, which has since collapsed. Instead—and contrary also to the familiar 1914 analogies—the Yugoslav conflict (deplorable and uncivilized as it is) turns out to be the first of a new kind of conflict—encapsulated and contained. Rather than being the source of violent escalation, it is becoming an "internal matter of the community of nations."[21]
- While unilateral use of force has visibly ceased to be a viable political option in the Euporean context (aside from some local conflicts that have been suc-

[20] Pierre Hassner, *Change and Security in Europe. Part I: The Background* (London: The Institute for Strategic Studies, *Adelphi Papers*, no. 45, February 1968), 24.

[21] Hans Dietrich Genscher in the German Bundestag on September 4, 1991. With his observation on the need to rethink the concept of noninterference in internal matters, Genscher is reinforcing a view that the French Foreign Minister Roland Dumas had initiated in the aftermath of Desert Storm, which led to the passage of the Kurdish resolution (SR Rcs. 688 and 715). There is now an observable trend even among formerly traditionalist international lawyers to reconsider noninterference in

cessfully encapsulated), there has been a concurrent revolution in the use of force. For the first time, the UN authorized the use of force to enforce peace (the Korean case had been noticeably different), and thus legitimized coalition warfare engaging twenty-eight nations, although with a tightly circumscribed mandate. This authorization has since been described as a unique scenario with a villain and a stake that is unlikely to repeat itself. Its lasting importance, however, is more likely to rest with the major precedent it provides and the increasing chances for Russian cooperation in international peace enforcement.

- The coalition was unique in that it brought together a hybrid coalition of Western and Arab military forces—including Arab forces from countries that often had displayed rather hostile attitudes toward the West, as in the case of Syria. This, too, clearly has implications for future crisis management and peace enforcement. It should reshape many of the political perceptions that still play a role in current descriptions of the "Southern threat." This is not to say that risks and uncertainties in the area are negligible, but it underlines the need for differentiated assessments, the prospects for future coalition-building, and the appropriateness of discriminating responses.
- The Iraqi aggression is often regarded as the first of a new type of aggression, with an oil-rich Islamic country armed on a massive scale with modern weaponry and engaging the West in a conflict where Western interests are vulnerable and Western responses limited. Instead, there is reason to assume that similar preparations for aggression will not be met again by the kind of benign neglect that Saddam Hussein enjoyed. Surveillance is going to be increasingly tighter, and the chances for future coalition-building involving Arabs in the region will continue to exist, unless the handling of the Israeli-Palestinian issue prevents it. In addition, the military outcome of the Gulf War should be a powerful deterrent. As Lawrence Freedman has put it, "there is now no question that in regular warfare the West and the Third World are in different classes."[22] Rather than exemplify the dominant type of future aggression, the Iraqi experience will probably influence other nations in a war comparable to the manner in which Hiroshima conditioned the behavior of nations on the northern half of the globe. In other words, it is unlikely that a Kuwaiti-type aggression will result from another massive conventional force buildup.
- This may also mean that efforts in this area toward acquiring modern means of mass destruction will be redoubled. This is certainly the most important security concern by far in the eastern and southern Mediterranean littoral and beyond, and it is heightened by the imminent transfer of former Soviet nuclear weapons, special materials, and expertise into critical areas. This requires

favor of a qualified right to interfere in internal matters. It may be a long time until this idea is adopted in the UN, but it could become a more promising issue for the Helsinki II accord, thus setting an important precedent.

[22] Lawrence Freedman, "The Gulf War and the New World Order," *Survival* 33, no. 3 (May/June 1991): 202.

military preparation to be sure, but more important, it requires a combination of diplomatic conflict resolution and effective nonproliferation regimes.

- It has been argued that in the Gulf as in former Yugoslavia conflicts have unfolded because the end of the Cold War provided the freedom to act at low risk. However, while this may be so, it is also true that lowered risk means reduced danger of escalation into a major war. Lowered risk had also meant enhanced chances for cooperative crisis-management by former adversaries. To that extent the now familiar paradigm of forces being unleashed after the cap of bipolarity has been lifted needs careful reconsideration.

  It is certainly not the dominant trend. Rather, there is abundant evidence (as there began to be after the Moscow summit in May 1972) that local adversaries see their leverage in playing off major sponsors is gone and that the chance to use military forces successfully for political purposes is vanishing.
- The Soviet-American dialogue over German unification and then during the Gulf crisis was the finale of what used to be superpower bilateralism. There will remain, however, an essential relationship between Russia and the United States. While the former USSR is turning into an inward-looking, mixed system combining central as well as peripheral centers of action, the United States also will undergo major changes in its international conduct. Familiar oscillations aside (for example, between "declinism" at the end of the 1980s and "triumphalism" in 1991), the United States no longer is in the central position of managing a dominant conflict relationship with the resultant discipline of allied coalitions, and thus with the continued potential for playing one against the other.
- Moreover, the Gulf War has demonstrated what many prudent observers and officials have argued throughout the 1980s: that future crisis-management on a large scale can no longer be sustained by the United States alone. What the United States achieved in the Gulf was a broad system of ad hoc cooperation as a result of brilliant diplomacy. Without the voluntary support of many countries, however, only some of which belonged to the coalition of twenty-eight, the United States would have been simply unable to conduct Desert Shield and Desert Storm.[23] In particular, the logistical base provided by Germany and Spain—to mention only two—as well as the financial support of Japan, Germany, and Saudi Arabia (against the background of the American budget deficit) were imperative for the United States to exercise its central role. Clearly, no other country could have replaced the United States. In the end, the American role will remain critical, but in need of legitimacy derived from the UN, of massive support, and of consensus. Moreover, while traditional U.S. alliances, or in any case, NATO, were important for support (logistics, communication, and so forth), what was needed above all was an ad hoc or, to use President Bush's term, a "hybrid" coalition.[24]

---

[23] See *The Gulf War. Military Lessons Learned.* Interim Report of the CSIS Study Group on Lessons Learned from the Gulf War (Washington, D.C.: Center for Strategic and International Studies, July 1991), 5–10.

It is obvious that except for northern Norwegian and eastern Anatolian contingencies, all military contingencies in the future will originate outside the NATO area with uncertain rules of engagement. Given this increasing scope for crisis management, one may observe that the American role in Yugoslavia did not exactly reinforce confidence in American capacity for crisis management. Rather, it reinforced the need to provide the European Community (now the European Union) with more effective means in similar future contingencies.

In future circumstances, extreme contingencies will cease to be the defining ones, except for security arrangements of last resort. The question is whether NATO should be confined to an alliance of last resort that would dramatically reduce (though not obviate) its political and strategic utility, or whether it will be reformed in a manner that responds to the new political and strategic environment. This latter option would give it a role within a network of interlocking institutions that could still be dominant, and it would reinforce a key role for the United States in European affairs that is seen to be in all or most European countries' interest. Indeed, as a very senior American study group has recently pointed out, the "United States will need to be flexible in its institutional choices as it continues to play a role in Europe." [25]

- Since the end of World War II there was a Soviet dimension to most Mediterranean problems facing the West. At Potsdam, it became clear that the USSR was trying to reach out into the Mediterranean with demands for a base on Turkish territory and Soviet trusteeship over Libya.[26] The subsequent formation of NATO was shaped in large measure by events in the eastern Mediterranean, in particular in Greece and Turkey, when the USSR was seen to exacerbate turmoil. The Truman Doctrine was the visible response. It was obvious from the outset, however, that the Atlantic, the Mediterranean, and Central Europe were difficult to combine within one homogenous security system. It was the United States and Great Britain facing a Soviet threat in these disparate areas that tended to forge one coherent alliance. In 1948, however, Bevin still favored a Mediterranean security system distinct from an Atlantic alliance and with a separate status for European states not bordering the Atlantic. American views at the time turned in similar directions.[27]

The outcome in 1949 was different. But the relationship between AFCENT and AFSOUTH or, in broader terms, the center and the flanks, has already

[24] *National Security Strategy of the United States (*Washington, D.C., August 1991), 13.

[25] "Facing the Future, America Strategy in the 1990s." An Aspen Strategy Group Report (Lanham: University Press of America, 1991), 25.

[26] Don Cook, *Forging the Alliance* (New York: Arbor House, 1989); see also *Legislative Origins of the Truman Doctrine.* Hearings held in the Executive Session before the Committee on Foreign Relations of the United States Senate, 80th Congress, First Session, on S. 938 (Historical Series). On the historical background see, for example, Norman E. Saul, *Russia and the Mediterranean 1797–1807* (Chicago, 1970).

[27] See Cees Wiebes and Bert Zeeman, "The Pentagon Negotiations, March 1948: The Launching of the North Atlantic Treaty," *International Affairs* 59, no. 3 (1983): 351–363.

tended to be unorganic in many ways, and Turks and Norwegians alike have time and time again expressed their worries about preoccupation with the center. Ironically, the alliance's center and its southern part have hardly ever cooperated more closely than during Desert Shield and Desert Storm—that is, in a non-NATO case. The temptation for NATO is obvious, but so are the shortcomings. The Russian military threat is gone. Russian support for nations or parties to civil war in the Balkans and the eastern and southern Mediterranean is an unlikely contingency in the foreseeable future. Countries in the area thus have lost their Russian card in diplomatic gambles. Instead there will be increasing political, economic, and strategic cooperation among major external powers in regional crises. This does not mean that the successor to the USSR or constituent republics will not rediscover respective interests. They will. Within the "Silk Road" constellation, however, antagonism and confrontation will not pay. Commonality will.

Security Options for Southeastern Europe

Future contingencies in the Balkans or in crisis-ridden areas generally need to be assessed in terms of the surrounding constellation of forces. It makes a difference of profound strategic importance whether the "Silk Road" constellation, or some less desirable variation, is anticipated. If the latter, one needs to spell out one's assumptions about what has changed. The least prudent approach would be to assume a cooperative, highly interactive Eurasian-North American zone in the north and a new hostile environment on the southern periphery with a substitute threat from the south. This could easily turn into a self-fulfilling prophecy that could indeed pose difficult problems.

Southeastern Europe and the eastern and southern Mediterranean littorals are widely regarded as areas from which future military instability and conflict are likely to spring. They are critically important for two reasons. First, they could require security action. Second, they could also invite fatally incorrect assessments, if not responses.

To that extent, regional and subregional conflicts in Southeastern Europe will increasingly fall within the realm of crisis management by the European Union, with the CSCE or the United Nations, or both, as a legitimizing framework. There are three reasons for this. First, the Yugoslav case demonstrates the need to hasten the process of creating a political union capable of exercising joint crisis management. Second, given the nonmilitary conditions of insecurity in candidate countries, the EU is likely to have leverage that no other organization possesses. Most important, the growth of the EU is governed by transfer of sovereignty. This confines nationalism without destroying national identities. It displays standards for countries' future accession as members or associated nations that ought to be upgraded in the light of the Yugoslav experience.

The EU not only should develop toward a security union, but it should be understood to be based on common security principles—as it actually is. It is also conceivable that in a developing CSCE system as well as in case of a strengthening of the UN, the EU (as well as the CIS) may eventually acquire some corporate membership status.[28] Conversely, the CSCE, with its potentially increasing legitimizing capacity, could conceivably authorize or mandate the EU, and in more extreme cases, NATO, to take action. Some embryonic version of that has already occurred in the case of Yugoslavia.

In this manner, a European security system would develop that defines roles in terms of successive phases of possible conflicts. It would create a kind of multiple multilateralism. To the extent that NATO ceases to be organized in terms of extreme major contingencies and adapts as a nonunitary multiinstitutional system with sequential arrangements, it will remain an important element. After all, one reason that many East European countries want to be closely connected to NATO is to be in one organization with the United States.

In this respect, there is no difference in principle between Central and East European and Southeast European countries, except that the latter are more diverse in terms of former alignments as well as their potential for reform and, consequently, their eligibility to join Western organizations.[29]

The Maghreb is clearly a main concern for the Latin European states. Problems there could increasingly become as absorbing as German concerns over Central and Southeastern Europe developments, thus pulling European interests again in different directions. With EC '92 these concerns spread throughout the Community and thus created priority conflicts that will be hard to resolve. Yet, in some crucial areas such as migration, common policies should be within reach.

The Middle East will remain the most crucial area, although in the postwar situation the chances for political settlements have improved. The war has changed the character of the region in one important respect. Given the web of complex interrelations between the "Silk Road" system and the Middle East, that region has moved closer to becoming a subsystem or extension of the emerging order. It is inconceivable that major external powers will cease to shape outcomes there, and these efforts will be increasingly governed by common or at least compatible objectives. The peace process that started at Madrid made this abundantly clear.

It would be a singular mistake to stipulate a uniform southern threat to justify the need for collective defense in the West. But Desert Shield has demonstrated that NATO's dissuasive effects do indeed reach far beyond its so-called treaty area. There will be a continuing need for some collective defense system involving the United

---

[28] This idea of corporate membership was launched by Konrad Adenauer in 1952 when he proposed EDC corporate membership within NATO. See Hans-Peter Schwarz, *Adenauer, Der Aufstieg: 1876–1952* (Stuttgart: Deutsche Verlag-Amstalt, 1986), 879. A similar issue with even more complex implications will undoubtedly come up with the formation of the successor to the USSR.

[29] Given that Turkey's membership within the EC is regarded as unlikely in the near future, it is important to recognize that with the political map of the Balkans changing, Turkey's political and strategic leverage is growing and, contrary to practice, dwarfs Greece's role. Its real importance, however, will be defined in the Western-Russian-Arab triangle. See *Wall Street Journal*, 2 Jan. 1992, p. 1.

States. For a complex organization of sixteen sovereign member states, however, it is too much to expect reform to keep pace with the changes in the European and international environment. What was envisaged at the London summit in July 1990 pointed in the right direction. The subsequent implementation—driven by the Gulf experience as well as by an interest in corporate survival—was marked by increasing conservatism. In contrast, changes in NATO's environment continued to unfold in a dramatic manner. The reforms resulting from the Rome summit (November 1991) would have been inadequate even without the recent events in the former USSR. As a result of the collapse of the USSR, they have become even more obsolete. It is necessary, therefore, to develop new guidelines for future developments. Any current agreement on command structure, force structures, strategy and, most important, on the future rationale for NATO is only transitory, and must be reassessed in light of future changes in Europe.

Glossary

AFCENT	Allied Forces Central Europe (NATO)
AFSOUTH	Allied Forces Southern Europe (NATO)
APL	Albanian Party of Labor
BCP	Bulgarian Communist Party
BSP	Bulgarian Socialist Party
CADA	Action Committee for Democratization of the Army (Romania)
CDU	Christian Democratic Party (Germany)
CFE	Conventional Forces in Europe
CIS	Commonwealth of Independent States
CJTF	Combined Joint Task Force (NATO-WEU)
CPC	Conflict Prevention Center
CSBM	Confidence and Security Building Measure
CSCE	Conference on Security and Cooperation in Europe
CSCM	Conference on Security and Cooperation in the Mediterranean
EBRD	European Bank for Reconstruction and Development
EC	European Community
EFTA	European Free Trade Area
EMU	Economic and Monetary Union
EPC	European Political Cooperation
EPU	Economic and Political Union
EU	European Union
FDP	Free Democratic Party (Germany)
FSC	Forum for Security Cooperation
FSN	National Salvation Front (Romania)
FDSN	Democratic National Salvation Front (Romania)

FYROM	Former Yugoslav Republic of Macedonia
G–7	Group of 7 (industrial nations; Britain, Canada, France, Germany, Italy, Japan, United States)
G–24	Group of 24 (i.e., OECD)
GDP	gross domestic product
GDR	German Democratic Republic
HDZ	Croatian Democratic Community
IMF	International Monetary Fund
INF	intermediate-range nuclear forces
JCG	Joint Consultative Group (on CFE)
JNA	Yugoslav People's Army
LYC	League of Yugoslav Communists
MBFR	Mutual and Balanced Force Reduction
MFN	most-favored-nation (trade status)
MRF	Movement for Rights and Freedoms (Bulgaria)
NACC	North Atlantic Cooperation Council
NATO	North Atlantic Treaty Organization
NFZ	nuclear-free zone
OECD	Organization for Economic Cooperation and Development
PASOK	Pan-Hellenic Socialist Movement (Greece)
PHARE	Aid for Economic Reconstruction of Poland and Hungary (EC)
PRNU	Party of Romanian National Unity
PSBR	public-sector borrowing requirement
PSDR	Party of Social Democracy of Romania
SACEUR	Supreme Allied Command, Europe
SHAPE	Supreme Headquarters, Allied Powers, Europe
SPD	Social Democratic Party (Germany)
SRI	Romanian Intelligence Service
UPF	Union of Democratic Forces (Bulgaria)
UNPA	United Nations protected areas

UNPROFOR United Nations Protection Force

USSR Union of Soviet Socialist Republics (or Soviet Union)

VMRO-DPMNE Internal Macedonian Revolutionary Organization—Democratic Party for Macedonian National Unity

WEU Western European Union

Index

About the Editor and Contributors

Editor

F. Stephen Larrabee, the editor of this volume, is a senior staff member in the International Policy Department at RAND. He previously served as Vice-President and Director of Studies at the Institute for East-West Security Studies in New York. From 1978 to 1981 he was a member of the National Security Council Staff, dealing with Soviet and East European Affairs. He has also held teaching positions at Cornell University, Columbia University, New York University, Georgetown University, The Johns Hopkins School of Advanced International Affairs (SAIS), and the University of Southern California. Dr. Larrabee has published widely on East-West relations, especially the Balkans. His most recent books include *East European Security after the Cold War* (RAND, 1994); (with Robert Blackwill) *Conventional Arms Control and East-West Security* (Durham: Duke University Press, 1989); and *The Two German States and European Security* (New York: St. Martin's Press, 1989). He is also the author of "Long Memories and Short-Fuses: Change and Instability in the Balkans," *International Security* (Winter 1990/91), and "Balkan Security," *Adelphi Papers* No. 135 (1976).

Contributors

Elez Biberaj is chief of the Albanian Service at Voice of America (Washington, D.C.). He holds a Ph.D. in political science from Columbia University and is the author of *Albania: A Socialist Maverick* (1990) and *Albania and China: A Study of the Unequal Alliance* (1986). He has also contributed articles to several publications, including *East European Quarterly; Survey, the World Today; Problems of Communism;* and *Conflict Studies.* His most recent publication is "Albania at Crossroads," *Problems of Communism* (September–October 1991).

Christopher Cviic, born and educated in Croatia (Yugoslavia), has lived in Britain since 1954. He was East European correspondent for *The Economist* from 1969 to 1990. Since 1984 he has also been the editor of *The World Today,* the monthly international affairs magazine published by the Royal Institute of International Affairs (RIAA) in London. His most recent publication is *Remaking the Balkans* (London: Pinter for the RIIA, 1991).

P. Nikiforos Diamandouros is currently a professor at the University of Athens. He was previously director of the Greek Institute for International and Strategic Affairs and staff associate responsible for Western Europe and the Near and Middle East at the Social Science Research Council (U.S.A.). His most recent publications include "Transition to, and Consolidation of, Democratic Politics in Greece, 1974–83," in Geoffrey Pridham, ed., *The New Mediterranean Democracies* (London: Frank Cass, 1987); "La transición del autoritarismo a la democracia en Grecia," in Julian Sanatamaria, ed., *La transición a la democracia en el sur de Europa y América Latina* (Madrid: CIS, 1982); and "Greek Political Culture: Historical Origins, Evolution, Current Trends," in Richard Clogg, ed., *Greece in the 1980s* (London: Macmillan, 1983).

Graham E. Fuller served three years as a foreign service officer in Istanbul in the 1960s, and was the national intelligence officer at the Central Intelligence Agency for long-range Middle East forecasting. He has recently completed a RAND study on *Turkey Faces East: New Orientations Toward the Middle East and the Old Soviet Union* (1992). He is the author of *The Center of the Universe: The Geopolitics of Iran* (Westview, 1991) and *The Democracy Trap: Perils of the Post-Cold War World* (Dutton, 1992). He is currently completing a study on modern Turkey as seen through the eyes of its novelists.

Thomas J. Hirschfeld is a senior researcher and project director at the Center for Naval Analysis (CNA) in Washington, D.C. Before joining CNA he was a senior staff member in the International Policy Department at RAND in Santa Monica. He has been a guest scholar at the Woodrow Wilson Center (Smithsonian) and was the 1986–1987 Tom Slick Professor at the University of Texas (Austin). He was deputy U.S. representative to the MBFR negotiations in Vienna (1979–1982), deputy assistant director of the Arms Control and Disarmament Agency (1977–1979), and a member of the Department of State Policy Planning Staff (1976–1977). In addition to staff assignments in the Department of State, Washington, he has served at the U.S. Embassies in Stockholm, Bonn, and Phnom Penh.

Ian O. Lesser is a member of the International Policy Department of RAND specializing in European and Mediterranean affairs. Prior to joining RAND, he was a senior fellow in International Security Affairs at the Center for Strategic and International Studies. He has also been a senior fellow of the Atlantic Council and a staff consultant at International Energy Associates in Washington, D.C. He is author of *Resources and Strategy* (New York: St. Martin's Press, 1989) and has published widely on the foreign and security policies of Southern European countries and Turkey. His most recent works include *Bridge or Barrier? Turkey and the West after the Cold War* (RAND, 1992) and *Mediterranean Security: New Perspectives and Implications for U.S. Policy* (RAND, 1992).

Daniel N. Nelson is director of Graduate Programs in International Studies at

Old Dominion University in Norfolk, Virginia. He was previously an adjunct professor at Georgetown University's Russian Area Studies Program and at the Johns Hopkins School for Advanced International Studies in Washington, D.C. During 1991 he served as the senior foreign and defense policy advisor for the majority leader of the House of Representatives, Richard Gephardt. Previously he was a senior associate at the Carnegie Endowment (1990) and (from 1977–1989) professor of political science at the University of Kentucky. Among his recent books are *Security After Hegemony* (1992), *Balkan Imbroglio* (1991), *Romanian Politics in the Ceausescu Era* (1989), *Elite Mass Relations in Communist Systems* (1988) and *Alliance Behavior in the Warsaw Pact* (1986).

Uwe Nerlich is deputy director at the Stiftung Wissenschaft und Politik (SWP) in Ebenhausen, Germany. He is a standing member of the European Strategy Group (ESG) and from 1986 to 1988 served as its chairman. He is also European director of the Nuclear History Program. He has published widely on defense, arms control and East-West relations. Among his most recent works are (with James Thomson) *The Soviet Program in American-German Relations* (New York: Crane, Russak & Co., 1985) and (with James Thomson) *Beyond Nuclear Deterrence* (New York: Crane, Russak & Co., 1977).

Duncan M. Perry is assistant director of the Analytic Research Department at the Radio Free Europe/Radio Liberty Research Institute in Munich, Germany. He holds a Ph.D. in history from the University of Michigan and is the author of *The Politics of Terror: The Macedonian Revolutionary Movements, 1893-1903* (Durham: Duke University Press, 1988) and many articles on Balkan and East European themes.

James B. Steinberg is director of the Policy Planning Staff in the U.S. Department of State. Before joining the State Department in 1993, he was a senior staff member in the International Policy Department at RAND specializing in the European Community and transatlantic political and economic issues. This chapter was written while he was at RAND and does not reflect the views of the U.S. government. Prior to joining RAND, Mr. Steinberg served as a senior national security advisor on the staff of Democratic presidential candidate Michael Dukakis. From 1985 to 1987 he was a senior fellow at the International Institute for Strategic Studies (IISS) in London, following five years as the national security and military affairs counsel to Senator Edward M. Kennedy. His publications include *"An Ever Closer Union." European Integration and Its Implications for the Future of U.S.-European Relations* (RAND, 1993); (with Scott Harris) *European Defense and the Future of Transatlantic Cooperation* (RAND, 1993); and "The Future of European Defense Cooperation," in Jonathan Alford and Kenneth Hunt, eds., *Europe in the Western Alliance: Towards a European Defense Entity* (New York: St. Martin's Press, 1988).

Loukas Tsoukalis is Jean Monnet Professor of European Organization at the University of Athens, and president of the Hellenic Centre for European Studies. He is also director of Economic Studies at the College of Europe in Bruges. His latest book is *The New European Economy* (Oxford University Press, 1991).

Thanos Veremis is director of the Hellenic Foundation for Defense and Foreign

Policy in Athens, Greece. Prior to joining the Hellenic Foundation, he was a professor at the University of Athens, a visiting scholar at Princeton and Harvard Universities, and a research associate at the International Institute of Strategic Studies in London. His publications include *Greek-Turkish Relations* (in Greek) (Athens, 1986); *Greek Security Considerations: A Historical Perspective* (Athens, 1980, 1982); *Dictatorship and the Economy* (in Greek) (Athens, 1982); and *The Interventions of the Military in Greek Politics* (in Greek) (Athens, 1977, 1983).

Radovan Vukadinovic is a professor of international relations in the faculty of political sciences at the University of Zagreb in Croatia and director of the postgraduate program in international relations there. He is author of numerous books on Yugoslavia and the Balkans, including most recently *The Breakup of Yugoslavia: Threats and Challenges* (Clingendael: The Haag, 1992), and *La fin de la Yougoslavie et l'instabilité balkanique* (Paris: Fondation Nationale des Sciences Politiques, 1992.)